AND YOU WILL BE MY WITNESSES IN (ACTS 1–7)

Acts 1   Modern Jerusalem.
"Do not leave Jerusalem, but wait for the gift my Father promised."

Acts 2   Old Jerusalem.
Here, the 120 were filled with the Spirit and began to speak in other tongues.

Acts 2   Model of Herod's Temple.
After Pentecost, believers continued to meet in the temple courts. (Center of Photo)

Acts 3-4 The Golden Gate, pictured, was near the Beautiful Gate. There the healing of a cripple led to church growth.

Acts 5 Jerusalem with Judean hills.
This chapter records that
Ananias and Sapphira died,
but the apostles healed many.

Acts 6-7 Saint Stephen's Gate (Note hundreds of bullet holes). Many think Stephen was stoned here.

AND IN ALL JUDEA AND SAMARIA, (ACTS 8–12)

Acts 8   Stadium at Samaria.
Persecution caused Philip to preach in Samaria. Healings opened their hearts.

Acts 9   Roman gate at Damascus.
Paul met Jesus on the road to Damascus.

Acts 9 The wall in Damascus.
Believers lowered Paul over this wall in a basket so he could escape.

Acts 9   Straight Street in Damascus.
Ananias prayed for Paul on Straight Street.
He was healed, baptized,
and filled with the Spirit.

Acts 10-11 Caesarea.
Cornelius was saved and filled with the Spirit in Caesarea. Peter was amazed!

Acts 12 Herod the Great's harbor at Caesarea. Here, an angel struck Herod Agrippa I and he died.

AND TO THE ENDS OF THE EARTH. (ACTS 13–28)

Acts 13 In Antioch, Syria there was a temple to Apollo. Antioch became the base for Paul's three missionary trips.

Acts 14 Coast near Paphos, on the island of Cyprus. Paul and Barnabas went here near the start of their first missionary trip.

Acts 14 Remains in Antioch, a city of Galatia. Galatian churches included Antioch, Iconium, Lystra, and Derbe.

Acts 15 The Damascus Gate in Jerusalem. Paul may have used this gate to attend the famous Church Council in Jerusalem.

Acts 16 The Egnatian Way linked the Macedonian cities of Philippi and Thessalonica to Rome.

Acts 17 The Parthenon, a temple in Athens. Paul preached about the Unknown God in Athens. Some philosophers mocked him. Others were humble and trusted in Jesus.

Acts 18 In Corinth, a temple to Venus once stood on this mountain. In this huge, sinful city, the power of the gospel changed people.

Acts 19 Ruins of the Celsus Library at Ephesus. Paul, unlike Apollos, emphasized being filled with the Spirit at Ephesus.

Acts 20 Ephesus, the main city of Asia. Paul used this city for three years as a base to preach, teach, and write.

Acts 21-23 A Jew dressed like the high priest. In Jerusalem, Paul stood before the high priest and Sanhedrin.

Acts 24-26 Caesarea. Here, Paul stood before Felix, Festus, and King Agrippa. He shared his testimony.

Acts 28 The Colosseum in Rome. Paul strengthened the church in Rome shortly before great persecution came.

ACTS OF THE HOLY SPIRIT

Student Manual

by Dr. George O. Wood
and Dr. Quentin McGhee

**Instructional Design by
Dr. Quentin McGhee,
Senior Editor**

PUT YOUR FAITH TO WORK!

Faith & Action Series

Faith & Action
637 Meadowview Ln
Chestnutridge, MO. 65630 U.S.A

Cover Photo

The descending dove represents the Holy Spirit (Matt. 3:16). He has come from the Father in heaven (Rev. 4:1-11; 5:11-12). Twenty-four elders, four living creatures, and thousands of angels surround the Father's throne. The Spirit is coming to believers on earth to fill them with God's presence and power. This baptism in the Holy Spirit is the gift Father promised to believers (Acts 1:4-5). It enables us to witness for Jesus in all nations.

Components That Complement This Book

Visit www.FaithAndActionSeries.org to see components with this book:

eVisuals— project all figures in color with captions. Download from our website.

2 **Kindle** color versions from Amazon: Matches the printed book for your computer or large tablet. Or for your tablet, phone, or computer www.amazon.com (search Faith & Action Team)

 Teacher's Guides—To purchase a TG submit our online form for approval as a teacher, pastor or administrator.

www.faithandactionseries.org/teachers.html

 ♥ **Thank You** ♥
Special thanks to BGMC and LFTL
for helping fund the Faith & Action Ministry.

Contact Information

Address: Faith & Action Team
637 Meadowview Ln
Chestnutridge, MO. 65630 U.S.A.

Telephone: (417) 881-4698
E-mail: Orders@FaithAndActionSeries.org
Web: www.FaithAndActionSeries.org

Table of Contents

Chapter
    Lesson

Unit 1: The Pre-Witness Days of the Church in Jerusalem (Acts 1)

Unit 2: The Witness of the Church in Jerusalem (Acts 2–7)

Unit 3: The Witness of the Church in Judea and Samaria (Acts 8–12)

Unit 4: The Witness of the Church to the Ends of the Earth (Acts 13–28)

Photo Credits

	Figure #	Color Page
Ken Berg	7.6	Acts 1, Acts 21–23
Robert Cooley	3.7, 5.7, 6.1, 7.7, 9.2, 9.8, 10.1, 11.6, 11.7, 11.8, 11.9, 11.10, 11.11, 11.14, 11.16, 12.3, 12.8, 12.9, 12.10, 12.11, 12.13, 13.13, 13.14	Acts 2, Acts 8, Acts 9a, b, c, Acts 10–11, Acts 12, Acts 13, Acts 14b, Acts 16, Acts 17, Acts 18, Acts 19, Acts 20
Corel Photo Stock	2.5, 6.3, 9.7, 10.6, 11.12, 11.18, 11.20, 12.6, 12.7, 13.5	Acts 14a, Acts 28
Roger Duclos	10.7, 11.13, 11.17, 12.3	
Ralph Harris	6.12, 12.12	
Faith McGhee		Acts 24–26
Planet Art - Doré	1.1, 3.1, 5.6, 7.1, 8.1, 11.1, 12.1, 13.1, 13.11	
Jerry Rausin		Acts 21–23
Rockafellow Studio	2.1, 3.2	
Clyde Smith	2.6, 5.1	Acts 5
Pat M. Smith	2.1	
Lucinda Zilverberg	1.2, 1.6, 2.7, 4.6, 4.7, 6.10, 9.14, 13.2, 13.7, 13.12	Acts 2b, Acts 3–4, Acts 6–7, Acts 15

Copyright Information

First Edition 2001
Third Edition 2005

Faith & Action Series—Acts of the Holy Spirit, Third Edition
©2018 Faith & Action Team

Course # BIB1063
ISBN 978-1-60382-024-0
Item # 4413-16E0

List of Figures

Faith & Action Series Overview

Bible	Theology	Church Ministries	General Education
Pentateuch	Systematic Theology: Articles in the Fire Bible (Life in the Spirit Bible)	Evangelism, Discipleship, & Church Planting	Survey of the New Testament
Historical Books	Theology 1: God, Bible, & Angels	Children's Ministry	Survey of the Old Testament
Major Prophets	Theology 2: Man, Sin, Christ, & Salvation	Pastoral Ministry	Wisdom Books (Introduction to Philosophy)
Minor Prophets	Theology 3: Holy Spirit, the Church, & Last Things	Leadership 1: Loving God & People	Homiletics: Preparing Biblical Messages
Synoptic Gospels: Life & Teachings of Christ	Hermeneutics 1: General Principles for Interpreting Scripture	Leadership 2: God's Love Crossing Human Boundaries (Conflict Resolution)	Principles of Teaching
Gospel of John: The Word Became Flesh	Hermeneutics 2: Interpreting Genres of Scripture	Biblical Counseling	Marriage & Family
Acts of the Holy Spirit		Introduction to Missions	Cross-Cultural Communications
Romans & Galatians: The Gospel According to Paul		Youth Ministry	The Bible & Science
First and Second Corinthians		Read the Light: Teaching Literacy	World Literature (Comparing the Holy Scriptures of Judaism, Christianity & Islam)
Prison Epistles: Ephesians, Colossians, Philippians & Philemon		Practicum 1: Preaching	Financial Management
Paul's Eschatological & Pastoral Epistles: 1 & 2 Thess., 1 & 2 Tim., Titus		Practicum 2: Evangelism, Discipleship, & Church Planting	
Hebrews		Practicum 3: Pastoral Ministry	
General Epistles: James—Jude		Practicum 4: Children's Ministry	
Revelation & Daniel (Eschatology)		Practicum 5: Youth Ministry	

Faith & Action
Four-Year Degree Plan (121 Credits)

First Year

First Semester

Course #	Course Title	Credits
BI 1013	Synoptic Gospels	3
TH 1013	Hermeneutics 1	3
BI 1023	Acts	3
GE 1013	Homiletics	3
MI 1013	Practicum 1: Preach 4 or more sermons on studies of this semester	3
		15

Second Semester

Course #	Course Title	Credits
BI 1033	Prison Epistles	3
MI 1023	Evan., Disc., & Church Planting	3
MI 1033	Practicum 2: Evan., Disc., & Church Planting	3
TH 1023	Pentecostal Doctrines + Fire Bible Articles	3
BI 1043	Ministerial Ethics + Pastoral Epistles	3
	AG Hist., Miss. & Gov. + Board Meetings	1
		16

Second Year

First Semester

Course #	Course Title	Credits
GE 2023	Old Testament Survey	3
GE 2033	New Testament Survey	3
TH 2033	Theology 1: God, Bible & Angels	3
BI 2053	Romans & Galatians	3
BI 2063	Introduction to Missions with Practice	3
		15

Second Semester

Course #	Course Title	Credits
BI 2173	Revelation & Daniel (Eschatology)	3
MI 2043	Leadership 1	3
MI 2053	Leadership 2 (Conflict Resolution)	3
MI 2063	Pastoral Ministry	3
MI 2073	Practicum 3: Pastoral Ministry	3
		15

Third Year

First Semester

Course #	Course Title	Credits
BI 3083	Pentateuch	3
MI 3083	Church Admin., Law & Finance with Practice	3
BI 3073	1 & 2 Corinthians	3
TH 3043	Theology 2: Humans, Sin, Christ & Salvation	3
TH 3053	Apologetics + Hermeneutics 2	3
		15

Second Semester

Course #	Course Title	Credits
MI 3093	Prayer, Worship & Practice	3
BI 3093	*Wisdom Books (Introduction to Philosophy)	3
GE 3043	Cross-Cultural Communications	3
GE 3053	*Marriage & Family	3
TH 3063	Theology 3: Holy Spirit, the Church, & Last Things	3
		15

Fourth Year

First Semester

Course #	Course Title	Credits
MI 4103	Children's Ministry	3
MI 4113	Practicum 4: Children's Ministry	3
MI 4123	Biblical Counseling with Practice	3
BI 4103	Hebrews	3
GE 4063 / GE 4073	*The Bible & Science **or** *Financial Management	3
		15

Second Semester

Course #	Course Title	Credits
MI 4133	Youth Ministry	3
MI 4143	Practicum 5: Youth Ministry	3
BI 4113	John	3
BI 4123	General Epistles	3
GE 4083	*World Literature (Comparing the Holy Scriptures of Judaism, Christianity & Islam)	3
		15

Electives may be approved and substituted on a case by case basis.

Course letters: BI is Bible; TH is theology; MI is ministry; GE is general education.

Course numbers: The first number is the year of study; middle numbers show the sequence in a category; last number is the credits.

Example: BI1023 is a Bible course. The first 1 shows it is in the first year. 02 reveals this course is the second in the sequence of Bible courses. The final number, 3, shows the course is 3 credits.

About This Book

1. **The Lesson Headings** divide each chapter into several parts. Each of these lessons focuses on principles related to one theme. We number the lessons consecutively throughout the book.

2. **The Lesson Goals** are listed at the beginning of each chapter. Also, when a lesson begins, the goal for that lesson is printed there. You will find that there is at least one goal for each lesson.

3. **Key Words** are defined in a section called "Definitions" at the end of the book. The symbol * comes before all words that are defined. To help some students, we have also defined a few words that are not key words.

4. **Teaching Method:** These courses are designed for the *guided discovery* method of learning. This method focuses on the student, rather than the teacher. When this course is used in a classroom, lectures are not intended. Rather, most of the class time should be used for students to discuss the questions in the margins and related questions from the teacher and other students. At least 25 percent of the student's grade should be on how faithfully the student has tried to answer questions *before* class.

    It is VERY important for each student to own his or her book. We encourage Bible schools to require students to buy their texts at the time they pay tuition. It is a shame for students to leave school without their books, because they need them for a lifetime of ministry. Owning the book enables a student to write notes in it and underline important ideas. Also, when students own their books, they do not waste class time by copying things that are already written in the text. Rather, they spend their time discussing questions related to the Bible and ministry.

    In a classroom the teacher and students should discuss key questions together. The best teachers never answer their own questions. Some students will complain at first when the teacher requires them to think, read, and search for answers. But a good teacher knows that children who are always carried never learn to walk. And students who are always told the answer learn to memorize, but not to think and solve problems. In many ways, a good teacher is like a coach—guiding others to succeed.

    The questions in this course are like a path that leads straight to the goal. If the questions are too hard for a student, the teacher can ask easier questions that are like stairs toward harder questions. Also, the teacher should ask questions that guide students to apply the text to local issues. Often, a good teacher will add a story or illustration that emphasizes a truth for students.

5. **Schedule:** This *Faith & Action Series* course is for three credits. For a Bible school course, it is good to plan 40 contact hours between the teacher and students. This allows one lesson for a class hour.

6. **The Questions:** Most questions in the margins are identified by the hammer ➤ and nail ➤ symbols. Questions are steps toward a goal. As a student answers the questions, he or she is sure to reach the goals. The hammer introduces *content questions* and the nail precedes *application questions*. Our logo for this book includes the hammer hitting the nail. A student must grasp content before being able to apply it. The answers to all content questions are in the text, near the question. We encourage students to answer nail or application questions from their local settings.

    In some books there is the symbol of a shovel ➤ before certain questions. Questions beside the shovel symbol are *inductive questions*. The word *induce* means "to lead." These questions lead students to discover truth for themselves.

7. *Sabio* is a Spanish word that means "wise man." This symbol in the margin signifies a proverb or wise saying.

8. **The Illustrations**, such as stories and examples, are preceded by the candle symbol .

9. **Figures** include pictures, photos, charts, and maps. We number the figures in order throughout the chapter. For example, the first three figures in chapter one are numbered 1.1, 1.2, and 1.3. There is a list of significant figures near the front of the book.

10. **The Test Yourself** questions come at the end of each chapter and are indicated by the balance symbol . There are always ten of these questions. As a rule, there are two test questions for each goal in the chapter. If students miss any of these questions, they need to understand why they missed them. Knowing why an answer is right is as important as knowing the right answer.

11. **Essay Test Topics** are at the end of each chapter, indicated by the pencil symbol . Note that these essay topics are the lesson goals of the chapter. A student should be able to summarize these goals, writing 50-100 words on each one. These essay topics test students at a much higher level than the multiple choice, Test Yourself questions.

12. **Sample Answers** to the hammer questions, some comments on the nail questions, and answers for the Test Yourself questions and Essay Topics are in the Teacher's Guide. Students should answer questions so they will grow and become strong in their mental skills.

13. **Bible quotations** are usually from the New International Version (NIV). We also use the New American Standard Bible (NASB) and the King James Version (KJV). We encourage students to compare biblical passages in several versions of the Bible.

14. **The Scripture List** includes key Scripture references in this course. It is located near the back of the book.

15. **The Bibliography** is near the endnotes page. It is a complete list of books to which the authors refer in this course. Some students will want to do further research in these books.

16. **Endnotes** identify the sources of thoughts and quotes. They are listed by chapter at the end of the book.

17. **The Unit Exams and Final Exam** are in the Teacher's Guide. In the Teacher's Guide there are also other useful items for the teacher and potential projects for the students.

18. **Course Description (BIB1063):** This is a thorough study of the content, purposes, principles, and applications of Acts. The course emphasizes the role of the Holy Spirit then and now. Attention is given to the geographical, numerical, cultural, and theological growth of the Church from Jerusalem to Rome. The journeys of Paul are examined as the background of his epistles.

19. **Course Goals** for the entire course are listed below. The goals in each chapter will enable a student to reach these broader goals. By the end of this book, a student should be able to:

- Comment on the author, date, setting, structure, and purposes of Acts. Analyze the extent to which Luke's purposes have been fulfilled in your life and church.
- Relate the sequence, content, and theology of Acts to the rest of the New Testament. Compare the theology of Acts with your theology.
- Analyze five places in Acts where believers were first filled with the Holy Spirit. Experience personally the filling of the Holy Spirit.
- Identify the Church's problems and solutions in growing from one language and culture to many. Relate these to your context.
- Identify the main people, cities, and regions in Acts.
- Explain how Acts gives the background and setting of several New Testament letters.
- Trace the steps by which the gospel spread from Jerusalem to Rome. Evaluate the spread of the gospel in your part of the world.
- Identify and apply the main reasons for Church growth in Acts.
- Apply the principles of guidance in Acts to making decisions today.
- Illustrate from Acts that God uses hard times for His purposes. Apply this principle to believers today.
- Identify and apply some of the missionary principles in Acts.
- Preach and teach biblical messages rooted in Acts.
- Trace Paul's travels from Antioch to Rome.

20. **Authors**

Dr. George O. Wood provided tapes and manuscripts of his preaching and teaching through Acts. His insights and illustrations were vital to this course. He is the son of missionary parents to China and Tibet. He completed his undergraduate degree from Evangel College (now Evangel University). Later, he earned a doctorate in theology from Fuller Theological Seminary, and a juris doctorate from Western State University College of Law. He was assistant district superintendent of Southern California for 4 years and pastored Newport-Mesa Christian Center in Costa Mesa for 17 years. Dr. Wood has authored a number of books including a college textbook on Acts. Dr. Wood served as General Secretary of the Assemblies of God from 1993, until he was elected as General Superintendent in 2007.

 **Dr. Quentin McGhee** is the founder, senior author, instructional designer, and an editor of the *Faith & Action Series*, a curriculum of 40 books at completion. He earned a B.A. in Biblical Studies from Southwestern College in Oklahoma City, and a B.S. in Math from Oral Roberts University (ORU). Later he completed his M.Div. at the Assemblies of God Theological Seminary, where he taught beginning Greek and was selected by the faculty for Who's Who Among Students. He earned a D.Min. from ORU in 1987 and in 2015 was inducted into the ORU Hall of Fame in the College of Science and Engineering. Dr. McGhee and his wife, Elizabeth, pioneered a church in Oklahoma. They served as missionaries in Kenya for 15 years where they helped start many churches, developed an extension Bible school for full-time ministers, and assisted in curriculum development. Since 2005, Quentin and Elizabeth have served as Assemblies of God missionaries with the Latin America/Caribbean region. Dr. McGhee is developer and director of the *Faith & Action Series*, while Elizabeth assists with graphic design, desktop publishing, translations, and sales.

21. Contributors and Consultants

 **Dr. Stanley M. Horton** approved this course for biblical and theological accuracy. His degrees include a B.S. from the University of California, an M.Div. from Gordon-Conwell Theological Seminary, an S.T.M. from Harvard University, and a Th.D. from Central Baptist Theological Seminary. He is Distinguished Professor of Bible and Theology Emeritus at the Assemblies of God Theological Seminary in Springfield, Missouri. Dr. Horton has written 400 articles and book reviews, and authored 46 books on topics such as Genesis, Amos, Matthew, John, Acts, 1 & 2 Corinthians, Revelation, and the Holy Spirit.

 **Dr. Robert E. Cooley** provided over 30 photos for this course and confirmed its historical and cultural accuracy. His degrees include a B.A. in Biblical Studies and Archaeology from Wheaton College, an M.A. in Religious Education from Wheaton College Graduate School, and a Ph.D. in Hebrew Studies and Near Eastern Archaeology from New York University. Dr. Cooley served as President and Professor of Biblical Studies and Archaeology at Gordon-Conwell from 1981-1997. He currently serves in many outstanding positions, including Distinguished Professor of Biblical Archaeology, Jerusalem University; Counsel to the President for Strategic Leadership, Eastern Nazarene College; Distinguished Visiting Scholar, and Counsel to the President, Bethel College and Seminary; Chancellor and Professor of Biblical Studies and Archaeology at Gordon-Conwell Theological Seminary. He has written articles in publications such as *The Bulletin of the Near East Archaeological Society, The New Encyclopedia of Archaeological Excavations in the Holy Land, Theological Education,* and *The Oxford Encyclopedia of Archaeology in the Near East.*

 **Dr. William W. Menzies** confirmed the biblical and theological accuracy of this course. His degrees include a B.A. from Central Bible College (CBC), a B.A. and an M.A. from Wheaton College, and a Ph.D. from the University of Iowa. He did additional graduate work at New York Theological Seminary, Golden Gate Theological Seminary, and Pacific School of Religion. He pastored for 7 years. His teaching and administrative experience include: 12 years at CBC; Chairman of the Biblical Studies Department at Evangel University from its beginning in 1970 to 1980; teaching at the Assemblies of God Theological Seminary from 1974-1983; Vice President for Academic Affairs and Professor of Biblical and Historical Theology at California Theological Seminary, 1985-1987; President and Professor of Bible, Theology, and History at Asia Pacific Theological Seminary (APTS) from 1989-1996. In addition he has taught and lectured numerous times in the USA, Asia Pacific, Southern Asia, and Eurasia. Dr. Menzies served as the co-founder and first president of the Society for Pentecostal Studies (SPS), the first editor of SPS's journal, *Pneuma,* and consulting editor of *Christianity Today.* He served as co-chairman of the Editorial Committee for *The Full Life Study Bible.* Among the many books he has written are *Bible Doctrines: A Pentecostal Perspective,* Gospel Publishing House, 1993, and *Spirit and Power,* (co-authored with Dr. Robert P. Menzies), Zondervan, 2000. Dr. Menzies currently serves as Chancellor for APTS.

22. Special thanks to Pastors Ron Woods, Phil Taylor and Don Couch.
Ron pastors the Assembly at Broken Arrow, which gave substantially toward the development of this course. Pastors Phil and Don spent hours researching, compil-ing notes, and editing, while leading their congregations to support the Acts project through prayers and offerings.

Unit 1:
The Pre-Witness Days of the Church
in Jerusalem (Acts 1)

Chapter 1 of this book lays the foundation for our study. You will do several things such as:

- *Analyze the title, author, and date of Acts.*
- *Analyze five purposes for which Luke wrote Acts.*
- *Explain two of the three ways to outline Acts.*
- *Identify six speakers of the messages in Acts.*

Chapter 2 focuses on the period from the Resurrection to Pentecost (Acts 1). In this chapter you will:

- *Analyze the command, the gift, and the Baptizer in Acts 1.*
- *Explain the plan, the place, the power, and the purpose of witnessing. Relate these to self and others.*
- *Identify and do three things that precede being filled with the Spirit.*

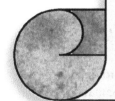

Chapter 1:
Understanding Acts

Introduction

Acts is a book of action. It has it all!
- Miracles, revivals, conversions, and resurrections!
- Martyrs, escapes from prison, angry mobs, and trials before kings!
- Shipwrecks, prophecies, beatings, and demonic conflicts!

It is a book about people. Its 75 characters include:
- Apostles, evangelists, and laypeople;
- Chief priests, kings, and governors;
- Slaves, jailers, and prisoners!

It is a book about Church growth.
- Acts begins with a Church so small it could fit in one upper room.
- It ends with a Church that had spread to the center of the Roman Empire!
- It begins with a local Jewish church of one language and one culture.
- It ends with an international Church of many tribes, languages, and cultures!

Above all, Acts is a book about the Holy Spirit.
- He continues to do through the Church what Jesus began.
- He enables apostles and laypeople to do supernatural ministry.
- He seeks to fill every believer with power to witness for Jesus.

Figure 1.1   The Ascension

Lessons:

Approaching Acts
Goal: *Analyze the title, author, and date of Acts.*

Appreciating Acts
Goal: *Analyze 5 purposes for which Luke wrote Acts.*

Analyzing Acts
Goal A: *Explain 2 of the 3 ways to outline Acts.*
Goal B: *Identify 6 speakers of the messages in Acts.*

            Key Words

Holy Spirit	epistles	province
Jerusalem	laypeople	Samaria
Judea		

Approaching Acts
Goal: *Analyze the title, author, and date of Acts.*

A. The title of Acts

When Luke first wrote Acts, it had no title. About A.D. 150 believers began to call Luke's book *The Acts of the Apostles*. Believers probably chose this title because the first chapter of Acts gives the names of the apostles (Acts 1:13). But as we read through Acts, we never see the names of most apostles again! After Acts 1, the only apostles called by name are Peter, John, James, and Paul.[1] Acts 1–12 focuses on Peter, and Acts 13–28 features Paul.

Q 1 ⟋ *What is the best title for Acts?*

In truth, the Holy Spirit is emphasized more than any of the apostles are. Luke introduces the Holy Spirit in the first verse of Acts. He shows us that even Jesus depended on the Holy Spirit (Acts 1:2). Then he reminds us that the apostles did not continue the ministry of Jesus without the power of the Spirit. Jesus commanded them not to leave Jerusalem until the Spirit filled them (Acts 1:4-5). Thus, from the beginning of Acts, Luke stresses that the Holy Spirit is the key to ministry. Jesus ascended to heaven. But He sent the Holy Spirit to live in and empower each believer. In Acts, Luke refers to the Spirit more than 50 times! Therefore, many agree that the best title for Acts is *The Acts of the Holy Spirit*![2]

B. The author of Acts

Most Bible teachers agree that Luke is the writer of Acts. In humility, Luke does not place his name at the beginning of his Gospel or Acts. He was not an apostle, like Paul. But he wrote more words in the New Testament than Paul wrote.[3] We do not know if Luke ever preached a sermon or performed a miracle. His name was not known for power or authority. Therefore, there was no reason to place it at the beginning of his writings.

Q 2 ⟋ *Summarize any 3 of the 5 reasons why we believe Luke wrote Acts.*

There are at least five reasons we believe Luke wrote Acts.

- The writer of Acts traveled with Paul on some of his missionary trips. We know this from passages like *"After Paul had seen the vision, we got ready at once"* (Acts 16:10). The word *we* shows us the writer was with Paul. See passages such as Acts 20:5; 21:18; 27:1; and 28:16. Luke was a Gentile doctor who sometimes traveled with Paul (Col. 4:14). This is one reason we believe he wrote Acts.[4]

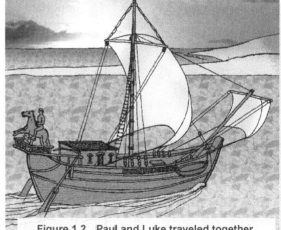
Figure 1.2   Paul and Luke traveled together.

- Whoever wrote Acts also wrote one of the Gospels. Acts 1:1 says, *"In my former book, Theophilus, I wrote about all that Jesus began to do and to teach."* The Church has always believed that the former book mentioned in Acts 1:1 is Luke's Gospel. Both Luke and Acts are written to the same person, *Theophilus. Luke wrote these two volumes as a historical set. We understand them best together.

- The writer of the Gospel of Luke was not an apostle. We know this from Luke 1:1-3. There, Luke says that others handed down the things that he wrote. He was not an eyewitness. Likewise, there is nothing in Acts that suggests the writer was an apostle. Luke fits this description. This adds to the evidence that he wrote Luke and Acts.

- Believers from the early church to the present have accepted Luke as the author of our third Gospel and Acts.

- Luke and Acts are arranged alike. Look at Figure 1.3. As you study the chart, notice the similar ways an author arranged Luke and Acts. Luke compares the ministry of Christ to the ministry of the body of Christ, the Church.

Luke		Acts	
Greeting to Theophilus	1:1-4	Greeting to Theophilus	1:1-2
Early life of Jesus	1:5–3:38	Early life of the Church	1–8
Anointing of Jesus	3:22	Anointing of the Church	2:4
First sermon at Nazareth	4:14-30	First sermon at Pentecost	2
Confirming miracles and healings	4:31-41	Confirming miracles and healings	3–4
Success and popularity	5	Success and popularity	2–4
Growing opposition from the Pharisees and Jewish leaders	6	Growing opposition from the Pharisees and Jewish leaders	4–8
Travel through Galilee, Judea, and Perea	3–8	Travel on missionary trips	8–23
Arrest and threefold trial before the Sanhedrin, Pilate, and Herod	22–23	Arrest and threefold trial before Felix, Festus, and Agrippa	24–26
Climax of ministry at Calvary	23–24	Climax of ministry in Rome	28

Figure 1.3   A comparison of the outlines of Luke and Acts[5]

We have looked at five reasons we believe Luke wrote Acts. Now let us consider when he wrote it.

C. The date of Acts

Q 3 ✒ *Acts was probably written between which two events (give dates)?*

Acts records the first time Paul was in prison in Rome about A.D. 60-63. Therefore, Acts must have been written after this. Rome burned in A.D. 64. At that time a *Caesar named Nero blamed Christians. And he began to persecute them. The good relationship Paul had with the Roman government suggests that Acts was written before Rome burned. Also, Luke does not mention the destruction of Jerusalem. This took place in A.D. 70. So we think Acts was written before this big event. Most Bible teachers think that Luke wrote Acts about A.D. 63.

Students should also be familiar with other dates related to Acts. Figure 1.5 gives a few important dates and references in Acts.

**Figure 1.4
Head of Nero**

Date [+] (A.D.)	Event	Acts	Letters Paul Wrote[6]
30	The ascension of Christ	1:9	
31-32	The conversion of Paul	9:1-19	
35	Paul's first visit to Jerusalem	9:26	
44	Paul's second visit to Jerusalem	11:30	
46-47	Paul's first missionary trip	13:4–14:27	Gal. (after first trip)
49	The first great Church council	15:1-29	
49-53	Paul's second missionary trip	15:36–18:22	1 & 2 Thess.
53-57	Paul's third missionary trip	18:23–21:17	1 & 2 Cor., Rom.
58	Paul's arrest in Jerusalem	21:17–23:35	
58-60	Paul's prison term in Caesarea	24–26	
60	Paul's trip to Rome	27:1–28:15	
60-63	Paul's first prison term in Rome	28:16-31	Eph., Phil., Col., Philem.
63	The writing of Acts by Luke		
63-65	Paul's ministry between prison terms in Rome	(After Acts)	1 Tim., Titus
65-67	Paul's second prison term and death in Rome	(After Acts)	2 Tim.

Q 4 ✒ *How many years passed from Christ's resurrection to Paul's imprisonment of Acts 28?*

Figure 1.5   Various dates related to Acts

+ approximate dates

Appreciating Acts
Goal: *Analyze 5 purposes for which Luke wrote Acts.*

Setting

There is a great danger in studying Acts. It is so full of action and stories that we can miss the big picture. A newspaper has many stories. These are often unrelated. In contrast, Luke chose a few stories for special reasons.

Acts gives us a history of the first 30 years of the Church.[7] Luke did not tell everything he knew. For example, he told us that Paul taught until midnight at Troas (Acts 20:7).[8] But Luke did not tell us anything Paul taught there. A book on the subjects Paul taught at Troas that one night would be longer than all of Acts! Imagine how many books it would take to tell all that happened in the Church during the first 30 years! Acts contains less than 1 percent of what happened in the early church (See John 20:30; 21:25). Why did Luke leave most things out, but include only a few stories and events? Why did the Holy Spirit guide Luke to write about certain things? We can identify at least five purposes for which Luke wrote Acts.

A. Acts serves as a bridge between the Gospels and Paul's letters.

Q 5 *How does Acts serve as a bridge between the Gospels and the Epistles?*

In its early stage, the New Testament had only two parts. It included the four Gospels and the letters of Paul. So there were great gaps in the written history of the Church. Paul wrote letters to some churches. But many believers did not know how or when other churches started.

Review Figure 1.5. Notice that Luke wrote Acts after Paul wrote most of his letters. Acts 13–28 tells us about Paul's travels. In Acts we see how Paul started the churches in Galatia, Thessalonica, Corinth, Ephesus, Philippi, and Colosse. Also, Acts introduces us to Timothy and Titus. Later in the New Testament we read Paul's letters to the churches and people that Acts introduced. Thus Acts gives us the background for Paul's letters. Acts has a special place in the New Testament. One of Luke's

Figure 1.6 Acts is a bridge between the Gospels and the rest of the New Testament.

purposes was to give us a bridge between the Gospels and Paul's letters.

B. Acts traces the growth of the Church.

Luke reveals that the Church grew in at least four ways.

Q 6 *What are 4 types of church growth that Acts describes?*

First, **the Church grew in numbers.**   On the Day of Pentecost, the Church fit in one upper room. Then thousands of Jews were saved in Jerusalem (Acts 2:41, 47; 4:4). Acts 6:7 reveals that numbers increased, including many priests. Persecution scattered the believers. These witnessed and made converts everywhere they went (Acts 8:1, 4). Throughout Acts we see the number of believers increase.

Second, **the Church grew *geographically, in new places.**   It started in Jerusalem. Acts explains how persecution scattered believers from Jerusalem to other places (Acts 8:1). It also explains how Paul's journeys helped expand the Church. Still, the Church was in Rome before Paul arrived there (Acts 28:14-15). Thus, Acts tells how the Church grew from Jerusalem to Rome, the center of the Roman Empire. (See chapter 5, Lesson 14, point B.) It is not an accident that Acts 1 begins with Jerusalem and Acts 28 ends in Rome. Luke arranged his stories to show the growth of the Church.

Third, **the Church grew socially.**   The early church was a Jewish church (Acts 1:1–7:60). How did the Church open up to other races? Acts 2 tells that Jews and Jewish

Q 7 ✎ *How has your church grown in the 4 areas mentioned in Acts? Explain.*

converts from 15 different locations heard the gospel. Acts 6:1 reveals that the Church included two Jewish groups. One group spoke Greek and the other spoke Hebrew. Acts 8 tells us that Philip preached to Samaritans, and later, to an Ethiopian. Acts 10 tells us about Peter's vision related to Cornelius, a Roman centurion. This vision led to a change of attitude toward Gentiles. Even the Gentiles could be saved (Acts 11:18). This was amazing to Jewish believers! Thus the walls of prejudice began to fall. Still, Acts 11:19-21 shows that the Church was limited by racial prejudice. A few Jews began to witness to Greeks! This was radical theology! But by Acts 13, we see Paul beginning to preach to the Gentiles after Jews reject the good news (Acts 13:43-46). Thus the Church grew to include those from all tribes, nations, languages, and cultures.

Fourth, **the Church grew in its theology.**   In the early days the believers were Jewish. It took time for them to understand the relationship between law and grace. Acts 15 focuses on an important question. Do Gentiles need to be circumcised and follow the law of Moses (Acts 15:5)? Peter's answer was "No!" (Acts 15:11). Still, the Jewish church leaders asked Gentile believers to follow some guidelines (Acts 15:19-21). Why? Partly so that there could be unity between Jewish and Gentile believers.[9] Thus Acts shows us how the theology of the Church grew to include all people. One of Luke's purposes was to show how the Church grew in numbers, new places, culture, and theology.

C. Acts explains and defends the Church.

Q 8 ✎ *What questions related to government does Acts answer?*

- Acts explains and presents the Christian faith to all. Luke explains the background, growth, and beliefs of the Church. He does this in a way that invites people to receive and follow Jesus.
- Read Acts 4:8-12. Notice how it defends Christianity to Jews. Now read Acts 25:8-11. It defends the faith to Gentiles. The Spirit guides Luke to answer the religious questions of Jews and Gentiles.
- Acts also answers questions that government leaders would ask about Christianity. Acts shows that the Church is peaceful. Believers respect government leaders. In Acts, riots and civil problems are always caused by enemies of the Church.

Luke probably wrote Acts while Paul was in prison in Rome. When Paul went to trial, Acts would support his defense. Likewise, Acts would help defend believers in other places. So we see that a third purpose of Acts was to defend the faith.

D. Acts serves as a guide for faith and practice.

Q 9 ✎ *Should Acts be used as a basis for doctrine? Explain.*

Acts gives us guidance in what the Church should believe and do. Some argue that we should not use Acts as a guide because it is history. But recall that Luke did not write a complete history. He wrote a selective history. Paul used history for the purpose of teaching.[10] He referred to the historical book of Genesis. He reviewed the history of Abraham to teach that we are justified by faith (Rom. 4).[11] Likewise, Luke used history to teach certain themes.[12] He chose a few stories and events for special purposes. One of his purposes was to emphasize what the early church believed. Why is it helpful to know what the early church believed? Because the first believers were under the same covenant we are under! The Church in Acts teaches us to believe in the following:

- The Scriptures, prayer, sharing, and fellowship;
- The work of the Holy Spirit in glorifying Christ;
- Knowing and worshiping God;
- Witnessing, signs and wonders, being filled with the Spirit;
- Speaking in tongues, prophesying, and other spiritual gifts;
- Solving Church growth problems, evangelizing, and teaching new believers;
- God's power—He is working during persecution; He loves those in all nations.

Luke did not know how long the Church would remain on earth. But one of his purposes was to teach future believers. The power and principles of Acts are for the Church until Christ returns.[13]

E. Acts emphasizes that the Holy Spirit is the key to being witnesses for Jesus.

The Gospel of Luke tells what Jesus began to do on earth, in a physical body. Acts tells us what Jesus continued to do from heaven. He did this through His spiritual body, the Church, by the Holy Spirit (Acts 1:1).[14]

Acts teaches that the Spirit uses both apostles and laypeople (Acts 2:17-18). For every apostle in the upper room, there were nine laypeople. On the one hand, Luke organizes Acts around the ministry of two apostles. Acts 1–12 is mostly about Peter. Acts 13–28 tells of Paul's ministry. Still, Luke includes the ministries of many others (See Figure 1.7).

Q 10 ⬋ *Who are some of your favorite lay ministers in Acts? Explain.*

Person(s)	Ministry	Acts
108 of the 120	Prayed and witnessed for Christ	1–2
Barnabas	Was generous; became a friend to Paul; ministered to and with Paul	4, 9, 11–15
The 7 deacons	Collected money and gave it to widows	6
Stephen	Served as a deacon; prayed for the sick; witnessed and taught for Jesus	6–7
Philip	Served as a deacon; took the gospel to Samaria	8, 21
Ananias	Prayed for and baptized Paul	9
Tabitha	Sewed clothes for widows	9
Simon the tanner	Provided housing for Peter	10
Cornelius	Gave alms; invited others to his home	10
Scattered believers	Told the gospel to Jews and Greeks	11
Mary, Mark's mother	Had a prayer meeting in her home	12
Unnamed believers	Prayed for Peter's release from prison	12
Silas	Traveled and ministered with Paul	15–18
John Mark	Traveled with and helped Paul and Barnabas	12, 15
Simeon, Lucius, Manaen	Prophesied and taught	13
Lydia	Provided housing for preachers	16
Philippian jailer	Fed apostles and washed their wounds	16
Timothy	Traveled with Paul and helped him	16–20
Jason	Provided housing for ministers	17
Unnamed believers	Escorted Paul to Athens	17
Priscilla and Aquila	Gave housing and support to Paul	18
Apollos	Testified for Jesus at Ephesus and Corinth	18–19
Unnamed brothers	Encouraged and recommended Apollos	18
Sopater, Aristarchus, Secundus, Gaius, Timothy, Tychicus, Trophimus	Traveled with Paul; sometimes carried messages for him or other believers	20–21
Unnamed disciples	Gave 7 days lodging to ministers	21
Unnamed disciples	Prophesied of trouble in Jerusalem	21
Philip's 4 daughters	Prophesied of trouble in Jerusalem	21
Agabus	Prophesied of trouble in Jerusalem	21
Mnason	Provided housing for ministers	21
Paul's nephew	Warned Paul of a plot to kill him	23
Aristarchus	Sailed with Paul from Caesarea toward Rome	27

Continued on next page

Continued from previous page

Person(s)	Ministry	Acts
Luke	Wrote Acts and traveled with Paul	1, 20, 21, 27, 28
Some brothers	Invited Paul and others to stay a week	28
The brothers	Walked out to meet Paul near Rome	28
Unnamed disciples	Paid 2 years for a rented house for Paul	28

Figure 1.7   People in Acts who were not apostles, but who were used by the Holy Spirit

Q 11 *What is Luke's greatest purpose in Acts?*

Luke's greatest purpose is to emphasize the ministry of the Holy Spirit through believers. In his Gospel, Luke stated that Jesus depended on the Spirit (Luke 4:1, 14, 18). Also, in his Gospel, Luke predicted that the Spirit would come to believers (Luke 11:13; 24:49). But in Acts, Luke emphasizes the Spirit 55 times! Take a few minutes to study Figure 1.8 at the end of this section. It emphasizes that the Holy Spirit must be the source of all we do for Christ. Read this list every time you study this book.

The fastest growing churches today emphasize the ministry of laypeople. Some of these growing churches have over 100 ministries that laypeople do. Laypeople visit the sick, feed the poor, and teach people to read. They teach students who have problems with their studies. Laypeople help widows, adopt orphans, and counsel troubled youth. They paint schools in the community. They build buildings for young churches. They sew and cook to raise funds for the church. Laypeople tell Bible stories to children in their neighborhoods. They have Bible studies in their homes. They meet with those who are divorced, pregnant outside of marriage, depressed, or out of work. They fix people's broken bicycles or cars. Some doctors set up clinics in local churches. One or two evenings each week they do dental or medical work free. Others pray with those in need. These are only a few of the things that laypeople can do. It is past time for laypeople to serve more. As we are filled with the Spirit, He can lead us into many ministries. Every member of the body of Christ should have a ministry. Each believer should answer the question, "What am I doing to serve God and others?"[15]

Q 12 *What would be missing in your life and church without the ministry of the Spirit?*

The Holy Spirit wants to work through all believers today. His fullness gives us the boldness to serve and witness for Jesus. The early church had few of the things we value today. But the Church spread like a fire across the world. Read through Figure 1.7 again. Note the events and stories that would be missing from Acts without the ministry of the Spirit. The Spirit is the key to helping each believer be a worker.

Conclusion

It is good to know the reasons why Luke wrote Acts. *First*, Acts serves as a bridge between the Gospels and Paul's letters. *Second*, Acts tells how the Church grew in numbers, in new places, in culture, and in theology. *Third*, Acts explains and defends the Church. *Fourth*, Acts serves as a guide for faith and practice. We will emphasize these four purposes as we study Acts. But these are all small compared to Luke's *fifth* purpose. He emphasizes the power of the Holy Spirit. If we miss Luke's emphasis on the Holy Spirit, we miss his greatest purpose!

A person may weave several strands into one strong rope. Likewise, Luke wove five themes into one strong story. It is the story of how the Holy Spirit empowered the Church to witness for Jesus from Jerusalem to Rome.

Acts	Reference to the Holy Spirit
1:2	*. . . after giving instructions through the **Holy Spirit** to the apostles he had chosen.*
1:5	*"For John baptized with water, but in a few days you will be baptized with the **Holy Spirit**."*

Continued on next page

1:8	"But you will receive power when the **Holy Spirit** comes on you; and you will be my witnesses in Jerusalem, and in all Judea and Samaria, and to the ends of the earth."
1:16	"Brothers, the Scripture had to be fulfilled which the **Holy Spirit** spoke long ago through the mouth of David concerning Judas, who served as guide for those who arrested Jesus—"
2:4	All of them were filled with the **Holy Spirit** and began to speak in other tongues as the **Spirit** enabled them.
2:17	"'In the last days, God says, I will pour out my **Spirit** on all people. Your sons and daughters will prophesy, your young men will see visions, your old men will dream dreams.'"
2:18	"'Even on my servants, both men and women, I will pour out my **Spirit** in those days, and they will prophesy.'"
2:33	"Exalted to the right hand of God, he has received from the Father the promised **Holy Spirit** and has poured out what you now see and hear."
2:38	Peter replied, "Repent and be baptized, every one of you, in the name of Jesus Christ for the forgiveness of your sins. And you will receive the gift of the **Holy Spirit**."
4:8	Then Peter, filled with the **Holy Spirit**, said to them: "Rulers and elders of the people!"
4:25	"You spoke by the **Holy Spirit** through the mouth of your servant, our father David: 'Why do the nations rage and the peoples plot in vain?'"
4:31	After they prayed, the place where they were meeting was shaken. And they were all filled with the **Holy Spirit** and spoke the word of God boldly.
5:3	Then Peter said, "Ananias, how is it that Satan has so filled your heart that you have lied to the **Holy Spirit** and have kept for yourself some of the money you received for the land?"
5:9	Peter said to her, "How could you agree to test the **Spirit** of the Lord?"
5:32	"We are witnesses of these things, and so is the **Holy Spirit**, whom God has given to those who obey him."
6:3	"Brothers, choose seven men from among you who are known to be full of the **Spirit** and wisdom."
6:5	They chose Stephen, a man full of faith and of the **Holy Spirit**; also Philip, . . .
6:10	But they could not stand up against his wisdom or the **Spirit** by whom he spoke.
7:51	"You are just like your fathers: You always resist the **Holy Spirit**!"
7:55	But Stephen, full of the **Holy Spirit**, looked up to heaven and saw the glory of God, and Jesus . . .
8:15	When they arrived, they prayed for them that they might receive the **Holy Spirit** . . .
8:16	Because the **Holy Spirit** had not yet come upon any of them; they had simply been baptized . . .
8:17	Then Peter and John placed their hands on them, and they received the **Holy Spirit**.
8:18	When Simon saw that the **Spirit** was given at the laying on of the apostles' hands, he offered . . .
8:19	"Give me also this ability so that everyone on whom I lay my hands may receive the **Holy Spirit**."
8:29	The **Spirit** told Philip, "Go to that chariot and stay near it."
8:39	When they came up out of the water, the **Spirit** of the Lord suddenly took Philip away, and . . .
9:17	"the Lord Jesus . . . has sent me so that you may see again and be filled with the **Holy Spirit**."
9:31	It [the church] was strengthened; and encouraged by the **Holy Spirit**, it grew in numbers . . .
10:19	While Peter was still thinking about the vision, the **Spirit** said to him, "Simon, three men . . ."
10:38	"God anointed Jesus of Nazareth with the **Holy Spirit** and power, and how he went around . . ."
10:44	While Peter was still speaking these words, the **Holy Spirit** came on all who heard the message.
10:45	The circumcised believers who had come with Peter were astonished that the gift of the **Holy Spirit** had been poured out even on the Gentiles.
10:47	"Can anyone keep these people from being baptized with water? They have received the **Holy Spirit** just as we have."
11:12	"The **Spirit** told me to have no hesitation about going with them. These six brothers also went . . ."
11:15	"As I began to speak, the **Holy Spirit** came on them as he had come on us at the beginning."
11:16	"Then I remembered what the Lord had said: 'John baptized with water, but you will be baptized with the **Holy Spirit**.'"
11:24	He was a good man, full of the **Holy Spirit** and faith, and a great number of people were brought . . .

Continued on next page

Continued from previous page

Acts	Reference to the Holy Spirit
11:28	One of them, named Agabus, stood up and through the **Spirit** predicted that a severe famine would . . .
13:2	While they were worshiping the Lord and fasting, the **Holy Spirit** said, "Set apart for me Barnabas and Saul for the work to which I have called them."
13:4	The two of them, sent on their way by the **Holy Spirit**, went down to Seleucia and sailed from . . .
13:9	Then Saul, who was also called Paul, filled with the **Holy Spirit**, looked straight at Elymas and said . . .
13:52	And the disciples were filled with joy and with the **Holy Spirit**.
15:8	"God, who knows the heart, showed that he accepted them by giving the **Holy Spirit** to them . . ."
15:28	It seemed good to the **Holy Spirit** and to us not to burden you with anything beyond the following . . .
16:6	Paul and his companions traveled throughout the region of Phrygia and Galatia, having been kept by the **Holy Spirit** from preaching the word in the province of Asia.
16:7	When they came to the border of Mysia, they tried to enter Bithynia, but the **Spirit** of Jesus would not . . .
19:2	"Did you receive the **Holy Spirit** when you believed?" They answered, "No, we have not even heard that there is a **Holy Spirit**."
19:6	When Paul placed his hands on them, the **Holy Spirit** came on them, and they spoke in tongues . . .
20:22	"And now, compelled by the **Spirit**, I am going to Jerusalem, not knowing what will happen to me."
20:23	"I only know that in every city the **Holy Spirit** warns me that prison and hardships are facing me."
20:28	"Keep watch over yourselves and all the flock of which the **Holy Spirit** has made you overseers."
21:4	Through the **Spirit** they urged Paul not to go on to Jerusalem.
21:11	he took Paul's belt, tied his own hands and feet with it and said, "The **Holy Spirit** says, 'In this way . . .'"
28:25	"The **Holy Spirit** spoke the truth to your forefathers when he said through Isaiah the prophet: . . ."

Figure 1.8   References to the Holy Spirit in Acts

Lesson 3   Analyzing Acts

Goal A: *Explain 2 of the 3 ways to outline Acts.*
Goal B: *Identify 6 speakers of the messages in Acts.*

We have looked briefly at the author, date, and purposes of Acts. Now, let us look at three ways to outline the book. We will begin with the easiest outline and end with the hardest.

A. Acts 1:8 is a good three-part outline of the entire book of Acts.

"But you will receive power when the Holy Spirit comes on you; and you will be my witnesses in Jerusalem, and in all Judea and Samaria, and to the ends of the earth" (Acts 1:8).

The chart that follows shows how we can divide Acts into three parts.

Part	Place to Witness	Chapters in Acts
1	Jerusalem	1–7
2	Judea and Samaria	8–12
3	The whole earth	13–28

Figure 1.9   Acts 1:8 is a good outline of the book of Acts.

In the *first* part of Acts the Church was in Jerusalem (Acts 1–7). At Pentecost, 3,000 believed, were baptized, and joined the Church. By the power of the Spirit, the apostles did miracles and healed the sick. They cast out demons in the name of Jesus. Many Jews continued to receive Jesus as their Savior and Lord (Acts 2:47). The good news spread rapidly. Many priests were converted and became obedient to the faith (Acts 6:7).

Q 13 *What are the 3 parts mentioned in Acts 1:8? (State the chapters for each part.)*

The *second* part of Acts focuses on Judea and Samaria (Acts 8–12). God allowed persecution to scatter the Church. The Jews stoned Stephen in Jerusalem. But burying his body was like planting a seed. A great harvest followed. Believers fled from Jerusalem throughout Judea and Samaria. Wherever they went, they witnessed about Jesus (Acts 8–12).

The *third* part of Acts is about the ministry of Paul (Acts 13–28). In these chapters we see this great apostle witnessing *"to the ends of the earth"* (Acts 1:8). Thus Acts shows how the good news spread. The Spirit enabled believers to witness in Jerusalem, then in Judea and Samaria, and on to the rest of the known world. The good news about Jesus traveled from Jews to Gentiles, and from Jerusalem to Rome.

Figure 1.10   Key cities and *provinces in Acts

B. We can outline Acts by comparing the supernatural ministries of Peter and Paul.

Figure 1.11 divides Acts into two parts. The first part, Acts 1–12, is mostly about Peter's ministry. The second part, Acts 13–28, covers the ministry of Paul. This chart does not cover all the things Peter and Paul did. But it emphasizes some similar ways in which the Holy Spirit worked through these apostles.[16]

Q 14 *Comparing Peter's ministry with Paul's divides Acts into which parts?*

Ministry of Peter (Acts 1–12)	Acts	Ministry of Paul (Acts 13–28)	Acts
Preached Jesus to the Jews	2–5	Preached Jesus to the Gentiles	13–28
Healed a man lame from birth	3:1-10	Healed a man lame from birth	14:8-18
Peter's shadow brought healing	5:15-16	Handkerchiefs and aprons brought healing	19:11-12
Dealt with Simon, a sorcerer	8:9-24	Dealt with Bar-Jesus, a sorcerer	13:6-11
		Cast a demon out of a girl	16:16-18
Raised Dorcas to life	9:36-41	Raised Eutychus to life	20:9-12
		Healed many on the island of Malta	28:1-9

Figure 1.11   Chart comparing the supernatural ministries of Peter and Paul

We have looked briefly at two ways to outline Acts. A third way of outlining Acts is according to its speeches or messages.

Q 15 ➤ *Who are at least 6 people who gave speeches in Acts?*

C. We can outline Acts by the 24 messages in it.

Luke records at least 24 different messages in Acts (See Figure 1.12). These include messages by Peter, Stephen, James, Paul, and others. Many of these messages were not planned. Rather, believers spoke as the Holy Spirit filled and inspired them. (Compare Matthew 10:20 and Luke 12:11-12.) Luke used these 24 messages as a major way to organize Acts.

We will study each of these in this course. For now, take a few minutes to study Figure 1.12. Being aware of these 24 messages will help you study Acts.

Message	Speaker	Reason or Theme	Place	Acts
1	Peter	Apostle to replace Judas	Jerusalem	1:16-22
2	Peter	Tongues on the Day of Pentecost	Jerusalem	2:14-36
3	Peter	Healing of lame man in the temple	Jerusalem	3:12-26
4	Peter	Defense to the Sanhedrin for preaching	Jerusalem	4:8-12
5	Gamaliel	Counseling the Sanhedrin about Peter and John	Jerusalem	5:35-39
6	Stephen	Arrested by the Sanhedrin	Jerusalem	7:2-53
7	Peter	Called to Cornelius' house	Caesarea	10:34-43
8	Peter	Defense to circumcised believers	Jerusalem	11:4-17
9	Paul	Sabbath message to Jews	Pisidian Antioch	13:16-41
10	Paul & Barnabas	Crowd wanted to worship them	Lystra	14:14-17
11	Peter	Meeting of Church leaders	Jerusalem	15:7-11
12	James	Meeting of Church leaders	Jerusalem	15:13-21
13	Paul	The unknown god	Athens	17:22-31
14	Gallio	Rejecting the Jews' case on Paul	Corinth	18:14-16
15	Demetrius	Angry followers of Diana	Ephesus	19:25-27
16	Town clerk	Riot at Ephesus	Ephesus	19:35-40
17	Paul	Good-bye to Ephesian elders	Miletus	20:18-35
18	Paul	Mob trying to kill Paul	Jerusalem	22:1-21
19	Paul	Defense to the Sanhedrin	Jerusalem	23:1-6
20	Paul	Defense before Governor Felix	Caesarea	24:10-21
21	Paul	Defense before Governor Festus	Caesarea	25:8, 10-11
22	Paul	Defense before King Agrippa	Caesarea	26:1-23
23	Paul	Bad storm on Mediterranean Sea	Near Malta	27:21-26
24	Paul	Testimony to Jewish leaders	Rome	28:17-28

Figure 1.12   Chart of 24 messages or speeches in Acts[17]

Test Yourself: Circle the letter by the *best* completion to each question or statement.

1. The best title for Acts is
a) *The Acts of the Apostles.*
b) *The Acts of the Holy Spirit.*
c) *The Acts of Peter and Paul.*
d) *The Acts of the Early Church.*

2. Which of the following is TRUE about the writer of Acts?
a) He traveled with Paul.
b) He was an apostle.
c) He favored the church in Jerusalem.
d) He was sometimes called Theophilus.

3. Acts was written about A.D.
a) 43.
b) 53.
c) 63.
d) 73.

4. One big purpose of Acts is to show the spread of the gospel from
a) Jerusalem to Rome.
b) Antioch to Tarsus.
c) Galilee to Judea.
d) synagogue to synagogue.

5. The greatest purpose of Acts is to
a) defend Paul and other believers.
b) show the spread of the gospel.
c) emphasize the power of the Spirit in believers.
d) serve as a bridge between the Gospels and the Epistles.

6. God intends Acts to be used for
a) history, but not doctrine.
b) doctrine, but not history.
c) neither doctrine nor history.
d) both doctrine and history.

7. A good outline of Acts is found in Acts
a) 1:1.
b) 1:8.
c) 2:4.
d) 2:38.

8. One complete section in the outline of Acts covers chapters
a) 1–6.
b) 5–13.
c) 8–12.
d) 20–28.

9. We can outline Acts by comparing the ministries of
a) Peter and Stephen.
b) Peter and Paul.
c) Stephen and Philip.
d) Paul and Barnabas.

10. Those who gave speeches in Acts include
a) Peter, Sapphira, and Gallio.
b) Paul, Aquila, and Priscilla.
c) Stephen, Demetrius, and Gamaliel.
d) Peter, Paul, and Ananias

 Essay Test Topics: Write 50-100 words on each of these goals that you studied in this chapter.

Approaching Acts
Goal: *Analyze the title, author, and date of Acts.*

Appreciating Acts
Goal: *Analyze 5 purposes for which Luke wrote Acts.*

Analyzing Acts
Goal: *Explain 2 of the 3 ways to outline Acts.*

Goal: *Identify 6 speakers of the messages in Acts.*

Chapter 2:

From the Resurrection to Pentecost
(Acts 1)

Introduction

A person's last words have always called for special attention. Last words often reveal what is most important in the heart of the speaker. Do you remember Jacob's last words found in Genesis 49? He gathered all of his sons around his bed. Each one leaned forward so he would not miss anything. Jacob's last words lived on in their hearts for the rest of their lives.

The last words of Joseph were also very important.

[24]*Then Joseph said to his brothers, "I am about to die. But God will surely come to your aid and take you up out of this land to the land he promised on oath to Abraham, Isaac and Jacob."* [25]*And Joseph made the sons of Israel swear an oath and said, "God will surely come to your aid, and then you must carry my bones up from this place"* (Gen. 50:24-25).

Figure 2.1   The gift our Father promised: the baptism in the Holy Spirit

Joseph's last words, like those of his father, Jacob, had great weight.

But what about the last words of Jesus? Do Christians know what was on His heart as He left? Jesus appeared to His disciples for 40 days after His resurrection. During this time, He spoke His last words on earth. These last words reveal what was most important in the heart of our Lord. He commanded them to remain in Jerusalem until they received the promise of the Father. He wanted His followers to receive the power of the Holy Spirit. Then they could tell others about Him. In this chapter, we will look closely at the promised gift of the Holy Spirit and how believers can receive it. We want to give special attention to the Master's last words.

Lessons:

The Gift Our Father Promised (Acts 1:1-5)
Goal: *Analyze the command, the gift, and the Baptizer in Acts 1.*

The Work of the Church (Acts 1:6-11)
Goal: *Explain the plan, the place, the power, and the purpose of witnessing. Relate these to self and others.*

Steps to Pentecost (Acts 1:12-26)
Goal: *Identify and do 3 things that precede being filled with the Spirit.*

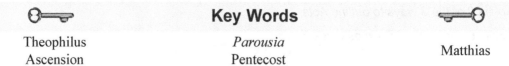

Key Words

| Theophilus | *Parousia* | Matthias |
| Ascension | Pentecost | |

26

The Gift Our Father Promised (Acts 1:1-5)

Goal: *Analyze the command, the gift, and the Baptizer in Acts 1.*

Setting

Luke and Acts are both written to Theophilus, a friend of Luke. The name Theophilus is a combination of two Greek words. *Theo* means "God," and *philo* means "love." Thus, Theophilus means "one who loves God." This was a common name in New Testament times.[1] Since Acts is written to *the one who loves God*, each believer feels included.

Recall that Acts is the second book of history Luke wrote to Theophilus. In Luke 1:3 the word *excellent* describes Theophilus. This suggests that he was an official or wealthy person of high position.[2] Perhaps the Spirit used Theophilus to spread copies of Luke and Acts.

The ministry of the Holy Spirit is a major theme of Luke. In his Gospel, Luke mentions the Holy Spirit a few times more than Matthew or Mark mentions Him. But in Acts, Luke emphasizes the Spirit over 50 times! As believers, we must understand the importance of the Spirit's ministry in and through us. If we miss this in Acts, we have missed Luke's biggest theme. If we miss the daily filling of the Holy Spirit, we miss God's best plan for us.

In this lesson, Luke takes us back to some of the last words of Jesus. Let us study about the command, the gift, and the baptizer.

A. The command

Look again at the command Jesus gave. Luke records it twice.

"I am going to send you what my Father has promised; **but stay in the city until you have been clothed with power from on high"** (Luke 24:49).

[4]On one occasion, while he was eating with them, he gave them this command: "Do not leave Jerusalem, **but wait for the gift** *my Father promised, which you have heard me speak about. [5]For John baptized with water, but in a few days you will be baptized with the Holy Spirit"* (Acts 1:4-5).

What was the command? He commanded them to stay in Jerusalem until they received the gift our Father promised. He commanded them not to leave Jerusalem without the gift. This gift was the baptism in the Holy Spirit.

People like gifts. You do not usually need to command them to receive gifts. They want to receive them. You do not need to command people to eat free food. Just offer it and they will eat it all. You do not need to command people to accept free money. Just offer it and they will take it. So why did Jesus need to command His followers to wait for a gift from God? Let us consider three reasons why Jesus made waiting a command instead of a request.

***First,* they did not realize how big the task was.** They thought Jesus died for Jews only! In the beginning, the disciples were full of prejudice. It took years for them to begin sharing the good news with Gentiles. They did not realize it was God's plan for them to tell strangers and outsiders. Jesus had already told them to tell everyone (Matt. 28:19-20). But the truth had not gotten past their prejudice. Perhaps they had enough power to tell their families and friends. But strangers and sinners are hard to talk to. So the disciples needed more of the Holy Spirit.

Likewise, all of us need to be filled with the Spirit. His love for the lost gives us the power to love those who are not like us. The Spirit enables us to witness to those who are a different color than we are. He enables us to witness to those who speak a different language, eat different food, dress differently, and think differently. If the task were not

Q 1 *What does the name Theophilus mean?*

Q 2 *According to Luke, what command did Jesus give His disciples before He left?*

Q 3 *Summarize 3 reasons why Jesus commanded the disciples to receive the gift Father promised.*

Q 4 *In what way was the task to witness bigger than the disciples realized?*

Q 5 *Do believers you know witness to those with different values and customs? Explain.*

so big, we could get by with less power. But God loves the whole world. Therefore, we must be filled with the Spirit to witness as God desires.

Second, they did not realize how hard the task would be.   The disciples were filled with joy. Jesus had risen from the dead. They saw Him ascend into heaven. Their hearts were full of emotion. But emotion makes people blind to reality. Like a young couple in love, they were unaware of the problems ahead. Like children, they did not realize they had enemies. When they began to witness, their vision would clear. They would soon be called drunks, blasphemers, and liars. Some would be dragged to prison. Many of them would lose their lands, homes, and earthly possessions. Loved ones and fellow Jews would reject them. Many would be beaten. Some would die. The task would be harder than they thought. Spiritual warfare was ahead. They needed more of the Spirit's power to succeed!

Q 6 *What is the key to witnessing in hard times?*

When times are easy, we tend to feel less of our need for God. But persecution causes believers to seek more of the Spirit's power. In Ethiopia some think that there were less than 1 million believers in 1974. Then the Communists gained control of the nation. Most churches lost their buildings and properties. Persecution was severe. But by 1992 the number of believers had grown to over 6 million! There were several denominations. However, believers in most of these denominations have been baptized in the Holy Spirit. They are Pentecostal in practice. That is, they boldly witness for Jesus and pray in tongues often. The Evangelical Union of Ethiopia includes several denominations with millions of members. This Union invited a Pentecostal group to come and build a Bible school to train their pastors. Persecution and hard times cause believers today to be as Pentecostal as the early church was. The harder the task is, the more believers need the Spirit's power.[3] The steeper the mountain, the more power it takes to climb it.

Q 7 *How long do you think the disciples expected to witness? Explain.*

Third, they did not realize how long the task would take.   The disciples had enough knowledge and power to start witnessing. They knew for sure that Jesus had conquered death. They walked and talked with Him after His resurrection. But they needed more of the Spirit's power to finish the task. A little power is enough to begin a task. But people who lack power quit a job before they finish it.

The disciples thought Jesus was about to set up His earthly kingdom (Acts 1:6). He had conquered death. Surely it would not take long to conquer the Romans. The early believers expected Jesus to return any minute. They had no idea that they would witness and watch for a lifetime. The task took longer than they expected. Therefore, the Lord commanded them to get extra power.

It is wise to live ready to meet the Lord. But we should seek all the power God has for us while we are waiting and witnessing. We might wait and work longer than we expect. Like the five wise virgins, we should get extra oil. We might need it if the groom delays (Matt. 25:5). The demands of life may surprise us. It is good to take a lunch when starting on a long walk. It is smart to fill a car with gas before starting a journey. We should fill up with all the spiritual power God has for us.

Both humans and ants know the importance of harvest time (Prov. 6:8). They gather extra food when it is available. Later, when there is no grain in the fields, they have plenty to eat. Thus planning for physical power is wisdom common to humans and insects. But consider the timing of Pentecost. This was the time the Jews celebrated the harvest. At the end of the barley harvest they had the big feast of Pentecost (Deut. 16:9-10).[4] They had filled all of their barns and grain bins. They had plenty of food for the flesh. At that exact time, God poured out the Holy Spirit. What a wonderful way to emphasize our need for a spiritual harvest. At Pentecost we reap the Spirit that God has for us. We fill up with the Spirit. Then we are spiritually ready for the future. Let us plan as much for the spiritual part of us as we do for the fleshly part. The task ahead may take longer than we think.

Some of the disciples were apostles. Think about it! These were Christian men who had walked with Jesus for over 3 years. They had preached Christ and baptized people. They already knew the Holy Spirit. It was the Spirit's power that had enabled them to minister. They healed the sick and cast out demons through a temporary anointing of the Spirit's power (Luke 9:1-2). Therefore, they could have thought they had enough of the Spirit. They could have thought that others needed the gift, but that it was not necessary for them. But even the apostles needed the baptism in the Holy Spirit. They needed a deeper relationship with the Spirit they already knew. Therefore, Christ commanded even the apostles to wait for the promised gift.

Q 8 ✎ *Are some people you know spiritual enough that they do not need the baptism in the Holy Spirit? Explain.*

Jesus did not just *suggest* that His disciples remain in Jerusalem. He did not tell them they *might* want to consider waiting. The Lord *commanded* His disciples to wait for the baptism in the Holy Spirit. He gave them a direct order to obey. Likewise, God's will is that each believer today be filled with the Spirit. Each person should be born again. Then each should seek until he or she is filled with the Spirit.

B. The gift

It is easier for us to wait for something if we understand its value. One great writer said the most precious gift a person can receive after salvation is the gift of being filled with the Holy Spirit.[5] Luke refers to this promised gift in several ways. Notice some of the ways he describes this deeper relationship with God.

Q 9 ⤸ *How does Luke most often refer to the baptism in the Holy Spirit?*

- *the promise of my Father* (Luke 24:49)
- *the promise of the Father* (Acts 1:4)
- *the promise of the Holy Spirit* (Acts 2:33)
- *the gift of the Holy Spirit* (Luke 11:13; Acts 1:4; 2:38-39; 8:20; 10:45; 11:17; 15:8)
- *baptized with the Holy Spirit* (Acts 1:5; 11:16)
- *filled with the Holy Spirit* (Acts 2:4)

Note that Luke most often refers to the baptism in the Spirit as a gift from our Father. There are at least seven references in Luke and Acts that refer to the baptism in the Spirit as something the Father gives us. The front cover of this book emphasizes this truth.

As a believer seeks to be filled with the Spirit, he or she should remember this is a gift. One Christian wanted to be filled. But he forgot that the filling is a gift. He got down on his knees and began to beg. With deep groans he began to plead with God. The man sounded sad. A visitor might have thought he was hurt or sick! This confused seeker thought he needed to convince God to give the gift. Then a friend helped. He gently stopped the brother who was begging. He reminded him that we do not need to beg for a gift that someone offers us. We just need to receive it with thanks. The seeking Christian began to smile. The light of faith had entered his spirit. Now he was ready to receive. Within a few minutes the Holy Spirit filled him. Praise the Lord for the precious gift of being filled with the Spirit. We are not worthy, but we are thankful.

C. The Baptizer

Recall that Luke sometimes refers to this inner filling as being baptized in the Spirit (Acts 1:5).+ A person is baptized in water on the outside of his or her body. But the baptism in the Spirit happens inside a believer.

A pastor may baptize a believer in water. The person being baptized must understand what to do. To be baptized one must submit to the pastor. As the person submits, the

---

+ Baptism *in* the Spirit is a better translation than *by* the Spirit. Likewise, baptism *in* water is a better translation than *by* water. Compare Acts 1:5 with Mark 1:8. There people went down into the water. The Greek word is *en*, and is commonly translated *in* throughout the New Testament.

pastor will lower him or her into the water. Then the pastor will help lift the person up. However, a pastor cannot baptize a person who does not submit. In other words, there are two parts to a baptism. There is the pastor's part, and there is the believer's part. Water baptism is possible only as two people work together.

Likewise, there are two parts to being baptized in the Spirit. To whom does a believer submit? Who baptizes a believer in the Spirit? John the Baptist gave us the answer to this question.

> *"I baptize you with water for repentance. But after me will come one who is more powerful than I, whose sandals I am not fit to carry. He will baptize you with the Holy Spirit and with fire"* (Matt. 3:11).

Q 10 ⟋ *Do pastors baptize believers in the Spirit? Explain.*

This verse tells us that Jesus is the One who baptizes a believer in the Holy Spirit. We come to Him to be filled with the Spirit. But how does a person submit to Jesus to be baptized in the Spirit? How does a believer cooperate with the Lord? The believer's part is to come to Jesus, receive the Spirit, and speak in the new language the Spirit gives. We will study this in chapter 4, Lesson 11, point B. But first, let us learn more about the reason Jesus wants us to be filled with the Spirit.

Q 11 ⟋ *What is a believer's part in being baptized in the Spirit?*

Lesson 5   The Work of the Church (Acts 1:6-11)
Goal: *Explain the plan, the place, the power, and the purpose of witnessing. Relate these to self and others.*

Setting

This lesson is about the work of the Church. It is important to recognize that the Church existed before Pentecost. Luke's Gospel ends with a convinced group of believers. Jesus had opened their eyes to the Scriptures (Luke 24:45). They were no longer a group of easily scattered disciples. Rather, they were a body of commissioned believers. Before Pentecost, the believers were united, worshiping, and waiting to be clothed with God's power from on high (Luke 24:49). "In other words they were already the Church."[6] The purpose of Pentecost was not to create the Church. Pentecost was to empower the Church that already existed.

In his Gospel and in Acts, Luke emphasizes only one purpose of the Holy Spirit. He stresses that the Holy Spirit empowers believers to serve.[7] Specifically, Luke emphasizes that the Spirit empowers us to serve as witnesses of Jesus.

Q 12 ⟋ *What one purpose of the Spirit do Luke, John, and Paul all emphasize?*

Luke, John, and Paul emphasize different ministries of the Holy Spirit. These three writers all emphasize that the Holy Spirit gives us power to serve. In Luke's Gospel, the entire ministry of Jesus is because the Spirit is upon Him (Luke 4:18-19). John adds the Spirit's role in salvation. Paul includes what Luke and John teach. And he adds the Spirit's role in helping us live a holy life to serve. Thus, Luke emphasizes one role of the Spirit, John emphasizes two roles of the Spirit, and Paul tells of three.

Writer	Ministry of the Holy Spirit	Selected Scriptures
Luke	1) Service (The Spirit enables us to witness to the lost and help believers.)	1) Luke 1:15-17, 39-56, 67-80; 2:25-38; 3:21-22; 4:18-19; 11:5-13; 24:45-49 (And all references to the Spirit in Acts)
John	1) Service 2) Salvation (The Spirit draws us to Christ and then helps us travel on the road to heaven.)	1) John 1:32; 7:37-39; 14:12-31; 15:26; 20:21-22 2) John 3:5-8; 16:8-11; 1 John 2:20
Paul	1) Service 2) Salvation 3) Sanctification (The Spirit enables us to live a holy life that pleases God.)	1) Rom. 15:19 2) Rom. 8:23; 1 Cor. 6:11; 12:13; 2 Cor. 1:22; Titus 3:5 3) Rom. 8:1-17; Gal. 5:22-23; 2 Thess. 2:13

Figure 2.2   The Spirit's ministry, according to Luke, John, and Paul

Luke emphasizes that the Holy Spirit enables us to serve.[8] In Acts, the focus of service is witnessing about Jesus. Let us look at four things about witnessing in Acts 1:6-11.

A. The plan to witness (Acts 1:6-7)

Notice the question the disciples asked Jesus in Acts 1:6, *"Lord, are you at this time going to restore the kingdom to Israel?"* The Old Testament prophets promised a kingdom to Israel. This kingdom included land (Ezek. 36:24-27). The Gospels record that Jesus said a lot about the kingdom of God. The Lord promised the disciples a kingdom (Luke 12:32). Recall that James and John had tried to get top positions in the new kingdom (Matt. 20:20-28). We can understand why the disciples asked if it was time to restore the kingdom to Israel. The Romans were ruling over the Jews. Thus, the Jews were anxious for freedom. The disciples wanted to know if it was time for Israel to become the head instead of the tail.

Q 13 *Why did the disciples want the kingdom restored?*

Notice the answer of Jesus. He told them that it was not their business to know God's specific time or plan for the earthly kingdom (Acts 1:7). The times and dates of the kingdom are God's business, not ours. As Christians, we are often tempted to worry about things that are God's business, not ours.

Jesus turned their thoughts from north to south. He turned their thoughts from God's business to their business. Their business, and ours, is not to know the future. The business of believers is to receive power and be witnesses for Jesus. *"But you will receive power when the Holy Spirit comes on you; and you will be my witnesses in Jerusalem, and in all Judea and Samaria, and to the ends of the earth"* (Acts 1:8). The word "But" in Acts 1:8 is like a hinge. In that one word, Jesus turns our thoughts from God's business to our business.

Q 14 *How is the word "But" like a hinge in Acts 1:8? Explain.*

What do witnesses do? Faithful witnesses tell what they know about something. They describe what they saw, heard, or felt. As Christians, we are witnesses that Jesus has risen from the dead. We are witnesses that He has saved us from sin. Our main business is to tell others about Jesus. God wants us to testify that Jesus saved us from sin and gave us eternal life. He wants us to tell the world the message of John 3:16.

On the one hand, we witness through our holy lives and good deeds. Christians witness when they give food to the hungry. They show the love of God by visiting the sick or helping an orphan. On the other hand, the witness of deeds is not complete without words.

Q 15 *Are believers you know fulfilling God's plan to witness? Explain.*

Imagine a silent witness in court. The witness is called to the front of the room. The lawyer asks the witness if he has seen something. The witness nods his head yes and smiles. Then the lawyer asks the witness to tell what he knows. The witness just smiles and remains silent. Each time the lawyer or judge asks a question, the witness only smiles. This would be foolish! How can we know what a witness knows if he does not tell it? To witness for Jesus, we must speak the right words for Him at the right times. Believers should not be afraid to witness for Jesus. Frog eyes in the river never keep a cow from drinking![9]

There are many things that are God's business, not ours. But witnessing about Jesus is our business, not God's! The main work of the Church is to witness that Jesus is either the Savior or the Judge of each person.

B. The place to witness (Acts 1:8)

Throw a rock into a pond of water. The rock will cause a circle of waves to go out in all directions. These waves will continue, moving further away from where they started. So it is with the power of the Holy Spirit and witnessing. God "threw the rock into the pond" when God poured out the Holy Spirit on the Day of Pentecost. Acts 1:8 describes three waves of witnessing that expanded. *First,* the witnessing about Jesus began in Jerusalem (Acts 1–7). *Second,* the witnessing spread to the districts of Judea, Samaria

Q 16 *Can you use a map to show someone the 6 stages of witnessing in Acts? Try it!*

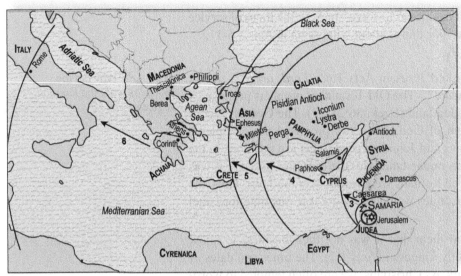

Figure 2.3   The Church spread from Jerusalem to Rome in six stages.[11]

and throughout Palestine (Acts 8–12). *Third,* the witnessing spread throughout the Roman world and to Rome itself (Acts 13–28).[10] So Acts 1:8 describes three waves or stages of witnessing. This is the simplest way to look at how witnessing expanded. Keep in mind that Luke wrote a selective history. No doubt the Church grew in many directions. But Luke chose to write about church growth in the direction of Rome. Acts also includes a more complex report of how witnessing expanded. Unlike Acts 1:8, this report emphasizes six stages of expanded witnessing (See Figure 2.3 and Figure 2.4).

Wave of growth in geography, numbers, and unity	The role of the baptism in the Holy Spirit (or filling of the Spirit)	Summary in Acts about growth in numbers and faith
1. **Jerusalem:** The church begins with great growth. It struggles to include Jews who speak Greek. (Acts 1–7)	**Event:** Christ promises the baptism in the Spirit (Acts 1:5), and this gift is given at Pentecost (Acts 2:1–41). **Sermon:** Peter explains that Joel's prophecy is being fulfilled—God is pouring out His Spirit on all flesh (Acts 2:17, 18, 28, 39).	*"So the word of the Lord spread. The number of disciples in Jerusalem increased rapidly, and a large number of priests became obedient to the faith"* (Acts 6:7).
2. **Samaria:** The church reaches out to the Samaritans, an African eunuch, and Saul. (Acts 8:1–9:31)	**Event:** Philip, a deacon, evangelizes the Samaritans. Peter and John pray and the Samaritans are baptized in the Holy Spirit. This helps the Samaritans be accepted as brothers (Acts 8:14–17).	*"Then the church throughout Judea, Galilee and Samaria enjoyed a time of peace. It was strengthened; and encouraged by the Holy Spirit, it grew in numbers, living in the fear of the Lord"* (Acts 9:31).
3. **Caesarea:** The church extends to the Gentile part of Palestine up to Antioch. (Acts 9:32–12:25)	**Event:** The household of Cornelius receives the Holy Spirit and speaks in tongues (Acts 10:44–48). **Sermon:** Peter explains that the miracle continues to fulfill Christ's promise of Spirit baptism and shows that God accepts Gentiles (Acts 11:16-18).	*"But the word of God continued to increase and spread"* (Acts 12:24).
4. **Antioch, Syria, and Galatia:** Jerusalem leaders accept Gentiles as equal believers—without keeping Jewish customs. (Acts 13:1–16:5)	**Sermon:** The church council hears the reports of Peter, Paul, and Barnabas about the Gentiles. Peter recalls that because Gentiles had a like Pentecostal experience, they are accepted without circumcision (Acts 10:14-48; 11:16-18; 15:8-19). Note that this Council also applied to the churches of Galatia, which Paul had just planted on his first missionary trip, A.D. 46-48.	*"So the churches were strengthened in the faith and grew daily in numbers"* (Acts 16:5).
5. **Ephesus:** Paul plants churches in Eastern Europe and Asia Minor. (Acts 16:6–19:41)	**Event:** Another Pentecost takes place in Ephesus (Acts 19:1-7).	*"In this way the word of the Lord spread widely and grew in power"* (Acts 19:20).
6. **Rome:** Paul meets with kings, and the Word of God reaches Rome. (Acts 20–28)	**Events:** No Pentecost is reported in these chapters. But the result of previous fillings is seen, since Paul and others prophesied, and Paul healed many.	*"Boldly and without hindrance he preached the kingdom of God and taught about the Lord Jesus Christ"* (Acts 28:31).

Figure 2.4   Acts records that the Church expanded in six waves, by the baptism in and power of the Holy Spirit.

Acts also includes a more complex report of how witnessing expanded. Unlike Acts 1:8, this report emphasizes six waves of expanded witnessing (See Figure 2.3

and Figure 2.4). Note that throughout Acts, Luke links the expanding witness of the Church to the spiritual power of the baptism in the Holy Spirit. It is the power of the Spirit that strengthens believers to witness for Jesus (Acts 1:8). Even when Paul wrote to the Romans, he said, *"I long to see you so that I may impart to you some spiritual gift to make you strong"* (Rom. 1:11). The power of the Spirit gives us the strength we need to witness for our Lord. The fullness of the Holy Spirit was the source of the early church's power to witness. And being filled with the Spirit is our greatest need today to be witnesses for Christ.

Each morning the sun rises to announce a new day. As this happens, we believers should ask God to help us be faithful witnesses that day. Then as the sun sets, each Christian should think back through the day. Ask yourself, "Was I a faithful witness for Christ today? Was I alert and praying as I met each person?" Each day a person should use this sunrise and sunset method. Then we will become more aware of opportunities to witness.

All day we breathe in God's free air. Let us shape some of the air into words about Jesus. We eat God's food. Then let us use the strength from some of it to tell others about our Savior. We receive so much from God. Day by day we should look for opportunities to tell others about God's love for them and us.

Once each month God puts the full moon in the sky. Each time you see it, ask yourself how many people you talked to about Jesus that month.

Witnessing does not stop in Jerusalem. As believers, we help witness in Judea, Samaria, and the whole earth. We do this by helping missionaries through praying and giving. This is our business. It is the main thing we have to do in life.

C. The power to witness (Acts 1:8)

It takes more than desire to be a faithful witness for Christ. It takes more than a prayer at sunrise and a review at sunset. Witnessing for Jesus requires spiritual power.

All work requires some kind of power. It takes power to dig a hole or take a walk. A weak person without power cannot work well. Both people and machines need power to work. It takes power for cars, buses, trains, and airplanes to move. The best bus will not move without power. All work requires power.

Different kinds of work require different kinds of power. The power that enables a person to walk will not move a bus. The power that will move a bus will not help a person walk.

There is only one kind of power that will enable a Christian to be a faithful witness. This is the power that comes from the Holy Spirit. No other kind of power will work. We must depend on the power the Spirit gives. It is not enough to be born again. It is not enough to know Jesus as Savior and be baptized in water. We reach our highest ability to witness for Jesus by being filled with the power that came at Pentecost. In the next lesson, we will study more about this power God wants to give each believer.

Q 17 ⟩ *What kind of power enables a believer to witness for Jesus?*

Around the world, those baptized in the Spirit witness with zeal and power. The Spirit does signs and wonders through common believers. The Spirit raises up an army of witnesses. Many times these may not have formal education. They are like the fishermen who first followed the Lord.[12] And they have the same spiritual power those first disciples had.

D. The purpose of witnessing (Acts 1:9-11)

One of God's main purposes for us is to witness about Jesus. We introduced this thought before in Lesson 5, point A, *The plan to witness*. Still, we want to emphasize this point one more time. Why? Because we believers need to be reminded about God's plan and purpose for us. The disciples were amazed as Jesus ascended into the clouds. Suddenly, two messengers from heaven appeared. They asked the disciples, *"Why do you stand here looking into the sky?"* (Acts 1:11).

On the one hand, we can understand why the disciples were gazing at the clouds. Jesus had been with them for several years. Now He was gone. Also, it was most unusual to see a person rise into the sky! This was an unusual and emotional time.

On the other hand, it was time to move on. It was not right for the disciples to stand gazing into heaven. Why? Jesus had sent them into all the earth. He called them to witness, not gaze at the clouds! He did not command them to focus on heaven. He commanded them to share a message of hope to a lost world. Their focus was to be out, not up. Thus the angels asked them, *"Why do you stand here looking into the sky?"*[13]

Q 18 *Do believers you know spend too much time thinking about the future? Explain.*

Christian, beware! Do not spend too much time thinking about what is above you. Instead, spend your time helping those beside you. Your work is to witness to others about Jesus. Do not waste time asking too many questions about heaven, about prophecy, or the times and dates (Acts 1:7). Do not let questions about what is above or ahead pull you away from helping those beside you. There is work to do in the power of the Spirit.[14] God's purpose for you is to witness!

Remember the order of four events.

- *First*, Jesus rose up into heaven. This event is the **Ascension* (Acts 1:9).
- *Second*, Jesus sends the Holy Spirit down to give believers the power to witness. This event is **Pentecost* (Acts 1:8).
- *Third*, Jesus sends believers out to witness. This is the Church's *Mission* (Acts 1:8).
- *Fourth,* Jesus will come down to earth again. This is the Second Coming, or **Parousia* in Greek (Acts 1:11).

The angels told the disciples an important message. "You have seen Jesus go up, and you will see Him come down. But between His comings, the Spirit must come down, and you must go out—into the world for Christ."[15]

A man dreamed he died and went to heaven. There, an angel took him to a beautiful temple. But the man noticed that one small stone block was missing in the wall of the temple. "Why is this small block missing from the temple?" the man asked. The angel replied, "That was the work God wanted you to do on earth. But you wanted to do bigger things instead." Then the man woke up from the dream. From that day forward he decided to do God's work day by day. Christian, part of the work God has for you today is to be a witness. Be faithful to tell others what you know about Jesus, even if there is only one person to talk to.[16]

One church member was deeply troubled and came to the pastor. "I cannot understand what the third toe of the beast represents in Daniel 2:42," said the worried believer. The pastor smiled and then asked two questions. "Do you understand that Jesus is coming back to earth some day?" "Yes," replied the believer. "Do you understand that only those who receive the Savior will go to heaven?" "Oh, yes," answered the believer. "Then let's spend our time trying to witness to the lost instead of worrying about the toes of the beast," said the pastor.

The purpose of witnessing is to get people ready to meet Jesus. Soon He will return just as He left. Blessed is that servant who is busy with the Master's work when the Lord returns (Matt. 24:46).

Figure 2.5   Modern Jerusalem

Lesson 6 — Steps to Pentecost (Acts 1:12-26)

Goal: *Identify and do 3 things that precede being filled with the Spirit.*

Setting

We remember Pentecost as the day God met His waiting children. At Pentecost, the Spirit of God filled believers. They received the promise Jesus gave them. At Pentecost their lives overflowed with His praise and presence. Like a river, the Holy Spirit flowed out of their inner beings (John 7:37-39). They praised God in languages they had never learned. They boldly witnessed for Jesus. Surely this type of Pentecost is the desire of every believer. We can identify three actions of believers that guided them to be filled with the Spirit.

A. They obeyed.

Explanation. The journey to Pentecost begins with steps of obedience. The Lord commanded the disciples to remain in Jerusalem (Luke 24:49; Acts 1:4). He commanded them to wait and receive the gift of the Spirit. Therefore, they did exactly what He said. They returned to the city and waited (Acts 1:12-13). Waiting might not have seemed like much to do. There was good news to tell. Jesus had risen from the dead. These disciples had talked with Him over a period of 40 days. No doubt they were ready to tell others. But waiting with an attitude of prayer was enough. It would have been wrong to do more. It is always enough to do what God says to do. We err if we try to do more or less than God commands.

Obedience is the birthmark of God's children. It is the evidence that a person is born again. Those who love God obey His commands (John 15:9-17).

A man stood beside a dog. What he wanted most from the dog was obedience. He wanted the dog to do exactly what he said. The owner did not care how smart, strong, or fast the dog was. The thing he valued most in dogs was obedience. Now the time for the test had come. The dog stood beside the owner. Suddenly, the owner threw a bone about 50 feet from the dog. The eager dog watched the bone hit the ground. But the animal did not move. He had learned to wait for the master's instructions. Then the owner commanded, "Go get it!" The dog ran to the bone and got it. "Bring it here," commanded the owner. The faithful dog brought the bone back to the owner. The owner was proud of the dog because it obeyed.

Obedience is the opposite of *disobedience*. Obedience says yes. It is humble and bows to God. But disobedience says no to God. It is stubborn and stands with a stiff neck and folded arms. The Bible says we were disobedient before we came to Christ. At that time we were children of Satan and of disobedience (Eph. 2:1-2).

Look up the word *disobedience* in a concordance. It is a word linked to sin, shame, and judgment. Through disobedience, Adam brought sin into the world (Rom. 5:19). Because of disobedience, Moses could not enter the Promised Land (Num. 20:12). Disobedience caused King Saul to lose the kingdom (1 Sam. 13:11-14). Disobedience stained David's name with a sin that every generation has seen. Do not be deceived. God's wrath comes on those who disobey Him (Eph. 5:6).

Illustration. Obedience precedes blessing. Abraham was blessed after he obeyed. He left Ur and went to a new land. Then he became the father of many nations. Thus obedience came before the blessing. Moses was blessed after he obeyed. God told him to return to Egypt. First Moses obeyed God, then blessings followed.

Q 19 *What did the disciples do in obedience before Pentecost?*

The relationship between obedience and blessing is a big theme in Scripture. We could illustrate it a hundred times from the Bible. The widows were blessed by Elijah and Elisha because they obeyed (1 Kings 17; 2 Kings 4). The lepers were cleansed because they obeyed Jesus (Luke 17:11-14). Saul received his sight because he obeyed (Acts 9:1-19). The disobedient miss the good things God has planned for them (Matt. 22:1-14; 23:37-39; Acts 13:46). The wise obey God and receive of His goodness.

Application.   Do you desire to be filled with the Spirit? Acts 5:32 says that God gives the Holy Spirit to those who obey Him. We can never earn the blessings God gives us. However, obedience is a key to receiving from God. Is there a blessing you desire from the heavenly Father? Search your heart. Has the Holy Spirit spoken to you about doing something? Mary's advice to the servants can help us all. "Do whatever he tells you" (John 2:5). The path of obedience always leads to the blessings of God.

An old song says, "Trust and obey, for there's no other way to be happy in Jesus, but to trust and obey."[17]

B. They prayed.

Explanation.   A second step toward Pentecost is prayer. As the disciples obeyed, they prayed. Notice that Luke answers several questions for us.

- Where did they pray? In an upstairs room in Jerusalem.
- Which apostles were there? All of the twelve except Judas. Matthias replaced him (Acts 1:26). We will discuss this more in point C that follows. For now, notice that Peter is first on the list. John and James follow him. These three apostles were the closest to Jesus.
- Who was praying with the apostles? Jesus appeared to a group of more than 500 after His resurrection (1 Cor. 15:6). Perhaps the 120 in the upper room were a part of that group. These included men and women.

Luke gives Mary, the mother of Jesus, and His brothers special attention. Some falsely teach that Mary was always a virgin. These falsely teach that she did not have any children other than Jesus. These false teachings contradict the Scriptures. Matthew does not say that Joseph never had sexual relations with Mary. Matthew says Joseph did not know her (sexually) *until* she gave birth to Jesus (Matt. 1:25). This indicates that they had the normal sexual relationship of a man and wife after Jesus was born.

Mary was a better woman than the false teachers say she was. She was a good wife to Joseph. No healthy woman who continually refuses to have sex with her husband is a good wife. Those who say Mary never had sexual relations with Joseph dishonor her. She was a good wife to him. The Bible gives the names of several of her children. These were the brothers of Jesus (Mark 6:3). They did not believe in Him before His death on the cross (John 7:5). But later, they believed. Jesus appeared to His brother, James, after the Resurrection (1 Cor. 15:7). James and Jude, the Lord's brothers, both became leaders in the church at Jerusalem (See Acts 12:17; 15:13; 21:18; Gal. 2:9; James 1:1 and Jude 1).[18] Each of these was as much the Lord's brother as Mary was His mother! What a joy to know they believed in Jesus after the Resurrection. They were in the prayer meeting that led to Pentecost!

How did they pray? Luke says they prayed constantly. That is, they were in an attitude of prayer. Paul refers to this as praying without ceasing (1 Thess. 5:17). Their constant prayer included praying in the upper room and the temple (Luke 24:53).[19]

There is a funny story about a contest. It was to decide who could pray the Lord's prayer the best. Each person was to pray the Lord's prayer without stopping. The winner was to receive a horse. The first man started well. But in the middle of the prayer he asked, "Will you also give me the bridle?" He lost the contest because he stopped praying. Sometimes we get distracted from praying!

Praying constantly should be a way of life for believers. This type of prayer includes talking to and listening to God. It includes petitions with groaning (James 5:16; Rom. 8:26). But it also includes joyful praise. Prayer can be so intense that one's sweat is like

Q 20 ✎ *Is there any area of your life in which you are not obeying God?*

Q 21 ➤ *Why does it dishonor Mary to say she remained a virgin all her life?*

Q 22 ➤ *Is it possible to pray throughout the day? Explain.*

great drops of blood (Luke 22:44). But prayer can also be quiet, peaceful, and relaxed. Praying means staying in touch with God. It is being aware of God and sensitive to Him throughout the day. Sometimes, like Adam or Enoch, we pray as we walk with God. One preacher liked to ask people, "Do I meet you praying?" God does not intend for us to go through every day groaning in prayer. But constant prayer is possible to those who learn that it includes passion and peace.

Did the prayers of the disciples cause God to send the Spirit more quickly? The Father had probably already chosen the Day of Pentecost to pour out the Spirit. But prayer caused the disciples to be aware and ready for what God wanted to do. Prayer keeps us in step with God. It enables us to be a part of what the Father is doing (John 5:19).

Illustration. One man was constant in prayer until it became a habit. He prayed always, even in doing small things like drinking a glass of water.

A prophet once told a story. He said a servant was told to guard a prisoner. But while the servant was busy here and there, the prisoner escaped (1 Kings 20:39-40). Likewise, you and I can be too busy. We should never be so busy with something that we cannot pray while we are doing it. The most important part of prayer is praying![20]

Application. If we depend on education, we get what teachers can do. If we depend on finances, we get what money can do. If we depend on ability, we get what talent can do. If we depend on people, we get what humans can do. But if we depend on prayer, we get what God can do! Therefore, let us use things like education, money, and talent. Let us appreciate and honor people. But let us depend on prayer.[21]

Some have the attitude that God will do whatever He wants. These do not feel the need to pray. But the Bible teaches us to pray constantly. We must ask, seek, knock, and listen. Then God will do what He wants, when He wants.

C. They based their beliefs on the Bible.

Explanation. The early disciples believed that the Scriptures are the words of God. Notice what Peter says when he stands in the upper room before Pentecost.

Q 23 ⟍ *Why do we honor Scripture above tradition and human opinions?*

"Brothers, the Scripture had to be fulfilled which the Holy Spirit spoke long ago through the mouth of David concerning Judas, who served as guide for those who arrested Jesus—" (Acts 1:16).

Peter says that the Holy Spirit spoke through David. As believers, we base our faith on the Bible. We place Scripture on a level above humans. The Bible is our guide to God and to heaven. Notice what the apostles said about the authority of Scripture.

*All Scripture is **God-breathed** and is useful for teaching, rebuking, correcting and training in righteousness* (2 Tim. 3:16).

[20]*Above all, you must understand that no prophecy of Scripture came about by the prophet's own interpretation.* [21]*For prophecy never had its origin in the will of man, but men spoke from God as they were **carried along by the Holy Spirit*** (2 Pet. 1:20-21).

Figure 2.6 Modern Jerusalem with Judean Hills in background

Paul tells us that God breathed Scripture to us. Peter says that the Holy Spirit carried the writers as they wrote. These great apostles affirm that the Bible is in a class by itself. The Scriptures are the words of God Almighty! We value them above the words of men and angels (Gal. 1:8-9). Our lives must be guided by *"It is written"* (Matt. 4:4, 7, 10; 1 Cor. 3:19). Like a king, Scripture must rule over the servants of tradition and human opinion (Matt. 15:1-9).

The Scriptures teach that someone needed to replace Judas. Judas was an apostle, chosen by Jesus. He had a part in the ministry (Acts 1:17). He even received the promise that the twelve apostles would sit on twelve thrones (Luke 22:29-30).[22] But like Esau, he lost his inheritance. Judas was a traitor and a spiritual deserter (Ps. 69:25; Acts 1:16, 20). He reminds us that it is necessary to continue in the faith. Even apostles can fall away. Paul knew this. He taught that only those who stay in the race win the prize of heaven (1 Cor. 9:24-27). Judas fell as far as a human can fall. He fell from being an apostle to being an eternally lost sinner. Therefore, someone needed to sit on the throne meant for Judas.

Judas killed himself. This proves he was sorry, yet he did not repent. But how did he die? Matthew tells us that Judas hanged himself (Matt. 27:1-10). Luke says that the intestines of Judas spilled out in a field. Together, Matthew and Luke give us a more complete picture. Many Bible teachers think that Judas hanged himself on the edge of a cliff.[23] Later, either the rope or the branch broke. Thus Judas fell and burst apart in the field below.[24] The field was bought in his name with the money he threw back into the temple (Matt. 27:5-7; Acts 1:18). Amazing, isn't it? Today a person wants something so much he could kill to get it. Tomorrow he could kill himself for the way he got it. The hot bread Satan sells will turn to ashes in your mouth. Ask Adam (Gen. 3), Balaam (Num. 22–24), Achan (Josh. 7), Samson (Judg. 16), Ananias (Acts 5), or Judas (Matt. 27).

Q 24 *Do you think Matthias was the right person to replace Judas? Explain.*

Was Matthias the right man to replace Judas? Two questions are common. *First,* did they use the right process (Acts 1:26)? Casting lots was a common way of making decisions in Old Testament times (1 Chron. 26:13-16; Neh. 11:1; Prov. 16:33; Jonah 1:7). The disciples used this method because the Spirit had not come in fullness yet. However, after Pentecost, we never hear of this method again. Throughout the New Testament, believers rely on the Holy Spirit for guidance.[25] *Second,* did they choose the right apostle? Some think that Paul was the apostle to fill the place of Judas. Paul was indeed a great apostle. But he was not the apostle to replace Judas. Paul was an apostle to the Gentiles (Acts 9:15). It would not seem right to put him on a throne judging Jews. Paul never considered himself a part of the twelve apostles (1 Cor. 15:7-8).[26] Luke wrote 30 years after Pentecost. He was a close friend of Paul. If Paul should have replaced Judas, Luke would have told us. Paul did not meet the qualifications to be one of the twelve. He was not an eyewitness of the ministry, death, and resurrection of Jesus (Acts 1:21-22). In the Old Testament, God worked through twelve tribes. In the New Testament, Jesus worked through twelve apostles. Luke was inspired by the Spirit to tell us how they replaced Judas. Matthias was the right apostle to replace Judas. He was still a part of the twelve in Acts 6:2. But as these twelve faithful men died, no one replaced them. The Bible does not teach that each apostle should be replaced when he dies. Judas was replaced only because he was a lost soul. When James, the brother of John, died, no one replaced him (Acts 12:2). He would rise again to sit on his throne.[27]

Q 25 *Does the Bible teach that each apostle should be replaced at death?*

Q 26 *Do the Scriptures guide all that you believe about the Holy Spirit? Explain.*

Illustration. The Scriptures are our guide to Pentecost. An evangelist stood in front of a church. The pastor had called him to put out a fire (See 1 Thess. 5:19). This Pentecostal fire started in a home. Several of the church members had been praying together. They were hungry to receive more of God. Among them were the town leader, the church song leader, and the Sunday school leader. As they prayed and studied Acts, the Holy Spirit filled them. They overflowed with great joy. Some said they felt like they had been baptized in love. In the midst of this, they began praising God in new languages. These happy believers wanted everyone to have the blessing of Pentecost. The Scriptures had led them to a new relationship with God. But the evangelist spoke loudly with authority. He said, "You do not need to speak in tongues because I do not speak in tongues!"

Application. What will be our standard for Pentecost? Will we use the Scriptures as our standard, or some human leader? Acts 2 says that all of the 120 were filled and began to speak in tongues (Acts 2:4). It is important to allow the Scriptures to lead us. Why? Because leaders have limits. They can lead only to places they know. But the Scriptures are the Word of God. When we follow the Scriptures, God is leading us! We pray that all leaders will follow Scripture. We agree to give honor to whom honor is due (Rom. 13:7). But we ought to obey God rather than men (Acts 4:19)! In Revelation we read that *"these are the words"* of God Almighty (Rev. 2:1, 8, 12, 18; 3:1, 7, 14).

Figure 2.7   The "Cardo"—ruins of the main street in ancient Jerusalem

Figure 2.8   Western Wall Plaza in Jerusalem

Test Yourself: Circle the letter by the ***best*** completion to each question or statement.

1. According to Luke, the Lord's last command to His disciples was to
a) *love one another.*
b) *go and make disciples of all nations.*
c) *wait for the gift my Father promised.*
d) *go into all the world and preach.*

2. Luke most often refers to the baptism in the Holy Spirit as
a) a gift.
b) a fruit.
c) an experience.
d) tongues.

3. The One who baptizes believers in the Holy Spirit is
a) the Father.
b) the Son.
c) the Spirit.
d) the local pastor.

4. Luke teaches that the main work of the Church is to
a) show love and kindness to all people.
b) speak out against sin and evil practices.
c) pray for the Lord to send forth harvesters.
d) tell people the truth about Jesus Christ.

5. The relationship of Jerusalem to Judea is that of
a) a city to another city.
b) a district to another district.
c) a city to a district.
d) a district to a nation.

6. In Acts, Luke traces the growth of the church from Jerusalem to
a) Antioch.
b) Philippi.
c) Athens.
d) Rome.

7. God wants believers to focus on
a) events related to the end of time.
b) the relationship between Israel and other nations.
c) the return of the Jews to Palestine.
d) preparing people to stand before God.

8. A key to receiving the blessing of Pentecost is
a) sacrifice.
b) obedience.
c) good deeds.
d) location.

9. Who of the following was NOT praying in the upper room at Pentecost?
a) The original twelve apostles
b) Mary, the mother of Jesus
c) The brothers of Jesus
d) Some women believers

10. Believers should seek to be filled with the Spirit because
a) church leaders encourage them.
b) the Scriptures guide us this way.
c) other believers have been filled.
d) Satan does not want this for us.

 Essay Test Topics: Write 50-100 words on each of these goals that you studied in this chapter.

The Gift Our Father Promised (Acts 1:1-5)

Goal: *Analyze the command, the gift, and the Baptizer in Acts 1.*

The Work of the Church (Acts 1:6-11)

Goal: *Explain the plan, the place, the power, and the purpose of witnessing. Relate these to self and others.*

Steps to Pentecost (Acts 1:12-26)

Goal: *Identify and do 3 things that precede being filled with the Spirit.*

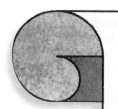

Unit 2:
The Witness of the Church in Jerusalem
(Acts 2–7)

Acts 1:8 is a helpful outline of the entire book (Figure 1.9).

In Chapter 3 of this book you will discover the key to spiritual power (Acts 2). You will:
- *Analyze the purpose and the evidence of being baptized in the Spirit.*
- *Evaluate at least five reasons why speaking in an unknown tongue is valuable.*
- *Answer ten questions people ask related to being filled with the Spirit.*

Chapter 4 continues the study of the key to the early church's success. This will lead you to:
- *Explain what happened at Pentecost, why it happened, and how it can happen to each believer.*
- *Explain and follow four steps to receiving the baptism in the Holy Spirit.*
- *Explain three priorities and three results of the early church. Apply these to your ministry.*

In Chapter 5 you will begin to walk in the footprints of the apostles. On this path you will:
- *Summarize and apply what Acts 3:1-10 teaches about people's beliefs, needs, and responsibilities.*
- *Analyze three truths related to God's part and our part in helping the needy. Relate this to your local context.*
- *Explain and apply what Acts 3–4 teaches about forgiveness, salvation, discouragement, God's sovereignty, and being Spirit filled.*

Chapter 6 looks closely into Acts 4:32–5:42. Why was the Church growing so fast? To answer this question you will:
- *Analyze six keys to unity in Acts 4:32-37. Relate these to your church and ministry.*
- *Explain and apply three truths related to purity in Acts 5:1-11.*
- *Evaluate the relationship of the miraculous to church growth in Acts and today.*
- *Analyze and illustrate three truths about persecution in Acts.*

Chapter 3:
From Weakness to Witness—Part 1
(Acts 2)

Introduction

Two drunks sat drinking beer in a bar. This was what they liked to do the most. Between drinks, one drunk spoke to the other. "What do you think about speaking in tongues?" he asked. The other drunk answered, "It is of the devil." But the first drunk quickly replied, "Oh, no. It couldn't be. If it were, you and I would do it!"

The drunk had a point. Unbelievers cannot receive the baptism in the Holy Spirit. Paul says, *"The man without the Spirit does not accept the things that come from the Spirit of God, for they are foolishness to him and he cannot understand them, because they are spiritually discerned"* (1 Cor. 2:14).

However, being filled with the Spirit is not far away from anyone. There are only two requirements for receiving this promise: be saved, and be spiritually hungry.[1] Do you meet these two conditions? May each reader open his or her heart to receive more of the Spirit while studying this chapter.

Figure 3.1   The coming of the Spirit at Pentecost

Lessons:

The Holy Spirit at Pentecost (Acts 2:1-4)
Goal: *Analyze the purpose and the evidence of being baptized in the Spirit.*

The Value of Speaking in Tongues (Acts 2:4)
Goal: *Evaluate at least 5 reasons why speaking in an unknown tongue is valuable.*

Ten Questions Related to Being Filled With the Spirit (Acts 2:4)
Goal: *Answer 10 questions people ask related to being filled with the Spirit.*

Key Words

baptism in the Spirit
Pentecostals

Charismatics
tongues

The Holy Spirit at Pentecost (Acts 2:1-4)

Goal: *Analyze the purpose and the evidence of being baptized in the Spirit.*

Setting

Recall that Jesus died on the Day of the Passover. After His resurrection, He ministered on earth 40 days. Then the 120 waited in the upper room for about 10 days. They waited until the Day of Pentecost.

The word *Pentecost* means "50." Pentecost was a harvest feast that took place 50 days after the Passover. In the Old Testament, Pentecost was also called the Feast of Weeks (Exod. 34:22; Deut. 16:16). Note that there was a week of weeks, that is, 7 weeks, between Passover and Pentecost. On the 50th day after the Passover they waved a sheaf of grain and two loaves of bread before the Lord (Lev. 23:15, 17).[2]

A. What is the purpose of being baptized in the Spirit?

The Feast of Pentecost was related to the wheat harvest. Likewise, the Day of Pentecost is related to spiritual harvest. Jesus said *"The harvest is plentiful, but the workers are few. Ask the Lord of the harvest, therefore, to send out workers into his harvest field"* (Luke 10:2). Pentecost prepares harvesters for the fields.

Q 1 ⟩ *What theme do the feast of Pentecost and the Day of Pentecost share?*

The Holy Spirit filled the 120 believers on the Day of Pentecost. Then they began to speak in Gentile tongues. This was a sign that the Spirit enables believers to witness to all nations.[3]

Before Pentecost, Peter was not a faithful witness. He knew the Lord and traveled with him more than 3 years. He and the other disciples had baptized some believers in water (John 4:1-2). Jesus had given Peter and many other disciples a temporary measure of power (Luke 10:1-22). They used that power to witness and help people. But this temporary anointing was only a taste of the Spirit's power. It did not last for long. Recall that Peter lacked the power to speak up for Christ. Because he lacked power, he denied that he knew the Lord. He refused to witness for Christ to a few men, or even to one woman (Luke 22:55-62).

Q 2 ⟩ *How did the gift of the Spirit transform Peter?*

Q 3 ⟨ *What do you think is the purpose of the baptism in the Spirit?*

But notice the change in Peter on the Day of Pentecost. The mouse has been changed into a lion! The man who denied Christ before a few now proclaims Him to a crowd. Filled with the Spirit, Peter is ready to witness. His spiritual battery has been charged. Now he has the power to witness. He stands up before the crowd and talks about Jesus. With great boldness he tells them that they, with the help of wicked men, killed Jesus (Acts 2:23). Now, they need to repent! Truly, the Holy Spirit brings boldness to speak about Jesus. The purpose of being baptized in the Spirit is to give a believer power to witness.

Q 4 ⟩ *How does Luke build upon an Old Testament model of the gift of the Spirit?*

We fully appreciate the Day of Pentecost when we understand the Old Testament Feast of Pentecost. That feast was to celebrate the harvest. Likewise, the Day of Pentecost is about harvest. God poured out His Spirit to enable believers to harvest people. Thus the Old Testament gives us the background to understand the New Testament.

Likewise, studying the Old Testament teaches us about the coming of the Spirit in the New Testament. Figure 3.3 compares the Old and New Testaments on three themes. It shows that the working of the Spirit under the old covenant was similar to His working under the new covenant.[4]

Figure 3.2   The Old and New Testaments emphasize three themes about the Holy Spirit.

	Theme 1: TRANSFER of the Spirit (for the work of serving)	Theme 2: SIGN to confirm the Spirit's presence and God's call to serve	Theme 3: ABILITY from the Spirit
Old Testament	a. The Spirit was transferred from Moses to the 70 elders. (Num. 11:10-30)	a. The Spirit enabled the 70 elders to help bear the burden of the people. (Num. 11:17)	a. They prophesied. (Num. 11:25)
	b. The Spirit was transferred from Moses to Joshua. (Num. 27:16-20; Deut. 34:9)	b. A sign is not recorded, but the people knew Joshua had been filled with the spirit of wisdom, so they listened to him. (Deut. 34:9)	b. The Spirit filled Joshua with wisdom to lead. (Deut. 34:9)
	c. The Spirit was transferred from Saul to David. (1 Sam. 10:10; 16:13-14)	c. When the Spirit came upon Saul, he prophesied. (1 Sam. 10:1-6; 9-10) David prophesied. (2 Sam. 23:1-2).	c. The Spirit changed Saul into a different person, making him fit to lead. (1 Sam. 10:6) Also, the Spirit gave David power to lead. (1 Sam. 16:13)
	d. The Spirit was transferred from Elijah to Elisha. (2 Kings 2:8-9,14-15)	d. Elisha was able to part the Jordan River as Elijah had done. (2 Kings 2:8, 14)	d. The Spirit gave Elijah and Elisha power to prophesy and perform signs and wonders.
New Testament	a. The Spirit anointed Jesus to preach the good news, release the captives, heal, and set free. (Isa. 11:2; 42:1; Luke 4:18-19) At Pentecost, the Spirit was transferred from Jesus to His disciples.	a. Luke records the sign of the dove coming upon Jesus. (Luke 3:22) The 120 disciples of Jesus spoke in tongues when the Spirit came upon them for service. This was an outward sign that the Spirit had come. (Acts 2:4)	a. The Spirit gave the disciples the ability or power to witness for Jesus. (Acts 1:8)
	b. The Spirit was transferred from Jesus, through Peter and John, to Samaritan disciples. (Acts 8:17)	b. Something happened that convinced Simon to offer money. (Acts 8:18-19)	b. The Spirit gave Samaritan believers the power to do their part in spreading the good news of Jesus.
	c. The Spirit was transferred from Jesus, through Ananias, to Saul. (Acts 9:17)	c. Saul's eyes were healed. (Acts 9:18; See 1 Cor. 14:18)	c. The Spirit equipped Saul to carry the Lord's name to Gentiles and their kings. (Acts 9:15)
	d. The Spirit was transferred from Jesus to Cornelius and other Gentiles. (Acts 10:44-46)	d. Cornelius and those with him spoke in tongues. (Acts 10:46)	d. The Spirit enabled these Gentiles to be witnesses for Jesus.
	e. The Spirit was transferred from Jesus, through Paul, to Ephesian believers. (Acts 19:6)	e. They spoke in tongues and prophesied. (Acts 19:6)	e. The Spirit gave them power to witness for Jesus.

Figure 3.3   Three themes linked to the Spirit in the Old and New Testaments

In the Old Testament, the Spirit did not come upon people to make them sons of Israel. Rather, the Spirit came to give the ability to serve. Figure 3.3 mentions that the Spirit came upon the 70, Joshua, Saul, and David, along with Elijah and Elisha. In all of these cases, the purpose of the Spirit was to give people the ability to serve. The

Spirit enabled many to serve in the Old Testament. He gave special skills to those who made Aaron's priestly garments (Exod. 28:3). The Spirit gave different skills to the craftsmen who worked on the Tabernacle (Exod. 31:3; 35:31). The same Spirit gave the Judges military insight and might (Judg. 3:10; 6:34; 11:29; 13:25; 14:6, 19; 15:14). Likewise, the Spirit did not come upon the Messiah to make Him God's Son. Instead, He came upon Jesus to enable Him to serve (Luke 4:18-19). All of this background helps us understand Luke's writings. Luke never mentions the coming of the Spirit to make us children of God. Rather, Luke describes God's Spirit coming in the same way He came upon Old Testament believers. In Luke and Acts, the Spirit does not come to give spiritual birth to people or the Church. Luke always describes the Spirit coming on those who are already believers. Why? The purpose is clear. Luke emphasizes that the Spirit enables believers to witness and serve.[5]

B. What is the first evidence of being baptized in the Spirit?

There are many places in Acts that mention the Holy Spirit. However, the chart that follows shows the places in Acts where believers were first filled with the Holy Spirit. Look over the chart. Then we will briefly study each part of it.

#	Acts	Setting	Outward Evidence of the Inner Filling
1.	2:1-4	The Day of Pentecost	All 120 spoke in new languages as soon as they were filled with the Holy Spirit.
2.	8:14-19	Believers at Samaria	Something happened that caused Simon to offer money.
3.	9:17-19	The conversion and filling of Saul	We know that Paul often spoke privately in unknown languages (1 Cor. 14:18).
4.	10:44-46	The home of Cornelius	They spoke in new languages.
5.	19:1-7	Believers at Ephesus	They spoke in new languages and prophesied.

Figure 3.4   The five places in Acts where believers were first filled with the Holy Spirit

Q 5 ⟍ *Which 5 chapters in Acts record the times believers were first filled with the Spirit?*

1. Read Acts 2:1-4.

On the Day of Pentecost 120 believers prayed in an upper room. They were waiting to be baptized in the Holy Spirit. Suddenly, they heard a sound like a great wind. The sound of wind was a symbol of God's presence. In Job 38:1 God spoke out of a great swirling wind. In 1 Kings 19:11 a great wind came before the presence of God. Likewise, fire is a symbol of God's presence. God spoke to Moses from a flaming bush (Exod. 3:2). The Lord came down as a fire on Mount Sinai (Exod. 19:18). Thus the sound of wind and the sight of fire alerted the believers that God was near. He had once accepted Solomon's temple (1 Kings 9). Now, He showed that He accepted the young Church and each believer as His new temple.[6] These two signs came *before* the baptism in the Spirit. But they were never repeated in Acts.

Q 6 ⟍ *In Acts 2, what did each believer do when filled with the Spirit?*

Each of the 120 believers was filled with the Holy Spirit. As soon as they were filled, they all began to speak in tongues.[7] The purpose of the baptism in the Spirit was to enable them to witness. Therefore, it is not surprising that the fullness of the Spirit affected their speech.

Today, there are over 520,000,000 Pentecostals and Charismatics.[8] These people are bold witnesses for Jesus. Also, they believe in speaking in new languages, just as believers did at Pentecost and throughout Acts.

2. Read Acts 8:14-19.

Philip preached Christ to the people at Samaria. Many men and women believed. Even Simon, who practiced evil magic, believed. After these received Jesus as their Savior, Philip baptized them.

The Samaritans, as all believers, received the Holy Spirit when they believed in Jesus. The Holy Spirit is the One who makes the presence of Christ real in each believer. All who belong to Jesus have the Holy Spirit (Rom. 8:9).

The question is not, "Does a believer have the Spirit?" Nor is the question, "How much of the Spirit does a believer have?" The question is, "How much of a believer does the Spirit have?" When we first come to Christ, we are thinking about our sins. Soon after, new believers begin thinking about telling others the good news. The Samaritans had been born again. But they had not yet received the fullness of the Spirit. They needed Him to expand within them and fill their lives.

Do not stumble over the different ways Luke describes our relationship to the Spirit. From one point of view, Luke describes the Spirit as a gift Father promised. From a second point of view, Luke describes this wonderful relationship as a baptism. From a third point of view, he calls it a filling from within. Here in Acts 8 he says the Spirit came upon them (Acts 8:16). Each of Luke's descriptions helps us understand our relationship to the Spirit.

Q 7 ↖ *What do you think caused Simon to believe the Samaritans had received the Spirit?*

What happened when the Samaritan believers were filled with the Spirit? We cannot know for sure. But it seems that Simon, the former magician, saw and heard something. Something got his attention. Many Bible teachers think the Samaritans spoke in tongues. Some non-Pentecostals believe Simon heard the Samaritan believers speaking in new languages.[9] On the Day of Pentecost, tongues attracted the attention of the crowd. In Samaria, it probably attracted the attention of Simon. He had already seen Philip do miracles. He did not offer money for this power. What caused him to offer money to the apostles?[10] He probably heard people he knew speaking in languages they did not know!

3. Read Acts 9:17-19.

We are studying the five times in Acts when believers were first filled with the Holy Spirit. We have looked at believers in Jerusalem and Samaria. The third case is Saul who became Paul.

God commanded a disciple named Ananias to help Saul. From Acts 9:17, we see that the Lord Jesus sent Ananias to Paul for two reasons. Ananias prayed for Paul to see again and also to be filled with the Spirit. The fact that Ananias said, *"Brother Saul,"* shows that he knew Saul had already believed in his heart.

Q 8 ↖ *When do you think Paul first began speaking in tongues? Explain.*

Luke does not repeat everything that happened. He does not tell us that Paul was filled with the Spirit or that he spoke in tongues. The biblical writers often skip over the obvious details. In fact, Paul never states in his writings that he was filled with the Spirit. He gives his testimony several times to unbelievers. Therefore, he does not mention the deeper things of God like speaking in tongues. Speaking in tongues was so common in the early church that Paul did not need to mention it! It was plain to everyone that apostles spoke in tongues. If it were not for a problem at Corinth, there would be no record in the Bible that Paul spoke in tongues. However, because of 1 Corinthians 14:18, we know that Paul spoke in tongues more than others did. When did he start speaking in tongues? It is logical to believe Paul spoke in tongues when he was first filled like the other apostles (Acts 2:4.)[11]

4. Read Acts 10:44-46.

Q 9 ↗ *How did Peter know the Gentiles had been filled with the Spirit?*

The fourth instance in this section occurs at the house of Cornelius in Caesarea. Peter tells us that the Holy Spirit *"came on"* all who heard the message. This is the way Luke described what happened to the believers at Samaria when Peter and John went there (Acts 8:16). But how did Peter and the other Jews know for sure that the Gentiles had been filled with the Spirit? They knew because they heard them speaking in tongues (Acts 10:45-46). Peter tells the account later in Jerusalem. There he emphasizes he was sure the Gentiles were baptized in the Holy Spirit. He knew they had received the same baptism, and the same gift. How could Peter be sure? Because the Spirit *"came on"* them just as he *"came on"* the apostles at Pentecost (Acts 11:15-16). Likewise, we can be sure today that we have been baptized in the Holy Spirit if we speak in a new language.

5. Read Acts 19:1-7.

The last example we will consider in this lesson happened in Ephesus, about 23 years after Pentecost.[12] Here is another clear example that the baptism in the Spirit is a different experience than being born again. The twelve men had believed, and Paul baptized them in water. Who can deny that they were Christians at that point? But something was missing in their lives. They needed to be filled with the Spirit that was already with them. So Paul placed his hands on them, and they were filled with the Spirit. What was the evidence? They spoke in tongues and prophesied (Acts 19:6).

Q 10 ↗ Were the 12 men at Ephesus filled with the Spirit when they were born again? Explain.

We have seen a biblical pattern in this lesson. We have looked at the five different times in Acts where believers were first filled with the Spirit. In three of these, we are sure believers spoke in tongues as they received the gift of the Spirit. These three times included Jerusalem, Caesarea, and Ephesus (Acts 2, 10, 19). In the other two cases some evidence implies that they spoke in tongues (Acts 8, 9). In all five cases, believers did not seek to speak in tongues. The main purpose of the baptism in the Spirit was not to enable believers to speak in tongues. The main purpose of the Spirit was to give them power to witness for Jesus. However, tongues was the biblical sign. It showed that believers had been filled with the Holy Spirit they were seeking.

Q 11 ↖ How would you summarize the biblical evidence of being filled with the Spirit?

Lesson 8

The Value of Speaking in Tongues (Acts 2:4)
Goal: *Evaluate at least 5 reasons why speaking in an unknown tongue is valuable.*

There are several reasons we value speaking in a new language as the Holy Spirit enables us.

A. We value speaking in tongues because the Bible teaches it.

The Bible is our standard of faith and practice. We study it to see how to know God and walk with Him.

John Wesley compared himself to an arrow flying through the air. He said he was a spirit that came from God and would return to God. He saw his life like an arrow in the air, headed toward eternity. Wesley wanted to know one thing: the way to heaven. He believed that God wrote a book to teach us the way. His prayer was, "O give me that book! At any price, give me the book of God!" Once he had the Bible, he became a man of one book. That is, the Bible became the one book he lived by. Wesley's attitude toward the Bible is a good example for us. We should base our faith and actions on what the Bible teaches us.[13]

Studying the Bible, we find that all of the apostles except Judas spoke in tongues. Paul was probably the most educated and greatest of the apostles (2 Cor. 11:23). Under the power of the Spirit he started many new churches and wrote about one-third of the New Testament. His life was so holy that he told Christians at least five times to follow his example (1 Cor. 4:16, 11:1; Phil. 3:17, 4:9; 1 Thess. 1:6; 2 Thess. 3:9). This great apostle was an example to us in many ways, including speaking in tongues. He thanked God that he spoke in tongues more than all of the Corinthians (1 Cor. 14:18). Praying in tongues was a key to Paul's ministry. The Bible does not teach that Paul preached in tongues. But he prayed to God in tongues privately. Why? This built him up spiritually (1 Cor. 14:2, 4). Then when he was with other believers, he was able to edify

Q 12 ↗ Did all of the apostles speak in tongues? Explain.

them. Likewise, we value praying in tongues privately to build ourselves up. Surely this should be the attitude of all who follow Christ.

Q 13 *Give 3 examples in Acts showing that laypeople spoke in tongues when the Spirit filled them.*

The Bible teaches us that not only the apostles, but also many other Christians prayed in tongues. On the Day of Pentecost, all 120 believers spoke in tongues (Acts 1:15; 2:4). At the home of Cornelius the Spirit came on *all* who heard the message, and they spoke in tongues (Acts 10:44-46). At Ephesus the twelve believers spoke in tongues (Acts 19:6-7).

Thus the Bible teaches that the Church began with believers speaking in tongues as the Spirit filled and enabled them. We value this practice today because the Bible teaches us that the early church valued it. As we have noted earlier, there are more than 520 million believers today who value speaking in tongues because the Bible teaches it.[14]

B. We value speaking in tongues because it is a form of prayer to God.

Q 14 *Which verses in Corinthians show that speaking in tongues is a form of prayer?*

First Corinthians 14:2 says that anyone who speaks in a tongue is speaking to God, not man. Speaking to God is a form of prayer. Thus the Holy Spirit enables us to pray to God in tongues (1 Cor. 14:14). Paul encourages us to pray in the Spirit on all occasions (Eph. 6:18). Likewise Jude encourages us to build ourselves up by praying in the Holy Spirit (Jude 20). Speaking in tongues is praying in the Holy Spirit. We value all forms of prayer.

Q 15 *Do you know anyone who discourages believers from praying in the Spirit? Explain.*

Over and over the Scriptures encourage us to pray to our Father in heaven. Jesus said we should always pray and not give up (Luke 18:1). Paul told us that we should pray continually (1 Thess. 5:17). Surely all Christians can agree that any biblical form of prayer is valuable. Is it possible that there is even one Christian who would discourage others from privately praying to God in tongues?

C. We value speaking in tongues because it edifies the believer who does it.

Q 16 *Do you think that praying in tongues is selfish? Explain.*

First Corinthians 12 mentions nine different spiritual gifts. But praying in tongues is the only gift described as building up the one who uses the gift.[15] It is not selfish for Christians to build themselves up. Jude tells us to build ourselves up in our most holy faith. How? By praying in the Spirit (Jude 20)! Surely praying in tongues is praying in the Spirit. Therefore, praying in tongues is very valuable to believers.

Too often, Christians are too weak to help others. Weak Christians are like the believers in Hebrews 5:11-14. These believers were weak and young. They could drink milk but could not eat meat. They were part of the problem instead of part of the answer. Instead of helping others, they needed someone to help them. They took a lot of some pastor's time. They were like a garden that needed a lot of hoeing but produced little.

It is dangerous to be a Christian who does not edify himself or herself. Satan travels about as a roaring lion, looking for someone to devour (1 Pet. 5:8). Lions often look for the weakest animal in a herd. But you, Christian, have a valuable gift. Pray in tongues and build yourself up. Then you will be strong enough to overcome Satan. And you will also be strong enough to help a weaker believer.

D. We value speaking in tongues as a sign to unbelievers and believers.

Q 17 *In what way is speaking in tongues a sign to you as a believer?*

To unbelievers, an unknown tongue may be a sign that God is present (1 Cor. 14:22). On the Day of Pentecost, the speaking in tongues was a sign to the Jews. This sign showed that God was speaking through the disciples of Jesus.

Tongues are also a sign to believers. This does not contradict what Paul said in 1 Corinthians 14:22. There are times when tongues are a sign to unbelievers. Paul emphasizes this. But tongues were also a sign to Peter. How did Peter know that Cornelius and his family had received the gift of the Holy Spirit? He knew because of the sign of speaking in tongues (Acts 10:44-46).

The Spirit works in many ways. He convicts of sin. He comes to live within each believer at the time of the new birth. He causes us to remember. He gives us power to witness. But a biblical sign of being filled with the Spirit is important. Why? Without it a believer could not clearly discern being filled with the Spirit from other spiritual experiences.[16] So we value tongues as a sign to believers.

Two pastors we will refer to as James and John were talking. John had been filled with the Spirit. He enjoyed praying in a new language. James testified that once when he was praying he felt great joy in God's presence. James believed this joy was the sign that he had been filled with the Spirit. But John said it was not the common biblical sign in Acts. He encouraged James to continue seeking to be filled with the Spirit. A few days later, James was filled and spoke in a new language. His joy overflowed. James was very thankful that God gave a biblical sign to show that the Spirit has filled us.

Speaking in tongues is an important sign. People who cut hair put out a sign. The sign will not cut a person's hair. But the sign assures others that the one who cuts hair is near. Likewise, there is always a sign in front of a public place to eat food. The sign will not feed a person, but it is evidence that a cook is nearby. Likewise, speaking in tongues is a biblical sign. God chose it to show that the Holy Spirit has filled a person.[17]

E. We value speaking in tongues as a way each believer can cooperate with God.

Usually, there are two parts to a miracle. There is God's part and our part. God's part is the big part, but He gives us a small part. In some miracles, the person's part was to fill a jar with water (John 2) or wash in a pool (John 9). In the baptism in the Holy Spirit, God's part is to enable a believer to speak a new language. The believer's part is to speak. God chose a part for us that anyone can do. The young or the old, the rich or the poor, the educated or the illiterate can do this small part God gives. Almost any person can speak anywhere and anytime. There are even cases of a person who was deaf and mute who often spoke in tongues and interpreted in public.[18]

Q 18 *What is a believer's part in being filled with the Spirit?*

F. We value speaking in tongues as an exercise in humility and faith.

Like the cross, tongues is a stumbling block to the proud. To some, tongues may seem even more foolish than the preaching of the cross (1 Cor. 1:18-25). The human mind is proud. Knowledge puffs up (1 Cor. 8:1). By contrast, we feel humbled at what we do not understand. The mind does not enjoy bowing to what it does not understand. Speaking in tongues brings the most respected believer down to the ground of a common person. Presidents, professors, doctors, lawyers, and children all speak in tongues at the same level. The Scriptures emphasize humility as a key to fellowship with God (Matt. 18:1-4; James 4:6). Therefore, we place high spiritual value on all biblical practices that emphasize humility. Examples of these may include suffering, washing feet, fasting, and praying in tongues (2 Cor. 12:7-10; John 13:12-17; 1 Cor. 14:14).

Q 19 *Does your mind protest when you pray in tongues? Explain.*

Praying in tongues links humility and faith. It is like walking on water. It reminds us to depend on God rather than self. We tend to trust in our minds, money, education, talents, and skills. None of these helps a person speak in tongues. Praying in tongues is a reminder to depend on God. It encourages being poor in spirit—that is, depending on God. Praying in tongues is humble faith in action.

Q 20 *Of what does praying in tongues remind us?*

G. We value speaking in tongues because it is a step toward other spiritual gifts (1 Cor. 12:8-10).

Like tongues, all of the other spiritual gifts defy the mind. One who prays often in tongues learns to cooperate with the Spirit. Some teachers say speaking in tongues is the doorway to all the spiritual gifts. One teacher said speaking in tongues is the root and stem for all the other gifts. It is the way we are nourished.[19] Those who pray often in

Q 21 *Do those you know who minister spiritual gifts in public speak in tongues in private? Explain.*

tongues learn to edify the Church with other spiritual gifts. One believer spoke a word of knowledge in public. But first, that believer spoke privately in tongues. In contrast, will a person who cannot speak in tongues *privately* speak a prophecy *publicly?* A short step is easier than a long one.

H. We value speaking in tongues because it shows that a believer has completely submitted to the Spirit.

The word *baptize* is associated with a ship that sinks out of sight. To *baptize* means "to take completely under." To be baptized in water, all of a person must go under the water. To be baptized in the Spirit, all of a person must come under the Spirit's influence. But the tongue is the most unruly part of a person (James 3:8). No human can tame the tongue! Speaking in tongues shows that a believer has submitted the mind and even the tongue to the Holy Spirit. Thus that person has been baptized—placed completely under the Spirit's control. This may be only for a few moments. The remaining challenge is to stay under the Spirit's control! A long journey begins with the first step.

I. We value speaking in tongues because it lessens the gap between apostles and laypeople.

Q 22 *What shows that a common believer can be as full of the Spirit as an apostle?*

On the Day of Pentecost the apostles were filled with the Spirit. They spoke in new languages. But common men and women also spoke in tongues on that day. Likewise today, God fills all who seek Him. Witnessing is not just for apostles, pastors, and teachers. God has work for every believer. In the age of the Spirit, God promised to pour out His Spirit even on slaves, both male and female (Acts 2:18). Speaking in tongues shows us that a common believer can be as full of the Spirit as an apostle.[20]

J. We value speaking in tongues because it reminds us that our fellowship with God is more spiritual than mental.

Q 23 *Do you think our fellowship with God is more spiritual or mental? Explain.*

The relationship of believers to God is spiritual. God is Spirit. We are eternal spirits living in temporary bodies. As John Wesley said, "I am a spirit."[21] Jesus said those who want to worship God must do so in spirit (John 4:23-24).

Praying in tongues reminds us that the spirit can be full when the mind is empty (1 Cor. 14:14). We need to remember that the mind is only a tool to help us walk in the Spirit. Our minds are very limited. Often our minds cannot find words to express the love we feel toward other humans. And the love we feel toward God is greater. It is a spiritual language of prayer and praise to Him. Praying in tongues is spirit to Spirit. It is a deep fellowship with God that goes beyond what the mind can understand (See Phil. 4:7). Spiritual knowledge and intelligence do not depend on a physical brain. God is spirit without a physical brain, and no one else is as intelligent as He is. When a believer's brain is dead in the grave, his or her spirit will be worshiping in the presence of God. Praying in tongues underlines the truth that our fellowship with God is spirit to Spirit.

Lesson 9 — Ten Questions Related to Being Filled With the Spirit (Acts 2:4)
Goal: *Answer 10 questions people ask related to being filled with the Spirit.*

God promised believers the gift of the Holy Spirit (Acts 2:4, 38). However, to receive a promise from God, we must take it by faith. Sometimes believers have questions that prevent them from receiving a promise. Therefore, we will take a little time to discuss some questions. We do not want to argue with anyone. But it is good to help those with sincere questions. Let us look at ten questions believers often ask related to the Holy Spirit.

1. Did I already receive the Holy Spirit when I was born again?

Yes, the Holy Spirit enters each person when he or she is born again. The Spirit is called the Spirit of sonship (Rom. 8:15). When a person receives Jesus as Savior, the Holy Spirit enters that believer. The Spirit brings the inner witness and assurance that a person is God's child (Rom. 8:16). Therefore, each believer has a measure of the Holy Spirit (Rom. 8:9-17). In contrast to us, Jesus received the Holy Spirit without measure or limit (John 3:34).

Q 24 ↖ *Have you met some who did not know that all believers have the Spirit? Explain.*

2. Why do we need more of the Spirit if we already have Him?

The main reason we need more of the Spirit is that we need to grow in grace. God wants to give us a greater measure of the Spirit than we received at salvation. He wants us to be filled with the Spirit. Jesus breathed the Holy Spirit into His apostles and told them to receive the Spirit (John 20:22). But they still needed to be baptized in the Holy Spirit on the Day of Pentecost. God wants to fill us up with the Holy Spirit. At conversion, we become God's children. Next, God wants us to begin to grow and mature. Then we can witness and help others become His children. Paul prayed for the Ephesian believers to grow and be filled with the Spirit. He wrote, *"That you may be filled to the measure of all the fullness of God"* (Eph. 3:19).

Q 25 ↗ *Why do believers need more of the Spirit?*

Some believers met together to pray. They had all been saved from their past sins. But they were hungry for more of God's Spirit. One prayed, "O God, please give me just a little bit of your Spirit."[22] Notice the contrast between this prayer and Paul's (Eph. 3:19). God does not want to give us only a *little* of the Spirit. He wants us *"to be filled to the measure of all the fullness of God."* This sounds like a lot of the Spirit! God wants us to have so much of the Spirit that *"streams of living water will flow from within"* us (John 7:37-39).

Notice that in Ephesians 3:19 Paul was praying for believers. These believers had already received the Spirit. But believers need to grow in grace (2 Pet. 3:18). Those who do not grow and go forward may go backward (2 Pet. 3:17-18). To faith we must add goodness. To goodness we must add knowledge. To knowledge we must add self-control, and so on (2 Pet. 1:5-9). It is the Holy Spirit who ministers grace to us. He is called *"the Spirit of grace"* (Heb. 10:29). Remember that the fruit of the Spirit results from the Spirit's presence in believers (Gal. 5:22-23). Likewise, the gifts of the Spirit result from the Spirit's presence in believers (1 Cor. 12:7-11). So a key to growing in grace is being filled with the *"Spirit of grace."*

Q 26 ↗ *Why is being filled with the Spirit a key to growing in grace?*

John the Baptist was filled with the Spirit even from birth (Luke 1:15). Still, he *"grew and became strong in spirit"* (Luke 1:80). *"Jesus grew in wisdom and stature, and in favor with God and men"* (Luke 2:52). The anointing on Him at age 30 was greater than the anointing he had at 12. He grew in favor with God! Imagine that! And we as servants are not above our Master (Matt. 10:24). Paul was filled with the Spirit near the time of his conversion (Acts 9:17). But he *"grew more and more powerful"* (Acts 9:22). Apostles and laypeople need to grow in grace. *"Eagerly desire the greater gifts"* such as prophecy (1 Cor. 12:31; 14:39). We can each be a greater blessing today than we were yesterday. Seek to be filled with the *"Spirit of grace!"*

Someone may be asking, "After I have been filled with the Spirit, do I need to daily seek more of the Spirit?" Yes! We receive the Spirit when we come to Christ. Then we seek to be filled with the Spirit. The first filling of the Spirit is called the baptism in the Holy Spirit. At this time, a believer speaks in a new language. But it is not enough to be content with yesterday's filling. Why? As we said above, we need to grow in grace. Also, note that all sources of power on earth need to be renewed. Batteries become weak. Cars run out of gas. Yesterday's kerosene, electricity, firewood, or food will not give you the power you need today. Likewise, there is only one baptism in the Spirit.

Q 27 ↖ *If you have been filled with the Spirit, should you be content? Explain.*

Q 28 ↗ *How many times should a person be baptized in the Spirit? Explain.*

But there should be many fillings. The apostles were filled a second time with the Spirit in Acts 4:31. The Spirit's filling gave them new boldness to witness for Jesus. Likewise, Paul prayed for us to keep being filled with the Spirit (Eph. 5:18). Do you desire to eat today after you were full yesterday? How much more should we have a daily appetite to be filled with the Spirit! Those who hunger and thirst for the right relationship with God will be filled daily (Matt. 5:6).

3. Does the New Testament teach there is only one baptism?

Q 29 ➤ *What does Paul mean when he says there is only one baptism (Eph. 4:5)?*

Ephesians 4:5 says there is *"one Lord, one faith, one baptism."* To understand this verse, a person must understand the purpose of Ephesians. Paul wrote to the believers at Ephesus to emphasize a great truth. In Christ, God brought Jews and Gentiles together into one body. In the past, the Gentiles were far off from God. They had no hope (Eph. 2:11-12). A wall stood between them and the Jews. But Jesus broke down the wall (Eph. 2:14). Now both Jews and Gentiles can come to God through Christ. There are many lords on the earth. But there is only one Lord over the Church. There is not one Lord for Jews and a different one for Gentiles. There is only one Lord for both. Likewise, there is not one baptism for Jews and a different one for Gentiles. There is only one baptism for both. This probably refers to water baptism (Rom. 6:3-4).

Q 30 ➤ *Which 4 baptisms did the 12 believers at Ephesus receive?*

However, the New Testament refers to at least five different baptisms.

- John's baptism in water was for repentance. It was a baptism to get people ready to receive Jesus (Luke 3:3-6). This baptism was no longer needed after Jesus began His ministry.

- Water baptism in the name of Jesus comes after a person has received Christ. As Philip said, after one believes, he or she may be baptized (Acts 8:37; 16:31-33).

- The Holy Spirit baptizes (places) each new believer into the body of Jesus Christ (1 Cor. 12:13). This happens at conversion, at the moment a person receives Christ and is born again.

- Jesus wants to baptize believers in the Holy Spirit (Matt. 3:11; Acts 1:5). This is a baptism of power for those who are already a part of His body. For many the baptism in the Holy Spirit is their third baptism. For example, consider the believers at Samaria. They had received Jesus as Savior. This means that the Holy Spirit had baptized them into the body of Christ. This was their *first* baptism. *Second,* Philip baptized them in water. *Third,* the apostles prayed for them and Jesus baptized them in the Holy Spirit (Act 8:9-17). For the twelve men at Ephesus, the baptism in the Spirit was their *fourth* baptism (Acts 19:1-7)! These baptisms included the baptism of John, the baptism by the Spirit into the body of Christ, the baptism by Paul in water, and the baptism by Jesus in the Spirit.

- For some believers, there is a baptism of suffering (Mark 10:38-39).

Type of Baptism	Person Baptizing	Purpose	Scriptures
1. John's baptism	John	Sign of repentance; Preparation for Christ	Luke 3:3-6
2. Baptism into the body of Jesus	Holy Spirit	Becoming a part of the Church, or body of Jesus	1 Cor. 12:13
3. Water baptism	Pastor	Sign of becoming a Christian	Matt. 28:18-20; Rom. 6:1-4
4. Baptism in the Holy Spirit	Jesus	Power to witness	Acts 1:4-5, 8
5. Baptism of suffering	God	Identifying with the sufferings of Jesus	Mark 10:38; John 18:11

Figure 3.5   Five different types of baptism in the New Testament

4. Why did God link speaking in a new language to being filled with the Holy Spirit?

There are several possible reasons. We will review a few.

- The purpose of being filled with the Spirit is to become witnesses for Jesus to the ends of the earth (Acts 1:8). In other words, believers will witness for Christ in all languages of the earth. Thus speaking in a new language is a sign that a believer will have a part in this global witnessing.[23]
- The tongue is the most rebellious member of the body (James 3:1-12). Thus allowing the Holy Spirit to control the tongue may be a picture of complete surrender to God.
- Almost every miracle has two parts: God's part and our part. Speaking in a new language allows both God and the believer to have a part.
- Speaking in a new language reminds us of a great truth. We cannot do anything for God without His help. There is always the temptation to depend on self. We may trust in money, education, skills, titles, and so on. But our trust should be in God. Without Him, we can do nothing (John 15:5). As often as believers speak in new languages, they remember to depend upon the invisible God. It helps us focus on the unseen (2 Cor. 4:18). Speaking in tongues reminds us that we do not succeed by might or power, but by God's Spirit (Zech. 4:6).
- Speaking in a new language is a form of praying. Praying is speaking to God. He who speaks in a tongue speaks (prays) to God (1 Cor. 14:2, 14). Jude refers to praying in the Spirit as a way we build ourselves up (Jude 20). How wonderful that God chose praying in a new language to edify us!

Q 31 ↗ *Why do you think God linked tongues to being filled with the Spirit?*

5. Are spiritual things like healings, miracles, and speaking in a new language for today?

Some teach that spiritual gifts died with the apostles. They base this false teaching on a true passage. Take a minute to read 1 Corinthians 13:8-12.

> [8]*Love never fails. But where there are prophecies, they will cease; where there are tongues, they will be stilled; where there is knowledge, it will pass away.* [9]*For we know in part and we prophesy in part,* [10]*but when perfection comes, the imperfect disappears.* [11]*When I was a child, I talked like a child, I thought like a child, I reasoned like a child. When I became a man, I put childish ways behind me.* [12]*Now we see but a poor reflection as in a mirror; then we shall see face to face. Now I know in part; then I shall know fully, even as I am fully known* (1 Cor. 13:8-12).

Q 32 ↗ *What will life be like when the perfect comes?*

First Corinthians 13:8-12 contrasts two times: now and then. Now we live in an imperfect time. But then, when Jesus returns, perfection will come. Now we do not see well. But then we will see face to face. Now we do not understand well. But then we will know as we are known. Now we live in an imperfect body. But then we will have a perfect body (1 Cor. 15). Now we have a great need for spiritual gifts and power. Then we will not need spiritual gifts.

Now (The Imperfect Appears)	1 Cor.	Then (The Perfect Comes)	1 Cor.
We need prophecy, tongues, and knowledge.	13:8-9	We shall not need spiritual gifts.	13:10
We talk, think, and reason like children.	13:11	We shall put childish ways behind us.	13:11
We see but a poor reflection, as in a mirror.	13:12	We shall see face to face.	13:12
We know in part.	13:12	We shall know fully, as we are known.	13:12
We live in a physical body.	15:44	We shall live in a spiritual body.	15:44
We are waiting for the trumpet.	15:52	We shall hear the trumpet sound.	15:52
We can die.	15:53	We shall never die.	15:53

Figure 3.6   First Corinthians 13 and 15 contrast the present with the future.

Q 33 ↗ *Does the Bible teach that we still need spiritual gifts? Explain.*

How long do we need spiritual gifts? Until Jesus returns. Some have said that we do not need spiritual gifts because the Bible has come, and the Bible is perfect. But it is the Bible that tells us to eagerly desire spiritual gifts (1 Cor. 14:1)! How long did Paul want the Corinthians to have spiritual gifts? Read 1 Corinthians 1:7 for a clear answer. *"Therefore you do not lack any spiritual gift as you eagerly wait for our Lord Jesus Christ to be revealed."* We need spiritual gifts until Jesus is revealed at His second coming (1 Cor. 1:7).

6. Is speaking in a new language only for those who are not mature? Is it the least of the gifts?

Some who do not speak in tongues say tongues is the least of the gifts. The Bible does not say that speaking in tongues is the least of God's gifts. But if it did, should we refuse a gift from God because it was small? We should give thanks for all gifts God offers us, whether they are great or small.

Q 34 ↖ *How would you answer one who says speaking in tongues is for young or weak believers?*

Is speaking in tongues only for those who are not mature? The apostle Paul prayed in tongues privately. He spoke in tongues more than all of the Corinthian believers did (1 Cor. 14:18). In other words, the one who was the most mature prayed in tongues the most! Let us follow his example and pray much in the language the Holy Spirit gives us.[24]

7. Does God give each believer a new language when he or she is filled with the Spirit? Or does God give different spiritual gifts to each believer?

On the one hand, God does give different spiritual gifts to each believer. All are not apostles, prophets, teachers, or leaders in the church. Not all do miracles, speak in tongues, or interpret tongues to edify the church (1 Cor. 12:27-31).

Q 35 ↗ *When Paul asks, "Are all teachers?" is he referring to teaching at home or in the church? Explain.*

On the other hand, each believer does things in private that he or she does not do in public. A believer may not pray for the sick in church, but all believers can pray for the sick outside of church services (Mark 16:17-18). A believer may not teach in the church, but most adult believers teach at home. A believer may not lead in the church, but each father and mother leads the children at home. Thus believers do the same things at home, but different things in church services.

First Corinthians 12–14 reminds us that all believers do not speak in an unknown language in a church service. Paul spoke in tongues more than all the Corinthians (1 Cor. 14:18). But in church, he preferred to speak in a language others knew. Thus Paul contrasts his private praying in tongues with public church services.

Q 36 ↗ *Which biblical verses show that all who are filled with the Spirit speak in tongues?*

Few have the specific gift of speaking in tongues to edify the entire church. But it is common in the Bible for all believers to speak in tongues when they are filled with the Spirit (Acts 10:46; 19:6). On the Day of Pentecost, all 120 believers were filled with the Spirit and spoke in tongues (Acts 2:4). God enabled each believer to speak in a new language. Why? Because praying in a new language edifies a believer (1 Cor. 14:4). Like Paul, each Christian should be filled with the Spirit and pray in tongues privately. Focus on your own personal needs when you are alone. But in church, seek to edify others.

Do you want more evidence that God desires each believer to speak in a private prayer language? Ask any of the 523,767,000 Charismatics or Pentecostals![25] Few of us have ever spoken in tongues for the whole church. But many of us pray in tongues daily to build ourselves up in private. We follow the apostle Paul's example.

8. Should I avoid all spiritual gifts because they might bring division or confusion? Should I seek love instead of the gifts?

Q 37 ↗ *Should we avoid spiritual gifts since they might cause division or confusion? Explain.*

God does not want us to choose between love and spiritual gifts. Confusion and division come when believers do not walk in love. It is not spiritual gifts that bring confusion and division. Neither is it generous giving that causes division (1 Cor. 13:3). We should not stop giving because our offerings might cause division. Division and confusion can result from anything if people do not walk in love.

It is true that a believer should neither give nor speak in tongues without love (1 Cor. 13:1). But this did not keep Paul from speaking in tongues more than all the rest (1 Cor. 14:18). Love is the path we must walk on as we practice spiritual gifts.[26] It is the excellent way or path in life for all of us. Jesus walked in love and power. Do not choose between love and spiritual gifts. That would be like choosing between mercy and witnessing. Let us choose both. Let us choose love, mercy, humility, spiritual gifts, and all the other good blessings the Holy Spirit offers!

9. Will God embarrass me by causing me to speak in a new language in public?

The Holy Spirit enables a believer to speak in a new language. But the Spirit does not force a believer to speak. The Holy Spirit is as gentle as a dove. He does not force anyone to do anything. God always allows us to make choices.

One man feared to speak in tongues. He was afraid it would be him speaking, not God. But it is never God who does the speaking in tongues. God enables the believer to speak in the unknown language. The believer may always choose to speak or be silent (1 Cor. 14:28, 32). Also, believers may speak as loudly or as quietly as they choose. They may shout in tongues or whisper.

Remember that there are two parts to most miracles. God's part is to fill a believer with the Spirit. He guides the believer in speaking a new language. The believer's part is to speak the language. Therefore, a believer will never be embarrassed by speaking in tongues. A believer may choose to speak or be silent.

Q 38 *Does the Spirit force a believer to speak in a new language? Explain.*

10. How can I be sure the new language is from God, not Satan or the flesh?

Remember the story of the two drunks who were talking in a bar. One of them asked the other if speaking in tongues was from the devil. The other replied, "No, if speaking in tongues was from the devil, we would do it!"[27]

Those who seek the devil find him, not God. And those who seek God find Him, not the devil. Jesus promised that when we pray to our Father in heaven, He will not deceive us.

Q 39 *If we ask God to fill us with the Spirit, should we fear being deceived? Explain.*

[11] *"Which of you fathers, if your son asks for a fish, will give him a snake instead?* [12]*Or if he asks for an egg, will give him a scorpion?* [13]*If you then, though you are evil, know how to give good gifts to your children, how much more will your Father in heaven give the Holy Spirit to those who ask him!"* (Luke 11:11-13).

Seek God, and you will find Him, not Satan (Luke 11:9-10).

Test Yourself: Circle the letter by the *best* completion to each question or statement.

1. The purpose of Pentecost is
a) to speak in an unknown tongue.
b) to be baptized in the Spirit.
c) to be fully saved from sin.
d) to receive power for witnessing.

2. The chapters in Acts about believers being filled with the Spirit are
a) 1, 2, 6, 10, and 26.
b) 2, 8, 9, 10, and 19.
c) 2, 7, 11, 13, and 15.
d) 2, 11, 15, 21, and 26.

3. The first biblical sign that believers have been baptized in the Spirit is
a) speaking in tongues.
b) a new joy for God.
c) increased love for others.
d) new power to witness.

4. We are sure believers who received the Spirit spoke in tongues at
a) Ephesus.
b) Samaria.
c) Antioch.
d) Rome.

5. The main reason we value speaking in tongues is
a) history records it.
b) believers practice it.
c) the Bible teaches it.
d) the mind despises it.

6. Which of the following is NOT a reason why we value speaking in tongues?
a) It is a form of prayer.
b) It is a form of witnessing.
c) It is an exercise in faith.
d) It is a step toward other gifts.

7. Tongues remind us that fellowship with God is more
a) emotional than spiritual.
b) physical than spiritual.
c) mental than spiritual.
d) spiritual than mental.

8. The Holy Spirit enters a person when that person is
a) born into the world.
b) born again.
c) baptized in water.
d) filled with the Spirit.

9. The New Testament mentions how many different types of baptism?
a) 1
b) 3
c) 5
d) 7

10. When that which is perfect has come, we will
a) continue to need spiritual gifts.
b) have partial knowledge.
c) have new bodies.
d) talk, think, and reason as children.

 Essay Test Topics: Write 50-100 words on each of these goals that you studied in this chapter.

The Holy Spirit at Pentecost (Acts 2:1-4)
Goal: *Analyze the purpose and the evidence of being baptized in the Spirit.*

The Value of Speaking in Tongues (Acts 2:4)
Goal: *Evaluate at least 5 reasons why speaking in an unknown tongue is valuable.*

Ten Questions Related to Being Filled With the Spirit (Acts 2:4)
Goal: *Answer 10 questions people ask related to being filled with the Spirit.*

Figure 3.7   Photos of Jerusalem

Jerusalem: Ruins at the southeastern corner of
the old city wall

Jerusalem: A portion of the Model City showing how
Jerusalem looked at the time of Christ. The Fortress of
Antonia is to the back left.

Chapter 4:
From Weakness to Witness—Part 2
(Acts 2)

Introduction

Pastor Jack Hayford found his seat on the airplane. He was on his way home. A man we will call Bill sat down beside him in a business suit. They greeted each other. Soon the plane rose into the clouds. As they talked, Bill shared that his mother was a Native American. She was of the Kiowa tribe in Oklahoma. Suddenly, the Holy Spirit impressed Pastor Jack. "Speak to Bill in tongues" was the message from the Spirit. Jack was shocked. Praying in tongues was a private matter. And Bill

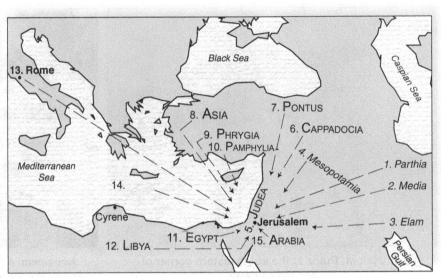

Figure 4.1   At Pentecost, Jews came from 15 different places.

was a stranger. Questions raced through Jack's mind. Would Bill think the pastor was crazy? Why would God ask such a strange thing? Jack wrestled with these and other questions. He and Bill talked for about an hour. But still Pastor Jack was struggling with the message from the Spirit. Bill was not a believer. He politely refused two free books Jack offered to send him. Speaking in tongues to an unbelieving stranger felt very awkward. Jack struggled with a way to obey this clear message from the Spirit. As he prayed, the idea came to relate tongues to Bill's Native American background. Finally, Pastor Jack asked to speak a few words. Bill agreed to tell Jack if the words were a part of the Kiowa language. Pastor Jack spoke about 60-80 words in the unknown language the Spirit gave him. Bill recognized many of the words. He said it was a pre-Kiowan language. Bill told Jack that the message was about the light coming from above. Jack explained that this was a language the Spirit gave him. This incident opened Bill's heart. He changed his mind and asked Pastor Jack to send him the two books about Jesus.[1]

Lessons:

Peter's Message to the Crowd (Acts 2:5-41)
Goal: *Explain what happened at Pentecost, why it happened, and how it can happen to each believer.*

The Promise Is for You (Acts 2:38-39)
Goal: *Explain and follow 4 steps to receiving the baptism in the Holy Spirit.*

The Priorities and Results of the Early Church (Acts 2:42-47)
Goal: *Explain 3 priorities and 3 results of the early church. Apply these to your ministry.*

 Key Words

hyperbole
last days
gift of the Holy Spirit

apostles' teaching
breaking of bread

Peter's Message to the Crowd (Acts 2:5-41)

Goal: *Explain what happened at Pentecost, why it happened, and how it can happen to each believer.*

Setting (Acts 2:5-13)

Acts 2:5 says that in Jerusalem there were Jews from every nation under heaven. This type of writing is called an overstatement or *hyperbole. In an overstatement, the speaker states something bigger than it actually is. He does this to emphasize a point. The listeners or readers know that the speaker or writer is not lying. He is just using the method of overstatement to underline the truth. Emphasizing a truth by overstating it was a common method of Jewish teachers. For example, the Old Testament says Solomon made silver as plentiful as stones in Jerusalem (1 Kings 10:27). This is an overstatement to emphasize the prosperity of Solomon's reign. Likewise, Jesus said the Pharisees strained out a gnat but swallowed a camel (Matt. 23:24). The Lord overstated a truth to make a point. Likewise, in Acts 2:5, Luke overstates his point. He was aware of nations like Ethiopia that were not represented in Jerusalem. But he overstated the point for a purpose. He emphasized that at the Passover, Jews were present from many nations. These were Jews who had been scattered by war and persecution. Each year, many of these Jews returned to celebrate the Passover in Jerusalem. Figure 4.1 shows the 15 places Luke mentions.

Q 1 What is a hyperbole and how does Luke use it?

The crowd was amazed and confused. They probably knew that most of the 120 were from Galilee by the way that they dressed.[2] But the 120 were speaking in many different languages (Acts 2:6). The listeners were amazed to hear their own languages. But they were also confused. How was it possible for the 120 to be speaking the languages of other nations?

Some teachers seem to be as confused as the crowd was at Pentecost. They falsely teach that the 120 were all speaking one language. They also wrongly say that the miracle was in the hearing, not the speaking! This contradicts the Bible. It was not the crowd that was filled with the Spirit and heard new tongues! The Bible says the 120 were filled with the Spirit and spoke in new languages as the Spirit enabled them (Acts 2:4). This caused the crowd to gather. Acts 2:6-7 emphasizes that the crowd heard the 120 speaking in different languages. The miracle took place in the speakers, not the listeners! The speakers were filled with the Spirit. The listeners were filled with amazement and confusion.

Q 2 What caused a crowd to gather on the Day of Pentecost?

Others in the crowd mocked. Because they could not understand the meaning, they decided there was no meaning.[3] Some are like this today. They criticize and mock what they do not understand. But Peter showed they were wrong. Those who get drunk are not out in the street talking at nine in the morning!

Q 3 Do you know some that criticize what they do not understand? Explain.

Next, Peter and the other eleven apostles (including Matthias) stood up. Peter spoke under the anointing of the Holy Spirit. The same Spirit that enabled him to speak in tongues enabled him to prophesy to the crowd (1 Cor. 12:10; 14:3). He did not sit down and plan three points for his message. Rather, the Holy Spirit inspired him to speak.[4] Let us look at three things Peter explained.

A. Peter explained *what* happened at Pentecost (Acts 2:14-21).

The Spirit had come down! This was what Joel had prophesied. Joel's prophecy covered a long period of time. The last days began with the first coming of Christ and will end with His Second Coming (Acts 2:17).[5] Joel emphasized that God will pour out His Spirit. Joel prophesied that the Church Age would be a time of supernatural events. Under the old covenant, signs, wonders, and miracles were rare. But supernatural events are a characteristic of the age of the Spirit, the last days.

Q 4 To what do "the last days" refer (Acts 2:17)?

God promised He would not be partial or have any favorites as He poured out His blessings. Note the following five areas in which God said He would treat all alike and have no favorites.

Q 5 ➤ What are 5 areas in which God said He would not show favoritism?

***First,* God promised He would not favor one nation over another.**   He said He would pour out His Spirit on all flesh or people (Acts 2:17).

***Second,* God promised He would not favor men over women.**   He said He would pour out the Holy Spirit on both sons and daughters (Acts 2:18). Both sexes would prophesy. Recall that there were women among the 120 who spoke in tongues.⁺

***Third,* God promised He would not favor the old above the young.**   He said the young would see spiritual visions and the old would dream spiritual dreams (Acts 2:17). The baptism in the Spirit is for all ages. Many children have been filled with the Spirit at an early age. Likewise, many elderly people have been baptized in the Spirit.

***Fourth,* God promised He would not favor the rich over the poor.**   He promised to pour out His Spirit even on male and female slaves (Acts 2:18). Israel was once a nation of slaves that God delivered from Egypt. Now Israel was under Roman rule. But through Pentecost, both rich and poor become God's slaves or property. Jesus bought us at Calvary. At Pentecost, He takes full possession of believers.

All of the Epistles refer to believers as slaves. The one Greek word *doulos* means "slave" or "servant." Even the apostles and brothers of Jesus call themselves slaves or servants of Jesus (James 1:1; Jude 1). As His slaves, we should claim no rights for ourselves. Rather, we should focus on serving our Lord and Master, Jesus Christ.

***Fifth,* God promised not to favor the early over the late.**   He blesses both the first to hear and the last. Acts 2:19-20 refers to signs that will take place at the end of the last days. But Acts 2:21 assures us that whoever calls on the name of the Lord will be saved. In the years just before Jesus returns, conditions on earth will get worse. Because evil will increase, the love of most will grow cold (Matt. 24:12). The last days will be terrible days (2 Tim. 3:1-5). But even in the worst of times, God will help those who call on Him. Whoever calls on the name of the Lord will be saved, whenever (Acts 2:21)! Likewise, Acts 2:39 says there is no time limit on receiving the gift of the Holy Spirit. This gift is for parents, their children, and those of every generation and race.

Wow! What good news this is to all. God is not biased. He has no favorites. He will pour out His Holy Spirit on all. Pentecost is for everyone. Those of any race, either sex, any age, any social level, any time may drink of His Spirit. Whosoever will may come! Welcome!

B. Peter explained *why* Pentecost happened (Acts 2:22-36).

Acts 2:14-21 centered on the Holy Spirit. But Acts 2:22-36 focuses on Jesus. Peter tells the crowd four truths related to Jesus.

***First,* God approved Jesus through miracles, wonders, and signs (Acts 2:22).**   These are the three words used in the Bible for supernatural acts.

Q 6 ➤ Are all Jews guilty of killing Jesus? Explain.

***Second,* God allowed Jesus to be crucified by unbelieving Jews in Jerusalem (Acts 2:23).**   God had planned for Jesus to die. But this does not lessen the guilt of those who crucified Him. We should note, however, that not all Jews are guilty of killing Jesus. The Bible never puts this guilt on the Jews in general. For example, look at Acts 13:27-29. There, in talking to Jews, Paul says "they," not "you," killed Jesus. Only the unbelieving Jews in Jerusalem were guilty of killing the Messiah.⁶

⁺ Recall that Paul says prophecy and speaking in tongues are equal blessings if the listeners understand (1 Cor. 14:5-6). Perhaps Peter was inspired to recognize that at Pentecost the tongues served as a prophecy for those who understood.

***Third,* God raised Jesus from the dead (Acts 2:24-32).** Peter quotes David in Psalm 16:8-11. David prophesied about the Messiah's resurrection. When Peter spoke, David was in his tomb in Jerusalem. Therefore, the people understood that David was not prophesying about himself. The Holy Spirit used this explanation and illustration to convict many.

***Fourth,* God exalted Jesus and gave Him the Spirit to pour out (Acts 2:33-36).** Note the Trinity in Acts 2:33. The Father exalted the Son to sit at His right hand. This was the greatest place of power and honor. (In Christ, we are also seated at the right hand of God, Eph. 2:6.) Then the Father gave the promise of the Spirit to the Son (See John 16:7). Finally, the Son pours out the Spirit on us. The Father gave the promise. But Jesus is the One who baptizes us in the Spirit (John 1:33).

Q 7 *How does Acts 2:33 describe the Trinity?*

C. Peter explained *how* Pentecost can come to each person (Acts 2:37-41).

One preacher falsely taught that our relationship with God has two parts. He said our part is to get lost, and God's part is to do the rest. But the Bible puts much responsibility on each person. Words like repent, be baptized, receive, and save yourselves emphasize what God commands us to do (Acts 2:38-40). Only those who ask, seek, and knock receive what God wants them to have. Peter spoke about two levels of blessing God desires for us.

***First,* Peter spoke about salvation.** His message to the crowd caused guilt. His words were like a knife that cut their hearts (Acts 2:37). The Holy Spirit convicted them of their sins (John 16:5-11). He caused them to feel guilty. Guilt from God is a gift. He sends guilt to stop us from traveling the path of sin.

Q 8 *Do you think guilt is good or bad? Explain.*

Some turned away from God when they began to feel guilty. This was a terrible mistake. It is natural for a person who feels guilty to look down or turn away. Isaiah felt guilty, unclean, and afraid in God's presence (Isa. 6:1-5). Likewise, Peter felt guilty in the Lord's presence. Peter's first response was, *"Go away from me, Lord; I am a sinful man!"* (Luke 5:8). God knows we are sinful. But His desire is not to go away from us because of our sins. His great desire is to forgive and cleanse us. Jesus did not come to condemn us, but to save us (John 3:17). Therefore, we should never turn away from God when we feel guilty. Guilt is God's invitation to repent.

Others made the right decision. They turned toward God with their guilt. They asked, *"Brothers, what shall we do?"* (Acts 2:37). This is the question that all sinners should ask when they feel guilty. Peter had preached hard truth to them, but still called them brothers (Acts 2:29). Perhaps this helped them call the apostles brothers. We should always talk to others like they are brothers.

Peter told them to repent and be baptized (Acts 2:38). These are the two steps God commands sinners to take. Repentance means a change of mind. Those who repent change their minds about sin. They turn away from sin toward God. It is impossible to face sin and God at the same time. No person can face north and south at the same time. We must choose one or the other. Those who repent choose to face God and walk toward Him.

Q 9 *What step did Peter link with repentance?*

Q 10 *Is it possible to face sin and God at the same time? Explain.*

Two men were talking about their past sins. One man said, "If I could live my life over, I would do more of those sins." The other said, "If I could live my life over, I would avoid those sins." One man was still facing sin. The other had repented. He had changed his mind about sin. He had turned from sin toward God.

When we turn from sin toward God, we are facing the Savior. His name is called *Jesus* because He saves His people from their sins (Matt. 1:21). But we have a part in our salvation. What is it? We must choose to turn from sin toward Jesus (Acts 2:40). But only He can free us from the power and penalty of our sins.

After Jesus saves a person, that believer is ready for water baptism. Baptism is the first step of obedience after receiving Jesus as Savior. Water baptism was a big, radical step for Jews. Why? Because the Jews taught that water baptism was just for Gentiles. Jews were born Jews. Only Gentiles who wanted to become Jews were baptized. Thus John the Baptist shocked people. He told the Jews that they needed to repent and be baptized![7] However, he refused to baptize people until *after* they repented (Matt. 3:5-10). Likewise, believers are baptized *after* they are born again.

Baptism is an outward picture of an inner experience. A believer is baptized *for* or *because* his or her sins have been forgiven (Acts 2:38).[8] Baptism shows that the old, sinful life was buried with Christ. As Christ went down into the grave, believers bury their old life in water. Then, coming up out of the water shows we are rising with Christ to live a new, holy life (Rom. 6:1-4).

Q 11 ↘ *What is "the gift of the Holy Spirit"?*

Second, Peter talked to the crowd about receiving "the gift of the Holy Spirit" (Acts 2:38). There are five places in Acts that Luke refers to the baptism in the Spirit as a gift.

- Jesus told the disciples to *"wait for the gift my Father promised"* (Acts 1:4).
- Peter told Jews they would receive *"the gift of the Holy Spirit"* after they repented and were baptized (Acts 2:38).
- Peter rebuked Simon the former sorcerer. Simon wanted to buy the ability to impart *"the gift of God"* to others (Acts 8:18-20). Peter taught him that God's gifts could not be bought or sold. They are free! Anyone who wants the gift of the baptism in the Spirit can have it. (Notice that believers in Samaria did not receive the gift of the Spirit until after they were baptized in water.)
- Peter was sure that *"the gift of the Holy Spirit had been poured out even on the Gentiles. For they heard them speaking in tongues and praising God"* (Acts 10:45-46).
- Peter recalled that John baptized in water, but Jesus baptizes in the Holy Spirit. *"God gave them* (the Gentiles) *the same gift as he gave us* (the Jews)*"* (Acts 11:16).

Q 12 ↘ *Does the baptism in the Spirit enable a person to become a Christian?*

Some Jews were offended when John the Baptist said they needed to be baptized. They said they were already children of Abraham (Matt. 3:9). But John's baptism was not to make them Jews. It was because they had a need in their lives. Likewise, some believers today are offended when told they need to be baptized in the Spirit. They say they are already Christians. But the baptism in the Spirit is not to make people Christians. It is for those who are already believers. The apostles were already followers of Christ, but they needed the gift of the Spirit (Acts 1:4). The Samaritans had believed and been baptized in water. *Afterward,* they were baptized in the Spirit (Acts 8:15-16). Paul preached Jesus to twelve men in Ephesus. They were born again and baptized in water. *Afterward,* he prayed for them and they were filled with the Spirit and spoke in tongues (Acts 19:1-7). Every person needs to be baptized twice. *First,* repent, believe, and be baptized in water. *Then* seek to be baptized in the Spirit. Water baptism is for the outside of the body. Spirit baptism is our Father's gift for us on the inside. Read Luke 11:9-13.

Q 13 ↖ *How does Luke 11:9-13 strengthen your faith?*

Ask your Father for the gift of the Holy Spirit. Keep asking until you receive. Ask with a smile on your face and confidence in your heart. Earthly fathers give good gifts to their children who ask. How much more will He give the Holy Spirit to those who keep asking! He will give you the same gift that He gave the 120 at Pentecost! God does not show favoritism (James 1:5).

Come to Jesus to be baptized in the Spirit. *"Jesus Christ is the same yesterday and today and forever"* (Heb. 13:8). He will change your weakness to witness.

The Promise Is for You (Acts 2:38-39)

Goal: *Explain and follow 4 steps to receiving the baptism in the Holy Spirit.*

Setting

Before Jesus left, He told His disciples to stay in Jerusalem.

⁴On one occasion, while he was eating with them, he gave them this command: "Do not leave Jerusalem, but wait for the gift my Father promised, which you have heard me speak about. ⁵For John baptized with water, but in a few days you will be baptized with the Holy Spirit" (Acts 1:4-5).

The disciples obeyed. They returned to Jerusalem and waited. On the Day of Pentecost they were together in an upper room. Suddenly, just as Jesus promised, the Holy Spirit came. They were all filled with the Spirit. They began to speak in languages they did not know as the Spirit enabled them. The 120 continued speaking in tongues as they went outside. A crowd began to gather. There were Jews in Jerusalem from many different nations. These scattered Jews had returned to Jerusalem to celebrate the Passover. Many became a part of God's plan to spread the gospel.

The crowd witnessed the miracle of Pentecost. They were amazed and confused. How could the disciples speak languages they did not know? This still amazes us today!

There are two parts to this lesson. We will review Peter's message to the crowd. Then we will study how each believer can be baptized in the Holy Spirit.

A. A review of Peter's message to the crowd (Acts 2:12-41)

Peter's message centered on two questions that the crowd asked.

***"What does this mean?"* (Acts 2:12).** This was the *first* question of the crowd. They wanted to know why believers were speaking in new languages. Peter explained that the baptism in the Spirit was from God. It was the gift the Father had promised. He told the crowd that this miracle fulfilled a prophecy of the Old Testament (Acts 2:16). God made a promise through Joel. *"In the last days, God says, I will pour out my Spirit on all people"* (Joel 2:28; Acts 2:17).

The promise was for all. Young and old, male and female could receive. Everyone who called on the name of the Lord would be saved. And all could receive the gift of the baptism in the Spirit (Joel 2:28-32; Acts 2:17-21).

Peter continued answering their question. He preached good news to the people. Many of these people already knew about Jesus. They had seen the miracles, wonders, and signs that God did through Him (Acts 2:22). In God's plan, Jesus had been handed over to the unbelieving Jews. With the help of wicked men, they had nailed him to a cross. *"But God raised him from the dead"* (Acts 2:24). Then Jesus was exalted to the right hand of God. Peter declared that this same Jesus had received the promised Holy Spirit. Then Jesus had poured out the gift of the Spirit. That was what the crowd was seeing and hearing (Acts 2:32-33)!

Thus Peter answered their first question, *"What does this mean?"* Now, let us look at the second question of the crowd.

***"What shall we do?"* (Acts 2:37).** Many accepted Peter's answer to their first question. Now they understood that God was pouring out His Spirit. They were convicted of their sins. And they wanted to receive the blessings God had planned for them. So they asked, *"What shall we do?"*

³⁸Peter replied, "Repent and be baptized, every one of you, in the name of Jesus Christ for the forgiveness of your sins. And you will receive the gift of the Holy Spirit. ³⁹The promise is for you and your children and for all who are far off—for all whom the Lord our God will call" (Acts 2:38-39).

Q 14 *In Acts 2:12, to what does the word "this" refer?*

Q 15 *What was the answer to the question of Acts 2:12?*

Q 16 *What does it mean today when a believer speaks in a new language?*

Q 17 *To whom does God offer the gift of the Holy Spirit (Acts 2:39)?*

For whom is this gift? Who can be baptized in the Spirit? Was it *only* for the apostles? No! This is not a gift only for a special class of people. God does not offer the gift to only a few "holy men." Peter said that the promise was for all. The promise of being filled with the Holy Spirit is not just for the apostles, or the 120. The promise was for the Jews, their children, their grandchildren, and those of every generation. God's promises are for all He calls, and God calls all. He wants all to be saved and filled. *"All"* includes *us!* The gift of the baptism in the Spirit is for anyone who wants it.

Imagine that I am standing in front of you with a gift. I say it is for you. I extend it for you to take. All you have to do is believe me, reach out, and take it! Likewise, God offers us the free gift of the baptism in the Holy Spirit. He wants to fill us with the Spirit's presence. But it is up to us to accept the gift. He offers salvation to all, but only a few take it. He offers the baptism in the Spirit to all. Are you ready to receive this gift?

B. How to receive the gift of the baptism in the Holy Spirit

Let us consider four steps to being baptized in the Spirit.

Q 18 *What 2 things did Peter say would come before the gift of the Spirit (Acts 2:38)?*

***First*, obey what Peter told the crowd (Acts 2:38).**   Repent, receive Jesus as Savior, and be baptized in water. Have you been born again? If not, turn toward God now. Repent of your sins and accept God's forgiveness (1 John 1:9). Have you been baptized in water to show that your sins are forgiven? If not, then obey the Lord and be baptized in water. Baptism in water is important. It is the first act of obedience for a new believer. As we obey what God commands, it gives us confidence when we pray (1 John 3:21-22).

Q 19 *Has comparing Acts 2:38 and Matthew 28:19 helped you? Explain.*

Should a person be baptized in the name of Jesus or in the name of the Father, the Son, and the Holy Spirit? *In the name of Jesus* means "upon the authority of Jesus." Luke does not say much about baptism. Sometimes he does not explain what was already clear to the early church. Comparing Acts 2:38 with Matthew 28:19 is helpful. Together, these verses give a more complete picture. Jesus commanded His disciples to baptize people into the name of the Father, the Son, and the Holy Spirit. This means we baptize people into the worship and service of God, the Trinity.[9]

Q 20 *Summarize the promises in Acts 2:38-39, John 7:37-39, and Luke 11:11-13.*

***Second*, look at what God promises about the baptism in the Spirit.**   We need faith to receive this blessing from God. And faith comes by hearing God's Word (Rom. 10:17). What does the Bible say about the promise of the Spirit's fullness? Read Acts 2:33, 38-39; John 7:37-39; 14:16-17; and Luke 11:11-13.

Realize that the promise of the baptism in the Spirit is for you, right now!

Q 21 *Summarize the first 3 steps toward receiving the gift of the Spirit.*

***Third*, ask and get ready to receive this precious gift the Father is offering you.**   Luke 11:13 states that God will give the Holy Spirit to those who ask Him. So ask! Pray something like, "Father, I believe your promises are true. I believe the gift of the Holy Spirit is for me, today, right now. By faith, I have already received your gift of salvation. Now by faith, I trust you to baptize me in the Holy Spirit. I expect that you will enable me to speak in a new language. I open my life to you. I reach out in faith to receive the gift of the baptism in the Holy Spirit. I thank you in the name of Jesus. Amen."

Q 22 *What is the believer's part in being baptized in the Spirit? Explain.*

***Fourth*, by faith do your part to receive this gift.**   The story of Peter walking on the water illustrates the believer's part (Matt. 14:22-33). It took God's help for Peter to walk on the water toward Jesus. Likewise, only God can enable you to speak in a language you do not know. God is ready to do His part. But you also have a part in the miracle. Did Jesus force Peter to leave the security of the boat? Did Jesus pick up Peter's feet and cause him to step out onto the water? No! All Jesus did was invite Peter to walk to Him. Jesus invited Peter with one of God's favorite words, "Come" (Matt. 14:29). Then Peter's part was to use his feet and begin walking. The miracle was not that Peter walked. Peter was using his feet in the way he used them each day.

Likewise, the miracle of speaking in tongues is not that you talk. You will talk with the same tongue and voice you use each day. It was Peter who took the steps. And it will be you who says the words. It was Peter's choice to start walking and his choice to stop walking. It is your choice to start talking and to stop talking. God will do His part, but you must do your part.

A believer called Albert sought for 3 years to be baptized in the Spirit. Many times he prayed, "Lord, I am ready. Baptize me in the Spirit. Begin speaking the new language." Albert thought Jesus would do the talking. He did not understand the difference in the Lord's part and his own part. Time after time Albert came to the Lord and said, "Go ahead, I am ready." But nothing happened. The Lord often put the new words and syllables into Albert' mind. Then He waited on Albert to start speaking. But Albert did not realize it was time to speak. Imagine two people playing a game like *checkers. They take turns. After one moves or takes a turn, it is the other person's turn to move. But nothing will happen if one of the players refuses to take his or her turn. They will just sit and look at each other! It took Albert 3 years to understand that his part was to speak! Then one glorious night he understood. He quietly whispered the words that came to his mind.[+] Then he stopped. His mind did not understand the new words. They sounded strange, like a language he did not know. Albert turned away from analyzing the new language. He realized his mind could never understand this spiritual experience. As Paul said, *"For if I pray in a tongue, my spirit prays, but my mind is unfruitful"* (1 Cor. 14:14). So Albert focused on Jesus and began again to speak in childlike faith. He spoke his words as praise offerings to God. Then he heard the Lord sigh and say to him, "O, so you finally believe me!" A great peace began to fill Albert as he prayed in the new language. He felt like he was being baptized in love. Alone in his room, he prayed in the new language for over an hour. It was as if a pure river of love was flowing through him. From that time forward his life was changed. He felt new love for old enemies. It became easier to follow Christ and live a holy life. No longer did living a Christian life seem like climbing a mountain. Also, the Spirit enabled him to conquer a bad habit in his life. Best of all, he became a more powerful witness for Jesus.

After Jesus puts new words or syllables in your mind, it is your turn! Speak them out in faith! Whisper the new words or shout them as loudly as you desire. The voice and the choice are yours. Jesus invited Peter to come to him on the water. The next step was up to Peter. It was Peter's turn. Nothing could happen until Peter picked up his foot and stepped away from the boat. You will be baptized in the Spirit only when you begin to speak.

It took faith for Peter to take the first step. On the one hand, he was stepping from the known to the unknown. This was scary! On the other hand, he was stepping from the known to the known. This was easy. Why? Because he was stepping toward the Jesus he knew. This was the key to Peter's faith. He was able to take a step of faith because he focused on Jesus. Jesus is the author and perfecter of our faith (Heb. 12:2). Likewise, you will receive the faith you need to speak in a new language as you focus on Jesus!

Q 23 Do you know people who had the same problem as Albert? Explain.

Figure 4.2
Checkerboard with checkers on it

Q 24 How is being baptized in the Spirit like walking on water?

+ Sometimes believers speak forth the language of the Spirit without thinking about the words. In these cases the language seems to completely bypass the mind.

You can trust Jesus. Remember, if you ask Him for a fish, He will not give you a snake (Luke 11:11). Jesus will give you the faith you need as you keep your eyes on Him. The Holy Spirit will enable you to speak in a new language (Acts 2:4). And Jesus will baptize you in the Spirit as you speak the words the Spirit brings to your mind.

Those who are baptized in the Spirit receive the same gift that the Father gave to the first believers. Also, they join a group of over 520 million Charismatic and Pentecostal believers.[10] Millions around the world will testify that this precious gift from God is the key to witnessing for Jesus. Pray in tongues daily as you enjoy the fullness of the Spirit in your life. Praying in the Spirit will build you up spiritually (1 Cor. 14:4; Jude 20).

Lesson 12 — The Priorities and Results of the Early Church (Acts 2:42-47)

Goal: *Explain 3 priorities and 3 results of the early church. Apply these to your ministry.*

Setting

Q 25 *Why do you think biblical teaching should be the first priority of the Church?*

The early church was a healthy, growing church. Why? Because of their priorities. When a church has the right values and focus, good things happen. In this lesson, we will study the values and priorities of the early church. Then we will see what happened because of these values.

A. Three priorities

1. The first priority mentioned is the apostles' teaching. *"They devoted themselves to the apostles' teaching and to the fellowship, to the breaking of bread and to prayer"* (Acts 2:42).

Churches may emphasize many things such as worship, witnessing, fellowship, and helping others. These are all good. But notice that Luke mentions the apostles' teaching first in the Church's priorities (Acts 2:42-47). Nothing should ever move biblical teaching into second place in the Church.

Q 26 *Which of the apostles' teachings are taught the least today? Explain.*

Notice that Luke emphasizes the teaching *of the apostles*. Believers *"devoted themselves to the apostles' teaching"* (Acts 2:42). What did the apostles teach? This is not a secret to us. The New Testament contains the teachings of the apostles. Figure 4.3 summarizes some of the things the apostles taught.

Teaching of the Apostles	Scriptures
1. The Scriptures are the inspired words of God, without any errors.	Acts 1:16; 4:25; 2 Tim. 3:16; 2 Pet. 1:20-21
2. There is one true God. He exists as a Trinity of three persons: the Father, the Son, and the Holy Spirit.	Matt. 28:19; John 14:16-17; Acts 17:24-31; 2 Cor. 13:14
3. All humans, except Jesus Christ, have sinned.	Acts 22:14; Rom. 3:23; Heb. 4:15; 1 Pet. 2:22
4. Salvation is available only through Jesus Christ. He shed His blood on the cross as God's Lamb, to redeem us from our sins. To be saved from sin and judgment, a person must repent, trust in Jesus as Savior, be baptized, and obey Jesus as Lord.	Acts 2:38; 3:23; 4:12; 10:43; 13:38-39; 22:14-16; 26:15-18; Eph. 1:7; Rev. 5:6-10
5. All who receive Jesus as Savior must be baptized in water.	Matt. 28:19; Mark 16:16; Acts 2:38; 8:12-13, 36-38; 9:18; 10:47-48; 19:5; 22:16
6. The Lord's Supper reminds believers of the Lord's death and return.	Matt. 26:26-29; Acts 2:42; 20:7; 1 Cor. 11:23-26

Continued on next page

Teaching of the Apostles	Scriptures
7. The baptism in the Holy Spirit comes with the immediate outward sign of speaking in a new language. This is a gift the Father wants to give each believer, after being born again. This gift brings power to witness, serve Christ, and live above sin.	Acts 2:4; 10:45-46; 11:15-17; 19:1-7 (See Figure 3.4)
8. Miracles, signs, wonders, healings, speaking in tongues, and other spiritual gifts are the Church's inheritance until Jesus Christ returns.	Acts 3:1-10; 4:30; 5:15; 6:8; 8:13; 12:1-17; 15:12; 19:11; 28:1-9; Rom. 1:11; 1 Cor. 1:7; 12:1–14:40; 1 Thess. 5:19-20; 2 Tim. 1:6; Heb. 2:4; James 5:14-16
9. God requires His children to live holy lives. This is possible as we choose to walk in the Spirit.	Acts 5:1-11; Rom. 8:1-2, 13; 12:1-2; 1 Cor. 6:9-11; Gal. 5:19-21; Titus 2:11-14; Heb. 12:14; 1 Pet. 1:15-16; Rev. 3:4-6
10. The Church is the spiritual family of God. It is a fellowship based on the blood of Jesus and created by the Spirit.[11] The Church serves in three directions. She evangelizes outward to the lost. She worships upward to God. She ministers inward to build up her members. All the ministry of the Church depends on prayer and the Holy Spirit.	Matt. 28:18-19; Acts 2:38-39, 47; 13:47; Rom. 12:1; 1 Cor. 14:12; 2 Cor. 5:11; Eph. 4:29; 1 Thess. 5:11; Heb. 13:15; Jude 20
11. Jesus rose victorious over death. He ascended to the right hand of the Father. He will return to reward believers. They will be with Christ forever.+	Acts 1:1-11; 2:20; 3:20-21; 23:6; 24:21-25; 26:8; 1 Cor. 15:51-52; 1 Thess. 4:16-17; Titus 2:13
12. Jesus will conquer Satan, the Antichrist, and evil. He will judge the disobedient. They will suffer in the lake of fire forever.	Matt. 8:12; 13:49-50; 25:31-46; 2 Thess. 2:1-12; Rev. 14:11; 20:10-14

Figure 4.3 Teachings of the apostles

God has NOT promised to bless many of the things churches do. But He has promised to bless His Word. He has promised that His Word will always accomplish its purposes (Isa. 55:11).

Biblical teaching is important from birth until death. It is necessary for believers from the womb to the tomb. A newborn baby desires milk. A newborn Christian desires the milk of the Word (1 Pet. 2:2). Healthy people desire food each day for their bodies. Likewise, healthy Christians desire biblical teaching every day. Believers never graduate from the school of God's Word.

The main thing Jesus told His disciples to do was make disciples (Matt. 28:19). There is a great danger in bringing people to Christ, but not teaching them. If a church does not teach her people, false teachers will teach them. There is one question that believers should continually seek to answer. *"What does the Scripture say?"* (Rom. 4:3).

What should you do if you do not feel a spiritual hunger for the Bible? Try three cures or remedies. *First,* examine your diet. What are you eating? That is, what are you feeding your mind and your soul? Eating candy or cake before a meal can ruin a person's appetite. Likewise, eating too much food the flesh likes can ruin your spiritual appetite. That is, watching too much television, reading the wrong books, or thinking too much about worldly things can destroy a person's appetite for godly things. Therefore, if you do not have a spiritual hunger, check your diet. You may need to cut some harmful things out of it. *Second,* eat some good food whether you are hungry or not. That

Q 27 ↗ *What 3 things can believers without spiritual hunger do?*

+ For a detailed study on end-time events, see the *Faith & Action* course on *Revelation & Daniel.*

is, read the Bible. Go to Sunday school. Many find that this will stir up the spiritual appetite. Eat a little good food, and you will want more. *Third,* examine your spiritual work schedule. Working too little or too much can affect a person's appetite. Working for God will cause you to be hungry for spiritual food. Working people naturally get hungry. On the other hand, a few believers try to work too hard for God. This may cause them to burn out. That is, they may lose their desire to work any for Him. Therefore, these believers need to relax more, take a walk in the woods, or take a vacation. Some think part of Elijah's discouragement came from working too hard (1 Kings 19:3-9). The best path is between working too little and too much.

2. Another priority of the early church was fellowship.   We have seen that the believers shared the same teaching. Their fellowship was based on three more things they shared.

They shared a common task. Their fellowship was more than just meeting to have fun. It was a partnership in the purposes of the Church (Figure 4.3, number 10). Believers had fellowship as they shared in the Church's message and work.[12] Fellowship is never an end in itself. It is never a goal that stands alone. People who believe the same things and work together enjoy fellowship.

Q 28   *How can you apply the story of Alfred to believers you know?*

Alfred complained. He told his pastor that there was not enough fellowship in the church. Alfred had already left one church to try another. Now he discovered that there was no fellowship in either. The pastor invited Alfred to come to the church on Saturday, in his work clothes. Alfred agreed. Several of the other members also came. They gathered to work on the church. They cleaned, cut grass, and did repairs. Alfred was surprised at how much fellowship he found that day. Fellowship is always a natural part of working together at a common task. Those who fight a fire or a war together will become closer to each other.

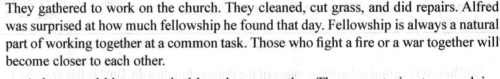

A doctor and his son worked long hours together. They were trying to save dying people from *cholera. Each day they got up early and went to bed late. Some days they did not take time for the noon meal. There was too much work for them to do alone. They needed common people to help with simple tasks. One day a stranger came to visit them. He was on his way to watch a soccer match. He said he believed in what they were doing and left a small offering. But there was not much fellowship between the doctor and the stranger. Why? Because the stranger did not help much with the task. Likewise, the Father and the Son are working to save people from sin. Some do not share in the task and have no fellowship with God. Others believe the Bible and do their part in God's work. These enjoy fellowship with God and His children (1 John 1:3).

Along with a common task, believers shared the breaking of bread. This was a part of the fellowship (Acts 2:42). *The breaking of bread* referred to the Lord's Supper and a meal. Believers shared a common Lord. They celebrated His death and return together at the Lord's Table (1 Cor. 10:21). The first believers could not receive the Lord's Supper in the temple. Therefore, they received it in their homes. Each home was a center of Christian fellowship and worship.[13] Believers often ate a meal together. Then they shared the Lord's Supper at the end of the meal. Recall that Jesus, at a meal, introduced the bread and the cup (Matt. 26:26-29). Thus He transformed the Passover meal into a reminder of the new covenant. We refer to communion as the Lord's Supper. Why? Because it was first associated with a supper. So what? We celebrate the Lord's Supper together. But let us not forget that believers ate a meal together. Many believers today can testify that Jesus, food, and fellowship go well together.

Notice that the believers were happy. They *"ate together with glad and sincere hearts"* (Acts 2:46). Grape juice is sweet. But some believers look like they have been drinking lemon juice. Perhaps they think it is wrong for believers to show joy when they come together. These remind us of Michal (2 Sam. 6:16-23). She was upset because David showed great joy before the people. This was too much emotion to please her. Likewise, Michal would not have approved of the first believers. The early church was a joyful church! They were not ashamed to show their joy. They were not too proud to rejoice and praise God (Acts 2:46-47).

Besides a common task, and the breaking of bread, believers shared their possessions. This was not communism in which the government owns everything. Neither was it socialism in which the government forces all to be at the same financial level. No one was required to sell anything (Acts 5:4). Some sold possessions, and some did not. Many believers still owned their homes in Jerusalem (Acts 2:46). But there were some believers from outside Jerusalem. These needed help to live. Some like Barnabas, Ananias, and Sapphira sold possessions to share (Acts 2:45; 4:36-37; 5:1-2).

Q 29 ⟍ *Did the first believers practice socialism? Explain.*

So the believers had fellowship as they shared four things. They shared the apostles' teachings, a common task, breaking of bread, and possessions. Woven together, these four things make a strong cord of fellowship. Figure 4.4 mentions other factors of fellowship.

Q 30 ⟍ *What 4 things did believers share?*

One another reference	Scripture
Love one another.	John 13:34
Rejoice with one another.	Rom. 12:15; 1 Cor. 12:26
Be kind to one another.	Eph. 4:32
Forgive one another.	Eph. 4:32; Col. 3:13
Encourage one another.	1 Thess. 5:11
Pray for one another.	James 5:16
Prefer one another in love.	Rom. 12:10
Do not judge one another.	Rom. 14:13
Do not spread evil against one another.	James 4:11
Do not grumble against one another.	James 5:9
Do not be puffed up against one another.	1 Cor. 4:6
Bear one another's burdens.	Gal. 6:2
Put up with one another.	Col. 3:13

Figure 4.4   Bible verses that guide our fellowship with one another

3. Prayer was the third priority of the early church. Time after time in Acts we find believers praying. Figure 4.5 summarizes a few of the times believers prayed.

When did the first believers pray?	Acts
They prayed as they waited to be filled with the Spirit.	1:14
They prayed as they chose an apostle to replace Judas.	1:24
They prayed as a way of life.	2:42
They prayed on the way to the prayer meeting.	3:1
They prayed when they were threatened and persecuted.	4:24-31
They prayed for those who served the tables.	6:6
They prayed when they were dying.	7:59
They prayed for new believers to be filled with the Spirit.	8:15; 9:17-19; 19:6
They prayed before eating.	10:9
They prayed when believers were locked in prison.	12:5
They prayed for their missionaries.	13:3
They prayed when they chose church leaders.	14:23

Q 31 ⟍ *Do believers today pray as much as the first believers prayed? Explain.*

Continued on next page

Continued from previous page

When did the first believers pray?	Acts
They prayed when they were bleeding in prison.	16:25
They prayed when they said good-bye to friends.	20:36
They prayed for the sick to be healed.	28:8

Figure 4.5   The early church was a praying church.

The references in Figure 4.5 are only a few of the times believers prayed. These first Christians prayed often. They did not have as much money, education, or freedom as many believers do today. They did not have printing power, electric power, waterpower, or gasoline power. But they had prayer power. Without prayer, the Church has the eyes of a blind man and the strength of a dead man.[14] But as we pray, God does His will on earth. The Church will do better on its feet if it will spend more time on its knees.

Prayer saves time. So we should never be too busy to pray. Luther had so much to do that he prayed 3 hours before he started. "Never look into the face of a man in the morning until you have looked into the face of God."[15]

One great preacher always felt that something was wrong during the day if a half-hour went by that he was not praying. We do not need to speak to pray. We do not need to kneel or be alone to pray. Minute by minute, let us commune with God. Prayer should be as constant during the day as breathing.[16]

A worker was on his knees, striking a stone. He hit it blow by blow with a hammer. Finally, it became the stone he wanted it to be. Likewise, we Christians work the best on our knees. Even the hardest hearts are changed as we continue to pray.[17]

Q 32 ✎ *Is it necessary to speak or kneel to pray? Explain.*

B. Results

The priorities of the early church brought at least three results.

1. God did signs and wonders through the apostles (Acts 2:43; 3:12-13).   Later, He did signs and wonders through many others (Mark 16:20; Acts 6:8; 8:6; 1 Cor. 12:7-11; James 5:14-16). These miracles were not just to see. They were for at least three purposes. First, to confirm the Word, the apostles' teaching. Second, to show love and mercy to those in need. Third, the miracles helped root the Pentecostal believers in the Word and the power of God (See 1 Cor. 2:4-5).18

Q 33 ↗ *What are 3 purposes of signs and wonders?*

A miracle or wonder can be either physical or spiritual.

- It was a wonder when God healed the man born a cripple (Acts 3:1-10). But it is just as great a wonder when a person crippled by bitterness, sexual sins, unbelief, alcohol, or drugs is delivered.
- It was a wonder when Jesus healed the man born blind (John 9). But it was also a wonder when Saul of Tarsus saw the light for the first time. Likewise, it was a wonder when Simon the Sorcerer saw the truth of the gospel.

Q 34 ✎ *Do you think physical wonders are greater than spiritual wonders? Explain.*

Some falsely say that signs, wonders, and miracles are not for today. But those who still believe the apostles' teachings still see physical and spiritual miracles today.

2. A second result was favor.   The early church enjoyed the favor of all the people (Acts 2:47). This is a general summary. It means that as a whole, the people in Jerusalem liked the early believers. The Church still had some enemies among the Sanhedrin. But most people favored the Church. Sinners liked seeing people healed. They liked seeing sinful lives changed. They liked seeing joy replace sadness. They liked seeing joy, fellowship, and sharing.

Q 35 ✎ *What are some keys for your church to find favor with others?*

How can a church find favor with people today? We will find favor with many people if we follow the example of the early church. What were the priorities of those first believers? They focused on the apostles' teaching. They shared fellowship in work, in homes, and in possessions. They prayed constantly. Let us do likewise. Then, like Jesus and the early church, we will grow *"in favor with God and men"* (Luke 2:52).[19]

3. The third result was church growth. Some focus on church growth. This is like putting the cart before the donkey. We should focus on the same values and priorities of the early church. Then, a natural result will be church growth. Fruit is a natural result of a good fruit tree. Growth is usually a natural result of a healthy church.

The early church grew in numbers. *"And the Lord added to their number daily those who were being saved"* (Acts 2:47). Let us note three things about Acts 2:47.

First, **the Lord is the One who adds people to the Church.** Sometimes people become church members *before* they are saved. There are many on church lists or roles whom the Lord has not added. This is sad. It is very important to realize that the Lord is the only One who can add people to His Church. He is the Savior. And He is the One who builds His Church. Every church member should be sure that the Lord has added him or her to the Church. We may welcome new members into fellowship. But only the Lord can truly add them to the Church.

Second, **Luke does not say how many "decisions" there were.** He does not say how many raised their hands or filled out a card. Luke only counts those who actually became part of the Church! The Bible teaches that those who are saved become part of a local church.[20]

Todd claimed he led 54 people to the Lord in one year. Mary asked, "How many of these converts attend church?" "Only three," replied Todd. "Then report that three were saved," said Mary.

Third, **the Lord adds a person to the Church as he or she is saved.** Saved from what? Saved from sin! *Saved* is a biblical word. Some teach that a person cannot be saved now. But Luke reminds us that salvation is for the present. As Jesus saves a person from sins, He adds that believer to the Church. God alone knows the names of those who are born again. God keeps an account of those who receive Jesus as Savior and Lord. He writes the names of believers in a book as He adds them to the Church. That book is called the book of life (Rev. 3:5; 20:12; 21:27).

Q 36 ✎ *How would you answer those who say we cannot be saved now?*

Saved! This one word *saved* is enough to make the heart dance. Saved! This word calls for music to celebrate. Some have been saved from terrible car crashes. Many were killed, but some were saved! Others have been saved from the dangers of fire or disease. To them, this word *saved* is sweet. But to be saved from sin and hell is even greater. We will sing it in life. We will whisper it in death. And for eternity we will celebrate that we are saved!

Figure 4.6
A model of the temple where the early church continued to worship

Test Yourself: Circle the letter by the ***best*** completion to each question or statement.

1. The prophet who foretold that God would pour out His Spirit was
a) Moses.
b) Amos.
c) Joel.
d) Daniel.

2. In pouring out the Spirit, God promised He would
a) favor adults more than children.
b) honor men more than women.
c) give the poor the first chance.
d) bless those in all nations.

3. The main reason Pentecost happened was that
a) God had exalted Jesus to heaven.
b) the Passover was at hand.
c) people from many nations came.
d) believers spoke in new tongues.

4. Usually, the baptism in the Spirit comes
a) at the time a person first accepts Christ.
b) at the time a person first feels the Spirit.
c) before a believer is baptized in water.
d) after a person has been baptized in water.

5. A passage that helps give faith to receive the Spirit's fullness is
a) Acts 4:2-5.
b) John 3:16-18.
c) Luke 11:11-13.
d) Acts 12:1-4.

6. An event that illustrates the believer's part in the Spirit-baptism is
a) Philip preaching in Samaria.
b) Peter walking on the water.
c) Stephen glowing like an angel.
d) Ananias searching for Paul.

7. In Acts 2:42-47, the first priority of the Church that Luke mentions is
a) the fellowship of believers.
b) the worship of the Father.
c) the teaching of the apostles.
d) witnessing to unbelievers.

8. Fellowship is best thought of as
a) a goal.
b) a result.
c) a meal.
d) a need.

9. A result of the priorities of the early church was
a) church growth.
b) persecution.
c) socialism.
d) fewer problems.

10. Signs and wonders of the Holy Spirit
a) ceased with the apostles.
b) were done first through Stephen.
c) have been replaced by the Scriptures.
d) continue for those who expect them.

 Essay Test Topics: Write 50-100 words on each of these goals that you studied in this chapter.

Peter's Message to the Crowd (Acts 2:5-41)

Goal: *Explain what happened at Pentecost, why it happened, and how it can happen to each believer.*

The Promise Is for You (Acts 2:38-39)

Goal: *Explain and follow 4 steps to receiving the baptism in the Holy Spirit.*

The Priorities and Results of the Early Church (Acts 2:42-47)

Goal: *Explain 3 priorities and 3 results of the early church. Apply these to your ministry.*

Figure 4.7 Gates entering the old city of Jerusalem

Eastern Gate (also called Golden Gate)—entering the old city from the east

Dung Gate—entering the old city from the south

Joppa Gate—entering the old city from the west

Damascus Gate—entering the old city from the north

Some call this St. Stephen's Gate because they believe Stephen was martyred here. Others call it Lion's Gate because of the lion carvings (high on wall on each side of gate).

Chapter 5:
The Ministry of Peter and John
(Acts 3:1–4:31)

Introduction

Some people think bad things should not happen to believers. But God uses our trials to perfect us.

Figure 5.1   The Golden Gate in the outside wall of Jerusalem

- The music of a guitar comes forth only as one strikes or plucks the strings.
- The juice of the grapes comes forth only as one crushes them.
- The flour of grain comes forth only after it is ground.
- The warmth of wood comes forth only as it is burned.
- The best of believers often comes forth as we suffer.[1]

Acts 3 begins with the healing of a crippled beggar. The crowd is amazed! About 2,000 men respond to Peter's message and are saved. But the winds of persecution are beginning to blow. Peter and John are arrested. They are brought before the Sanhedrin. Persecution began to change their lives. Things would never be the same again. But persecution brought forth the best in the Church.

Lessons:

Peter and John Minister to a Crippled Beggar—Part 1 (Acts 3:1-10)
Goal: *Summarize and apply what Acts 3:1-10 teaches about people's beliefs, needs, and responsibilities*

Peter and John Minister to a Crippled Beggar—Part 2 (Acts 3:1-10)
Goal: *Analyze 3 truths related to God's part and our part in helping the needy. Relate this to your local context.*

Peter Speaks to the Crowd, the Sanhedrin, and the Church (Acts 3:11–4:31)
Goal: *Explain and apply what Acts 3–4 teaches about forgiveness, salvation, discouragement, God's sovereignty, and being Spirit filled.*

 Key Words

Beautiful Gate   Sanhedrin
Sadducees   sovereign

Peter and John Minister to a Crippled Beggar—Part 1 (Acts 3:1-10)

Goal: *Summarize and apply what Acts 3:1-10 teaches about people's beliefs, needs, and responsibilities.*

Setting

Luke has already told us that the apostles did many wonders and miracles (Acts 2:43). Now he gives us an example. He tells about Peter and John healing a crippled beggar. This is the only miracle Luke describes in detail in Acts 1–7. He chose this miracle for a reason. It is like a hinge on a door. This miracle turns believers from Jerusalem toward Rome. How? Persecution started rising after this miracle. Thus, the healing of the crippled beggar is a very special miracle in Acts.

Most of Acts 3–4 is related to the healing of the crippled beggar. Let us look at the first three of eleven truths we will study related to this miracle.

A. People's beliefs mature slowly.

"One day Peter and John were going up to the temple at the time of prayer—at three in the afternoon" (Acts 3:1).

There were many animal sacrifices each day at the temple in Jerusalem. Among these were two burnt offering sacrifices for the nation of Israel.[2] One sacrifice was in the morning and the other in the evening. The Jewish day began at six in the morning. Godly Jews prayed early. Then they prayed again about 3:00 p.m. This was shortly after the evening sacrifice in the temple. Recall that Daniel prayed each day at these times (Dan. 9:20-21). Also, some Gentiles, like Cornelius, feared and respected God. These prayed each morning and afternoon (Acts 10:2-3, 22).[3]

Peter and John went to pray at the temple. They arrived just after the evening sacrifice. This verse of Acts 3:1 is like a lid on a pot. It covers a lot. You see, the Jewish Christians were still going to the temple week by week. They were still practicing Old Testament laws that Jesus came to fulfill. Later, the book of Hebrews emphasized that the New Testament is better than the Old. We have a better altar, a better High Priest, a better sacrifice, and a better temple. Hebrews teaches that there is no longer any need for the Old Testament sacrifices. Jesus is the end of sacrifices and the Law (Rom. 10:4). The Church would learn that as it matured. But in the early days of the Church, believers continued to sacrifice animals. If you doubt this, read Acts 21:17-26. There we see James and the elders of the Jerusalem church. They told Paul that all Jewish Christians still followed the Law (Acts 21:20)! They advised Paul to be purified by the Law. He took a vow. He probably bought eight pigeons and four lambs to sacrifice in the temple (Num. 6:9-12).[4] Paul did this to please the believers who were still under the Law. Jesus had died to free them from the Law. But they were still living under it. People's beliefs mature slowly!

When we first receive Christ, we do not see all the changes He will make in our lives. We do not get a whole new set of ideas dropped into our minds all at once. On the one hand, we become new creations in Christ (2 Cor. 5:17). God forgives our sins. We are born again. We begin to think in a new way. We begin to develop spiritual values instead of worldly values.[5] On the other hand, the new birth is only the beginning. It is the starting point of our spiritual growth. Then, line upon line, we gain knowledge. Sometimes our spiritual growth is hard to see. It is like the silent, slow growing of corn (Mark 4:26-29). But growth is certain for those who follow Jesus.

Do you know any believers whose theology needs to mature?

- Some believers still think malaria, cholera, and polio are caused by demons. They do not yet understand that tablets and vaccines prevent these diseases.

Q 1 *How is the healing of the cripple related to witnessing in all nations?*

Q 2 *At which 2 times did Jews normally pray?*

Q 3 *Did the Jerusalem believers still sacrifice animals? Explain.*

Q 4 *Do you think the priests of Acts 6:7 continued to sacrifice animals? Explain.*

Q 5 *In what areas do believers you know need to mature?*

- Some believers still think circumcision has religious value. A few even practice female circumcision. And it never did have religious value! These believers have not yet understood 1 Corinthians 7:19 or Galatians 5:6, 11.
- Some think it is not spiritual to study the Bible. They reject teachers. Some of these believers are even pastors! They preach the first text they see when they open their Bibles! They have not yet understood verses like Daniel 9:2, Ephesians 4:11, and 2 Timothy 2:15. They wanted someone to teach them to read. But they do not want anyone to teach them to study! They want to teach others as Paul taught Timothy (2 Tim. 2:2). But they themselves refuse to be taught!
- Some believers think it is wrong to eat certain vegetables or meats. They have not yet grown into the liberty of 1 Timothy 4:3-5.
- And what more shall I say? I do not have time to tell about those who do not teach children the Bible; or those who prevent sinners from entering churches; or those who insist on foot washing; or those who pray to the dead; or those who sleep with dead bodies; or those who use versions of the Bible they cannot understand; or those who cling to human customs that contradict Scripture; or those who refuse to pray with the family of a sinner who died; or those who think a believer suffers only when he or she sins; or those who think the richest are the most spiritual.

Q 6 What are some keys to helping believers mature?

Do you want to help these believers mature in their theology? Then love them! Be patient with them! Pray for them! Study the Bible with them. God will help them mature in time. Even men as spiritual as apostles grew slowly. Chameleons and turtles are fast compared to people making changes. People's beliefs mature slowly!

B. Some people have great needs.

What do we know about the beggar? We know that he was over 40 years old (Acts 4:22). Doctor Luke tells us that this man had been a cripple from birth (Acts 3:2; Col. 4:14). He had never walked one step. Each day people carried him to beg.

Q 7 What was life like for the crippled beggar? Explain.

Some people have a *diary or a journal. Each day they write in the diary a few thoughts, feelings, prayers, or things that happened. Suppose the crippled beggar kept a diary. Figure 5.2 contains some things he might have written. Pretend you are a crippled beggar. Sit down on the floor. Read Figure 5.2 as if you wrote it.

Age	Year (A.D.)	Writing
11	1	Today is my eleventh birthday. I still cry when I watch other children play. And it hurts my feelings when people throw coins in the dirt beside me. They act like they are throwing a bone to a dog. Don't they realize I am a person? Or maybe I am less than a person.
16	6	I am learning to be a beggar. People seem to give an extra penny if I look sad. Also, I keep my feet out where they can see them. But the way they look at my ugly feet makes me feel ashamed. Fate has forced me to display what I want to hide.
21	11	Perhaps this is not a good place to beg. People always look at this tall gate instead of at me! I wish I had a little of the gold they spent to build this gate. But gold is for buildings. Copper is for beggars.
26	16	This place stinks! I am so tired of smelling what the animals leave behind. And there is so much dust from the people walking by. I feel and smell like dirt.
31	21	Life is so boring down here. It must be nice to go into the temple.[6] I wonder what it looks like on the inside. Also, I wonder what it would be like to read.
36	26	Some think beggars get a lot of money. I would love to trade places with any of them. They could live in my dark shack and eat dried bread alone. They could wait for someone to carry them to the bathroom twice a day. How great it would be to work and not beg!
41	30	There was a lot of noise coming from the temple a few days ago. Some told me that a prophet named Jesus healed many that were lame or blind. They said I must be very sinful or He would have healed me. But everyone forgot me. No one came to carry me from the Beautiful Gate to the temple. Now, they say He has been crucified. My hopes died today when He died.

Figure 5.2   What the crippled beggar of Acts 3 might have written in a diary

Beggars are not the only people with needs. All around us there are hurting people. Some are crippled, blind, deaf, or mute. Others are poor, sick, hungry, naked, or in prison. Some are rich and healthy, but empty and lonely. Others are discouraged. Some come from homes of divided families. Many are lost without Christ. Do you notice the people around you that are hurting or in need?

C. God calls us to notice those in need.

Before going further, let us have a brief history lesson about Herod's Temple.

Locate the Beautiful Gate in Figure 5.4. It was the entrance into the temple area.[7] Outside the gate was the court of the Gentiles. They were forbidden to climb the stairs and pass through the Beautiful Gate. Signs in Greek and Latin warned Gentiles not to come further. If they disobeyed, they would probably be killed. The Beautiful Gate was one of the gates between the court of the Gentiles and the court of Jewish women.[8] Jewish women could pass through the Beautiful Gate into their court or area. There were offering chests there, so the women could give (Mark 12:41-44). But only Jewish men were allowed to continue. The men climbed the stairs and went into the court of Israel. Once a year, at the Feast of Tabernacles, Jewish men could walk around the altar in the priests' court.[9]

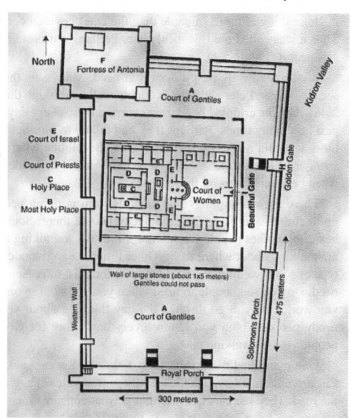

Herod's Temple

A Court of Gentiles
B Most Holy Place (Inner Sanctuary 20 cubits square)
C Holy Place (20 cubits wide, 40 cubits long)
D Court of Priests
E Court of Israel
F Fortress of Antonia (Held a garrison of Roman soldiers to subdue temple disorders. Priests' robes stored there as a sign of subjection to Rome.)
G Court of Women
H Golden Gate
I Beautiful Gate (Where Scribes held school and debates)

Figure 5.3   Drawing of Herod's Temple, looking down on it

Q 8 *Who was allowed to pass through the Beautiful Gate?*

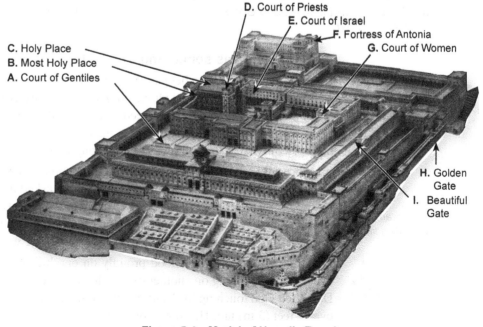

Figure 5.4   Model of Herod's Temple. The temple covered 35 acres (14 hectares).[10]

The Beautiful Gate was about 75 feet (23 m) tall. It had huge double doors. It was probably made of bronze. One historian, Josephus, says it had gold and silver in parts of it. He said it was more valuable than the gates covered completely with gold or silver.[11] Thus it was called the Beautiful Gate. Perhaps it was shaped like the Golden Gate that was near it (Figure 5.1).

Q 9 *Why was it easy for people to notice the gate instead of the beggar?*

It is easy to walk past a person in need. Many saw the Beautiful Gate, but did not see the beggar. Peter and John probably walked through this gate nearly every day (Acts 2:46). And the crippled beggar was carried there every day (Acts 3:2). They had walked past him many times. Perhaps they had talked to him before. Or maybe they were like those who did not pay attention to him. But notice what Luke tells us. *"Peter looked straight at him as did John"* (Acts 3:4). This is a wonderful verse! It is a great thing when believers focus on those in need!

Q 10 *What types of things cause believers not to notice those in need?*

There are many things that keep us from noticing people in need. Believers often go to church and do not see the needy people there. Sometimes we are looking at the beautiful clothes people wear. Other times we are talking to our friends. Sometimes we are thinking about where to sit. Other times we are wondering if we will get to sing the type of songs we like. We could make a long list of reasons believers walk past those in need. Do you see people in need when you walk? Do you notice people in need where you work? Do you go through the day thinking about your own problems? Are there needy people whom you ignore every day? Pray for God to direct your attention to people you are walking past.

One man liked motorcycles. A sticker on his car said, "Start seeing motorcycles." Car drivers often have accidents with motorcycles. They do not notice motorcycles on the road. They see cars because that is what concerns them.

Olivia attended church regularly. She heard a message about learning to see needy people. She asked God to open her eyes to the needy she was ignoring. That week she noticed children in her neighborhood. She invited them to her church. Several of them began attending church with her. They had been near her for years. Finally, the Lord helped her to think about their needs.

Lesson 14 **Peter and John Minister to a Crippled Beggar—Part 2 (Acts 3:1-10)**
Goal: *Analyze 3 truths related to God's part and our part in helping the needy. Relate this to your local context.*

A. Each of us has something to give those in need.

Q 11 *What can each believer say to those in need?*

What can you do for a beggar? You may not be able to say to the beggar, "Get up and walk!" But you can still say to him, *"What I have I give you"* (Acts 3:6).[12] Each believer has something to give people in need. We have different talents. We do not all minister to the same people. But remember that the Church is the body of Christ on earth. Acts is the story of what Jesus continues to do through His body on earth.

Moses did not have much. He did not think those in need would listen to him. He did not feel like he had enough to give. But the Lord asked him a question: *"What is that in your hand?"* (Exod. 4:2). It was only a shepherd's staff. But when Moses obeyed, God used it. Who would have thought a shepherd's staff could help? But it was the first step in delivering a nation from bondage. God wants to use what you have in your hand.

Q 12 *Name 4 examples of those who had only a little, but gave it.*

An army of Philistines stood proudly on one hill. Across the valley, the soldiers of Israel stood trembling on another hill. Goliath challenged anyone to come and fight him. David felt God touching his heart. He was only a youth, and Goliath was a giant. He was over 9 feet (3 m) tall. He wore a bronze helmet. His armor weighed about 7 kilos or 15 pounds. How could a youth help conquer a giant? But a sling and a stone were enough. David dared to try (1 Sam. 17:1-58). God wants to use what you have in your hand.

A prophet had plenty to eat because a widow gave a little grain (1 Kings 17:7-16). A multitude had plenty to eat because a little boy gave his lunch to Jesus (John 6:5-13). Do not apologize for what you do not have. Do not be ashamed if you have only a little to help the needy. There is no shame in having only a little to give. But there is great shame in having one talent and not using it for God (Matt. 25:14-30).

Q 13 What do believers you know have to give those in need?

A farmer was talking to a friend. The farmer boasted, "If I had a million dollars, I'd give it all to God. But I do not have it." The friend replied, "If you had one sheep would you give it to God?" "Stop talking like that," replied the farmer. "I have a sheep!"

You may not be able to say to the beggar, "Get up and walk!" But you can still say to him, *"What I have I give you"* (Acts 3:6). And remember, *who* you have is more important than what you have.[13] Jesus is the greatest gift you can share with a person who does not know Him.

B. God helps after we take a needy person by the hand.

[6]*Then Peter said, "Silver or gold I do not have, but what I have I give you. In the name of Jesus Christ of Nazareth, walk."* [7]*Taking him by the right hand, he helped him up, and instantly the man's feet and ankles became strong* (Acts 3:6-7).

People were giving a lot of money to the Church. But Peter was not using the money for himself. Therefore, he did not have silver and gold. It is a good testimony when God's servants do not grow fat on the Church's money.

Q 14 If believers were giving, why did Peter lack silver and gold?

Peter did not have silver or gold. But he gave what he had. He shared his faith. Sometimes your faith in God is the greatest help you can give someone in need.

It took courage for Peter to reach out his hand to the cripple. But he felt faith in his heart. Therefore, he reached out his hand in love. God did not do anything for the crippled beggar until Peter reached out his hand to him. And God will not help those around us until we reach out a hand. "The power was Christ's, but the hand was Peter's!"[14]

Q 15 What is the key to God doing miracles for the needy?

C. God often does more through small things than we expect.

The crippled beggar was more than a little bit happy!

[8]*He jumped to his feet and began to walk. Then he went with them into the temple courts, walking and jumping, and praising God.* [9]*When all the people saw him walking and praising God,* [10]*they recognized him as the same man who used to sit begging at the temple gate called Beautiful, and they were filled with wonder and amazement at what had happened to him* (Acts 3:8-10).

The healed beggar was full of joy. He took his first steps! He entered the temple for the first time! He was jumping around like a child on the playground. He probably wrote several pages in his diary that day!

Notice the effect of this miracle on the crowd. They were filled with wonder and amazement. Miracles help turn people to Christ. Two thousand men were saved because a common beggar was healed. Likewise, multitudes turned to Christ when Peter healed Aeneas and Dorcas (Acts 9:35, 42). Sermons reach some. But miracles help confirm the Word of God. Our greatest need today is not a better sermon. Preachers need to spend more time praying for power to heal the sick. The apostles spent time praying so they would have God's power. They knew that preaching and miracles work together (1 Cor. 2:1-5). The Church still needs miracles today as much as ever. There are so many different messages that sinners do not know what to believe. A picture is worth a thousand words. Five words of teaching in church are better than ten thousand words in an unknown tongue (1 Cor. 14:19). And one miracle, with a clear gospel message, may be worth two thousand souls (Acts 4:4)!

Q 16 What was the key to the salvation of 2,000 in Jerusalem?

We do not even know the beggar's name. Most of us would have planned for a revival in a different way. Perhaps we would have tried to win Jerusalem's top political leader to Christ. Or we might have prayed for a rich man to get saved. Or perhaps we

Q 17 Is the greatest need today a better sermon? Explain.

would have tried to get money from the government.[15] But God often works in small ways that we do not expect. Sinners pay attention when people's lives are changed.

We never know what God will do through our small acts of obedience. Some servants obeyed and filled up jars with water. Through this small deed of obedience, God supplied the needs of a wedding party (John 2:1-11). Peter obeyed and threw a hook into the sea. God used this obedience to supply money to pay their taxes (Matt. 17:24-27).

Pray for God to open your eyes to those in need. Then do what He speaks to your heart. Sow the seed, and leave the results to Him. Peter heard a small voice tell him to take the cripple by the hand. He believed in spiritual gifts and was walking in the Spirit. Therefore, he obeyed the inner voice. God did the rest. The Lord often does more than we expect when we listen and obey.

Lesson 15 Peter Speaks to the Crowd, the Sanhedrin, and the Church (Acts 3:11–4:31)
Goal: *Explain and apply what Acts 3–4 teaches about forgiveness, salvation, discouragement, God's sovereignty, and being Spirit filled.*

Setting

Peter confessed that he could not heal by his own power. He kept the focus on Jesus (Acts 3:12-13). The Sanhedrin noticed this. Peter and John were ordinary men. They were not known for their education. But the Sanhedrin realized that these men had been with Jesus.

> *When they saw the courage of Peter and John and realized that they were unschooled, ordinary men, they were astonished and they took note that these men had been with Jesus* (Acts 4:13).

Q 18 *Had Peter and John been to school? Explain.*

The Sanhedrin knew that Peter and John had not been to the school of the rabbis. They had never sat under a recognized teacher like Gamaliel. Thus the Sanhedrin considered Peter and John to be laymen.[16] These Jewish leaders noted that Peter and John had been with Jesus. And people had once asked a similar question about Jesus. *"How did this man get such learning without having studied?"* (John 7:15).[17] Jesus had never studied under a famous Jewish teacher. But God has many teachers who are not famous. Both Jesus and the disciples had studied the Scriptures under teachers.

Peter and John had been in the school of ministry with Jesus for over 3 years. And Jesus is the greatest rabbi or teacher. But the Sanhedrin recognized only one kind of school. It was the school they had attended! Likewise, there are many different types of schools today. Let us not make the same mistake the Sanhedrin made. We should not look with contempt at schools which emphasize ministry. The most formal schools are not the only schools.

The Sanhedrin members were wrong to say that the apostles had not been to school. But they were right in noting that these believers had been with Jesus. And this is the best thing anyone can ever say about a believer. Peter and John lived close to Jesus. And Jesus was the center of their message.

Peter's Description of Jesus	Acts
The holy servant of God	3:13; 4:27
The Holy and Righteous One	3:14
The author of life	3:15
The source of healing	3:16
The One waiting in heaven to return	3:20-21
The prophet Moses foretold	3:22-23

Continued on next page

Peter's Description of Jesus	Acts
The One all the prophets told about	3:24
Jesus Christ of Nazareth	4:10
Abraham's son who brings blessing to all the earth	3:25
The One whom God raised from the dead	4:10
The cornerstone which the builders rejected	4:11
The only One who can save sinners	4:12

Figure 5.5   Peter kept the focus away from himself and on Jesus.

There are many great truths in Acts 3–4. Of these, we will focus on only five.

A. God is willing to forgive all who repent.

A crowd gathered to watch the crippled beggar jump. They were amazed! Peter saw a good chance to preach. A healing or miracle is the best sermon introduction a preacher can have!

Peter preached a strong message. He accused the Jews of sin. In fact, he told them they had killed the author of life. What a contrast! They killed the One who created them and gave them life (Acts 3:15; John 1:1-5). Acts 3:15 shows us that Peter believed Jesus was God in the flesh. Thus, Peter accused his listeners of a great crime.

Killing Jesus was a terrible sin. But we must be careful not to accuse all Jews of killing Jesus. All Americans did not have slaves. Only a few were guilty. Many Americans fought to free the slaves. And most Americans have never seen a slave! Likewise, all Russians were not communists. All Germans did not fight in World War I. All Japanese did not fight in World War II. All Africans did not fight in Rwanda. All Jews did not crucify Jesus. Many Jews loved Him and believed in Him. Sometimes a few people in a nation commit a crime. But it is not fair to blame every person of that nation. We do not deserve the credit for what our best people have done. But neither do we deserve the blame for what our worst people have done!

Q 19 ⬉ *Do people you know blame an entire group for what only a few people of that group did? Explain.*

Peter's message turned from an accusation to an invitation. A true gospel message is always like this. God does not call us guilty so He can tell us "Goodbye." Telling us we are guilty is His way of saying "Hello" or "Welcome!" Jesus did not die to condemn us, but to save us (John 3:17). God causes us to look down with guilt, so we will look up for help.

There were two kinds of sins in the Old Testament. *First,* there were sins done on purpose. There was usually no forgiveness for a sin done on purpose. These were sins someone planned to do. Perhaps a man hated another man. If he killed this enemy, his guilt remained. There was no place this murderer could hide. There was no city of refuge for him. If he grabbed hold of the altar, he could be dragged away from it. There was no sacrifice or forgiveness for sins that people planned to do. The guilt of intentional sins remained (Num. 15:30-31). *Second,* there were sins of ignorance. These were accidental sins. They were sins that a person did not plan or intend to commit. For example a man's axhead might fly off and kill someone. This was an accident. He could be forgiven. Or a man's ox might gore someone with a horn. A man could be forgiven for this—the first time it happened (Lev. 4:2, 22, 27; 5:15-18; Num. 15:27-29).

Q 20 ⬈ *What type of sins in the Old Testament could not be forgiven?*

So what? Did the Jews who killed Jesus do it accidentally or on purpose? Did they plan to kill Him or did it just happen? They planned it! He was not killed by a stray arrow. They nailed Him to a cross! Their sin was on purpose!

But notice the words of Peter. *"Now, brothers, I know that you acted in ignorance, as did your leaders"* (Acts 3:17). Amazing! Peter calls their sin an act of ignorance. He puts their sin in the group of sins that God forgives. On the one hand, they murdered

Jesus on purpose. On the other hand, they did not recognize that He was the Messiah (Acts 13:27). God offers greater grace under the new covenant!

Q 21 *Under the new covenant, how does God treat our sins?*

Behold the good news of the gospel! God is willing to treat our sins as sins of ignorance. That is, He is willing to forgive us. Recall the attitude of Jesus on the cross. *"Father, forgive them, for they do not know what they are doing"* (Luke 23:34). God considers that we sinners do not fully know what we are doing. He reckons that we do not fully understand how much we hurt Him and others. Amazing grace, how sweet the sound! God is willing to forgive those who murdered His Son. Surely He will forgive our sins also.

What are God's conditions for forgiveness? He requires us to repent. This means to turn from our sins. Then, we must turn toward Him (Acts 3:19). Repenting and turning from sins is not the same as ceasing to sin. We cannot save ourselves from our sins. All can repent, but none can break the chains of his or her own sin. Alcoholics cannot save themselves from alcohol. Those with bitterness cannot deliver themselves from hate. A person with bad habits cannot break them. Each of us needs a Savior. And the name *Jesus* means "Savior." *"She will give birth to a son, and you are to give him the name Jesus, because he will save his people from their sins"* (Matt. 1:21).

Q 22 *Is repenting the same as breaking sin's power? Explain.*

Our part is to repent and turn from sin. His part is to save us from our sins. No one else can forgive us and free us from sins. *"Salvation is found in no one else, for there is no other name under heaven given to men by which we must be saved"* (Acts 4:12).

All will be lost who keep their backs to God and their faces toward sin. But all will be saved who keep their backs to sin and their faces toward Jesus.

B. God desires to refresh and bless people.

"Repent, then, and turn to God, so that your sins may be wiped out, that times of refreshing may come from the Lord" (Acts 3:19).

"When God raised up his servant, he sent him first to you to bless you by turning each of you from your wicked ways" (Acts 3:26).

Q 23 *What lie does Satan tempt people to believe?*

Since Eden, the devil has confused people. He twists their thoughts around. How? By telling them that sin is a blessing, and holy living is a curse. This is backwards! Sinning brings problems, curses, and troubles. It brings poverty, disease, and sorrows. The way of a sinner is hard (Prov. 13:15). *"The wicked are like the tossing sea, which cannot rest. . . . 'There is no peace,' says my God, 'for the wicked'"* (Isa. 57:20-21). The pleasures of sin are only for a short time (Heb. 11:25). Then a person must reap what was sown (Gal. 6:7). Still, Satan convinces some to follow him and run from God.

It is a blessing to have our sins wiped away. It is wonderful to be free from guilt and fear of judgment. It is a delight to make peace with God.

Jesus did not come to make people sad. He came that we might have abundant life (John 10:10). He came to bring us joy.

Q 24 *Do you know people who refuse blessings? Explain.*

Will a hungry person run from food? Will a sick person hide from a doctor? Will a cold person turn away from a fire? Will a tired person refuse a place to rest? Will a sad person refuse a new song to sing? Will a poor person refuse eternal wealth? And yet some people run from our loving heavenly Father. His only desire is to refresh and bless us! His only desire is for us to receive the good gifts He has for us. Salvation brings refreshing and blessing, now and later! The blessing of the Lord makes rich and adds no sorrow (Prov. 10:22).

C. The devil desires to discourage those who work for God.

[1]*The priests and the captain of the temple guard and the Sadducees came up to Peter and John while they were speaking to the people.* [2]*They were greatly*

disturbed because the apostles were teaching the people and proclaiming in Jesus the resurrection of the dead. [3]*They seized Peter and John, and because it was evening, they put them in jail until the next day* (Acts 4:1-3).

Q 25 *Did the Sadducees thank Peter and John for healing the cripple? Explain.*

Notice that it was the Sadducees who were upset. They did not believe in the resurrection, miracles, or a personal Messiah. Therefore, they were angry with Peter and John. These apostles had healed a cripple in the name of Jesus. And they were teaching the people that Jesus is the Messiah. Therefore, the Sadducees put them in jail! Later, the Sanhedrin warned them not to use the name of Jesus (Acts 4:17-20). Satan gets upset about good deeds in the name of Jesus. Peter and John were put in jail because they did an act of kindness to a cripple (Acts 4:9).

Do not expect praise from everyone for the good deeds you do. Nine out of ten lepers did not even say "Thank you" when Jesus healed them (Luke 17:11-19).

- One believer taught Bible stories to children. She taught about Jonah, Daniel in the lion's den, and others. A parent complained that these stories made her child afraid to sleep.
- Another believer visited in several homes for the church. Some of the people were rude to him.
- One believer took some food to hungry people. Others complained that they did not get any.
- Another believer led singing. Some said the songs were too slow. Others said they were too fast. Some did not like the songs chosen.
- One believer worked hard cleaning the church. Not one member noticed.

Q 26 *Do you think people will always appreciate your ministry? Explain.*

Do not expect everyone to clap when you do good deeds. People criticized both Jesus and John the Baptist for the good they did (Matt. 11:18-19). And the apostles were put in jail because they healed a cripple! So do your good deeds to please the Lord (Matt. 6:1-18; Luke 17:10; Col. 1:10). He will reward you. But beware of men (Matt. 10:17-22).

Thomas was not as blessed as most other children. From birth he could neither hear nor talk. When he was about 5 years old some people taught him to hoe. Year after year he worked long hours in the field. Some believers heard about him. They took him to a revival under a big tent. There, God completely healed him. Later, he married and began to testify of his healing. But many opposed him. Why? Because their churches taught that God does not heal today. One night the Lord awakened Thomas. An inner voice warned him to leave the house. He and his wife climbed a large hill nearby. A short time later people from the village surrounded their house. They blocked all the doors and windows so they would not open. Then they burned the house to the ground. Thomas and his wife were shocked! Was this people's response to the good news? Why did people hate them? But likewise the prophets were persecuted (Matt. 5:11-12). Satan does all he can to discourage believers. Nevertheless, we do not lose heart (2 Cor. 4:1).

Q 27 *What religious power did the Sanhedrin have?*

Figure 5.6 A scribe like Gamaliel

D. God is sovereign.

The Sanhedrin was the top Jewish court. It was made up of three groups. These were the religious rulers, elders, and teachers of the Law (Acts 4:5).[18] The Sanhedrin was a powerful group of religious leaders. They had authority to put people in jail. In Acts 6 we will see that the Sanhedrin was responsible for the death of Stephen.

Peter and John spoke boldly to the Sanhedrin. But the Sanhedrin commanded them not to speak or teach at all in the name of Jesus (Acts 4:18). Also, these hardened leaders added more threats (Acts 4:21).

Did Peter and John become anxious or afraid? We do not know. Sometimes people are bold, but become fearful afterwards.[19] Even the greatest of God's servants must overcome thoughts of fear (Acts 18:9-10; 2 Tim. 1:7).

Abram went boldly to war against several kings. This took great courage. He had only 318 men he had trained himself. But by faith he conquered those kings and brought

Lot home. Afterward, Abram began to be afraid. Questions knocked at his door. What would happen next? Would those kings with all their thousands of soldiers come and destroy him? But the Lord knew Abram was afraid. *"After this, the word of the LORD came to Abram in a vision: 'Do not be afraid, Abram. I am your shield, your very great reward'"* (Gen. 15:1). Abram replied, *"O Sovereign LORD"* (Gen. 15:2). Abram's fears became quiet as he focused on God. Our Father keeps us in perfect peace as we trust in Him (Isa. 26:3). The cure for fear is a fresh vision of who God is.

Q 28 ➤ *Do mature believers ever wrestle with fear? Explain.*

The apostles were afraid after the religious leaders killed Jesus.

Q 29 ➤ *What is the key to conquering fear (John 20:19-20)?*

[19]On the evening of that first day of the week, when the disciples were together, with the doors locked for fear of the Jews, Jesus came and stood among them and said, "Peace be with you!" [20]After he said this, he showed them his hands and side. The disciples were overjoyed when they saw the Lord (John 20:19-20).

Peace and joy conquer fear when we remember who the Lord is. (For more illustrations on this theme see Acts 18:9-11 and Acts 27:22-25.)

Peter and John reported all that the chief priests and elders had said. They did not hold back any information. Then, the believers prayed together, out loud. However, one person probably led them in the prayer of Acts 4:24-30.[20] When one believer leads in prayer, all believers in the group should be praying, not just listening!

Q 30 ➤ *What does "sovereign" mean?*

Notice that their prayer begins with *Sovereign Lord. These two words translate one word from the Greek language. The Greek word is *despotes*.[21] When we say God is sovereign, we mean He is the ruler in total control. He has all power and authority. It looked like the Sanhedrin was in control. But the believers turned their thoughts from the problem to the solution. They turned their minds from earth to heaven. They reminded themselves that God is still on the throne. *"Sovereign Lord,"* they said, *"you made the heaven and the earth and the sea, and everything in them"* (Acts 4:24).

Their prayer was God-centered. They put God between them and their problems. They could have whined and complained. They could have said, "O God, sinners have beaten us. We did not deserve to be treated this way." Or the apostles could have prayed like they once did, *"Lord, save us! We're going to drown"* (Matt. 8:25). Perhaps they remembered that Jesus rebuked them when they focused on their problems. Instead, they focused on God. As a result, God blessed them. When we pray, it is always good to center our thoughts on God. This puts things in perspective. As we focus on Him, our hearts are filled with faith. It is good to bring our needs to God. But our prayers should always begin focusing on who God is, and all He has done for us.

There is none like our God! If God is for us, no one will succeed against us (Rom. 8:31). Those who fight against God will lose the war!

[25]"'Why do the nations rage and the peoples plot in vain? [26]The kings of the earth take their stand and the rulers gather together against the Lord and against his Anointed One.'[27]Indeed Herod and Pontius Pilate met together with the Gentiles and the people of Israel in this city to conspire against your holy servant Jesus, whom you anointed" (Acts 4:25-27; See Rev. 11:18).

Sometimes it looks like Satan is in control. Sinners persecute believers. Things happen that we do not understand. Accidents happen. In these times, we need to remind ourselves that God is sovereign. We need to lift up the shield of faith so that the enemy will not wound us in the time of trials (Eph. 6:16).

Q 31 ➤ *How can the truth that God is sovereign encourage believers you know?*

God is sovereign. Even the death of Jesus was in the plan of God (Acts 4:28). It was God's will for Joseph to be sold into slavery. His brothers meant it for evil, but God meant it for good (Gen. 50:20). Likewise, God was still in control when Job suffered. And it was His will for believers at Philippi to suffer (Phil. 1:29; Compare with 1 Peter 2:18-25; 4:1, 14, 16). Hold on to your confidence (Heb. 10:35-39).

E. God desires to refill believers with the Holy Spirit.

Sometimes it is good to pray for God to change people or circumstances. But this is not how believers prayed in Acts 4:24-30. They did not pray for God to change the Sanhedrin. They prayed for God to change them. Too often, we pray for God to change others. Much of the time, we are the ones God wants to change!

God's plan to change us is through His Spirit. Are there areas in your life that need to be changed? Do not try to change them in your own strength. Pray for God to help you through His Spirit. Some may say, "I have already been filled with the Spirit. I speak in tongues." To these we reply, "Wonderful! But remember one thing. There is only one baptism in the Spirit, but many fillings."[22]

The apostles had already been filled with the Spirit on the Day of Pentecost. But Acts 4 records that all believers, including the apostles, were filled again. *"After they prayed, the place where they were meeting was shaken. And they were all filled with the Holy Spirit and spoke the word of God boldly"* (Acts 4:31).

We need to be refilled with the Spirit for two reasons. **The *first* reason is that we leak!** The face of Moses glowed when he came from God's presence (Exod. 34:29). For a time, the glory of God was great upon him. Moses put a veil over his face. But as time passed, the glory faded. Soon, Moses did not need a veil. Yesterday's meeting with God may not be enough for today. There may be a few times when you are like Elijah. You may receive enough power to travel 40 days (1 Kings 19:7-8). But as a rule, yesterday's bread is not enough for today's appetite. The work and trials of each day cause us to use up our spiritual power. Therefore, we need to be refilled often with God's presence.

Q 32 *What are 2 reasons why believers should be refilled with the Spirit?*

***Second,* we need to be refilled because we expand.** A person who sins a little expands. That is, soon he or she is able to sin a lot. In the beginning, Judas had only enough room in his heart for a little sin. He stole a few coins. But his *capacity for sin increased. In the end, there was room for Satan himself in the heart of Judas. Likewise, a person's capacity for God can increase.[23] A child increases in knowledge and strength day by day. Likewise, we can contain more of God as we grow in grace. Therefore, each of us should make it a habit to seek more of God. Those who hunger and thirst for God will be filled and refilled. "New, fresh fillings of the Holy Spirit are part of God's wonderful provision for all believers."[24]

Figure 5.7   Blind beggars at town gate

Test Yourself: Circle the letter by the *best* completion to each question or statement.

1. Acts 3 reveals that believers
a) still trusted in animal sacrifices.
b) understood that Christ ended sacrifices.
c) forced Gentiles to obey the Law.
d) refused to follow the law of Moses.

2. The beggar in Acts 3 was a cripple for
a) 4 years.
b) 14 years.
c) 24 years.
d) 40 years.

3. What caused many NOT to notice the crippled beggar of Acts 3?
a) The pool of Bethesda
b) The temple guards
c) The Beautiful Gate
d) Solomon's Porch

4. What should each believer say to a person in need?
a) "In the name of Jesus, rise and walk."
b) "What I have I give you."
c) "I wish there were a way to help you."
d) "May the Lord bless and keep you."

5. God did not help the cripple until
a) there was more silver and gold.
b) the cripple helped himself.
c) Stephen prayed for him.
d) Peter reached out his hand.

6. The key to adding 2,000 to the church was the
a) conversion of a government leader.
b) healing of a crippled beggar.
c) ability Peter had for preaching.
d) money donated by wealthy believers.

7. Under the Old Testament, there was NO forgiveness for sins
a) done against parents.
b) that cost someone a life.
c) done against children.
d) done on purpose.

8. The reason many people run from God is that
a) Satan confuses them.
b) God will not forgive them.
c) God's plan is for many to be lost.
d) the Christian life is dull.

9. *God is sovereign* means that
a) whosoever will may come.
b) all must do God's will.
c) He is the ruler in total control.
d) Satan is a lion with no teeth.

10. Believers should be refilled with the Spirit because
a) there are many fillings and baptisms.
b) we expand in our capacity for God.
c) we are not as spiritual as the apostles.
d) that which is perfect has come.

 Essay Test Topics: Write 50-100 words on each of these goals that you studied in this chapter.

Peter and John Minister to a Crippled Beggar—Part 1 (Acts 3:1-10)

Goal: *Summarize and apply what Acts 3:1-10 teaches about people's beliefs, needs, and responsibilities.*

Peter and John Minister to a Crippled Beggar—Part 2 (Acts 3:1-10)

Goal: *Analyze 3 truths related to God's part and our part in helping the needy. Relate this to your local context.*

Peter Speaks to the Crowd, the Sanhedrin, and the Church (Acts 3:11–4:31)

Goal: *Explain and apply what Acts 3–4 teaches about forgiveness, salvation, discouragement, God's sovereignty, and being Spirit filled.*

Figure 5.8   Photo from the Model City in Jerusalem—Herod's Temple. On the left are the columns of the Royal Porch.

Figure 5.9   (A close-up from Herod's Temple shown above) The steps and gate that were between the Court of Women and the Court of Israel

Chapter 6:
The Ministry of the Apostles
(Acts 4:32–5:42)

Introduction

Dorris Wood had poor vision. She could see only 50 percent with one eye and 20 percent with the other eye. This caused her to wear very thick glasses. Then a revival came to the Bible school she was attending. It was called Central Bible Institute and was located in Springfield, Missouri. The power of God was great. Instead of going to classes, teachers and students spent time in prayer and worship. As she prayed, it seemed that a voice within her said, *Dorris, take off your glasses.* She did nothing. People had prayed for her eyes

Figure 6.1   Jerusalem, north end of Temple Mount

many times. But her sight never got better. Then the voice spoke again. *Dorris, take off your glasses.* Again, she doubted that God was speaking to her. Finally, the voice came a third time. She responded, *If I take them off, I don't ever want to put them on again.* At that moment, she had a vision of Christ on the cross. Blood was flowing from His wounds. In her vision, Dorris took some of the blood and put it on her eyes. The presence of Jesus was very real to her. She did not even remember throwing her glasses across the room. She was healed instantly! But the vision continued for a long time as she prayed in an unknown language. Dorris never needed the glasses again. Her brother, Dr. George O. Wood, is one of the authors of this book. He recalls seeing the beautiful change in her.[1]

The acts of the Holy Spirit continue in the name of Jesus. And they draw many sincere seekers to the Savior.

Lessons:

The Church Grows Through Unity and Purity (Acts 4:32–5:11)
Goal A: *Analyze 6 keys to unity in Acts 4:32-37. Relate these to your church and ministry.*
Goal B: *Explain and apply 3 truths related to purity in Acts 5:1-11.*

The Church Grows Through Signs and Wonders (Acts 5:12-16)
Goal: *Evaluate the relationship of the miraculous to church growth in Acts and today.*

The Church Grows Through Persecution (Acts 5:17-42)
Goal: *Analyze and illustrate 3 truths about persecution in Acts.*

 Key Words

| Barnabas | Sapphira |
| Ananias | Great Commission Christians |

The Church Grows Through Unity and Purity (Acts 4:32–5:11)

Lesson 16

Goal A: *Analyze 6 keys to unity in Acts 4:32-37. Relate these to your church and ministry.*
Goal B: *Explain and apply 3 truths related to purity in Acts 5:1-11.*

Setting

"All the believers were one in heart and mind. No one claimed that any of his possessions was his own, but they shared everything they had" (Acts 4:32).

A. The Church grows through unity (Acts 4:32-37).

Acts 4:32-35 reminds us of Acts 2:42-47. Both of these passages emphasize the unity of believers. All of the believers were filled with the Holy Spirit (Acts 4:31). The Spirit helped unite them in at least six ways.[2]

First, **believers were willing to lay aside minor differences.** They agreed on the big things that really mattered. Sometimes believers become divided over little things. One church split over the color of paint on the walls. Two deacons fought over the name of the church. One teacher left because he wanted a bigger classroom. Two sisters argued over which songs were best. The apostles argued over the best positions (Matt. 20:20-28). Paul and Barnabas parted over taking John Mark along (Acts 15:36-40). Believers are all different. They seldom agree on all of the small things. But as we are filled with the Spirit, we can agree on the big things.

Second, **believers related the financial to the spiritual.** Jesus said that a person's treasure and heart go together (Matt. 6:21). Is a person spiritual? You cannot tell by how loudly a believer claps. You cannot know by how high he or she jumps. You cannot be sure by how well someone sings. But you can know a lot by how a person spends money. A spiritual person pays tithes. And a spiritual person gives offerings to help those in need. When the believers were filled with the Spirit, they shared.

Sometimes we have only a little of the Spirit and a lot of self. In these times we are stingy! We forget that "the one who eats alone dies alone."[3] Stingy people do not want to share Jesus or wealth. When we are full of self, we do not feel like sharing. We focus on our own needs. But those filled with the Spirit are generous. His presence causes us to share with others. The less of God's Spirit a person has, the stingier that person is. The more of God's Spirit a person has, the more generous that believer is. One of the reasons early believers were united was that they were generous.

Third, **believers shared by their free will.** No one was required or forced to share. In cults, members are often required to sell their possessions. In *communism, the government owns everything, and the people own nothing. In *socialism, there is only one level. No one has more or less than others. But the early church was not like a cult, communism, or socialism.

- They were not forced to give. The land of Ananias belonged to him. After he sold it, the money belonged to him (Acts 5:4). He was free to give all, part, or none.
- Some had more than others did. Some kept more than others did. Some spiritual believers still had houses for prayer meetings and fellowship (Acts 2:46; 12:12).
- Believers sold things at different times. Luke tells us that they sold things *"from time to time"* (Acts 4:34).

The world notices we are different when we share. The world says, "Get all you can and keep all you get." But the Spirit of God makes believers different from those of the world. The world knows we are His disciples because of our love for each other (John 13:35). For we are most like God when we give (John 3:16; 2 Cor. 8:8-9). Sharing is a sermon that touches unbelievers.

Q 1 *Give some examples of major and minor differences.*

Q 2 *How does being filled with the Spirit affect a believer's attitude toward money?*

Q 3 *Has being filled with the Spirit helped believers you know to share? Explain.*

The citizens of one country joined together in a war for their independence. They had one common enemy to fight. This one purpose united them. It helped them love one another. Someone wrote a song to describe their relationship. The song said, "I noticed such a great love among men and women. If they got even one bean, they would share it!"[4] The early church had such a love.

Q 4 *What was one reason the Spirit led believers to sell possessions?*

***Fourth,* God was guiding them.** Persecution was growing in Jerusalem. Soon believers would be arrested, killed, or chased out of town (Acts 8:1). Therefore, the Spirit led them to sell many possessions. Many would have lost what they did not sell. This reminds us of the Jewish believers of Hebrews 10:34. Some were put in prison. Others had their property seized and stolen by unbelievers. God alone knows the future. When He leads us to give, we should give. It is always wise to give what we cannot keep. Thus we gain a reward in heaven that we cannot lose!

Q 5 *Does your church put legs on its prayers? Explain.*

***Fifth,* believers put legs on their prayers.** That is, they shared with those in need. [34]*"There were no needy persons among them. For from time to time those who owned lands or houses sold them, brought the money from the sales* [35]*and put it at the apostles' feet, and it was distributed to anyone as he had need"* (Acts 4:34-35).

True Christianity is practical. Real faith helps those in need (James 2:15-16; 1 John 3:16-18).

The Church should not help lazy people. Paul said those who will not work should not eat (2 Thess. 3:10). But hard times come to hardworking people. Accidents, disease, and death visit every home. Therefore, Spirit-filled believers share with those in need. Today, you may be the one giving. Tomorrow, you may be the one receiving. Those who suffer deserve our help. It is always more fun to be the one giving.

Q 6 *Do believers in your church know how much is given, and who gets it? Explain.*

***Sixth,* believers managed the offerings with integrity.** The apostles did not accept money one by one in private. This would have led to questions and doubts. Rather, the offerings were given in public. At a meeting of believers, people brought offerings. Then they laid them at the feet of the apostles. Thus everyone could see when money was given. The money was put into a common fund. Then it was given out to those in need. This prevented accusations and criticism. No one could say, "I gave Thomas a bag of silver coins. I wonder if he kept it or used it for those in need?" It is important to handle offerings carefully before the eyes of God and people (2 Cor. 8:16-21). Managing money in an honest, open way promotes unity.

Q 7 *Have you learned to illustrate statements in your preaching? Explain.*

Luke likes to illustrate his statements. Earlier, he said that God was doing special miracles (Acts 2:43). Then he illustrates his statement with the crippled beggar Peter healed. Now, in Acts 4:32-35, he says people shared. Then he illustrates this truth with the story of Joseph, or Barnabas (Acts 4:36-37). All good preachers, teachers, and writers illustrate their statements of truth. In the Gospel of Luke, three out of every four words of Jesus are part of an illustration.[5]

Joseph, or Barnabas, was a Levite with property. Levites did not own inherited property in Palestine. Perhaps his property was in Cyprus.[6] Later, we will see that Barnabas sails to Cyprus with Paul. Luke introduces Barnabas early in Acts. Barnabas was a good example of those who cared for the needy.[7]

Q 8 *Do you think one who believes should receive a new name? Explain.*

In passing, note that Barnabas was the name the apostles gave Joseph. *Bar* means "son," and *nabas* means "encouragement" in the Aramaic language.[8] The Bible does not teach that it is necessary to have a new Christian name. There are only a few people— such as Abraham, Sarah, Peter, and Barnabas—who received new names. But the Bible does teach that new names are related to character or actions. Why did the apostles call Joseph "Barnabas"? They gave him a name based on his actions. Barnabas was known for encouraging people! Likewise, Jesus once called James and John the Sons of Thunder. Why? Because of their actions. They wanted to call down judgments on their enemies (Mark 3:17). The Lord has promised to give each believer a new name in

Q 9 *What new name would believers give you for your actions?*

heaven (Rev. 2:17). Perhaps our new names will be related to our actions on earth. God and others watch us. They see things about us that stand out. What new names would you give believers you know, based on their actions? Others might not give you a new name. But they could. Each of us is earning a name by his or her actions. Live in a way that earns a name you like!

B. The Church grows through purity (Acts 5:1-11).

Barnabas liked to encourage others. He was willing to take a lesser place. He did not feel the need to sit at the front of the room. He liked to help others become all they could become. Barnabas had a way of keeping the focus on others.

In contrast to Barnabas, Luke introduces Ananias and Sapphira. *Ananias* means "the Lord is gracious." Sapphira probably refers to a beautiful sapphire stone (Rev. 21:19).[9] But unlike Barnabas, their names did not match their actions.

Ananias and Sapphira were jealous. They wanted to be as respected as Barnabas was. Perhaps they wanted the apostles to give them special names, like Barnabas. This husband and wife were wise in their own eyes. They did not realize that they were standing at the gate of judgment. The story of Ananias and Sapphira emphasizes three great truths.

First, **God is the One who will judge all sins.** At key times in history, God uses judgments to remind us that He is our Judge. He judged Nadab and Abihu just after the new tent of worship was completed (Lev. 10:1-2). He judged Achan just after the Israelites entered the Promised Land (Josh. 7). He judged Eli's household and those who looked into the ark as Samuel began to rule (1 Sam. 4–6). He judged Uzzah for touching the ark just after David became king (2 Sam. 6:6-7). He judged Ananias and Sapphira just after the Church had begun (Acts 5:1-10). These sudden acts of judgment remind us that God is holy. He will judge the sins of every person.

Q 10 *What are 3 truths the story of Ananias and Sapphira emphasize?*

Q 11 *Do you think God judged sin at key times in your church? Explain.*

The principal of a Bible school was stealing money. Teachers were not receiving their wages. Students lacked food. Still, this sinning leader continued to steal. He did not repent of his sins. One day he was suddenly killed in a car accident. Only God knows if the wreck was a judgment. But we all know that if we would judge ourselves, we would not be judged (1 Cor. 11:31). *"The sins of some men are obvious, reaching the place of judgment ahead of them; the sins of others trail behind them"* (1 Tim. 5:24).

If sins of believers are obvious, the Church should judge them. God has given us this responsibility. Matthew 18:15-20 gives the steps for judging the sins of believers. First Corinthians 5 gives an example of a church member. Paul commanded the church to judge him. Why? There are two reasons. *First,* to restore the church to purity. A little yeast spreads through all the dough (1 Cor. 5:6). The sin of Ananias and Sapphira would have affected others. *Second,* judging a sinner may save that person from further sin (1 Cor. 5:5). Some believers refuse to submit to discipline. But others are saved by this act of love (Matt. 18:15; 2 Cor. 2:5-11).

Q 12 *State 2 reasons why a church should judge sinning members.*

God judged Ananias and Sapphira in an unusual way. Few sinners are judged in that manner. But He wants His Church to be pure. The Church is helping believers when it disciplines them for sinning. A loving parent disciplines each child who sins. And a loving church disciplines members who sin. The day is coming when Jesus will judge the secrets of our hearts (Rom. 2:16; 1 Cor. 4:5). It is better to be judged sooner than later.

Josh was a leader among the youth in a church. One day he got a very good job. He began to act very proud. Perhaps he forgot that pride changed an angel into the devil. In his pride, Josh began to have a bad testimony for Christ. He led several of the youth in the church to a disco to dance. There they danced and drank alcohol. Several became drunk. The church leaders learned of Josh's sin. In love, they chose to discipline him. Josh refused to submit. He left the church, saying the leaders were hypocrites. But like Ananias and Sapphira, Josh was a hypocrite.

Q 13 *Was it a mistake to discipline Josh? Explain.*

Second, the story of Ananias and Sapphira reminds us that God is concerned about truth.   Jesus said He is the truth (John 14:6). And the Holy Spirit is the Spirit of truth (John 16:13).

Q 14 *Did Ananias lie to man or God? Explain.*

Peter said Ananias *"lied to the Holy Spirit"* (Acts 5:3). Peter told Ananias, *"You have not lied to men* [only] *but to God"* (Acts 5:4).[10] Together, these verses of Acts 5:3-4 show us that the Holy Spirit is God. Thus when we lie to the Holy Spirit, we lie to God. God is present in His Church. He lives in His people. The Church is His temple and body. Therefore, a person who lies to a believer also lies to God who dwells in the believer.

Q 15 *Do you think Ananias and Sapphira were saved, but fell from grace? Explain.*

The devil is the father of lies (John 8:44). Satan lied *to* and *through* Ananias and Sapphira. He tempted them to deceive people. When the devil fails to defeat the Church from the outside, he tries from the inside. Ananias and Sapphira agreed with Satan. They seem to be believers who opened their hearts to Satan's lie. They made a little place for sin. But give sin an inch and it will take a mile. Give sin a centimeter and it will take a kilometer! In the end, Satan filled their hearts (Acts 5:3). Then there was no room left for the Holy Spirit.[11] Satan has many tools. But a lie is the handle that fits them all.[12]

When we walk in truth, we have fellowship with God. When we lie, we fellowship with Satan. Sooner or later God will judge Satan and all liars (Rev. 21:8).

Q 16 *Did Satan keep Sapphira in the dark? Explain.*

***Third,* God's children walk in light, but Satan's children walk in darkness.**   It appears that the burial customs were different then. Ananias was dead and buried in a short time. They did not even notify the widow! Sapphira came in about 3 hours after Ananias. She had no idea that he was dead and buried. Satan always keeps his servants in the dark.[13]

Q 17 *How did Peter know Sapphira would die suddenly?*

We are not certain about how Peter knew Ananias was lying. Perhaps it was a spiritual gift of knowledge. Or perhaps someone found out and talked about their secret sin. Sin is hard to keep hidden. People talk. Be sure your sins will find you out. That is, they will be revealed in public (Num. 32:23). We are not sure how Peter knew Ananias was lying. But he knew. And he also knew Sapphira was lying. She was in the dark and did not know what was happening. In contrast, Peter knew what had happened and what would happen next. God gave him a spiritual gift of insight. Perhaps it was a gift of knowledge. Notice that Peter knew Sapphira would die before it happened (Acts 5:9). Satan keeps his servants in the dark. But God keeps his servants in the light (John 15:15).

Conclusion

Q 18 *Are the standards in your church high enough? Explain.*

Some people imagine we must lower standards of holiness and truth to make progress. This has never been true. The Church is always stronger when we catch a vision of the holiness of God.[14] The Church's respect for God grew after the deaths of Ananias and Sapphira. *"Great fear seized the whole church and all who heard about these events"* (Acts 5:11).

Also, the Church did not become smaller because of purity and truth. It grew. *"Nevertheless, more and more men and women believed in the Lord and were added to their number"* (Acts 5:14).

This brings us to the next lesson.

Lesson 17

The Church Grows Through Signs and Wonders (Acts 5:12-16)

Goal: *Evaluate the relationship of the miraculous to church growth in Acts and today.*

Setting

Read Acts 5:12-16. It serves as a bridge. It connects the story of Ananias and Sapphira to the arrest of the apostles (Acts 5:17-18). Also, Acts 5:12-16 is a summary. It reminds us of passages like Acts 2:43-47 and 4:32-35.[15] From time to time Luke summarizes the growth of the Church.

"No one else dared join them [the believers], *even though they were highly regarded by the people"* (Acts 5:13). That is, no half-hearted actors like Ananias and Sapphira came near.[16] Unbelieving Jews feared to pretend they were Christians. They kept away from the Christians and left them alone.[17]

"Nevertheless, more and more men and women believed in the Lord and were added to their number" (Acts 5:14). Hypocrites stayed away from the believers. But more and more sincere sinners came to Christ.

People notice when God acts. In this lesson, we will examine the relationship between supernatural events and church growth. Let us look at three truths.

A. Jesus taught His disciples differently than many teach today.

Our Lord was a Jewish rabbi, and He taught like the rabbis. His disciples did not sit all day in a classroom. They attended seminary in the street![18] Students walked with Jesus. They followed Him. He taught them how to fish for men. And they watched Him heal people. Crowds marveled at Him. He taught with more authority than other teachers did (Matt. 7:29). He and His disciples talked about it. Next, He sent His disciples out to practice. They preached the good news, healed the sick, and cast out demons (Luke 9:1-6; 10:1-24). Returning, they talked about problems and successes. This cycle continued for 3 years. The disciples watched Jesus minister. They learned to preach, teach, and heal by following His example.[19] Thus they learned by listening, watching, and doing.

Before ascending, Jesus told them to go and make disciples. No doubt He intended for them to train others as He had trained them. But many have forsaken this method! Too many teachers teach theory in the classroom and model mostly in the chapel![20] Each teacher must be a model of ministry for students. We must discover again the relationship between words and deeds of power.

One man had a reputation for training horses. He taught horses to walk in a certain way, at a steady rate. What was his method? He began with an older horse that was a good example. Then he tied a younger horse to it. In time, the younger horse learned to walk the same as the older. Does this surprise us? How many other animals learn from walking beside a parent or mentor? Likewise, a daughter learns to cook by working beside her mother. A young man learns to be a carpenter by working beside one. Ministry in the power of the Holy Spirit is like this. Being around someone who does it well is the best way to learn it for yourself.[21]

A Bible school in Africa keeps the emphasis on ministry. All of their teachers are also pastors. This allows students to watch their teachers minister, and help them. The school has been very successful. It keeps a good balance between studies, skills, prayer, and ministry. Its students are well known for becoming good pastors.

Likewise, extension Bible schools keep the focus on ministry. Extension students leave their churches for 1 or 2 weeks a few times each year. During these times, they study courses to help them in ministry. This is on-the-job training. Thousands of pastors appreciate this practical training. It is a great blessing to help mature leaders who have families and responsibilities.

Q 19 *Explain Acts 5:13-14. Did people continue to join the Church?*

Q 20 *In what ways should a teacher be an example for students?*

Q 21 *How is learning to ride a bicycle like learning to minister?*

Q 22 *Do some schools give too much credit for grades and too little for ministry? Explain.*

Figure 6.3
Much learning occurs through imitation.

7. Pastor the new church and be supported financially by it.
6. Plant a new church at an assigned place.
5. Receive official Certificate of Ministry papers to preach.
4. Win new converts at a preaching point.
3. Lead worship and preach in small meetings.
2. Teach a Sunday school or Bible class.
1. Be filled with the Spirit; testify for Jesus in public.

Figure 6.2   Seven typical steps to becoming a Pentecostal pastor in Latin America

Signs and wonders followed as believers preached in new towns. Beginning at Pentecost, power evangelism spread the good news. Supernatural events showed that the kingdom of God had come. There were powerful signs of the Spirit from Jerusalem to Rome. All people—Jews, Samaritans, and Gentiles—saw God's power in action. The ministry of the disciples was supernatural. It was just like the ministry of Jesus, their teacher.[22]

Q 23 ➤ *Name 3 examples of supernatural events that caused church growth in Acts 1–7.*

"The apostles performed many miraculous signs and wonders among the people" (Acts 5:12). In his Gospel, Luke told how the Spirit anointed Jesus to preach good news, heal, and deliver (Luke 4:18-19). That same Spirit was upon the apostles. God's servants change, but the power of the Holy Spirit remains the same.

B. Supernatural events were a major key to church growth in Acts.

Acts	Supernatural Event	Result
1:3-8	Jesus rose from the dead and appeared to His disciples for 40 days.	They believed He was alive.
1:9-11	Jesus ascended into heaven. Angels instructed the disciples.	The disciples waited in Jerusalem to be baptized in the Holy Spirit.
2:1-4, 41	The 120 were filled with the Holy Spirit. They spoke in various languages.	About 3,000 believed and were baptized after Peter explained the miracle of Pentecost.
3:1–4:4	The crippled beggar was healed. Peter explained what happened.	The number of male believers grew to 5,000.
5:1-11	God struck Ananias and Sapphira dead for lying to the Holy Spirit.	Great fear (respect) seized the whole Church and all who heard.
5:12-18	The apostles performed many miraculous signs and wonders among the people.	More and more men and women believed in the Lord and were added to their number. Leaders became jealous and put the apostles in jail.
5:17-20, 27, 40-42	An angel opened the doors of the jail and told the apostles to go tell the full message in the temple.	The apostles were questioned, flogged, and ordered not to speak in Jesus' name. Still, they continued teaching.
6:8, 10, 15 8:1, 4	Stephen did great wonders and miraculous signs. He spoke with great wisdom by the Spirit. His face shone like an angel as they stoned him.	A great persecution broke out against the church in Jerusalem. All except the apostles were scattered. They preached the Word wherever they went.

Figure 6.4   The relationship of the supernatural to church growth in Acts 1–7

Q 24 ➤ *What are some ways the Holy Spirit works in your ministry?*

The supernatural power helped spread the good news. We are not saying that signs and wonders are the only reason for church growth. It is the gospel that changes lives. But supernatural events help persuade people that the gospel is true. A Muslim father accepted Jesus at a tent meeting. Why? His 12-year-old son was a cripple. He had never walked. But prayer in the name of Jesus instantly healed the boy. Miracles draw multitudes toward the kingdom of God.

[15]*As a result, people brought the sick into the streets and laid them on beds and mats so that at least Peter's shadow might fall on some of them as he passed by.* [16]*Crowds gathered also from the towns around Jerusalem, bringing their sick and those tormented by evil spirits, and all of them were healed* (Acts 5:15-16).

Crowds came from the towns around Jerusalem. They brought their sick and those tormented by demons. Notice that many of the people who were sick did not have demons.[23] What happened? *"All of them were healed"* or made whole (Acts 5:16)!

Earlier, we studied five purposes of Acts. *First,* Acts serves as a bridge between the Gospels and Paul's letters. *Second,* Acts tells how the Church grew in numbers, in new places, in culture, and in theology. *Third,* Acts explains and defends the Church against

The Ministry of the Apostles 95

its enemies. *Fourth,* Acts serves as a guide for faith and practice. *Fifth,* Acts emphasizes that the Spirit's power is the key to witnessing for Jesus.

The last of these five purposes is the most important. Acts is a story about the supernatural growth of the Church. The greatest of Luke's purposes is to emphasize our need for the Holy Spirit's power. We do our worst when we depend on ourselves. We do our best when we depend on the Spirit. The charts in this section emphasize that the Church grew because of the acts of the Holy Spirit.

Acts is a book about the power and acts of the Holy Spirit. Take away the supernatural from Acts, and little remains in it. Is the Holy Spirit working through you and your church? Are you depending more on Him or human power? What would be left in your ministry if the supernatural were taken out of it?

Q 25 ⟋ *Name 3 supernatural events from Acts 8–12 that caused church growth.*

Acts	Supernatural Event	Result
8:5, 13	Philip preached Christ and did miraculous signs in Samaria.	Many men and women believed and were baptized.
8:14-25	The apostles laid hands on the Samaritan believers to receive the Holy Spirit.	The Samaritans were filled with the Spirit. Simon offered money for the power to impart the Spirit through prayer.
8:26-38	An angel directed Philip to travel south toward Gaza. The Spirit told him to walk near the Ethiopian's chariot.	The Ethiopian believed and was baptized.
9:1-19	Jesus appeared to Saul on the road to Damascus. His brightness blinded Saul.	Saul was converted.
9:10-31	The Lord spoke to Ananias in a vision to pray for Saul.	Saul was filled and healed. He began to preach. The church was strengthened, encouraged, and grew in numbers.
9:32-35	Peter healed Aeneas. He had been in bed 8 years.	All who lived in Lydda and Sharon saw him and turned to the Lord.
9:36-42	Peter raised Dorcas from the dead.	Many people believed in the Lord.
10:1-48 11:1-18	By a vision Peter was led to preach to Cornelius.	Cornelius and his household believed and were filled with the Spirit. Peter and the Jerusalem leaders learned that God loves people in all nations.
11:27-30	Agabus prophesied a great famine.	Believers in Antioch and Syria sent money to help believers in Jerusalem.
12:1-17	An angel released Peter from prison as believers prayed.	Believers were amazed.
2:19-24	An angel struck down King Herod for accepting praise as a god.	Herod died, but the Word of God continued to increase and spread.

Figure 6.5   The relationship of the supernatural to church growth in Acts 8–12

C. Acts of the Holy Spirit help churches grow today.

Some do not want to talk about supernatural ministry for today. These honor the Holy Spirit with words. But they seek to lock Him within the pages of Scripture. They want His sudden and unusual miracles attached to the far-off days of the apostles. They like to write books about the ministry of Jesus and the apostles. But it is awkward for them to imagine the Spirit enabling believers to do miracles or speak in unknown languages today. They find it easier to say the age of miracles died with the apostles. These think the Bible is the safest place for the Holy Spirit. They think He belongs there, not in real life![24] However, supernatural events have never ceased. They have continued throughout Church history. Note the following selected, short summary.[25]

Q 26 ⟋ *Did healings and miracles die with the apostles? Explain.*

- Justin Martyr, A.D. 100-165, wrote that believers of his day cast out many demons and healed the sick.
- Irenaeus, 140-203, wrote that some in his day cast out demons and healed the sick. He said it was not possible to name the number of spiritual gifts God had given to believers throughout the world.
- Tertullian, 160-220, wrote about those set free from demons and healed in his day.
- Ambrose, 339-397, testified about healings and tongues in his lifetime.
- Augustine, 354-430, wrote about the blind, the sick, the demon-possessed, and the dead who were healed in his days.
- Francis of Assisi, 1181-1226, had many miracles in his ministry.
- Martin Luther, 1483-1546, cured the sick in the name of Jesus.
- John Wesley, 1703-1791, said that spiritual gifts were taken away for two reasons. *First,* because of a lack of faith and holiness. *Second,* because dry, formal men began to ridicule whatever gifts they themselves did not have. Furthermore, these leaders described God's gifts as insane and fake. Wesley's journal describes more than 200 healings in his ministry.

In recent years, thousands of healings and miracles have taken place.[26] These supernatural events have happened in various nations of the world. Many books tell of wonders of the Holy Spirit in our day.[27] For example, see *Acts Today* by Ralph W. Harris.[28] It tells of many healings, miracles, and messages in tongues being understood by visitors.

Q 27 ➤ *What percent of those obeying the Great Commission believe tongues, signs, and wonders are for today?*

Supernatural events help the Church grow. In many places, Pentecostal churches are growing faster than all others are. An example of this is Latin America. In 1969, 63 percent of all *Protestant believers in Latin America were Pentecostals. Pentecostals and Charismatics believe in miracles, healings, and praying in tongues. There are about 647,810,000 *Great Commission Christians. We define these as active church members who take the Great Commission seriously (Matt. 28:19-20). They obey Christ's command to share the good news with the lost. Of these, 523,767,000 are either Pentecostal or Charismatic.[29] In other words, five out of every six Great Commission Christians in the world are Pentecostal or Charismatic. This means that more than 80 percent of those working for church growth expect signs and wonders today. Many recognize David Barrett as the leading person in the world who gathers missions statistics. He predicts that by the year 2025, 91 percent of all Great Commission Christians will be Pentecostal or Charismatic.[30] These believe that the Holy Spirit works through believers now as He did in the early church.

Q 28 ➤ *By how many millions have Pentecostals and Charismatics increased in the past century?*

Q 29 ➤ *In Acts 13–28, what are 3 supernatural events that caused church growth? (See Figure 6.7.)*

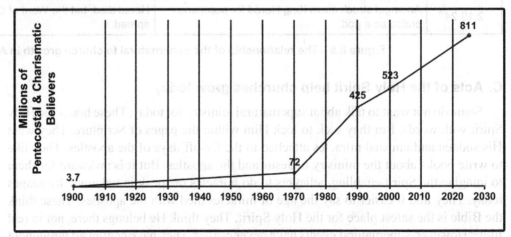

Figure 6.6   Growth of Pentecostal and Charismatic believers from 1900-2025[31]

Acts	Supernatural Event	Result
13:1-3	The Holy Spirit spoke through believers, saying, *"Set apart for me Barnabas and Saul for the work to which I have called them."*	Barnabas and Saul began their first missionary trip.
13:4-12	Paul, filled with the Holy Spirit, pronounced blindness on Elymas, the Jewish sorcerer.	Sergius Paulus, the proconsul or governor, believed in Christ.
14:1-7	God confirmed the message of His grace, enabling Paul and Barnabas to do miraculous signs and wonders.	Some believed the apostles.
14:8-22	God used Paul in Lystra to heal a man crippled from birth. The crowd stoned Paul, but he lived as the disciples gathered around him.	The crowds thought their gods had come down to earth. Paul taught that we must go through many hardships to enter God's kingdom
16:6-15	Through a vision the Holy Spirit forbade Paul to enter Asia and guided him to Macedonia.	In Macedonia, Lydia and her household received Christ and were baptized.
16:16-24	Paul cast a demon out of a girl who predicted the future.	Paul and Silas were beaten and jailed.
16:25-34, 40	Paul and Silas prayed and sang at midnight. An earthquake opened all the prison doors.	The jailer and his family believed in Christ and were baptized. Believers were encouraged.
18:9-11	The Lord spoke to Paul in a vision. He encouraged Paul to keep on speaking without fear.	Paul kept teaching in Corinth for a year and a half.
19:1-7	Paul preached to 12 men in Ephesus. He placed his hands on them and they were filled with the Spirit.	The 12 men spoke in tongues and prophesied.
19:8-12	Paul preached and taught 2 years and 3 months in Ephesus. God did special miracles.	All Jews and Greeks who lived in the province of Asia heard the Word.
19:13-20	The sons of Sceva tried to cast out a demon in the name of Jesus. They fled wounded and naked.	"The name of the Lord Jesus was held in high honor. . . The word of the Lord spread widely and grew in power."
20:7-12	Paul raised Eutychus from the dead.	The young man lived, and believers were greatly comforted.
21:1-15	Agabus and others prophesi*ed that Paul would be bound in Jerusalem.*	Believers were prepared to accept the Lord's will for Paul. Because of the prophecy, his trials strengthened their faith rather than shook it.
23:1-11	The Lord stood near Paul. He encouraged Paul and assured him that he would testify in Rome.	Paul was strengthened and prepared for the journey to Rome.
27:21-44	An angel stood by Paul. He told him that all the men on the ship would live through the storm.	All 276 men on the ship reached the shore safely.
28:1-6	Paul shook a viper off into the fire at Malta.	The people changed their minds about Paul, saying he was a god.
28:7-10	Paul healed the father of Publius and many other sick people.	The people honored Paul and his friends in many ways.

Figure 6.7   The relationship of the supernatural to church growth in Acts 13–28

Lesson 18
The Church Grows Through Persecution (Acts 5:17-42)
Goal: *Analyze and illustrate 3 truths about persecution in Acts.*

Setting

Persecution is like a river in Acts 1–28. It flows from Jerusalem to Rome. In the last lesson, we surveyed the supernatural in Acts. In this section we will survey persecution in Acts 1–28.

Unbelievers have always persecuted believers (1 John 3:12-13). Cain killed Abel (Gen. 4:8). Ishmael persecuted Isaac (Gen. 21:9; Gal. 4:29). Sinning Jews persecuted the prophets (Matt. 5:12). In Acts, unbelieving Jews were a major source of persecution. Acts illustrates three truths about persecution.

A. We cannot avoid persecution by being more spiritual than others.

Q 30 ➤ *What are 2 cases of persecution that led to church growth in Acts 1–7?*

Jesus was persecuted. The apostles were persecuted. *"In fact, everyone who wants to live a godly life in Christ Jesus will be persecuted"* (2 Tim. 3:12). Persecution is like temptation. It knocks at every door.

Acts	Source of Persecution	Reason for Persecution	Description of Persecution	Result of Persecution
1:3 2:23-41	Unbelieving Jewish leaders	Jesus claimed to be the Son of God and the Messiah. The masses believed Him.	They nailed Him to a cross.	He died, but rose from the dead. He ascended and sent the promised gift of the Spirit. Millions follow Him.
4:1-31	Sadducees	The apostles healed a cripple and preached the resurrection of the dead through Jesus.	They put Peter and John in jail. The Sanhedrin threatened them.	The disciples prayed for boldness. All were filled with the Holy Spirit.
5:17-41	Jewish high priest and Sadducees	Some Jewish leaders were jealous over the success of the apostles.	The Sanhedrin jailed the apostles and later beat them.	An angel released them. They rejoiced for being worthy of suffering for the Name.
6:9– 8:1, 4	Unbelieving Jews and the Sanhedrin	By the Spirit, Stephen did great wonders and miraculous signs, and spoke with wisdom about Jesus.	They brought him to the Sanhedrin, produced false witnesses, and stoned him.	In Jerusalem, great persecution broke out. All except the apostles were scattered, preaching wherever they went.

Figure 6.8   Persecution of believers in Acts 1–7

B. The supernatural rarely delivers believers from persecution.

There are three charts on persecution in this lesson. These cover the entire book of Acts. The charts contain about 26 examples of persecution in Acts.

Q 31 ➤ *How many times in Acts do miracles deliver believers from persecution?*

Q 32 ➤ *Does God promise to deliver believers from persecution or to be with them? Explain.*

God gave a supernatural release only three times in Acts! That leaves 23 times that believers struggled with persecution. The *first* miraculous release from persecution was in Acts 5:19. An angel released the apostles from prison. But he sent them back to the place they got into trouble! The next day they were beaten. The *second* miraculous release is in Acts 12:7. An angel released Peter from prison. But James, one of the top three apostles, was not released from the same prison. The *third* supernatural release from persecution is in Acts 16. Paul and Silas are let out of prison after a severe beating. But they are only out from midnight to dawn! What is the conclusion? Persecution is a mountain that God seldom removes. Rather, He gives us the strength to climb it! The power of the Holy Spirit seldom helps us avoid persecution. But His power and presence enable us to triumph through it. God delivered Shadrach, Meshach, and Abednego from the fiery furnace (Dan. 3). But He strengthened thousands of believers whom the Caesars burned to death. A few times in history God has removed the mountain of persecution. But usually, He gives us the strength to climb it. This year, it appears that at least 160,000 believers will be martyred for their faith![32]

So why does God rarely deliver His people from persecution? The Bible teaches that God does many things through persecution.[+] Suffering produces maturity (James 1:2-4). And suffering is like a fire that purifies (1 Pet. 1:6-7). Maturity and purity are things that persecution or suffering produce in us. The next point speaks of what God does through us as we suffer.

Q 33 ⟋ *Cite 2 cases in Acts 8–12 showing that persecution led to church growth. (See Figure 6.9.)*

Acts	Source of Persecution	Reason for Persecution	Description of Persecution	Result of Persecution
8:1, 5, 11	Unbelieving Jews in Jerusalem	They were jealous (5:17), angry (7:57), and did not believe in Jesus (1 Tim. 1:13).	They beat, killed, or imprisoned believers. Sometimes they took their property (Heb. 10:34).	Philip went to a city of Samaria and preached. Many believed.
8:3-4	Saul	He thought he was serving God!	He began to destroy the church, house to house. Believers were beaten, imprisoned, or killed (Acts 9:1-2; 22:4, 19; 26:10-11).	Believers were scattered. They preached the Word wherever they went.
9:23-25	Unbelieving Jews in Damascus	Saul was proving that Jesus was the Messiah.	They planned to kill him.	His followers lowered him in a basket through an opening in the wall. He went to Jerusalem.
11:19-21	See 8:1 above.	See 8:1 above.	See 8:1 above.	Those scattered told the good news in Phoenicia, Cyprus, and Antioch.
12:1-17, 24	King Herod	Herod desired to please the unbelieving Jews.	He had James' head cut off; later he put Peter in prison.	Believers were encouraged when God freed Peter from prison. The Word of God continued to increase and spread.

Figure 6.9   Persecution of believers in Acts 8–12

C. Jesus continues to build His Church during persecution.

Paul suffered a great amount of persecution (Acts 9:15-16). This persecution opened many doors for witnessing. Paul's trials escorted him into the presence of governors and kings.

Nothing can separate us from the love of God in Christ Jesus (Rom. 8:38-39). Not even death. *"Thanks be to God! He gives us the victory through our Lord Jesus Christ"* (1 Cor. 15:57). Persecution scatters believers. And they witness about Jesus wherever they go. Christianity is like a fire. If you poke it with a stick, the sparks spread the fire to new places. Acts shows that persecution spreads the Church.

**Figure 6.10
Jerusalem—St. Stephen's
Gate or Lion's Gate.
Some believe Stephen was
martyred here.**

+ See the *Faith & Action Series* book on *Revelation & Daniel*, chapter 3, Lesson 7 under A. It lists some of the purposes of suffering.

Acts	Source	Reason	Description of Persecution	Result of Persecution
13:44-49	Unbelieving Jews in Antioch of Pisidia	Jealousy over the crowds that gathered to hear the Word of the Lord from Paul	They talked badly against what Paul was saying.	The apostles turned to the Gentiles. Many believed. God's Word spread throughout the whole region.
13:50-52	Unbelieving Jews in Antioch of Pisidia	Jealousy over the Jewish crowds and Gentile believers	They used God-fearing women with influence and leading men to stir up persecution. They expelled the apostles.	The apostles shook the dust from their feet as a protest (See Luke 9:5). The disciples were filled with joy and the Holy Spirit.
14:1-7	Jews who refused to believe at Iconium	Unbelief	They stirred up the Gentiles and poisoned their minds. They planned to stone the apostles.	They fled to Lystra and Derbe and continued to preach the good news.
14:19-22	Jews from Iconium and Antioch	Unbelief and jealousy over the crowds	They stoned Paul and dragged him out of the city.	The disciples prayed for him. Paul got up and went back into the city. Later, he taught that we must go through hardships to enter God's kingdom.
16:16-40	Owners of a slave girl; a crowd; Roman magistrates	Masters of a slave girl became upset when Paul cast out a demon that was in her.	They beat Paul and Silas, put them in jail, and fastened their feet in stocks.	A jailer and his family were saved. Believers at Philippi were strengthened.
17:1-10	Unbelieving Jews of Thessalonica	Jealousy	They formed a mob and started a riot.	Paul and Silas escaped to Berea.
17:13-15	Unbelieving Jews of Thessalonica	Jealousy	They stirred up the crowd.	Paul and Silas escaped to Athens.
18:1-17	Unbelieving Jews of Corinth	Unbelief	Jews opposed Paul and became abusive. Later, they united and took him to court.	He shook out his clothes and turned to the Gentiles. Many Corinthians believed. Gallio threw the case out of court.
19:8-10, 20	Unbelieving Jews in Ephesus	They refused to believe.	They publicly slandered the Way.	Paul left the synagogue. He taught beside it for 2 years. Many Jews and Greeks believed.
19:23–20:1	Demetrius, a silversmith	He was losing money. People were not buying the idols of Artemis that he made.	They started a riot and rushed into the theater.	The city clerk dismissed the case. Paul encouraged the disciples and left for Macedonia.
20:3	Unbelieving Jews of Greece	Unbelief	They made a plot against Paul.	He changed his plans and returned to Macedonia.
21:27–23:35	Unbelieving Jews	Unbelief; Paul's ministry to the Gentiles	They seized Paul and stirred up the crowd. They dragged him from the temple and tried to kill him. Later, more than 40 men vowed to kill him.	The Romans moved Paul to a prison in Caesarea, in Herod's palace.
24	The high priest and some elders	Preaching Jesus	They accused Paul with a lawyer before Governor Felix.	Paul testified to the governor and others. He was bound for 2 years.

Continued on next page

Acts	Source	Reason	Description of Persecution	Result of Persecution
25–26	Chief priests and Jewish leaders	Preaching Jesus	They made serious charges that they could not prove. Paul was put in chains.	Paul testified to Festus. Then he appealed to Caesar. A few days later Paul testified to King Agrippa and city leaders.
27	Chief priests and Jewish leaders	Preaching Jesus	Paul was taken as a prisoner to Rome. The ship was lost to a great storm.	Paul became a friend with Julius, the centurion. Also, all 276 survived the storm because of Paul.
28:1-10	Chief priests and Jewish leaders	Preaching Jesus	Paul continued his journey to Rome as a prisoner.	Paul healed the sick on the island of Malta.
28:11-31	Chief priests and Jewish leaders	Preaching Jesus	Paul was chained and guarded for 2 years.	Boldly and without hindrance he preached the kingdom of God and taught about the Lord Jesus Christ.

Figure 6.11   Persecution of believers in Acts 13–28

"We must go through many hardships to enter the kingdom of God" (Acts 14:22).

Figure 6.12   Ruins of prison where Paul was kept in Caesarea

Q 34 ⟋ *In Acts 13–20, what are 3 cases showing that persecution led to church growth?*

Q 35 ⟍ *Has persecution caused church growth in your country? Explain.*

Test Yourself: Circle the letter by the *best* completion to each question or statement.

1. One of the reasons believers were united was that
a) they agreed on almost everything.
b) no one owned any possessions.
c) there were no private offerings.
d) they separated the financial and the spiritual.

2. Sharing by early believers resulted from
a) free will.
b) socialism.
c) communism.
d) apostolic rules.

3. Ananias died because he
a) lied to man.
b) lied to God.
c) gave too little.
d) stole from God.

4. Peter knew Sapphira would die because
a) Ananias had died.
b) God kills those who lie.
c) the Holy Spirit told him.
d) Sapphira blasphemed.

5. The apostles learned to heal the sick by
a) reading about Old Testament miracles.
b) being filled with the Holy Spirit.
c) listening to what Jesus said in private.
d) following the example of their teacher.

6. All in Lydda and Sharon turned to the Lord because
a) Peter preached the gospel to them.
b) one supernatural healing occurred.
c) Agabus prophesied a great famine.
d) the Samaritans believed Philip.

7. What percentage of Great Commission Christians believe that miracles still happen?
a) At least 20 percent
b) At least 40 percent
c) At least 60 percent
d) At least 80 percent

8. More than 200 healings are recorded in the journal of
a) Tertullian.
b) Augustine.
c) Luther.
d) Wesley.

9. Of the 25 cases of persecution in Acts, the supernatural delivered someone
a) 1 time.
b) 3 times.
c) 5 times.
d) 7 times.

10. Which of the following is NOT a major cause of church growth?
a) Prosperity
b) Unity
c) Miracles
d) Persecution

 Essay Test Topics: Write 50-100 words on each of these goals that you studied in this chapter.

The Church Grows Through Unity and Purity (Acts 4:32–5:11)

Goal: *Analyze 6 keys to unity in Acts 4:32-37. Relate these to your church and ministry.*

Goal: *Explain and apply 3 truths related to purity in Acts 5:1-11.*

The Church Grows Through Signs and Wonders (Acts 5:12-16)

Goal: *Evaluate the relationship of the miraculous to church growth in Acts and today.*

The Church Grows Through Persecution (Acts 5:17-42)

Goal: *Analyze and illustrate 3 truths about persecution in Acts.*

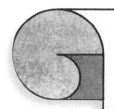

Unit 3:
The Witness of the Church in Judea and Samaria (Acts 8–12)

Acts 1:8 is a helpful outline of the entire book (Figure 1.9).

In Chapter 7 you will discover that church growth causes problems. Every pastor and church worker who studies with us will be blessed by this chapter. In it you will:
- *Contrast the way the apostles and Stephen's enemies handled conflict. Compare these methods with yours and those of leaders you know.*
- *Identify and apply what Stephen's speech says about change and God's location.*
- *Identify and apply three truths related to Stephen's speech and death.*

In Chapter 8 you will see the Church take a major step forward (Acts 8:1–9:31). They had been slow to obey the Great Commission. Finally, they begin to witness to those outside of Jerusalem! In this exciting chapter you will:
- *Explain four principles of evangelism in Acts 8. Evaluate your church and ministry in relation to these principles.*
- *State and apply two truths about God's concern for the lost.*
- *Analyze and apply the relationship between reading and understanding.*
- *Identify and apply six truths related to Saul's conversion and early ministry.*

In Chapter 9 you will see the young Church continue to expand (Acts 9:32–12:25). Recall that Acts traces the growth of the Church from Jerusalem to Rome. It is wonderful to see how the Spirit helped Jewish believers conquer their prejudice toward Gentiles. In this chapter you will:
- *Identify and apply four truths from Peter's ministry to Cornelius.*
- *Summarize four insights about the ministry in Antioch. Relate these to your context.*
- *Explain four contrasts in Acts 12. Apply these to self and others.*

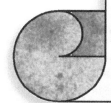

Chapter 7:
The Ministry of Stephen
(Acts 6:1–8:1)

Introduction

On February 14, 1994, David sat in an airport in Sierra Leone, West Africa. He was waiting for the airplane he would ride. His friend, Ian, was praying out loud as he walked around. This attracted the attention of a security officer named Moses. "What are you doing?" asked Moses. Ian replied, "I'm just talking to Jesus. I'm telling Him how much I love him." Moses was a Muslim. The idea of talking to Jesus amazed him. Moses and Ian talked a few minutes. Ian had been a believer for only 2 years. He wanted Moses to talk to a more mature believer. So they walked over to talk with David. David set down his coffee cup. But Moses held up a hand. "Wait! Don't say anything yet. I want to call some of my friends." Soon, Moses returned with about seven friends. David shared a simple message of the life, death, and resurrection of Jesus. Then he said, "Jesus

Figure 7.1   The stoning of Stephen

loves Muslims. And He often likes to heal Muslims to show them His love. Is anyone here sick or hurting?" Umar, who lifted baggage, spoke up. "I hurt my hip. It gives me constant pain." David was depending on the Holy Spirit. He prayed a short prayer for healing in the name of Jesus. Umar spoke up at once. He said, "It's gone! My pain is totally gone!" As a result of this healing, all eight of these Muslims received Jesus as Savior. The healing opened the door for Jesus to come in.[1]

Lessons:

Stephen Among the Seven (Acts 6:1-15)
Goal: *Contrast the way the apostles and Stephen's enemies handled conflict. Compare these methods with yours and those of leaders you know.*

Stephen's Speech—Part 1 (Acts 7:1-53)
Goal: *Identify and apply what Stephen's speech says about change and God's location.*

Stephen's Speech—Part 2 (Acts 7:1–8:1)
Goal: *Identify and apply 3 truths related to Stephen's speech and death.*

 Key Words

Stephen	Hebraic Jews	Alexandria
synagogue	Hellenistic	Cilicia
Grecian Jews	Cyrene	Asia

Lesson 19 **Stephen Among the Seven (Acts 6:1-15)**

Goal: *Contrast the way the apostles and Stephen's enemies handled conflict. Compare these methods with yours and those of leaders you know.*

Setting

Acts 1–8 includes three ways Satan seeks to defeat the Church. *First* is persecution. We have seen this in the early chapters of Acts. Church leaders are special targets of persecution. Peter, John, and the other apostles faced Satan's attacks. Some were beaten and some were put in jail. Persecution should never be a surprise to believers. *Second,* we saw that seduction is a tool of Satan. He seduced Ananias and Sapphira to be greedy and jealous. They believed his lies. God's act of sudden justice cleansed the Church. Thus the Church overcame Satan's seduction to worldly values. *Third,* Satan uses division and conflict. Acts 6 reveals two types of conflict. The first conflict is between believers. The second is between Stephen and some synagogue members. Let us see what we can learn from each of these conflicts.

A. How the apostles responded to conflict (Acts 6:1-7)

Conflicts are like temptations. That is, they come to all people. Even the most spiritual people disagree and have conflicts at times.

Believers may disagree on many issues. They may disagree on clothing styles, food, music, politics, Bible verses, worship, and a hundred other things. This is normal. But how should believers act when they disagree? And how should leaders solve conflicts between believers? We will search for answers to these questions. We will divide Acts 6:1-7 into three parts: the problem, the solution, and the result.

Q 1 *What are some issues on which believers you know disagree?*

First, let us look at the *problem.* Notice that the problem came because the number of disciples increased.

In those days when the number of disciples was increasing, the Grecian Jews among them complained against the Hebraic Jews because their widows were being overlooked in the daily distribution of food (Acts 6:1).

The problem came because the number of disciples increased. Church growth causes problems. Some church members like the church to remain small. Thus they avoid growth problems. They like a few people that all know each other. These tend to think and act the same. But Jesus calls us to reach out to the lost. Heaven celebrates each time a sinner comes to Christ (Luke 15). New converts usually cause conflicts. Still, conflict is a necessary part of growth. And not growing is a bigger problem than the problems caused by growth!

Q 2 *Should we avoid church growth because it causes problems? Explain.*

The conflict in Acts 6:1-7 was a relationship problem. It was between Jewish believers. Recall that the early church was made up mostly of Jews. They had not yet started reaching out to Gentiles. Acts 6:1 says the conflict was between the *Grecian Jews and the *Hebraic Jews. The Hebraic Jews were the ones who spoke Hebrew well. These were mostly natives of Palestine. They spoke Hebrew in their homes and Greek as a second language.[2] But the Grecian Jews did not know Hebrew well. Many of these were born outside of Palestine.[3] Recall that Luke earlier mentioned many places from which Jews came (Acts 2:5-11). These Grecian Jews usually spoke Greek. All of the Roman Empire spoke Greek. It was the language of business and government since *Alexander the Great.[4]

Q 3 *Did all Jews know the Hebrew language well? Explain.*

Different languages are always barriers in relationships. People understand each other better when they speak the same language. But language was not the only difference in the Grecian and Hebraic Jews. Even outside the Church, there were tensions between those who spoke Hebrew and those who spoke Greek.[5]

Q 4 Did all Jews share the same values? Explain.

It is impossible to separate a language from a culture. Those who grow up with a language will accept part of the ideas and values linked with that language. The Grecian Jews were Jewish. But they were less bound to Hebrew tradition. And they were more open to Greek ideas than the Jews of Palestine. The Greek word for a Greek person is *Hellene*. Therefore, Greek ideas are referred to as *Hellenistic. The Grecian Jews were Hellenistic. They spoke Greek, thought like Greeks, and acted like Greeks.[6] The Greeks ruled for about 300 years. This Hellenistic rule affected Jews. And it especially affected those whose fathers and grandfathers were scattered from a Jewish community. Jews who grew up in Palestine and spoke Hebrew were more loyal to the past. But Grecian Jews saw life differently. For example, Grecian Jews outside of Palestine saw the temple only once a year. So they might not have thought it was as important as it was to those who worshiped in it each week. Therefore, we should be aware that all Jewish believers did not share the same values. They were not united. Some Jews were Pharisees and others were Sadducees. Some were Grecian Jews and others were Hebraic.

Q 5 How do values of believers in your country differ?

Q 6 Why did the Grecian Jews complain?

The differences between the Grecian and Hebraic Jews led to a conflict. The Grecian Jews began to complain or murmur. They said their widows were being overlooked in the daily serving. Recall that believers shared with other believers who were in need. Some brought offerings from time to time. These offerings may have included money, clothing, or food.[7] Those who could work got a job. But each day, the widows could receive help.[8] Still, some of the Grecian widows were being neglected. Perhaps this was due to the language barrier. Some think that those in charge of the money and food were all Hebraic Jews.[9] Regardless of the reason, the Grecian widows were being neglected. This was a problem.

Q 7 Why is complaining worse than what a person complains about?

But complaining and murmuring was a worse problem. The Bible tells us to do all things without complaining (Phil. 2:14). Look up the word *complain* or *murmur* in a concordance. You will find that God often judges those who complain. Fire fell on some of the Israelites who complained (Num. 11:1). Others became sick because they complained about their food (Num. 11:4-20, 32-34). Another time God sent poisonous snakes to bite those who complained (Num. 21:4-9).

Q 8 Which is easier: to defend yourself or look at the problem? Explain.

God invites us to bring our needs to Him. He wants us to pray about our problems. But He likes to hear our requests mixed with thanksgiving (Phil. 4:6). God will judge those who growl like a dog. He will punish those who grumble, murmur, and complain. Complaining is not praying. Those who complain are not showing faith. They are like the disciples who awakened Jesus on the boat. They accused Him of not caring that they were perishing (Mark 4:38). Therefore, Jesus rebuked them for their lack of faith. Those who complain are not looking up to God for an answer. Rather, they are looking only at the problem. And this makes them part of the problem. Nevertheless, the apostles were patient with those who complained.

We have focused on the *problem*. Now let us move on to the *solution*. Note four things about the way the apostles handled the complaint.[10]

- The apostles did not become defensive. The apostles did not say, "We are doing the best we can. Stop speaking against God's anointed leaders." Rather than defend themselves, the apostles looked at the problem.

  One preacher said some faith teachers were making mistakes. He said some of their teachings contradicted the Bible. He gave specific examples and verses. The faith teachers became angry. They did not examine the problem. Rather, they defended themselves and claimed to be anointed. Then, they said that if the preacher did not stop criticizing them, his children would die.[11] But his children continued to do well!

Q 9 How did the apostles respond differently than Pharaoh?

- The apostles did not attack those who complained. Some leaders, like Pharaoh, punish those who want change (Exod. 5:1-21). When the Israelites complained, he did not listen to their need or problem. Rather, he became angry and punished them.

When they spoke of the need to worship, he took away their straw. When they said he was not fair, he beat them. They were working hard, but he said they were lazy. In contrast, the apostles did not turn against those who complained. They did not embarrass or punish them. They did not try to make them feel guilty. Instead, they listened carefully to discover the problem. Successful leaders separate the problem from the person. They recognized that God still loves those who are less spiritual than they should be.

- The apostles were open to change. There are times that believers, churches, and denominations must change. Parents, teachers, and other leaders must be open to change. As things and people grow, change often becomes necessary. The way we did things yesterday may not work tomorrow. New shoes may hurt the feet at first. And new ideas may hurt the mind for a while. But the price of progress is change.[12]

Q 10 ↖ *What types of changes must parents and pastors make?*

- The apostles let the people help make the decisions. There are two types of government in the New Testament. For new converts, Paul chose the leaders. Or, he had a church leader like Titus appoint them (Titus 1:5). This model of church government was for immature believers. They did not know the Bible well. But Acts 6 gives us a type of government for mature believers. The apostles wanted to focus on the Word and prayer. They did not want to help count and distribute money for the poor. Therefore, they allowed the people to choose seven men to serve at the financial tables.[13] This pleased the whole group (Acts 6:5).

Q 11 ↖ *When should believers be allowed to help solve church problems? Explain.*

The apostles gave two qualifications. They said the deacons should be full of the Spirit and wisdom. These two are not the same. The Holy Spirit fills a person in a moment. But wisdom grows with years. Some are full of the Spirit, but lack wisdom and maturity. Others have wisdom from experience, but lack the Spirit. It is wonderful to have leaders that are full of both the Spirit and wisdom!

Q 12 ↖ *Are all who are filled with the Spirit full of wisdom? Explain and illustrate.*

So the people chose the seven men. An amazing thing happened! All seven of the men chosen had Greek names. This shows us that the Hebraic Jews had great love for their Grecian brothers. The Hebraic Jews gave authority to the Grecian Jews. This is a great example of preferring others in love (Rom. 12:10).

Q 13 ↗ *What do the Greek names of the seven deacons show? Explain.*

We have looked at the *problem* and the *solution*. Now, let us consider the result. There are two things to note. *First,* a new level of ministry began. Some call these seven the first deacons. The apostles laid hands on them and prayed for them (Acts 6:6). Then the Holy Spirit anointed them. All believers do not have the same ministry. But God has a task and an anointing for each believer. New ministries often begin as leaders encourage laypeople to help solve problems.

Q 14 ↖ *Should leaders share authority with those of a different social group? Explain.*

Second, the church continued to grow. *"So the word of God spread. The number of disciples in Jerusalem increased rapidly, and a large number of priests became obedient to the faith"* (Acts 6:7).

When the Church grows, new problems arise. And when the Church solves its problems, it continues to grow. Problems are never meant to weaken. Their purpose is to help us grow from one level to another. Thus we see that church problems and church growth form a cycle. One leads to the other. But remember this. The fate of a person, a family, or a church depends on one thing. It depends on how leaders respond to people's needs and complaints.

Q 15 ↖ *Does solving church problems often lead to new ministries? Explain.*

B. How the synagogue members responded to conflict (Acts 6:8-15)

[8]*Now Stephen, a man full of God's grace and power, did great wonders and miraculous signs among the people.* [9]*Opposition arose, however, from members of the Synagogue of the Freedmen (as it was called)—Jews of Cyrene and Alexandria as well as the provinces of Cilicia and Asia. These men began to argue with Stephen* (Acts 6:8-9).

Q 16 ➤ *What does the name "Stephen" mean?*

In Acts 5 we looked briefly at the meanings of some names. *Barnabas* means "son of encouragement." His name revealed his character. Barnabas liked to encourage others. Likewise, in Acts 6–7, we see that Stephen's name fit him. *Stephanos* is a Greek word for "crown." Stephen was crowned with wisdom and the Holy Spirit.

Q 17 ➤ *Did the apostles choose Stephen to do signs and wonders? Explain.*

Acts is the story of how the Spirit helped the Church expand from Jerusalem to Rome. Jesus chose twelve men. Now, the Church has chosen seven more. Stephen was healing, preaching, and teaching. He did great wonders and miraculous signs among the people (Acts 6:8). They chose him to serve at financial tables. As he was faithful, God added to his ministry. God always subtracts from the negligent and adds to the diligent. Thousands of God's best workers today began with small responsibilities. One of Luke's purposes is to show that the Holy Spirit is not just for apostles. The Spirit expands God's work through each person.

New ministry always brings new opposition. Satan does not like God's work to expand. So he fights against all ministry. As Stephen's ministry grew, opposition arose.

Q 18 ➤ *What were the purposes of synagogues?*

Stephen's opponents were from a synagogue. *Synagogue* is an important word. It appears 56 times in the New Testament. *Synagogues were buildings where Jews met. The purposes of synagogues were worship, education, and government. Recall that the ten tribes became slaves to Assyria in 722 B.C. Later, in 586 B.C., Babylon captured Judah. The temple was destroyed. After the exiles to Assyria and Babylon, Jews were scattered. Later, they built small synagogues to replace the loss of the temple. The first known synagogues appeared in the century before Christ.

Unlike the temple, synagogues were in all parts of the land. They served as substitutes for the temple. However, there were no altars in synagogues. Prayer and Scripture reading replaced sacrifices. Each synagogue had a ruler, elders, and members. Children learned to read in the synagogues. Some think there were about 400 synagogues in Jerusalem in A.D. 70.[14]

Stephen's enemies came from the Synagogue of the Freedmen. Perhaps this synagogue was built to honor war prisoners or slaves.[15] It was probably a synagogue of the Hellenistic (Grecian) Jews.

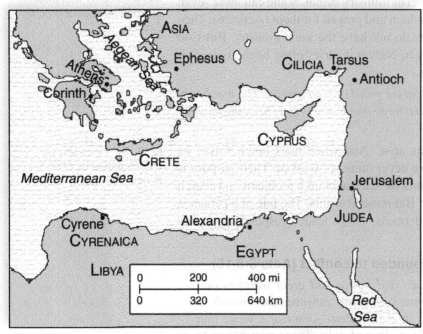

Figure 7.2   Members of the Synagogue of the Freedmen came from various places.

Jews from different places were members of the Synagogue of the Freedmen. Some were from Cyrene, the chief city of Libya and North Africa (See Figure 7.2). Others were from Alexandria, the capital of Egypt in that day. Some members came from Cilicia. This province included Tarsus, where Paul was from. He may have attended this synagogue and argued with Stephen. Paul may have been a member of this synagogue. We know that Paul was present when Stephen was stoned (Acts 7:58; 8:1). Finally, other members came from Asia. This was a province in the western part of Asia Minor. Ephesus was Asia's largest city.

Above, we saw how the apostles responded to conflict. But Stephen's opponents had a different attitude. Note four mistakes they made.

- They refused to submit to wisdom and the Spirit. *"They could not stand up against his wisdom or the Spirit by which he spoke"* (Acts 6:10). Stephen did not depend on himself. The Holy Spirit was speaking through him. His opponents could not stand up against the truth. But they would not bow down to it! These men were as stubborn as donkeys. Stephen's face glowed like an angel. Perhaps he looked like Moses when he came from the presence of God (Exod. 34:29-35; 2 Cor. 3:13). Or he may have looked like Jesus on the mountain with Moses and Elijah (Matt. 17: 2-3). But the light from Stephen's face did not change the darkness of their minds.

- They ignored the ideas and attacked the person. These opponents made Stephen look as bad as possible.[16] They could not stand up against his ideas in public. So they met secretly to discuss him. Then evil men persuaded false witnesses to distort what Stephen said (Acts 6:11). They gossiped about him and slandered him (Acts 6:12). Notice that they accused him of two things. They said he spoke against the temple and the Law (Acts 6:13). Stephen's response to these two accusations is in the next two sections.

Q 19 *How do you respond to those who disagree with you, and are wiser than you?*

- They resisted change like it was leprosy. The worst thing they could think to say was that Jesus wanted to *"change the customs"* (Acts 6:14)! They were members of the Synagogue of the Freedmen. But they were slaves of tradition and prejudice!

Q 20 *Have you known leaders who brought change? If so, how did they do it?*

  Most people resist change. And they persecute those who want to bring change. The apostles were beaten for preaching the resurrection of Christ. But Stephen was stoned for talking about change! Preaching the gospel often brings social tensions. People do not like to change.

- They used force and authority to silence truth. They lost the contest of ideas. So they turned from reason to power.[17] *"They seized Stephen and brought him before the Sanhedrin"* (Acts 6:12). But force is a poor weapon against truth. Communism and Islam use force against truth. These succeed only by political force. In contrast, Christianity allows discussion and free choice. The truth will always survive questioning.

Q 21 *Why is it unwise to silence truth with force?*

Truth is like a fire. Fighting against the truth is like putting hot coals in a paper box. Therefore, it is wise to never fight against the truth (2 Cor. 13:8). Force may bury truth for a time. Paul speaks of those who hold the truth down through their evil (Rom. 1:18). But sooner or later the truth will resurrect and rule.

Some people once fought against the truth. They said it was right to buy and sell other people. They used these slaves to get much wealth. Others protested that slavery was wrong. The argument continued for years. Meanwhile, the slaves worked. It seemed that truth itself had become the slave of power. But in the fullness of time, truth gained strength. One day it stood up. With a mighty voice it shouted that slavery was wrong. Truth said that all humans are created in the image of God. The power of God began to flow through the truth. A great war was fought. Truth broke the chains that bound it. All of the slaves became free. Sooner or later, truth always wins.

Q 22 *What types of wrongs in your country will truth change sooner or later?*

Conclusion

Conflicts come to all. People disagree on many things. So we should learn how to deal with conflict.

Responding rightly to conflict is a skill. The apostles did four things right. They did not become defensive. They did not attack those who disagreed with them. They were open to change. And they let others help make decisions. In contrast, the synagogue members made four mistakes. They refused to submit to wisdom and the Spirit. They ignored the ideas and attacked the speaker. They resisted all change. Finally, they used force to silence truth.

Q 23 *In conflicts, are you more like an apostle or a member of the Synagogue of the Freedmen? Explain.*

Think of some of your past conflicts. What did you do right? What mistakes did you make? What conflicts are you in now?

Stephen's Speech—Part 1 (Acts 7:1-53)

Lesson 20

Goal: *Identify and apply what Stephen's speech says about change and God's location.*

Q 24 ➤ *What are at least 3 historical facts in Stephen's speech?*

Setting

Stephen reviews the history of Israel. Every student of the Bible should be able to explain Stephen's review. Take time to review the Old Testament passages to which Stephen refers. Figure 7.3 summarizes some of the facts Stephen mentioned.

	Historical Facts	Scripture
1.	God appeared to Abraham in Mesopotamia. He called him to leave his relatives and country. Abraham obeyed and left the land of the Chaldeans (Babylonians).	Gen. 11:31–12:5 Neh. 9:7; Acts 7:2-5
2.	God promised to give Canaan to Abraham and his seed. First, however, they would be slaves for about +400 years![18] Then God would punish the nation that enslaved them.	Exod. 1:8-11; 12:40 Acts 7:5-6; Gal. 3:17
3.	Circumcision was a sign of the covenant between God and Abraham.	Gen. 17:9-14; Acts 7:8
4.	Abraham's descendants were Isaac, Jacob, and the 12 *patriarchs, or grandfathers of the Jews.	Gen. 21:2-4; 25:26 Acts 7:8
5.	The patriarchs were jealous of Joseph. They sold him as a slave into Egypt. But God was with him. He rescued Joseph, gave him wisdom, and made him ruler over all of Egypt.	Gen. 37; 41:39-43 Acts 7:9-10
6.	Joseph revealed himself to his brothers and rescued them from the famine. Jacob and his whole family, about 75 people, went down to Egypt.	Gen. 42–46 Acts 7:11-14
7.	The time for God to fulfill His promise to Abraham grew near. The number of Israelites greatly increased in Egypt. A new king arose who did not know Joseph. He persecuted the Israelites.	Exod. 1:7-22 Acts 7:17-19
8.	Then Moses was born and hidden for 3 months. Outside, Pharaoh's daughter found him. She raised him as her own son. He was educated in all the wisdom of the Egyptians and was powerful in speech and action.	Exod. 2:1-10 Acts 7:20-22
9.	At age 40, Moses thought his own people would recognize that God was using him to rescue them. But they did not. They rejected him as their ruler and judge. He fled to Midian. There, God gave him two sons.	Exod. 2:11-22 Acts 7:23-29
10.	At age 80, an angel appeared to Moses at the burning bush. This is the same Moses the Israelites rejected. God Himself sent Moses to be their ruler and deliverer.	Exod. 3 Acts 7:30-36
11.	Moses promised that God would send a special prophet from among their own people.	Deut. 18:15, 18 Acts 7:37-38
12.	The Jewish fathers refused to obey Moses. Instead, they rejected him and turned their hearts back to Egypt. They made a gold calf and worshiped it!	Exod. 32 Acts 7:39-41
13.	God rejected them. He left them to worship their idols. Also, He promised to send them into exile beyond Babylon.	Amos 5:25-27 Acts 7:42-43
14.	The Israelites had the tent in the desert. This tent contained the Commandments. Moses made the tent by the pattern God gave to him. The tent remained until the time of David.	Exod. 25:8-40 Acts 7:44-45
15.	David desired to build a place for God to dwell. But Solomon built the temple. Still, the Most High does not live in houses built by humans. Heaven is His throne and earth His footstool. He created everything!	1 Kings 8:17; 6:1-38 Isa. 66:1-2 Acts 7:46-50

Figure 7.3   Fifteen historical facts in Stephen's speech

We have reviewed the historical facts of Stephen's speech. Next, we want to examine six truths woven into his message. We will consider three of these truths in this lesson, and three in the next lesson.

+ Stephen uses the round number of 400. Paul refers to a period of 430 years (Gal. 3:17). Paul seems to say the 430 years includes the time from the promises to the Law. God promised Abraham that his seed would be in bondage 400 years (Exod. 12:40-41). God renewed this promise to Jacob (Gen. 46:1-4). Thus Paul probably refers to the period from Jacob's promise to the Law.

A. God may use laypeople to bring change.

It appears that Stephen was the first believer to preach in a synagogue.[19] The members of the Synagogue of the Freedmen accused him. They said he spoke against the temple and the Law. *"They produced false witnesses, who testified, 'This fellow never stops speaking against this holy place and against the law'"* (Acts 6:13).

On the one hand, it is clear that the false witnesses lied about Stephen. On the other hand, Stephen did have some new ideas about the temple and the Law. Stephen understood the mission of Jesus better than the apostles understood it. Jesus chose the apostles. God ordained them as leaders. But Stephen had more insight than all of the twelve apostles had.

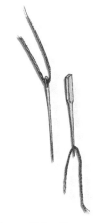

Figure 7.4 On a sewing machine, the thread and the point of the needle are on the same end.

In Acts 3 we saw that the apostles were still attending the temple services. Acts 21:17-26 confirms this. The Jerusalem believers were still living like they were under the Law. They were circumcising their sons. And they were still sacrificing animals. Likewise, Ananias was a Spirit-filled Jew. But he was living under the Law and was respected by all the Jews in Damascus (Acts 22:12). Today, we realize that Christ was the end of the Law (Rom. 10:4). We have the book of Hebrews. It makes it clear that temple sacrifices and earthly priests are no longer needed. But in Stephen's time, the Jerusalem church had not fully understood the work of Christ. They knew He was the Messiah. They knew He died for our sins and rose again. They knew He was Savior and Lord. But they did not clearly see how Jesus related to Moses. So they simply added the teachings of Jesus to those of Moses. Nor did they see how Jesus related to Gentiles. Why? What was keeping them from these insights? Their past way of thinking was controlling their views. They had believed in the temple and the Law for years. It was not easy for them to think in a new way.

Q 25 *How did Jerusalem believers relate Moses to Jesus?*

The longer one does something, the harder it is for that person to see a better way of doing it. Sometimes experience is good. But at other times experience is like a millstone tied to a person's neck. Experience can be like a prison that locks people in the past. The invention of the sewing machine was delayed for years. Why? Because people thought the eye of the needle must remain opposite the point of the needle. The phone companies did not invent the dial telephone. They were too used to dialing another way. It was a funeral director who thought of the idea of the dial telephone. People would not use the iron plow for years. Why? They were afraid it would poison the ground! Experience gives yesterday's answers to yesterday's problems. But the best leaders link creative thinking, current facts, and past experience.[20]

Q 26 *Is experience good or bad? Explain.*

Some call Stephen *the father of the book of Hebrews*. He was a Greek-speaking Jew. He was open to change. Unlike the Hebraic Jews, he did not have a commitment to tradition. Thus it was easier for him to see the big picture. Stephen understood that the temple and the Law were only temporary. They were things Jesus came to fulfill and change.

Q 27 *Why do you think some call Stephen the father of the book of Hebrews?*

A person's background shapes his or her values. The Church is richer because it includes many languages and cultures. It was the Grecian Jews, like Philip, who took the lead in cross-cultural evangelism. It was easier for them to see that the gospel was for Gentiles. Why? Because they were not prisoners of the past. The Greek influence had taught them to think in new ways.

Q 28 *Why was it easier for Grecian Jews to become the first cross-cultural evangelists?*

So what? We need to listen to those of different backgrounds from ours. The Church needs fresh insights from many nations and denominations. We also need the insights of new converts. They may have new ideas about how to do God's work. These ideas can enable the Church to expand. The old need the new, and the new need the old. We all need each other. The Church is a body, and all the parts have a purpose. Sometimes God brings new ideas through laypeople rather than leaders. Therefore, godly leaders are good listeners.

Q 29 *Why does the Church need the insights of various nations and people?*

The Maasai are a tribe in Kenya. They have large herds of cattle and live in remote places. When the grass or water dries up in one place, they move to another. Thus, an African proverb says, "The Maasai never live long at the same place." This proverb can encourage people to try new things and ideas.[21]

B. God works through change.

Q 30 *State 5 examples Stephen gave to show that God works through change.*

Stephen was full of wisdom. He wove his message into the history of Israel. In this way, he let history speak for him. His enemies thought the temple and the Law were permanent. They believed these things would never change. So Stephen gave five examples of God working through change.[22]

- In the beginning, God worked through men like Adam, Abel, Enoch, and Noah. But God changed His method. He decided to begin a new nation through one man. So God revealed Himself to Abraham (Acts 7:2-8). He called him to move from Mesopotamia to the Promised Land. Abraham changed locations. Thus he became the Father of the Jews. This was a big change in the way God related to people.
- Jacob and his twelve sons changed locations (Acts 7:9-16). This was a big surprise. But God helped them make the change.
- It was time for another change (Acts 7:17-43). Moses was born. He led the Israelites from Egypt back to Canaan! Many Israelites complained about the change!
- The fourth change was in regard to worship. The Israelites had sacrificed the Passover Lamb. Now, it was time for the Tabernacle (Acts 7:44-46). This tent was not permanent. It was moved from place to place. This emphasized that God changes locations.
- The temple was Stephen's fifth example of change. God allowed Solomon to build it (Acts 7:47). The temple was not God's home. It was only a symbol of His presence (Acts 7:48-50).

Q 31 *What 2 things does Stephen suggest that God might change?*

Stephen used five illustrations to suggest one point. God works through change. He changed many things in the past. Stephen suggested that the temple and the Law were not permanent. He suggested that God might make more changes.

Q 32 *What are some things the Church should begin planning to change?*

What kinds of changes does God want to make today? The Spirit must always be the One who leads us. But consider the following questions. Does Sunday school always have to be on Sunday morning? Should the Church be doing more to reach children? Does the Church always have to meet inside of a building? Do the standards for godly dress or hair ever change? Is preaching a sermon the best plan for every service? Are there more ways for laypeople to do God's work? What is the best way to reach neighbors who are unbelievers? Are we starting enough churches in the cities? How can we help our Bible school graduates start more churches? Should class time in Bible schools be used for lectures or discussions? What are some better ways for believers from different cultures to work together? Should we have more extension Bible schools? Does God allow believers to eat all foods? Is there a better way to create this book?

God is the same yesterday, today, and forever (Heb. 13:8; James 1:17). He is the same God. But He often changes the way He does things. Those who fear change fear the way God works. May He give us the grace to ask questions and allow new ideas. Try to add ten questions to the ones above. Remember, the truth will survive questioning!

C. God is too big to limit to one place.

Q 33 *Why did Stephen mention God's blessings in places like Shechem and Midian?*

The temple was in a special place. Jerusalem and Palestine were special places. But these were not the only places that were special to God. God pours out His blessings in many places. And God is too big to limit to one place. Stephen gave four examples to illustrate this truth.[23]

- Israel's father and patriarchs were blessed *outside* the land of Israel. Abraham was called in Mesopotamia. This is where he first met God. And God gave him promises *before* he lived in Haran (Acts 7:2-5). Likewise, God was with Joseph in Egypt (Acts 7:9-10). Also, Shechem was a worthy place to bury Jacob and his sons (Acts 7:15-16).

The Jewish unbelievers did not appreciate the good way Stephen spoke of Shechem. It was the capital of Samaria! And the Jews hated Samaritans! Again, Moses met with God in Midian (Acts 7:29-34). Stephen is careful to point out that God gave Moses two sons in Midian. Thus Jerusalem and Palestine are not the only places God likes. Mesopotamia, Egypt, Shechem, and Midian are all places special to God.

- The Law was given *outside* the land of Israel. Moses was in the desert when he received it (Acts 7:38).
- The Tabernacle was not built in Jerusalem. It was built in the desert. The Jews brought it with them when they came to Canaan (Acts 7:44-45).
- The temple was special. But it was not God's home. God did not live there! Stephen proved this by quoting Isaiah 66:1.

Q 34 *What was Stephen's point in saying the Law and Tabernacle were given outside Palestine?*

⁴⁸*"However, the Most High does not live in houses made by men. As the prophet says:* ⁴⁹*'Heaven is my throne, and the earth is my footstool. What kind of house will you build for me? says the Lord. Or where will my resting place be?* ⁵⁰*Has not my hand made all these things?'* " (Acts 7:48-50).

In other words, humans cannot build a house for God. We cannot tell God where He must dwell. The Creator creates His own place to live![24]

These four examples emphasize a point. It is not good to limit God to one location. God is bigger than the temple, Jerusalem, and Palestine.

How does this apply to believers today? For one thing, we should recognize that God loves people in all places. Also, we should not limit God's presence to a church building. The Bible teaches us to assemble together (Heb. 10:25). But a building is not the only place to meet with God. Too many believers wait to worship God until they enter a church building. God wants us to worship Him every day in every place. He invites us to sing and pray throughout the week. Those who seek God will find Him often outside the church building.

Q 35 *Should believers worship God at home and at work? Explain.*

Some believers have strange ideas. They talk holy in a church building. But outside the building, they act like God does not hear them. They honor God inside the church. But outside the building, they live like God does not see them. These believers are a lot like Stephen's enemies. They limit God to one special place! But acceptable worship must be in spirit and in truth (John 4:23). Worshiping God includes all that we do (Rom. 12:1-2).

Lesson 21

Stephen's Speech—Part 2 (Acts 7:1–8:1)

Goal: *Identify and apply 3 truths related to Stephen's speech and death.*

A. Children usually follow in the footsteps of their parents.

Why did Stephen review the history of Israel? What was his purpose? His purpose was to show a parallel. The Jewish leaders treated Jesus the same way some of the Old Testament Jews treated God's servants. Stephen told the Jewish leaders, *"You are just like your fathers"* (Acts 7:51). As the fathers rejected God, the children rejected God. Note this theme of rejection in Figure 7.5.

The greatest theme of Stephen's speech is rejection. Over and over some Jews resisted God and His Spirit. When people continue to reject God, their hearts become hard.[25] Then they do not hear God's voice clearly. Neither do they see spiritual truth.

Rejection	Acts
1. They rejected Joseph because they were jealous. But God was with him. He made him ruler over all Egypt.	7:1-16 (Note 7:9-10)
2. They rejected Moses whom God sent to be their ruler and deliverer.	7:17-39 (Note 7:23, 35, 39)
3. They rejected God and turned to idols. Therefore, God rejected them.	7:39-43
4. They rejected the Holy Spirit.	7:51
5. They rejected the Law and the Prophets.	7:52-53
6. They rejected Jesus.	7:52

Figure 7.5   Stephen emphasized that rejection was a habit of some Israelites.

Q 36 ➤ *In what way were the unbelieving Jews like their fathers?*

Q 37 ➤ *Give 2 examples of the greatest theme of Stephen's speech.*

Q 38 ➤ *Have the sins of your parents affected you? Explain.*

Q 39 ➤ *Do parents pass on sins to their children? Explain.*

[14] "*In them is fulfilled the prophecy of Isaiah: 'You will be ever hearing but never understanding; you will be ever seeing but never perceiving.* [15]*For this people's heart has become calloused; they hardly hear with their ears, and they have closed their eyes. Otherwise they might see with their eyes, hear with their ears, understand with their hearts and turn, and I would heal them'*" (Matt. 13:14-15).

Those who reject God separate themselves from His help and blessings. Rebellion against God is a road that leads straight to judgment.

It would be bad enough if the parents' sins affected only themselves. But parents have great influence over their children. Hannah, Samuel's mother, led him on the paths of righteousness (1 Sam. 2). From an early age she led him toward God. It was no accident that he served God all the days of his life. In contrast, Herodias, Salome's mother, led her away from God into sin (Matt. 14). Salome's mother caused her to have John murdered. It would not surprise us if Salome continued on the road to hell. It is the only road her mother ever showed her.

Some have asked about a generational curse. That is, they want to know if parents pass sins on to their children. For sure, each person chooses. Each person is responsible for his or her own sin. But the question still remains. Do parents pass on their sins to their children? No, parents do not transfer sins to their children. However, usually, children follow in the footsteps of their parents. Children, before they are old enough to choose well, imitate their parents. If Dad or Mom curses, the child will learn to curse. If Dad and Mom smoke or get drunk, the children will usually follow their examples. In fact, often, if a parent takes one step into the world, the child will take two. If Dad treats Mom with kindness, the son will learn to treat his wife that way. Children learn more from examples than words. One father told his child, "Do as I say, not as I do." But this is very hard for a child to do. Children look, talk, walk, and act like their parents. If Dad and Mom do not lead the children to God, who will lead them? Therefore, every parent should consider this. The destiny of the children is, to a large extent, in the hands of the parents. Stephen's words are usually true about children. *"You are just like your fathers"* (Acts 7:51).

In Christ, we have complete freedom from sins and spiritual bondage. Still, believers must depend on the Holy Spirit to avoid following the bad examples of ungodly parents.

A father and his young son were climbing a hill together. They came to a dangerous place. The father stopped to consider which way to go. The boy said, "Choose the best path, Dad. I'm following in your footsteps."[26]

B. We reflect what we gaze at (Acts 7:54-60).

Note the contrast between Stephen and his enemies. He was calm, loving, and filled with the Spirit. His face shone like an angel. His enemies were furious and filled with hate. They were gnashing their teeth. This means they were grinding their teeth together. Gnashing the teeth shows extreme emotion such as despair or rage (Luke 13:28; Job 16:9; Ps. 35:16). In this case, crunching their teeth together showed great hate. Likewise, their actions showed they hated him. They put their hands over their ears to shut out his words. They dragged him out of the city and began to stone him.

How was Stephen able to show love at such a time? He *"looked up"* (Acts 7:55). This is the key to showing love to those who hate us. And it was the Holy Spirit who enabled him to look up.

Q 40 ➤ *Do you tend to be rude to those who are rude to you? Explain.*

In many ways life is a mirror. It reflects back to us what we focus on. When others are ugly to us, we are tempted to gaze at or think about them. The fleshly response is to react to those who hate or hurt us. It is normal to mirror back to others the way they treat us. But the Spirit helped Stephen look away from his enemies. He looked up to heaven. This is the key to not returning evil for evil.

43 "You have heard that it was said, 'Love your neighbor and hate your enemy.'
44But I tell you: Love your enemies and pray for those who persecute you, 45that
you may be sons of your Father in heaven" (Matt. 5:43-45).

How shall we obey Matthew 5:44? How shall we love our enemies? How shall we be able to pray for those who attack and persecute us? Stephen showed us the way. He did not focus on those who were hurting him. Instead, he looked up! Then the love of God flowed through him to his enemies. He prayed for God to forgive them (Acts 7:60). His words remind us of Jesus on the cross (Luke 23:34).

 Q 41 *What is the key to being kind to those who offend us?*

Mark and Neil are believers. But they do not like each other. Neil said, "I hear that the New Jerusalem has twelve gates. There, if I see Mark coming in one gate, I will go out another!" With this attitude, Neil may never see the New Jerusalem.

Are you hungry for more knowledge? Do you long to know the deep secrets of God's Word? Good. But there is something more important than more knowledge. Have you learned Stephen's secret? Do you practice loving those who are rude to you? To learn this one lesson is more important than adding an entire book of knowledge!

Two believers talked. The younger, named Jerry, was angry with Edward. Edward did not think he had done wrong. Still, he asked Jerry to forgive him. He walked humbly and showed love to Jerry. Jerry agreed and left. Immediately, he began to act like Edward had refused to repent. Jerry called several other believers. Together, they came to the older believer's house. All of them began to criticize and accuse him. The older believer listened. Their words stung like cords of a whip. At first, he felt angry. He thought of many things to say. But he sat there, praying silently. As his spirit looked up, tears began to roll down his cheeks. Their words hurt. Yet he felt that the Lord did not want him to defend himself. Jerry was young and under a lot of stress. After about an hour, all the believers left. Edward cried for a while and continued to pray for several days. When he thought about their words, he felt bitter and angry. But when he prayed, he felt love and peace. In time, God healed his wounds. Over the next few months, God convicted each of the other believers. One by one they came to Edward and repented. Edward thanked God for helping him to imitate Stephen. It takes two to fight. And when believers return evil for evil, the damage may affect many. When two bulls fight, the grass suffers!

Q 42 *Do you think Edward chose the right path? Explain.*

C. God uses problems as a source of blessings.

Evil is not God's will. But He allows people to choose good or evil. Evil causes many problems that are not God's will. Still, God uses these problems to bring good. Acts 6–8:3 gives three examples showing that blessings come through problems.

Stephen's death is the *first* example. He died full of the Spirit. His final words were *"Lord do not hold this sin against them"* (Acts 7:60). But the greatest blessing of his earthly life came as he *"fell asleep"* (Acts 7:60). He *"looked up to heaven and saw the glory of God."* And he saw *"Jesus standing at the right hand of the Father"* (Acts 7:55-56). Other passages in Scripture speak of Jesus sitting at the Father's right hand (Mark 14:62; Luke 22:69; Heb. 1:3, 13; 8:1; 10:12; 12:2).+ Jesus sat down because His work was finished. But as Stephen was dying, Jesus stood up! Out of courtesy, we rise as a visitor enters the room. Likewise, it appears that Jesus stood to welcome Stephen into heaven.[27] The Lord Himself arose to welcome the first Christian martyr to heaven. Thus a great blessing came through Stephen's problem.

**Figure 7.6
Angry Jews stoned
Stephen, who was full of
the Holy Spirit.**

+ Note that these passages help support the doctrine of the Trinity. The Father and the Son are separate persons. Imagine a man trying to sit down to the right of himself!

"Blessed are those who are persecuted because of righteousness, for theirs is the kingdom of heaven" (Matt. 5:10).

Q 43 *Give an example showing that blessings come through problems.*

Saul is a *second* example that blessings come out of problems. We noted that some members of the Synagogue of the Freedmen came from Cilicia. The city of Tarsus is in Cilicia. Therefore, it is possible that Saul of Tarsus heard Stephen preach. We are sure that Saul heard Stephen's message. He saw Stephen's face glowing like an angel. It was Saul who kept the garments of those who stoned Stephen (Acts 7:58; 8:1). Soon after, Luke records the conversion of Saul (Acts 9:1-19). On the road to Damascus Jesus asked him a question.

"We all fell to the ground, and I heard a voice saying to me in Aramaic, 'Saul, Saul, why do you persecute me? It is hard for you to kick against the goads'" (Acts 26:14).

Figure 7.7   Farmers poked stubborn oxen with a goad.

Q 44 *How was Stephen's life like a goad to Saul?*

Notice what Jesus said about goads. The goads were sharp sticks. These were used to poke stubborn oxen. Then the oxen would continue moving. So what is the point? Jesus used Stephen's life as a goad for Saul. Saul was like a stubborn ox. He kicked against his master. Still, the testimonies of believers like Stephen made a mark on Saul. It was not easy for Saul to forget Stephen's glowing face, powerful life, wise words, and forgiving spirit. Stephen's death was a link to the conversion of the greatest apostle. Sometimes a person's death is like a seed. It brings a great harvest. Saul won thousands to Christ. And he wrote over a third of the New Testament. In heaven, Stephen will be one of the first people that Saul thanks. What a blessing came through Stephen's problem!

Luke gives us a *third* example of how blessings come through problems. This example comes in Acts 8. We will study this more in the next chapter. Still, we will mention this third example. Stephen's death marked the beginning of a great persecution. This persecution scattered most of the believers from Jerusalem. As they went, they shared the good news about Jesus. Thus Stephen's death marked the beginning of a new period. Persecution caused the Church to expand greatly. None of us enjoys problems. But we give thanks that God uses problems to bring blessings.

Test Yourself: Circle the letter by the *best* completion to each question or statement.

1. The first seven deacons included
a) men who were all Hebraic Jews.
b) men who were all Grecian Jews.
c) some Hebraic, some Grecian Jews.
d) some Jews, and some Gentiles.

2. In solving the problem of Acts 6, the apostles
a) had a private meeting to solve the problem.
b) rebuked those who complained of a problem.
c) allowed believers to help solve the problem.
d) defended themselves and prayed about the problem.

3. Leaders who punish those who want change are like
a) Stephen.
b) Pharaoh.
c) Moses.
d) Herod.

4. When Stephen's enemies met wisdom greater than theirs, they
a) laughed at it.
b) accepted it.
c) rejected it.
d) marveled at it.

5. Which of the following is TRUE about Stephen?
a) He had more insights than the apostles had.
b) He was one of the twelve apostles.
c) He spoke against the teachings of the apostles.
d) He was older than most of the apostles.

6. Stephen's speech emphasized that
a) God desired a tent, not a temple.
b) Moses was the greatest prophet.
c) the temple was God's dwelling place.
d) God works through change.

7. Stephen shows that God blesses in many places by referring to
a) Shechem and Midian.
b) Assyria and Babylon.
c) Jordan and Canaan.
d) Dan and Beersheba.

8. The greatest theme of Stephen's speech is
a) the Holy Spirit.
b) rejection.
c) temptation.
d) salvation.

9. Stephen's speech shows us that
a) parents pass on their sins to their children.
b) without a vision the people perish.
c) children usually follow the footsteps of their parents.
d) people usually recognize the leaders God sends.

10. What blessing resulted from Stephen's death?
a) The government stopped religious persecution.
b) The Church comforted Stephen's family.
c) Stephen's enemies repented of their sins.
d) A great persecution scattered believers.

 Essay Test Topics: Write 50-100 words on each of these goals that you studied in this chapter.

Stephen Among the Seven (Acts 6:1-15)

Goal: *Contrast the way the apostles and Stephen's enemies handled conflict. Compare these methods with yours and those of leaders you know.*

Stephen's Speech—Part 1 (Acts 7:1-53)

Goal: *Identify and apply what Stephen's speech says about change and God's location.*

Stephen's Speech—Part 2 (Acts 7:1–8:1)

Goal: *Identify and apply 3 truths related to Stephen's speech and death.*

Chapter 8:
The Ministries of Philip and Saul
(Acts 8:1–9:31)

Introduction

Hogwanobiayo was sick in Papua New Guinea. He was less than 50 years old. But his head and bones ached as if he were older. He had no energy. Dan Shaw was a missionary working with Wycliffe Bible Translators. Hogwanobiayo adopted Dan as one of his *little brothers*. The two men often worked together translating the Bible.

Figure 8.1   The conversion of Saul

Hogwanobiayo tried to overcome the sickness. He slept in various places. He hoped this would prevent a spirit from attacking him at night. He tried a paste made from local herbs. He paid a local witch doctor to contact the spirits. But none of these efforts helped. Instead, Hogwanobiayo got worse. Even medicine from his little brother, Dan, did not help. He lay in bed at home, weak with chills and fever. One day Dan brought him a portion of Scripture to check. It included John 5:1-15. Dan read. Hogwanobiayo was very still. He was hearing about the man who had been ill for 38 years. Suddenly Hogwanobiayo cried out, "That's me! That's me! That's me!" Dan asked, "What do you mean?" Hogwanobiayo answered, "He's been sick for a long time. He's tried everything. And I've tried everything. Do you think Jesus can heal me too? I want you to ask Jesus to heal me."

Dan thought, "Why me? I'm just a Baptist from a small town." But Hogwanobiayo insisted. He said that Dan was his little brother. And that it was the brother's responsibility to help another brother get healed. So Dan prayed a short prayer. They saw no change. Dan continued to pray for several days with his wife. Then Hogwanobiayo began to testify that he was healed. People saw him walking around with new energy. He was claiming that Jesus had healed him. Dan expressed doubt. Hogwanobiayo touched his cane to Dan's ribs. "Don't you believe?" he asked the missionary. With tears Dan confessed, "Yes, I believe!" As a result of this healing, the whole village was more open to the gospel.[1]

Lessons:

Philip's Ministry to the Samaritans (Acts 8:1-25)
Goal: *Explain 4 principles of evangelism in Acts 8. Evaluate your church and ministry in relation to these principles.*

Philip's Ministry to the Ethiopian (Acts 8:26-40)
Goal A: *State and apply 2 truths about God's concern for the lost.*
Goal B: *Analyze and apply the relationship between reading and understanding.*

Saul's Conversion and Early Ministry (Acts 9:1-31)
Goal: *Identify and apply 6 truths related to Saul's conversion and early ministry.*

 Key Words

Samaria	Samaritans	Ethiopian eunuch
evangelism	Simon the sorcerer	Damascus

Lesson 22 **Philip's Ministry to the Samaritans (Acts 8:1-25)**

Goal: *Explain 4 principles of evangelism in Acts 8. Evaluate your church and ministry in relation to these principles.*

Setting

Remember Luke's greatest purpose. It is to show how the gospel spread from Jerusalem to Rome by the power of the Spirit. Acts 1–7 tells how the gospel spread in Jerusalem. That is where Jesus said the disciples would begin to witness. Recall that Acts 1:8 gives a good outline of Acts.

"But you will receive power when the Holy Spirit comes on you; and you will be my witnesses in Jerusalem, and in all Judea and Samaria, and to the ends of the earth" (Acts 1:8).

Jesus said the Holy Spirit would give believers power to witness. They would testify about Him in Jerusalem, Judea, Samaria, and the ends of the earth (Acts 1:8). The Church had started to witness. They had taken step one. But they were still in Jerusalem.

Part	Place to Witness	Chapters in Acts
1	Jerusalem	1–7
2	Judea and Samaria	8–12
3	The whole earth	13–28

Figure 8.2   Acts 1:8 is a good outline of the book of Acts.

Acts 8 is a key chapter. It is a chapter about *evangelism. Evangelism* comes from a Greek word that means "to tell the good news." To evangelize is to tell someone the good news of Jesus Christ. Acts 1–7 shows us how the good news spread in Jerusalem. Acts 8 tells how believers began to evangelize in Judea and Samaria. Luke does not have time to tell about every believer. In Acts, he summarizes 30 years of Church history. So he chooses only a few examples. In Acts 6–7 he told us about Stephen. In Acts 8 Luke focuses on Philip. Read Acts 8:1-25.

The chart that follows shows several principles of evangelism in Acts 8.

Principle of Evangelism	Scripture
1. God uses circumstances to spread His kingdom.	Acts 8:1-4
2. Every believer is a witness for Christ.	Acts 8:1, 4
3. The Word is the seed.	Acts 8:4
4. One reaps where another has already sown.[+]	John 4:34-38; Acts 8:5, 40; 9:32-42
5. Believers should witness first in Jerusalem, in their own culture.	Acts 1:8; and Acts 1–8
6. The gospel is for the whole world.	Acts 1:8; 8:4
7. God cares about a multitude or one person.	Acts 8:5-6, 26-29
8. Miraculous signs help people accept the gospel.	Acts 8:6, 13
9. God rewards those who seek Him.	Acts 8:26-40
10. New believers need to be baptized in water and the Spirit.	Acts 8:12-13, 38
11. God guides Spirit-filled believers to witness for Him.	Acts 8:4, 8, 29
12. Those who receive Jesus Christ find great joy.	Acts 8:8, 39

Figure 8.3   Twelve principles of evangelism in Acts 8

It would take too long to discuss all of the principles of evangelism in Acts 8. We looked at principle eight in chapter 6, Lesson 17. In this chapter, we will focus on six principles from Figure 8.3. We will study four principles in this lesson and two in the next lesson.

[+] Philip reaped where Jesus had sown earlier. Peter reaped where Philip had sown earlier.

A. God uses circumstances to spread His kingdom.

God has a plan. And He uses events on earth to fulfill His plan (Eph. 1:11). God sees events on earth like pieces of a puzzle. He knows how they can fit together in the big picture. To us, events on earth may be like letters of the alphabet. But God is able to use events to make words and sentences.

Many things on earth do not make sense to us. Why? We do not see how they can relate to the plan of God. For example, consider the death of Stephen. The Bible says believers *"mourned deeply"* as they buried him (Acts 8:2). He was such a godly man. He brought health and healing to many. The Church was able to trust him with offerings. Perhaps many believers wondered why God let others murder Stephen. They *"mourned deeply."* But notice the contrast in their mourning and the *joy* in Samaria (Acts 8:8).

God had a plan to use Stephen's death. He took Stephen to a better place to live. And as a result of Stephen's death, a great persecution broke out.

And Saul was there, giving approval to his death. On that day a great persecution broke out against the church at Jerusalem, and all except the apostles were scattered throughout Judea and Samaria (Acts 8:1).

Q 1 *How did God use Stephen's death to fulfill His will?*

Stephen's death was like a match. It started a great fire of persecution. This fire became so hot that most believers fled.[+] But look what happened as believers fled.

[4]Those who had been scattered preached the word wherever they went. [5]Philip went down to a city in Samaria and proclaimed the Christ there. [6]When the crowds heard Philip and saw the miraculous signs he did, they all paid close attention to what he said. [7]With shrieks, evil spirits came out of many, and many paralytics and cripples were healed. [8]So there was great joy in that city (Acts 8:4-8).

The mourning in Jerusalem led to great joy in Samaria. Sinners who find Christ find great joy (Acts 8:8, 39). God used the persecution to scatter believers. And He used the scattered believers to witness about Jesus to the lost. God uses circumstances to spread His kingdom.

The persecution of believers in Jerusalem gives us mixed feelings. On the one hand, we are sorry that many lost their homes, lands, and possessions. A few, like Stephen, even lost their lives. We grieve with those who grieve. On the other hand, we rejoice with those who rejoice (Rom. 12:15). The joy in Samaria resulted from the tears in Jerusalem. Our temporary tears are a small price to pay for one sinner to find eternal joy.

Joseph's brothers sold him as a slave. But Joseph realized it was a part of God's plan. He said that it was God, not his brothers, who sent him to Egypt (Gen. 45:7-8). After his father's death, Joseph encouraged his fearful brothers. *"You intended to harm me, but God intended it for good to accomplish what is now being done, the saving of many lives"* (Gen. 50:20). Likewise, those who killed Stephen wanted to harm the Church. But God used their persecution to save many lives.

Q 2 *Give an example showing that God paints with dark colors as well as light.*

What an encouraging truth! God uses the good things of life to build His kingdom. These may include healings, miracles, and good deeds. But God is not limited. He uses all circumstances, both good and bad, to fulfill His plan. A skilled artist uses both the dark and bright colors. God paints with many colors.

B. Every believer is a witness for Christ.

The apostles remained in Jerusalem. All the rest of the believers were scattered (Acts 8:1). And those scattered *"preached the word wherever they went"* (Acts 8:4). They *preached.* This does not mean they prepared and preached sermons. The word *preach* means "to tell or declare." Today, we tend to think of pastors or ministers as

---

+ Only the apostles stayed in Jerusalem. It was dangerous to stay there. But it appears that they felt it was necessary. Perhaps other believers felt more secure because the apostles remained together, and in Jerusalem.

the only ones who preach. But preaching takes place whenever any believer shares the good news.

Where did the believers preach? That is, where did they tell about Jesus? Did they look for a pulpit? No! They looked for a person. It is time for us to get back to the real meaning of preaching. Today there is too much emphasis on listening to sermons in church buildings. God wants all believers to tell others about Jesus. He wants us all to preach the good news. We do not need to create sermons. There are already enough sermons! The great need today is for people to preach without pulpits and without sermons!

Q 3 ↗ Should every believer preach the Word? Explain.

Some believers think preaching is the job of only the pastor. They seem to think they pay him to tell others about Jesus. But the Holy Spirit wants all believers to tell others about Christ. Sinners expect pastors to preach. So they avoid them and do not pay much attention to them. But when a plumber talks about Jesus, sinners pay attention. When a farmer, a nurse, a doctor, a housewife, a student, or any layperson preaches, sinners do not expect it. It surprises them. So they pay attention. That is why preaching outside the church often helps more sinners than the preaching in the church.

Q 4 ↗ Why does the preaching of a layperson often help more sinners than a pastor's preaching?

Under the Old Testament, there were only a few priests. These served the people. But the New Testament is different. God wants every believer to be a priest (Rev. 1:6). Sinners seldom enter a church building. This includes the sinners that live or work around you. You may not consider yourself to be a very good preacher or priest. But you may be the only one who ever tells them about Jesus. You do not need to be a good preacher to be the best one they ever hear.

We thank God for pastors. They are one of God's gifts to the Church. They are shepherds of God's flock. But it is not the shepherds who give birth. It is the sheep!

Philip was not an apostle. He was not a pastor. He was only a deacon. He was an honest believer who was filled with the Spirit. He was willing to work. So they chose him to serve at the tables. In the beginning Philip probably had no dreams about ministry. Samaria was not his target. But he let the wind of the Spirit blow where it wanted to blow. He worked where there was a need. And as he served, his ability to serve increased.[2] God adds to the diligent.

Q 5 ↖ What happens to the abilities of those who serve? Explain.

A bicycle is easier to steer if it is moving. Likewise, a believer who is working for God is easier to guide. Do what the Spirit leads you to do. Talk about Jesus when the Spirit leads you. Then God will guide you to fulfill His will in your life. It does not matter whether you win a city or help only one person. The important thing is that you plant the seed. Be a witness for Jesus. Preach the Word day by day. Leave the results to God. Some of the seed will bring a harvest (Matt. 13:8).

The Church's work today is too much like a football match. Thousands of people gather and watch a few people on the field. The watchers cheer when a player does well. They groan when a player gets hurt. This is acceptable for sports fans. But God wants believers to stop watching and get in the game. God's team needs help. There are not enough players on the field!

Q 6 ↗ How is the Church's work today too much like a football match?

C. The gospel is for every person in the world.

Believers in Jerusalem started witnessing in the right place. Every believer should begin witnessing in his or her own culture. This is a principle of evangelism. It is easier to share the good news with those of our own culture. All believers should start witnessing in their Jerusalem. But our witness for Jesus should not stop at home.

Jesus said the gospel is for everyone, not just those of our culture. He told the disciples to preach the good news in all nations (Matt. 28:19-20). He said believers would be witnesses in Jerusalem, Judea, Samaria, and to the whole earth.

Q 7 ➤ *Why was it hard for Jews to witness to Samaritans?*

Jerusalem and Judea sounded good to the Jewish believers. But the Jews did not like the Samaritans. As John told us, *"Jews do not associate with Samaritans"* (John 4:9). In fact, Jews went out of their way to avoid even traveling through Samaria. In Scripture, moving toward Jerusalem is always up. Notice that Philip went down to a city in Samaria (Acts 8:5).

Samaria was a province about 30 miles (45 km) north of Judea. We are not sure which city Philip went to. It may have been the capital city, also named Samaria. Or Philip may have gone to Shechem.[3] The name Shechem was also a bad memory of Jews. Recall that the man named Shechem defiled Dinah, the daughter of Jacob (Gen. 34:1-5). The man, Shechem, was probably named after the town of Shechem in Samaria.[4] Wherever Philip went in Samaria, the Jews did not like it!

Q 8 ➤ *Why did the Jews refuse to associate with Samaritans?*

The Jews believed all Samaritans were unclean.[5] Why? The Samaritans were only part Jewish. Assyria captured the northern ten tribes of Israel in 722 B.C. As time went on, some of the Jews married with captives from other nations.[6] These mixed marriages had mixed beliefs. Jews of Jerusalem believed Samaritans had rejected Moses (See John 8:48). That is why Jews of Jerusalem destroyed Shechem in the second century before Christ. The Jewish book of Maccabees says, "God abhors those in Shechem."[7]

Samaritans followed the law of Moses much like the Jews did. But they said animal sacrifices should be on Mount Gerizim, not at the temple in Jerusalem. Joshua stood on Mount Gerizim and spoke of blessings of obedience (Josh. 8:30-35). Jotham once stood halfway up this mountain and spoke to the men of Shechem (Judg. 9:7). Even today, the Samaritans worship on Mount Gerizim, calling it Jebel et Tor. They claim it is Mount Moriah, where Abraham went to sacrifice Isaac.[8]

Q 9 ➤ *Which tribe or type of people do you have the most prejudice toward? Why?*

This background about Samaria helps us understand Acts 8:5. One might say it took persecution to cause Philip to go there.[9] And it took the Holy Spirit to cause him to preach there. Many believers have some form of prejudice. And it is not easy to conquer.

John was a missionary in South India. He was praying about a hard question. There were many levels of people in India. Each level of society was called a *caste. At the highest level were the *Hindu priests, called the *Brahmans. They performed duties and sacrifices for those who came to the Hindu temples. Below the priests were many other levels or castes. In descending order, these castes included rulers, businessmen, farmers, and workers. At the bottom of the caste ladder was a group called the *Untouchables*. They were considered unclean. They did work such as making leather from dead animals or cleaning restrooms. This allowed other people to remain clean.

Hindus believe that each person lives many lives. They think a person may live one life as a dog or a snake. Then at death, they believe the person returns to live life in another form, perhaps as a person or an animal. Hinduism teaches that people are not equal. Hindu scriptures say that each person deserves to live at the level he or she is born. They say this level results from the good or bad done in a previous life. Thus Hindus believe that the Untouchables did evil in their past lives. Hindus teach that a person should not try to move up to a better level during life. Each person should patiently live at one level until death. Then, perhaps he or she will be born into a higher level.

But the Bible teaches that all people are equal in God's eyes. In Christ, rich and poor, free and slaves, men and women are all equal heirs (Gal. 3:28). On the other hand, Paul encouraged believing slaves to remain slaves. He said they should continue serving their masters. And, he said their believing masters should be fair (Eph. 6:5-9).

So what was the hard question John was praying about? Several families from the Farmer caste had come to Christ. These were from a high caste. They had been baptized and had built a small church. A year later he preached in a village outside the town. The Untouchables lived there. At the end of his message, several asked him if the Untouchables could be saved. John said, "Yes! Jesus died to save all people." Then six families from the Untouchables accepted Christ. These were from the group that worked with leather. John was very happy. Then he asked believers of the Farmer caste to welcome the Untouchables into their church. They were shocked! This would make the believers from the Farmer caste unclean. Then their friends and family would no longer visit them or eat with them. The Jews did not associate with the Samaritans. And the Farmer caste did not associate with the Untouchables. The Farmer caste believers said they would leave the church if the Untouchables came in. Likewise, other people from higher castes would not like mixing with the Untouchables. So John prayed. Should he ask the Untouchables to have their own, separate church? Then he could try to bring unity in time. Or, should he insist that believers are all one in Christ?[10]

Q 10 Should John ask the Untouchables to have their own separate church? Explain.

D. New believers need to be baptized in water and the Spirit.

Some believers act like baptism in water is not necessary. Julius accepted Jesus as Savior. This new believer was 18 years old. But he did not get baptized in water until he was 32! Then he was baptized with his daughter. The pastor asked Julius why he waited so long to be baptized. Julius said he knew each believer should be baptized. But he just never got around to it.

Baptism in water is a command (Matt. 28:19; Mark 16:16). If a person refuses to be baptized, that believer is disobeying the Lord. It is one of the first steps of obedience a new believer takes. Parents enjoy watching a child take its first steps. Likewise, God enjoys watching His new children take their first steps.

Q 11 Do you think one who refuses to be baptized is a true follower of Jesus? Explain.

If you accept Christ when you are nailed to a cross, do not worry about being baptized. God will understand (Luke 23:39-43). But God commands believers in normal circumstances to be baptized. Figure 8.4 summarizes water baptisms in Acts. Notice that all of these believers were baptized in water soon after they accepted Jesus.

Those Baptized in Water	Acts
3,000 new believers at Pentecost	2:41
Samaritan believers	8:12-13, 16
The Ethiopian eunuch	8:36
Saul of Tarsus	9:18
Cornelius and his household	10:47-48
Lydia and her household	16:15
The Philippian jailer and his household	16:33
Corinthian believers	18:8
Ephesian believers	19:5

Figure 8.4   Water baptisms in Acts

Acts shows that the early church emphasized water baptism. We are saved by the blood of Jesus, and not by water baptism. Nevertheless, water baptism is very important. Those who refuse to be baptized in water should not plan on going to heaven. Water baptism is not the only step of obedience. But it is one of the first steps in walking with Jesus.

Many in Samaria, including Simon, believed. They accepted Jesus as Savior and Lord. Then they were baptized in water into the name of the Lord Jesus (Acts 8:12-13, 16). It is helpful to compare Acts 8:16 with Matthew 28:19. Together, these verses give us a more complete teaching on baptism. Mature believers realize that it is wise to compare Scripture with Scripture. Believers are baptized into the name of the Father, the Son, and the Holy Spirit. This shows we are under the authority of the Trinity.

Q 12 Why should we compare Acts 8:16 with Matthew 28:19?

The Samaritan believers had believed and been baptized. This shows us they were saved (Acts 16:30-33). Their names were in the Lamb's book of life (Rev. 21:27). Still, God had more for them. They lacked the power that God wanted to give them to witness. They had been baptized in water. But they needed the baptism in the Spirit.

Q 13 Are believers who have not been baptized in the Spirit saved? Explain.

Recall what Peter said about the relationship of water baptism and the Spirit baptism. Usually, baptism in the Spirit comes after a person repents and is baptized in water (Acts 2:38). The Jerusalem crowd did not understand how believers could speak in new languages. Peter explained it to them. He told them to repent and be baptized. Then they could receive the same gift of the Holy Spirit.

On the one hand, it is the Spirit who draws us to Christ. And it is the Spirit who brings the presence of Jesus into all who repent. Thus all new believers have the Spirit in their lives (Rom. 8:9). On the other hand, God wants to fill us with more of the Spirit's power. The first time the Spirit fills believers is referred to as the baptism in the Spirit (Acts 1:4-5). There is only one baptism in the Spirit. But there are many fillings. He gives us new power as we grow and have new needs. Both the Scriptures and 500 million Pentecostals and Charismatics testify that this is true. We discussed this in chapter 3, Lesson 7 of this book.

Some believers stumble over Acts 8:16.[11] They find this verse amazing or extraordinary.[12]

> [14]*When the apostles in Jerusalem heard that Samaria had accepted the word of God, they sent Peter and John to them.* [15]*When they arrived, they prayed for them that they might receive the Holy Spirit,* [16]*because the Holy Spirit had not yet come upon any of them; they had simply been baptized into the name of the Lord Jesus* (Acts 8:14-16).

The apostles prayed that the Samaritans would receive the Holy Spirit in the same way the 120 received Him. They wanted the Holy Spirit to come upon the Samaritans as He came on the disciples at Pentecost.

The experience of the Samaritan believers was not extraordinary or unusual to the apostles. It was the same experience! The apostles received the Spirit's fullness after they believed. All of the 120 had already believed in Christ before they were baptized in the Spirit (Acts 2:4). Likewise, the twelve at Ephesus had the same experience. They believed and were baptized. Afterward Paul laid his hands upon them and prayed. Then they were filled with the Holy Spirit (Acts 19:1-7). The baptism in the Holy Spirit normally comes after water baptism. The only exception noted in the New Testament is Acts 10:44-48. Believers of the household of Cornelius in Caesarea were baptized in the Spirit before water baptism! This is unusual. It is different from all other cases stated in the New Testament. Why should we call the Samaritan pattern unusual? Believers in Jerusalem, Samaria, and Ephesus all received the Spirit in the same pattern. About 500 million Spirit-filled believers today can testify the same way! And these are adult church members. How many children have been filled with the Spirit just like the Samaritans received? Perhaps a billion more! We know the Pentecostal experience at Samaria is biblical. But how many Pentecostals do there need to be before people will say their experience is usual? The baptism in the Holy Spirit after conversion is only unusual to those who have not received it! It is normal in the New Testament. And it is normal for the millions who have received the precious gift of the Spirit!

Tony prayed at the altar. He had received Jesus as Savior and been baptized in water. Now he was seeking to be baptized in the Holy Spirit. Tony was hungry for all that God had for him. As he prayed, he felt the presence of God in a powerful way. Great joy filled his heart. He told his pastor that he thought he had just been baptized in the Holy Spirit. Tony's pastor smiled. He was glad to see Tony receiving the blessing of God. Still, he encouraged Tony to keep seeking more of God. The pastor told Tony to expect to speak in a new language. He said God would fill Tony like He did believers at Jerusalem, Samaria, Caesarea, and Ephesus.

Philip could have prayed for the new believers to be filled with the Holy Spirit. But remember that they were Samaritans. The Jewish believers would have doubts about their salvation. There was the need for the Jerusalem church to accept and welcome Samaritans. Philip wisely waited for the Jerusalem church to take the first step. Soon, the good news about Samaria reached Jerusalem. Jewish believers must have been amazed. Even Samaritans could be saved! The apostles did not waste time. They acted at once. The Samaritans had accepted Jesus. Now, they needed to take the next step. They needed to be filled with the Holy Spirit.

Q 14 What did the apostles want for the new believers in Samaria?

Q 15 Give 3 examples in Acts showing that being filled with the Spirit comes after being saved.

Q 16 Do you agree with Tony's pastor? Explain.

The Samaritans received the Spirit when Peter and John prayed for them (Acts 8:17). Even Simon could see they had received. He saw some kind of evidence. How did he know they had received? It must have been something more than a bigger smile on their faces.[13] Scholars of various denominations think the Samaritans spoke in tongues.[14] Tongues seems likely by comparing other places in Acts that tell about the baptism in the Spirit (Acts 2:4; 10:46; 19:6). Simon was certain they had received the Holy Spirit. He offered money to pass the Spirit along through prayers. He had not offered money for the power to cast out demons or heal cripples (Acts 8:6-7, 13, 19). Therefore, it is likely that he heard the Samaritan believers speaking in new languages.

Q 17 ↖ How do you think Simon knew the Samaritans had received the Spirit?

Simon had become a believer. Philip was a man full of the Spirit. He would not have baptized Simon unless the former sorcerer was sincere. But Simon was still in bondage to his old way of thinking. For years he had been the center of attention. His evil ministry had been his way of getting money. Jesus had set the Samaritans free. Simon was bitter about losing his old ministry. So he offered to pay money for a new ministry. Peter told him his heart was not right for ministry (Acts 8:20-23). So Peter urged Simon to repent. He said that *perhaps* God would forgive Simon (Acts 8:22). Peter did not doubt that God would forgive. God always forgives those who confess and turn away from their sins (1 John 1:9). But Peter was not sure Simon would truly repent.[15] We hope Simon repented and was baptized in the Spirit.

Q 18 ↗ Why did Peter use the word "perhaps" in Acts 8:22?

As we leave this lesson, do not miss Acts 8:25. Peter and John have learned to love the Samaritans more, and include them. As these apostles returned to Jerusalem, they preached in many Samaritan villages. Praise the Lord! Their hearts had been opened! These apostles did not lead the way to the Samaritans. But they quickly learned to follow a deacon's example! Peter is not yet ready to witness to a Gentile like Cornelius. That is still down the road (Acts 10). But he is halfway there. The Spirit is patient with us. He helps us take small steps toward those of other cultures.[16]

Q 19 ↗ Was Peter ready to witness to a person like Cornelius? Explain.

Q 20 ↖ Are you ready to witness to those of other cultures? Explain.

Lesson 23 Philip's Ministry to the Ethiopian (Acts 8:26-40)
Goal A: State and apply 2 truths about God's concern for the lost.
Goal B: Analyze and apply the relationship between reading and understanding.

Setting

Philip was rejoicing in Samaria. The kingdom of God was expanding in a great new way. The gospel had broken through the boundary of Judea. The light was shining in the darkness of Samaria. Demons were fleeing. Healed cripples were dancing! Many new believers were worshiping God. What a wonderful place to be!

But remember the lesson Luke wrote in his first book. *"There will be more rejoicing in heaven over one sinner who repents than over ninety-nine righteous people who do not need to repent"* (Luke 15:7). Luke spent an entire chapter illustrating God's love for the lost (Luke 15).

The Samaritans were full of the Spirit. But an Ethiopian *eunuch was empty. And the Good Shepherd leaves the 99 to find the one lost sheep. Therefore, God had a new task for Philip. The Church is learning that the gospel is for everyone. From Philip's ministry, let us look at two truths about God's concern for the lost.

A. God cares about a multitude or one person.

[26]*Now an angel of the Lord said to Philip, "Go south to the road— the desert road—that goes down from Jerusalem to Gaza."* [27]*So he started out, and on his way he met an Ethiopian eunuch, an important official in charge of all the treasury of Candace, queen of the Ethiopians. This man had gone to Jerusalem to worship* (Acts 8:26-27).

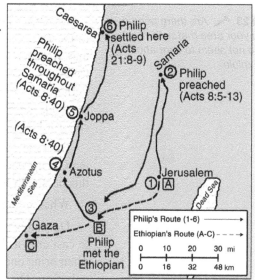

Figure 8.5 Philip's journeys

Q 21 ➤ *Why would we not expect Luke to tell a story about an Ethiopian?*

Luke's purpose in Acts is to show the spread of the gospel from Jerusalem to Rome by the Spirit. Luke had room to tell about only a few things in Acts. He had 30 years of history to cover in just a few pages. And Ethiopia is not on the path from Jerusalem to Rome. It is the opposite direction. Still, the Spirit would not allow Luke to leave out this one story. It takes Luke in the opposite direction from Rome and Luke's theme. But it illustrates the greatest theme in the Bible. God searches for those who search for Him. He looks for the hungry heart. He listens for the slightest whisper of one seeking Him. Is there a lost one reaching out to God? Then God will find that person. For our heavenly Father is not willing that even one should perish, but that all should come to Him and repent (Matt. 18:14; 2 Pet. 3:9).

A building crashed in Latin America. Several people were killed, but two young men were alive beneath the stones. They could not get out. For days they lay trapped, unable to move. All of these days they had no way to get food or water. But they were close to each other, so they could talk. One of them was very discouraged. But the other said, "Do not give up. If my father is alive, he will be looking for me." And in time, the father came and rescued them both. Likewise, the heavenly Father seeks the lost. It is not His will that one should perish.[17]

An Ethiopian was trying to find God. *"This man had gone to Jerusalem to worship"* (Acts 8:27). Ponder those words. *This man had gone to Jerusalem to worship!* There were thousands of Spirit-filled believers there. Yet not one of them had led this searching man to Jesus. Why? There are several reasons why believers do not notice sinners searching for God.

Q 22 ➤ *Give 3 possible reasons why Jerusalem believers did not help the Ethiopian.*

Perhaps the Jerusalem believers were thinking only about their own needs. Maybe some of the widows were still hungry (Acts 6:1). When believers focus on themselves, they do not pay attention to the lost.

Or maybe the Jerusalem believers were enjoying fellowship too much. They liked going from house to house for food and fellowship (Acts 2:46-47). Maybe this is why they did not see the Ethiopian. Sometimes this happens. Sinners walk right past believers day by day. And believers do not even notice them. Some sinners even visit a church, but no one takes the time to talk with them. Believers enjoy the fellowship of other believers. This is wonderful. But it is terrible when fellowship blocks out seeing the lost.

Q 23 ➤ *Are there people in your area that believers do not seem to care about? Explain.*

Or perhaps there is another reason why the Spirit could not lead Jerusalem believers to the Ethiopian. Perhaps he was the wrong color or the wrong race. Remember that they were Israelites and he was African. They were from different nations and different tribes. He was hungry for God. This Ethiopian had even bought some Scriptures. Perhaps he bought the scroll of Isaiah in Jerusalem. It was obvious that this man was reaching out for God. But some colors are hard for us to see. Did anyone in Jerusalem care for his soul (Ps. 142:4)?

But God cared. He cared so much that He called Philip away from a city to help one man. It appears that the Ethiopian was the first African Christian.[18] Perhaps God used this person in the government to help many in Africa.

When no one else cares, God cares. He cares about a city, or just one person.

Do you want to honor God? Do you want to praise and please Him? Do you desire to cast crowns before His throne? Would you like to pour costly perfume on His head? Then bring one lost person to His feet. This is the reward He desires for the price of His only Son. The lost are what God desires most.[19]

Malcolm looked for the right time to witness to Christopher, his neighbor. He began to pray for this lost sheep. But he did not feel the time was right. There was no bridge between them. So Malcolm and his wife invited Christopher and his wife over for supper. They cooked a nice meal for them. As they talked, Malcolm prayed in his heart. Still, he did not feel the Spirit leading him to talk to Christopher about the Lord. Christopher's heart seemed closed. For several months, Malcolm continued to pray for Christopher. He took time to visit with him often. Then Malcolm invited them over for supper again. They had become friends. Christopher saw a Bible on a table and began to ask questions. This was his first step toward Christ. In time, Malcolm led Christopher and his wife to the Savior. It took almost a year to win them for Christ. Sometimes believers are in too big of a hurry to witness. *"There is a time for everything"* (Eccl. 3:1-8). A time to flee to Samaria. And a time to walk toward Ethiopia. A flower opens slowly. But those who are patient smell its fragrance. A corn seed grows slowly. But those who are diligent and patient reap its harvest.

B. God guides Spirit-filled believers to those seeking Him.

God *"rewards those who earnestly seek him"* (Heb. 11:6). How? God speaks to searching sinners in various ways. Sometimes He prepares the lost through dreams or visions. And usually, God rewards searchers by guiding His witnesses to them. Figure 8.6 gives some examples of believers God guided to help sinners.

Person God Guided	Acts
Philip to the Ethiopian	8:26-29
Ananias to Saul of Tarsus	9:10-19
Peter to Cornelius	10:9-26
Paul to Lydia and others	16:9-15

Figure 8.6   God often guides Spirit-filled believers to seeking sinners.

Here is a great encouragement for God's witnesses. Do you want to help lead someone to Jesus? Then pray throughout the day. Be filled with the Spirit and listen to the Spirit. Not all lost people are searching for God. But God knows the ones who are seeking Him. And He wants to lead believers to seekers.

Q 24 *Has the Spirit led you to help a person who was searching for God? Explain.*

A husband and wife heard that a certain Muslim was in their local hospital. They had never met him, but decided to visit him. They asked a nurse to lead them to his room. The nurse replied, "There are two people here like the person you are describing. I will show you each and you will know which one you are seeking." The first man they met was not the one they were seeking. But he was seeking God. The husband greeted him and explained the mistake. They continued to talk for almost an hour! Before leaving, the couple asked the Muslim if he had any prayer requests. He explained a need. They prayed, and God met the need. They continued to visit him from time to time. On each occasion, he had a new prayer request. And each time, God met the need. They enjoyed one year of friendship, prayer, and eating together. As a result, the Muslim invited Jesus Christ into his life.

D. L. Moody was a faithful witness for God. He prayed throughout each day for the Spirit to help him lead one person to the Savior. One day he saw a picture that he liked more than any other he had seen. It was the picture of a man drowning in the water. With both hands, the drowning man clung to a cross. Moody liked the picture so much that he bought it. Later, however, he found a picture that completely spoiled his desire for the other picture. It was the picture of a person coming out of the dark waters. With one hand he clung to the cross. And with the other hand, he was pulling someone else out of the dark waters.[20]

Would you try to save a child crying for help inside a burning house? Then pray for God to lead you to that lost person crying for help. If you listen daily, God will lead you.

We have looked at two truths about God's concern for the lost. We turn now to the second goal of this lesson. Let us analyze and apply the relationship between reading and understanding.

C. Even those who read may not understand.

[30]*Then Philip ran up to the chariot and heard the man reading Isaiah the prophet. "Do you understand what you are reading?" Philip asked.* [31]*"How can I," he said, "unless someone explains it to me?" So he invited Philip to come up and sit with him* (Acts 8:30-31).

Philip was on foot. He did not have a horse, a car, or a bicycle. But he was a fruitful witness for Jesus. The Spirit led him to the searching Ethiopian.

The Ethiopian was wealthy and educated. Philip heard him reading. Today, 70 percent of all lost people cannot read.[21] The Church should be teaching more people to read. But even those who read may not understand. Notice the important question that Philip asked. *"Do you understand what you are reading?"*

Q 25 ✎ *Explain 3 reasons why believers may not understand what they read.*

Many people, including believers, read without understanding. Why? Unbelievers may not understand the Bible because it is a spiritual book (1 Cor. 2:14). Some may not understand the Bible because of cultural differences. Still, there are three common reasons why believers do not understand what they read.

- Some do not prepare their minds before they begin reading. Before you plant the seed of the Word, prepare the soil. That is, get your mind ready before you begin. Ask yourself questions like those that follow. What are these verses about? Who wrote them? What problem was he trying to solve? What illustrations did he use? How does God want me to apply these verses? Plow the soil before you sow the seed. And keep asking questions like these as you read. This will help you pay attention to what you are reading. Then you will understand more.

- Some do not understand because the language is too hard. This is often true for those, like the Ethiopian, reading in their second or third language. Your first language is the one you speak at home. If you study in a second language, some books will be hard for you to understand. Those reading in a second language must read some sentences several times to understand them. Also, they must read slowly and look up new words in a dictionary.

- Finally, many believers do not understand the Bible because the version they read is too hard. Some versions of the Bible are very difficult to understand. They use long sentences and long words. Many believers like these versions because they sound religious! But what good is reading the Bible if you do not understand it? Perhaps the Bible you read is hard to understand. If so, compare hard verses with another version. This will take longer. But it is better to read two verses and understand them than to read two chapters you do not comprehend.

Jesus gave a warning about those who hear Scripture but do not understand it.

Q 26 ✎ *According to Matthew 13:19, why is it important to understand what we read?*

"When anyone hears the message about the kingdom and does not understand it, the evil one comes and snatches away what was sown in his heart. This is the seed sown along the path" (Matt. 13:19).

We lose what we do not understand. The devil steals the seed of the Word from us if we do not understand it. Therefore, it is important to understand what we hear or read. Sometimes people memorize Bible verses but still do not understand them!

How can we know if a person understands? There are at least two ways.

Q 27 ✎ *How can a teacher know if a student understands a truth?*

***First,* ask questions.** Jesus liked to ask His disciples if they understood (Matt. 13:51). Philip asked the Ethiopian if he understood what he read. The Ethiopian was humble and honest. He admitted that he could not understand unless someone helped him (Acts 8:31). God helps the humble. But many people are too proud to admit they do not understand. Some students care more about what others think than understanding a lesson. God leaves the proud in the dark. But He leads the humble into the light (James 4:6). Therefore, if you are teaching, ask your students questions. (And if you are a student, do not be ashamed to ask questions.)

***Second,* ask someone to rephrase what he or she heard or read.** That is, ask someone to repeat a truth, but use different words. Sometimes people think they have understood, but they have not. If you ask them if they have understood, they may sincerely say "Yes." They may have even memorized what they heard or read. However, understanding is different from memorizing. We can repeat something that we do not understand. But restating a sentence in different words proves that someone has understood it.

The Ethiopian admitted that he did not understand what he read. Therefore, God gave him a teacher to help. Those who humbly seek understanding will find it. Later, they may become good teachers. Church tradition claims that the Ethiopian returned to his country and established a church there.[22]

Lesson 24 Saul's Conversion and Early Ministry (Acts 9:1-31)
Goal: *Identify and apply 6 truths related to Saul's conversion and early ministry.*

Setting

In Acts 8, Luke showed us the results of Stephen's death. Sometimes one stone rolling down a mountain can cause many other stones to start rolling. Stephen's death was like that. It started a great force of persecution. The persecution led to eternal blessings for the Samaritans, the Ethiopian, and others. Still, Saul continued to persecute believers. He had bad breath. Saul was so full of hate that he breathed out murder (Acts 9:1).

Saul got authority to persecute. His hatred was legal, by human law.

[1]*Meanwhile, Saul was still breathing out murderous threats against the Lord's disciples. He went to the high priest* [2]*and asked him for letters to the synagogues in Damascus, so that if he found any there who belonged to the Way, whether men or women, he might take them as prisoners to Jerusalem* (Acts 9:1-2).

Damascus was about 150 miles (241 km) northeast of Jerusalem. It was about halfway between Jerusalem and Tarsus, Saul's home.

Damascus was not just another city on Paul's path of persecution. It was the center or hub of much business. Business flowed out of Damascus to Syria, Mesopotamia, Anatolia, Persia, and Arabia. Locate these places on the map in Figure 8.9. Believers were already in Damascus. From there, Christianity would spread to many places. Therefore, Damascus was a key city in Saul's strategy.[23]

Q 28 Why was Damascus a key city in the strategy of Saul?

Saul was near Damascus when Jesus appeared to him. Luke tells us how Saul of Tarsus became Paul the apostle. Paul's conversion is one of the greatest events of Christianity. Most Bible teachers agree that Paul became the greatest of the apostles. Take a few minutes and read Acts 9:1-31. Then we will briefly survey and apply six great truths in these verses.

A. There is a reason why believers should never despair.

God and Satan are in a war against each other. Believers are in between. Both God and Satan work through key people. Satan's greatest human worker was Saul. In contrast, the apostles and deacons were key workers for God.

Q 29 How did Saul's conversion affect the war between God and Satan?

Satan seeks to destroy God's best workers. He uses any person or method that will help him. The devil used Jewish leaders to beat and imprison Peter and John. He stirred up a mob to stone Stephen. Satan used King Herod to murder one of God's top apostles (Acts 12:1-2). Our enemy rejoices when God loses key leaders. Perhaps you have known a key leader that Satan wounded or killed.

On the other hand, God sometimes takes our enemies out of the battle. The Lord decided it was time to take Herod out of the war. He sent an angel to strike him down. Worms ate him and he died (Acts 12:21-23). Herod's death was a loss for Satan and a victory for the Church. Likewise, the Church would have rejoiced if God had struck Saul down. But God had a better idea. *"As he* [Saul] *neared Damascus on his journey, suddenly a light from heaven flashed around him"* (Acts 9:3).

Consider the effect of Saul's conversion on the war between God and Satan. God took Saul away from Satan's army. And He chose Saul to be a general in the kingdom of God. Then He filled Saul with the power of the Holy Spirit. Thus Saul did a thousand times more for Christ then he ever did for Satan. The conversion of Saul was a huge victory for the Church.

Q 30 ➤ Before Saul was saved, was God preparing him to be an apostle? Explain.

God plans ahead. Calling Saul to be an apostle was not a late idea God had. The Church did not know it. But God planned Saul's conversion years before it happened. Paul was called to be an apostle from the time of his birth (Gal. 1:15). Figure 8.7 lists twelve things that made Paul an effective apostle. Notice that in many ways God prepared Paul before he was saved.

Qualification	Scripture
1. He learned the Jewish language and culture well.	Acts 21:40; Phil. 3:5
2. He learned the Greek language and culture well.	Acts 17:22-31; Titus 1:12
3. He was a Roman citizen.	Acts 16:37; 22:23-29; 25:10-12
4. He was trained in Jewish theology.	Gal. 1:14
5. He learned to make tents and support himself.	Acts 18:3; 1 Cor. 9:14-18; 2 Cor. 11:7-11 1 Thess. 2:9; 2 Thess. 3:8
6. He was called by God.	Acts 9:15-16; 22:14-15; 26:12-18; Rom. 1:1 1 Cor. 1:1 (and others)
7. He was filled with the Spirit.	Acts 9:17
8. He was given great grace.	1 Cor. 3:10; 15:10; 2 Cor. 12:9
9. He was given a thorn in the flesh that kept him humble and dependent on Jesus.	2 Cor. 12:7-9
10. He had a great love for people.	Rom. 9:1-4; 2 Cor. 11:28-29; Phil. 4:1
11. He had the heart of a servant.	Acts 21:17-26; 2 Cor. 6:3-10; 9:19-23; Gal. 2:2
12. He was diligent and persevered to run his race.	1 Cor. 9:24-27; 2 Cor. 11:23-33; Phil. 3:13-14

Figure 8.7   Twelve things that enabled Paul to be an effective missionary

Q 31 ➤ Why should believers not despair during dark times?

Believers should never despair. God plans far ahead. The Church would fail if it depended on humans. But God has promised to build His Church (Matt. 16:18). Things looked bad for the early church. Many believers had lost their homes, lands, and possessions (Heb. 10:34). Many were put in prison. It looked like evil was winning. But God is always ahead of the Church. We do not know what He will do next. Nevertheless, He will build His Church. The apostles were slow to obey the Great Commission. So God used some deacons to lead the apostles. Then God converted Satan's top man! No matter how dark the clouds look, never despair. Jesus will build His Church. There are youth today who will become great church leaders. There are laypeople God will use to do wonderful things in the Church. God surprises us with the people He calls. Have faith in God. And never give up on the worst sinner you know. That person might become the greatest apostle![24]

B. Christianity is more than an experience. It is the Way!

Several places in Acts refer to Christianity as the Way.

Verse That Refers to the Way	Acts
Saul wanted to imprison any *who belonged to the Way.*	9:2
Some unbelievers said evil things about *the Way.*	19:9
In Ephesus there arose a great disturbance about *the Way.*	19:23
Paul once *persecuted the followers of this Way to their death.*	22:4
Paul became *a follower of the Way.*	24:14
Felix was *well acquainted with the Way.*	24:22

Figure 8.8   Acts refers to Christianity as the Way.

Some try to reduce Christianity to a prayer or an experience. It is true that following Jesus begins with a prayer of repentance. And a person becomes a child of God by being born again. This is a wonderful experience. But Christianity is more than an experience. It is the Way to heaven. That is, it is a lifestyle.

Notice that the Bible does not say Christianity is *a Way*. It is not one way among many. Christianity is the *only* way to heaven. Jesus is the way, the truth, and the life. No one can come to the Father except through Him (John 14:6). Being a follower of the Way means being a follower of Jesus. A person may accept Jesus as Savior in a moment. But reaching heaven requires following the footsteps of Jesus for a lifetime.

There is a cheap, unbiblical grace that offers eternal life for a short prayer. However, Christianity is more than a prayer or an experience. It is the Way to live. Following Jesus means obeying His teachings day by day. Some are confused. They think they can accept Jesus as Savior, but not as Lord. These may attend church on Sundays. Yet they follow the ways of the world Monday through Saturday. Not everyone talking about heaven is going there. Receiving Jesus means following Him everyday, all day.

Christianity is not an intersection or a stop beside the road. It is a narrow road (Matt. 7:13-14)! And it is the only road or Way to heaven.

Q 32 *What is the difference between calling Christianity an experience and calling it the Way?*

C. Whoever persecutes a believer persecutes Jesus.

"He fell to the ground and heard a voice say to him, 'Saul, Saul, why do you persecute me?'" (Acts 9:4).

Notice that Jesus did not ask Saul, "Why do you persecute my Church?"[25] Jesus asked, *"Why do you persecute me?"* Jesus lives in each believer. So what people do to a believer, they do to Jesus. Several verses in the Bible teach this. Matthew wrote about helping believers who are hungry, thirsty, naked, sick, or in prison. He said what we do to the least believer, we do to Jesus Christ (Matt. 25:31-46). Luke said something like this in Acts 5:4. Ananias and Sapphira lied to Peter. But Peter said they lied to God. This is because God the Holy Spirit lives in each believer. What we do to a believer, we do to God.

Q 33 *Is it possible for people to persecute God? Explain.*

Jonas was married to a believer named Ellen. He became angry each time she went to church. Often he beat her for attending. Then he would lock her outside the house. She spent many hours in the cold. After Jonas went to sleep, the children would unlock the door for her. The pastor and believers in the church prayed much for Jonas. One day, Jonas asked Ellen, "Which home are the believers meeting in tonight? Would you ask the pastor to change and come here instead?" The pastor agreed. That night, Jonas confessed his sins to the believers. He said, "I am sorry for the way that I have been treating my wife. I realize that I am fighting against God. And I cannot win the fight against Him. Therefore, I want to surrender my life to God." He knelt and with tears opened his heart to God. Jonas became an active member in the church.

Paul wrote that sinning against a believer is sinning against Christ (1 Cor. 8:12). He first learned this truth on the road to Damascus. Saul held garments while unbelievers stoned Jesus (Acts 7:58). And it was Jesus whom Saul tried to force to blaspheme (Acts 26:11). Saul thought he was dragging men and women to prison. But it was Jesus whom Saul locked behind bars. Saul beat, bound, punished, and condemned Jesus, the Son of God. It was Jesus whom Saul persecuted to His death (Acts 9:4-5; 22:4; 26:14-15).

Many unbelievers do not understand this truth. For example, Muslims honor Jesus as a prophet. They say Jesus was a righteous man sent by God. But they condemn Muslims who accept Jesus as their Savior. Thus, they both honor and persecute Jesus. In condemning His followers, they condemn Him.

Q 34 *Is it possible to honor Jesus and dishonor His followers? Explain.*

Believers also need to learn this truth. Those who gossip about or slander a believer sin against Jesus. Those who refuse to forgive a believer refuse to forgive Jesus. Some were not aware that they met angels (Heb. 13:2). Imagine that! But many more have met

Q 35 *Do we sometimes meet the Lord of the angels and not realize it? Explain.*

the Lord of the angels and not realized His presence. Like the Corinthians, they fail to discern the body of Christ (1 Cor. 11:27-32). Jesus is present in the least believer.

It was the night before Christmas. In a dream the Lord appeared to a believer. Jesus promised to visit the believer four times on Christmas day. The believer awoke with joy. This day would be his greatest day on earth! Throughout the day, the believer watched for Jesus. But he never saw the Lord. He was very disappointed. That night he knelt by his bed to pray. He complained that the Lord had not kept His promise. Then a small voice spoke to his heart. "Do not say that I did not keep My promise to you," said the Lord. "I came to you four times, just as I promised. I was in the beggar to whom you gave the bread. I was in the old man whom you honored. I was in the Christian whom you encouraged with kind words. And I was in your wife whom you thanked for the food. Thank you for treating me so kindly today!"

D. New believers need to be connected with other believers.

¹⁰*In Damascus there was a disciple named Ananias. The Lord called to him in a vision, "Ananias!" "Yes, Lord," he answered.* ¹¹*The Lord told him, "Go to the house of Judas on Straight Street and ask for a man from Tarsus named Saul, for he is praying"* (Acts 9:10-11).

Q 36 ⟋ *Give 2 reasons why God sent Ananias to Saul.*

The Lord could have healed Saul's eyes without the help of Ananias. But He did not. Saul received his sight through the prayer of Ananias. The meeting of Saul and Ananias served at least two purposes. *First,* Ananias became a witness that Saul was blind and was healed. No one's testimony is valid without others who confirm it. Ananias had a good reputation. *"A man named Ananias came to see me. He was a devout observer of the law and highly respected by all the Jews living there"* (Acts 22:12).

Second, Saul learned his first lesson about relating to other believers. It was Ananias who prayed for Saul, baptized him, and fed him.

A young believer named Jerry told about going fishing. He said the fish were not biting. So he commanded them to jump in the boat. He claimed they came quickly from every direction. He said he had to command them to stop, or they would have sunk the boat. But no one else was there to see what happened. And no one ate any of the fish! An old believer named David responded with a story. He said his dog had many fleas. But he commanded the fleas to jump off of the dog into the fire. They obeyed immediately! But no one else was home to see the fleas jump. Do you believe either of these stories? It is easier to believe when there are two or three witnesses!

Believers need each other. We are members of one Body. Paul wrote that the foot and the hand help each other. Likewise, the ear and the eye bless each other (1 Cor. 12:14-20). Saul first learned this truth when he met Ananias. (This Ananias was a better person than the Ananias of Acts 5!) Luke also records how Barnabas helped Saul (Acts 9:26-27). The first person Saul saw when he opened his eyes was another believer. From then on, he valued relating to other believers. Saul spent several days with the disciples in Damascus (Acts 9:19).

Two things are very hard for a believer to do. It is hard for a believer to baptize himself and to bury himself. And between baptism and death, believers depend on each other in many ways. To follow the Way, believers need each other from the beginning to the end.

Two believers were talking. Thaddeus was rejoicing. He claimed that he had led 55 sinners to Christ in the past year. "That is wonderful," said Henry. "How do you do it?" Thaddeus said that he went door to door. He shared the gospel with the lost. Then he led them in a prayer. He said many prayed and accepted Jesus as Savior. Henry responded with two questions. "How many of these 55 people have been baptized? And how many attend church somewhere now?" "Only one of them," replied Thaddeus. "But they are all believers."

Q 37 ⟍ *If you were Henry, what would your next question be?*

E. Saul was baptized in water and the Spirit.

Acts 9 shows us some things that are important for new believers. We have noted that each believer needs to connect with other believers. Saul did this. Then he was baptized in water and the Spirit. Three important things for each believer are relationships, water baptism, and Spirit baptism.

Q 38 *What are 3 important things for each new believer?*

Ananias baptized Saul in water (Acts 9:18). And Jesus baptized Saul in the Spirit (Acts 9:17; Matt. 3:11). For Luke, *filled with the Spirit* and *baptized in the Spirit* mean the same thing. We usually refer to the first filling of the Spirit as the *baptism in the Spirit*. It is safe to assume that Saul was baptized in water like other believers. And it is safe to assume that at his Spirit baptism he spoke in a new language. There are at least three reasons we believe Saul spoke in a new language when he was filled with the Spirit. [26]

Q 39 *Do you think Paul spoke in a new language when he was filled with the Spirit? Explain.*

- *First,* God called Paul to be an apostle. He was an example for other believers. Therefore, it was important for Paul to have the spiritual experiences other apostles and believers had. All the other apostles, except Judas, were filled with the Spirit and spoke in new languages. Paul was not less than or inferior to other apostles (2 Cor. 11:5). Jesus appeared to the other apostles after the Resurrection. So Jesus appeared to Saul (Acts 9:17; 1 Cor. 15:8). Saul's spiritual experiences were not less than those of the other apostles. His spiritual experiences were more (2 Cor. 12:1).
- *Second,* Paul baptized new believers in water. Then he prayed for them to be filled with the Spirit. When he laid hands on them, they received the Spirit and spoke in new languages (Acts 19:1-7). It is likely that he learned this from Ananias. A person tends to minister to others what they have received and experienced (2 Cor. 1:4). This is common. But it is rare to lead others to a place one has never been!
- *Third,* he told the Corinthians he spoke in tongues more than all of them did (1 Cor. 14:18). It is likely that he began when he was first filled with the Spirit. This is when all the other apostles and disciples in Acts began to speak in new languages (Acts 2:4; 10:44-46; 19:1-7).

Paul connected with other believers in the body of Christ. Also, he was baptized in water and in the Spirit. Every believer should do these three things.

F. Persuading requires more study than telling.

"At once he began to preach in the synagogues that Jesus is the Son of God" (Acts 9:20).

Saul began to *preach* at once. *Preach* is the Greek word that means "to tell." New converts can begin to tell others about Jesus immediately. Saul had an experience to share. Jesus had changed his life. All believers have their own unique stories to tell. They can tell what Jesus has done for them. This is a powerful witness to others.

Andrew used his personal testimony to bring Peter to Christ (John 1:40-42). The Lord sent a man from the tombs to testify. He had been saved only a few minutes. But he was ready to be a witness for Jesus (Luke 8:38-39). The woman at the well brought many to Jesus. She had not been to Bible school. All she did was tell them what Jesus had done for her (John 4:39). Many sinners are led to Christ through the personal testimonies of believers. Even in front of kings, Paul told about his own conversion. Sharing his testimony was one of Paul's favorite ways to witness. No one can argue when you tell what Jesus has done for you. Every believer is a witness.

Q 40 *How long should a person be a believer before telling others about Jesus?*

Saul began his ministry by telling what Jesus had done for him. But he did not stop there.

²²Yet Saul grew more and more powerful and baffled the Jews living in Damascus by proving that Jesus is the Christ. ²³After many days had gone by, the Jews conspired to kill him (Acts 9:22-23).

Saul became more powerful. How? He did this by studying the Scriptures and by praying. At first, Saul told what had happened to him. This led some to Christ. However, others wanted more proof that Jesus was the Messiah. It is easier to share your personal experience than it is to prove the truth. Proving the truth requires study.

Q 41 ➤ *What made great men like Daniel and Paul wiser?*

Even apostles grow. As a believer studies the Bible, his or her understanding increases. The prophet Daniel was a spiritual man. He had many visions and dreams. But his understanding increased as he read the Scriptures.

I, Daniel, understood from the Scriptures, according to the word of the LORD given to Jeremiah the prophet, that the desolation of Jerusalem would last seventy years (Dan. 9:2).

There is a time for everything. There is a time for visions and a time for dreams. There is a time to pray and a time to study. Visions, dreams, and prayer were all a part of Daniel's life. But none of these was the key to his understanding about the captivity. Daniel understood when he studied what Jeremiah wrote. Even a man as spiritual as Daniel became wiser by studying.

Likewise, Paul was the greatest of the apostles. And study was one of the keys to his ministry. Luke does not take the time to tell us about Paul's studying. But Paul himself reveals this to us.

[17]Nor did I go up to Jerusalem to see those who were apostles before I was, but I went immediately into Arabia and later returned to Damascus. [18]Then after three years, I went up to Jerusalem to get acquainted with Peter and stayed with him fifteen days (Gal. 1:17-18).

Notice that there is a period of 3 years between Damascus and Jerusalem. Paul was baptized in water and in the Spirit in Damascus. At once he began to tell what Jesus had done in his life. Then he spent some time studying in the desert of Arabia. This probably happened between Acts 9:22 and Acts 9:23. Luke summarizes this period by saying, *"after many days had gone by"* (Acts 9:23). Paul probably spent much of the 3 years studying in the Arabian desert.[+] Clarence McCartney, a great preacher from Scotland, talked about these 3 years. He said Paul went into the desert with the Law, the Prophets, and Psalms in his bag. But he came out with Romans, Ephesians, Philippians, and Colossians in his heart![27] Figure 8.9 harmonizes Acts 9 and Galatians 1.

Every believer is a witness. But there is a great need for all believers to prove truth from the Bible. This ability increases only through Bible study. Jude tells us to *"fight hard for the faith God gave his holy people"* (Jude 3, NCV). God bless you for studying this book. As you study, God will approve of the way you handle the Scriptures (2 Tim. 2:15). Your studies will enable you to persuade others for Him.

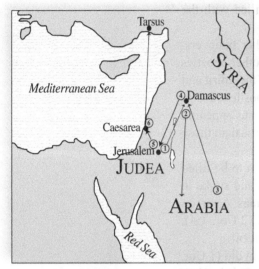

Journey of Paul		Scripture
①	From Jerusalem to Damascus	Acts 9:1-22
②	From Damascus to Arabia	Gal. 1:17-18
③	From Arabia to Damascus	Acts 9:23-25 Gal. 1:17 2 Cor. 11:32-33
④	From Damascus back to Jerusalem	Acts 9:26-29 Gal. 1:18-20
⑤	From Jerusalem to Caesarea	Acts 9:30
⑥	From Caesarea to Tarsus	Acts 9:30 Gal. 1:21-24

Figure 8.9   Paul's travels in Acts 9[28]

Q 42 ↖ *Why are you studying this course?*

+ This was the time of Aretas IV and the Nabataean Kingdom. Paul was relating his Jewish ideas to Christianity. Perhaps he witnessed to the Nabataean Arabs.

Test Yourself: Circle the letter by the **best** completion to each question or statement.

1. The death of Stephen was the beginning of a
a) revival in Jerusalem.
b) time of great peace.
c) time of prosperity.
d) great persecution.

2. Preaching the Word is the responsibility of
a) pastors.
b) evangelists.
c) missionaries.
d) all believers.

3. Jews avoided Samaritans because Samaritans
a) worshiped on Mount Gerizim.
b) did not speak Hebrew well.
c) were only partly Jewish.
d) were descendents of Cain.

4. Those who refuse to be baptized in water
a) should not plan on going to heaven.
b) will lose some of their rewards.
c) may still serve Jesus as Savior and Lord.
d) are like the thief saved on the cross.

5. Believers in Samaria were baptized in the Spirit
a) at the same time they were saved.
b) when they were baptized in water.
c) after they were baptized in water.
d) before they were baptized in water.

6. The best illustration of God's concern for one lost person is
a) Simon the sorcerer.
b) the Ethiopian eunuch.
c) Ananias or Sapphira.
d) Caiaphas, the high priest.

7. The Ethiopian was reading the Bible
a) but did not understand.
b) in the book of Ezekiel.
c) in his first language.
d) to justify himself.

8. Christianity is most like
a) an intersection.
b) a resting place.
c) a road.
d) a map.

9. Saul was set apart to be an apostle
a) on the road to Damascus.
b) from the time of his birth.
c) after 3 years of study.
d) when Ananias prayed for him.

10. Saul's eyes were healed when
a) he submitted to the Lord.
b) the Lord spoke to him.
c) Ananias prayed for him.
d) Barnabas befriended him.

 Essay Test Topics: Write 50-100 words on each of these goals that you studied in this chapter.

Philip's Ministry to the Samaritans (Acts 8:1-25)

Goal: *Explain 4 principles of evangelism in Acts 8. Evaluate your church and ministry in relation to these principles.*

Philip's Ministry to the Ethiopian (Acts 8:26-40)

Goal: *State and apply 2 truths about God's concern for the lost.*

Goal: *Analyze and apply the relationship between reading and understanding.*

Saul's Conversion and Early Ministry (Acts 9:1-31)

Goal: *Identify and apply 6 truths related to Saul's conversion and early ministry.*

Chapter 9:
The Ministries of Peter, Barnabas, Saul, and James

(Acts 9:32–12:25)

Introduction

Simba Mohammedovich was born and raised in Turkey, near the Black Sea. He practiced the Sunni Muslim faith. At the age of seven, he began to realize he had special spiritual abilities. The form of a man appeared to him many times in visions at night. This spirit person talked with Simba and gained his trust. The night visitor often asked, "Do you love me?" The boy was able to predict the future of students at school. Soon, many people were coming to him for spiritual guidance.

At the age of 23, Simba's uncle invited him to attend a university in Russia. Simba agreed. He arrived in the fall of 1991. He spoke only Turkish. Therefore, he spent many months learning Russian, English, and the local Caucasian language. He made many new friends. One of these was Martha. She was a European Christian. One day Simba asked her for a New Testament in Turkish. She began the process of trying to find one. Meanwhile, Martha invited Simba to a meeting where Christians prayed and had discussions. At first he refused. But after a time he attended. Their love for God and each other attracted him. He began to reach out to know God in a new way.

That night he had a vision. There was a spiritual struggle with the spirit that had been visiting him for years. He felt as though invisible forces were fighting over his body. He was sweating, felt sick, and could not see. Simba cried out for help. A man in bright light appeared

Figure 9.1   A Roman centurion like Cornelius

and helped him. Later that night, Simba called some of his new friends. They prayed with him and taught him from the Scriptures. When he was ready, they led him to Jesus. These believers also taught Simba to rebuke the evil spirit in the name of Jesus. At his home that night, the demon returned. But Simba resisted him in the name of Jesus. The demon left. Simba, a new believer, slept well that night.[1]

God still speaks through visions today. He revealed himself to Paul through a vision (Acts 26:19). He guided Ananias and Paul to each other through visions (Acts 9:10-12). In this chapter, we will see the Lord guiding Peter and Cornelius through visions.

Lessons:

Peter's Ministry to Cornelius (Acts 9:32–11:18)
Goal: *Identify and apply 4 truths from Peter's ministry to Cornelius.*

Barnabas and Saul's Ministry at Antioch (Acts 11:19-30)
Goal: *Summarize 4 insights about the ministry in Antioch. Relate these to your context.*

Peter's Escape and Herod's Death (Acts 12:1-25)
Goal: *Explain 4 contrasts in Acts 12. Apply these to self and others.*

 Key Words

Antioch
Caesarea

prophesy
phylacteries

Lesson 25 — Peter's Ministry to Cornelius (Acts 9:32–11:18)

Goal: *Identify and apply 4 truths from Peter's ministry to Cornelius.*

Setting

Luke gives several progress reports in Acts. Review Figure 2.4. Acts 9:31 is one of Luke's summaries about the Church's progress.

Then the church throughout Judea, Galilee and Samaria enjoyed a time of peace. It was strengthened; and encouraged by the Holy Spirit, it grew in numbers, living in the fear of the Lord (Acts 9:31).

Luke shows us how the Church spread. By the Spirit's power, the Church spread in Jerusalem (Acts 1–7). It took the Church a few years to develop a foundation. Believers learned to relate to each other. Then they began to reach out to others. The foundation precedes the building. This is true in the life of a person or a church. Pastors or churches may try to reach out too quickly. But the foundation is worth the time and effort it takes to build it. Bible school is worth the time it takes. And building relationships is worth the time it takes. In Acts 1–7 the Church developed a base to work from. Then they were ready for the next step.

Q 1 ➤ *Where was the city of Caesarea?*

In Acts 8–12 we see the Church expanding mostly in Judea and Samaria. God used Philip to take the gospel to Samaria. The Spirit's great signs and wonders opened Samaria to the good news. From Samaria, Philip briefly went south. The Spirit led him to the Ethiopian. Then Philip traveled north, preaching in all the towns as he went. He finally settled down to live in Caesarea. About 20 years later, Paul stayed in Philip's house there (Acts 21:8).[2]

Caesarea was a city on the coast of Judea. It was named in honor of Augustus Caesar, the Roman emperor. Herod rebuilt Caesarea with a good harbor. The city was a military base. It was located about 30 miles (48 km) north of Joppa, and about 50 miles (80 km) northwest of Jerusalem. In Acts 10–11 we will study about Peter's ministry to Cornelius in Caesarea. Let us look at four truths in this section.

Figure 9.2
Ruins of the ancient street leading to Herod the Great's harbor at Caesarea

A. Believers grow little by little.

Spiritual growth is not sudden. A believer does not move from one spiritual level to another as a person climbs stairs. Growth is slow. A believer rises like yeast. He grows more slowly than corn. You may chop a tree down in a few minutes. But it takes a tree years to grow up. Likewise, a believer grows one day at a time.

All believers grow slowly, even apostles. An apostle does not necessarily mature faster than other believers do. In fact, both Stephen and Philip were more mature than the apostles in some ways. Stephen appears to be the first believer to preach in a synagogue. He had advanced understanding of Christ's relationship to the Law and the temple. And it was Philip, not the apostles, who first preached to the Samaritans. All believers grow in grace. In fact, even Jesus grew in wisdom, stature, and favor with God and man (Luke 2:52).

Q 2 ➤ *Do apostles grow faster than other believers? Explain.*

A calf cannot give birth to another calf. A newborn donkey cannot pull a cart. A small child cannot read this book. *"As is the man, so is his strength"* (Judg. 8:21).

Peter is a good example of a growing believer. He grew faster than the other apostles did. God used Philip's ministry to awaken Peter. Remember that Peter and John went to Samaria after Philip. Before this they had preached to Jews only. But Peter's experience in Samaria opened his heart. After Samaria he was never the same. He and John preached in many Samaritan villages on the way back to Jerusalem (Acts 8:25).

Acts 9:32 reports that Peter traveled about the country. It is good to see him preaching outside of Jerusalem! As he stepped out in new areas, God did miracles in his life.

The Spirit used Peter to expand the Church in Caesarea and other cities of Samaria. Locate Lydda and the Plain of Sharon in Figure 9.3. All living in these towns turned to the Lord when Peter healed Aeneas (Acts 9:35). Also, locate the city of Joppa on the map. Dorcas was a believer who lived in Joppa. She was known for her good deeds, especially making clothes (Acts 9:36, 39). Believers have different talents.[3] Dorcas was not a teacher or a prophetess. But she had a ministry to others. People mourned when she died. They sent for Peter, who raised her from the dead. As a result, many believed in the Lord (Acts 9:42). Luke continues to emphasize that the Church spread by the power of the Holy Spirit. The Spirit uses signs and wonders to confirm the Word. These help many to believe. Many missionaries and evangelists today can testify to this. The Word of God and the works of God belong together.

In Acts 9 we saw Peter doing miracles. But in Acts 10 we see God doing a miracle in Peter! Jesus told Peter and the others to preach in all the world. But their view of the world was small. Little by little, step by step, Peter's view of the world grew. In Acts 10 we see Peter becoming a Great Commission Christian. He has finally realized that the gospel is for the whole world! His view of the world grew in stages. Figure 9.4 shows some steps in Peter's growth. Little by little he moved from helping his fellow Jews to helping the Gentiles. It was only about 50 miles (80 km) from Jerusalem to Caesarea. But it took Peter about 10 years to make the trip!

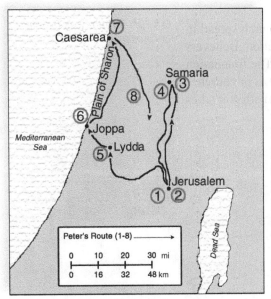

Figure 9.3   The Spirit used Peter to spread the gospel in Caesarea (See Figure 9.4).

Q 3 *Why did it take Peter 10 years to walk the 80 kilometers from Jerusalem to Caesarea?*

Q 4 *Which steps in Peter's growth do you think were the hardest for him? Explain.*

8. He returned to Jerusalem to tell of his ministry to the Gentiles (Acts 11:1-18).

7. He preached the gospel to Cornelius, a Gentile in Caesarea (Acts 10).

6. He stayed in the home of Simon the tanner whom Jews considered unclean (Acts 9:36-43).

5. He began to move about the country and preach in places such as Lydda (Acts 9:32-38).

4. He preached in other Samaritan towns as he returned to Jerusalem (Acts 8:25).

3. He followed Philip and prayed for the Samaritans who were half Jewish (Acts 8:14-24).

2. He preached the good news to fellow Jews in Jerusalem (Acts 2–5).

1. He stood up among Jewish believers and guided them (Acts 1:15-26).

Figure 9.4   Eight stages in the growth of Peter's worldview (See Figure 9.3)

Growth is slow! But it is certain for those who walk in the Spirit. Keep praying, studying, listening, and witnessing. Like Peter, you will continue to mature.

B. Sometimes a person must choose to obey culture or God.

Culture is made up of the values, beliefs, and behavior patterns of a group of people. It includes traditions handed down from generation to generation. Sometimes culture agrees with the Bible. At other times culture teaches the opposite of God's Word.

Peter believed it was better to obey God than man. He declared that truth to the Sanhedrin (Acts 4:18-20). Still, he was obeying man, not God! Jesus had told them to preach the good news to all nations (Matt. 28:19-20). Years had passed. Yet they had not obeyed. Peter had enough courage to stand up against the Sanhedrin. But he found it hard to stand up against his own culture. Little by little he chose between his culture and the command of Christ.

- His culture taught that the Jews do not associate with the Samaritans (John 4:9). He broke through this cultural barrier and prayed for the Samaritans. When he obeyed, they were filled with the Spirit (Acts 8:17).

- His culture taught that it was wrong to stay with Simon the tanner (Acts 9:43; Lev. 11:40). A tanner worked with the skins of dead animals. Jewish law said tanners were unclean. Peter broke through this cultural barrier. He understood that the blood of Christ made all Jews clean. The house stunk! But the Spirit led Peter to stay there.

  Mature Christianity does not divide people into groups of clean and unclean. In Hinduism, the priests will not associate with tanners. They say leather workers are unclean. The priests say tanners are part of a group called The Untouchables.[4] But Christ and Christians do not have this attitude toward others. Jesus ate with tax collectors and sinners. He touched those whom society called unclean (Matt. 8:1-3). And the unclean touched Him (Matt. 9:20). They did not make Him unclean. Rather, He made them clean! And He taught His disciples to serve others, not look down on them. It is good to see Peter, an apostle, staying with a tanner!

- His culture said it was wrong to go into the house of a Gentile.

  [27]*Peter went inside and found a large gathering of people.* [28]*He said to them: "You are well aware that it is against our law for a Jew to associate with a Gentile or visit him. But God has shown me that I should not call any man impure or unclean"* (Acts 10:27-28; Compare Luke 10:25-37).

It is good to honor culture that does not conflict with God. But there are times a believer must choose between culture and God (Matt. 15:1-9). *"We must obey God rather than men!"* (Acts 5:29).

Samson was a believer, but his mother, was not. She came to help name his firstborn son. His mother wanted to select a name that would please his dead ancestors. The process was a long one. First, she would mix milk, beer, and honey in a pot. Then, she would select a short stick, about a foot long. One end of the stick would be in the pot. She would hold the other end and say the name of a departed ancestor. Then she would release the stick. A falling stick meant the ancestors rejected the name. But the time would come when the stick stood upright in the pot. Their tribe believed that the spirit of a departed ancestor caused the stick to stand up.

Culture and God's Word often conflict. Time and space do not allow us to discuss the possible examples. But what do you think? Should believers obey a culture that commands them to circumcise boys and girls? Is it acceptable for a believer to drink blood? Should believers drink wine? Is it right for people of different tribes or races to marry? Does the Bible allow believers to eat all foods? Can a believer have more than one wife? Should a woman wear a cloth over her head? Is it right for a woman

Q 5 *Describe some ways you have grown as a witness for Jesus.*

Q 6 *What do we mean by "culture"?*

Q 7 *Give 3 examples of how Peter learned to obey Christ rather than culture.*

Q 8 *Have you ever had to choose between obeying the Bible or culture? Explain.*

Q 9 *Discuss any of the questions in the paragraph before point C.*

to wear makeup? Should believers attend the funerals of unbelievers? These are a few questions about the Bible and culture. Add your questions to the list. Discuss some of these with other believers. All believers have the same Bible. But different cultures may have different answers.

C. God does not show favoritism.

Q 10 How many soldiers did a centurion command?

Cornelius was a Gentile. He was also a centurion. A centurion was an officer in the Roman army. The word *centurion* comes from the Latin word *centum*, meaning "100." Words like century and centimeter are also based on *centum*. A centurion was over at least 100 men. The Romans grouped soldiers into *legions. A legion contained 6,000 soldiers. Each legion was divided into ten parts called *regiments. The commander of a regiment was over about 600 men. That was too many men for one person to command well. So the Romans divided each regiment into groups of about 100. They put a centurion over each group of 100 soldiers (See Figure 9.5).

1	2	3	4	5	6	7	8	9	10
100	100	100	100	100	100	100	100	100	100
100	100	100	100	100	100	100	100	100	100
100	100	100	100	100	100	100	100	100	100
100	100	100	100	100	100	100	100	100	100
100	100	100	100	100	100	100	100	100	100
100	100	100	100	100	100	100	100	100	100

Figure 9.5   A Roman legion had 6,000 soldiers. There were 10 regiment commanders (top row). Each regiment commander had about 6 centurions under him. A centurion was over at least 100 soldiers.[5]

Q 11 What is one reason why Luke chose to write about several centurions?

Luke mentions several centurions. One of his purposes for writing Acts was to commend Christianity and Paul to the government. Luke's references to the Roman centurions support this idea. He always shows a good relationship between the centurions and Christianity (Figure 9.6).

Centurion	Scripture
1. The centurion with a sick servant: This centurion built a synagogue for the Jews. He asked Jesus to "speak the word."	Luke 7:1-10
2. The centurion at the cross: He praised God and declared that Jesus was a righteous man.	Luke 23:47
3. Cornelius, a centurion of the Italian Regiment: He was saved and baptized in the Holy Spirit.	Acts 10:1-48
4. The centurions who protected Paul and permitted him to speak to the crowd: One of these spoke up for Paul's rights as a Roman citizen.	Acts 21:30–22:29
5. The two centurions who commanded the army that escorted Paul from Jerusalem to Caesarea	Acts 23:17-35
6. Julius, a centurion of the *Imperial *Regiment: He was kind to Paul and spared his life.	Acts 27:1-3, 43

Figure 9.6   Centurions Luke describes

Q 12 Was Cornelius saved before Peter arrived? Explain.

Cornelius was a centurion who respected God. Many military men are godly. Sometimes their relationship with authority helps them understand God (Matt. 8:8-9). Cornelius was a centurion and a Gentile who sought to honor God. He had some knowledge about God. He knew about the life and ministry of Jesus (Acts 10:37-38). Still, he had not placed his trust in Christ. Cornelius was a good man in many ways. He was not far from the kingdom of God. Still, he needed a Savior. God saw the good deeds Cornelius did. And He heard the prayers this military man prayed (Acts 10:4). So God sent Peter to tell him how to be saved (Acts 11:14). God sees and loves every person on earth. He sees the good deeds and hears the prayers of sinners. He does not want any to perish. The heavenly Father searches for those who seek to please Him.

Peter had grown faster than the other apostles. He knew other believers would criticize him. It is common for immature believers to criticize mature believers. So Peter took six witnesses with him! He wanted some support when he gave account! Peter was wise to take the witnesses. Even apostles should give an account of their actions. So they all went together to the large home of Cornelius. Many people were inside (Acts 10:24).

³⁴*Then Peter began to speak: "I now realize how true it is that God does not show favoritism ³⁵but accepts men from every nation who fear him and do what is right"* (Acts 10:34-35).

In what way did God *accept* Cornelius? He accepted him as a person trying to walk in truth. God did not leave Cornelius in the dark. He guided him into the light.

Q 13 ➚ *What does Acts 10:35 mean?*

How does God respond to those seeking Him? The story of Cornelius gives us the answer. God accepts all who reach out to Him. He accepts rich and poor, educated and illiterate, Jews and Gentiles. He accepts all tribes, nations, and colors. This does not mean that a person can be saved in any religion. It means that God sees people in all religions. He reaches out to those who reach out to Him. God guides believers to seeking sinners. He guided Philip to the Ethiopian. He guided Ananias to Saul. And He guided Peter to Cornelius. God accepts all who seek Him. And He guides believers to show them the Way.

The believers in Jerusalem were angry.⁺ They criticized Peter for visiting and eating with Gentiles (Acts 11:1-3). Peter told them the whole story. And he had six witnesses! Jerusalem believers were amazed. Notice their response. *"When they heard this, they had no further objections and praised God, saying, 'So then, God has granted even the Gentiles repentance unto life'"* (Acts 11:18).

The word *even* in Acts 11:18 is revealing. It shows that these Spirit-filled believers were full of prejudice. Their words amaze us. But remember, believers grow slowly. Luke has brought us to the top of a mountain. From here, the Church will spread to the whole world. It is a thousand miles from Jerusalem to Rome. But the hardest part of the journey was the first fifty miles from Jerusalem to Caesarea! The mountains between cultures are steeper than all other mountains! But by the Spirit the steepest mountain can become flat (Zech. 4:6-7). Acts tells how the gospel spread from one culture to many.

Q 14 ➘ *Are Spirit-filled believers you know prejudiced toward others? Explain.*

D. The evidence of the gift of the Holy Spirit is speaking in tongues.

Peter and the six men with him had no doubts. They were certain the Gentiles had received the gift of the Spirit. They knew because they heard them speak in tongues!

Q 15 ➚ *How were Peter and his six witnesses sure the Gentiles had been filled with the Spirit?*

⁴⁵*The circumcised believers who had come with Peter were astonished that the gift of the Holy Spirit had been poured out even on the Gentiles. ⁴⁶For they heard them speaking in tongues and praising God* (Acts 10:45-46).

The Holy Spirit is in all believers (Rom. 8:9). And there are various evidences that the Spirit is within a believer. His presence gives us an inner assurance that we are God's children (Rom. 8:16). This assurance is an evidence of His presence. Likewise, our love for God, His Word, believers, and the lost are evidence of God's Spirit within. Again, the fruit of the Spirit is evidence of the Spirit's presence. But none of these is the evidence of the baptism in the Holy Spirit. The presence of the Spirit and the baptism in the Spirit are two different things. The Spirit is present in all believers. But not all believers have been baptized in the Spirit.

+ All but the apostles fled from Jerusalem for a time. Perhaps things settled down after Saul's conversion. Then some believers returned.

Q 16 ↗ *Must there be a long wait between being saved and being filled with the Spirit? Explain.*

The baptism in the Spirit is for those who have already believed in Jesus. Recall that Luke refers to the baptism in the Spirit as the gift of the Spirit. The 120 believed and later received the gift of the Spirit (Acts 2:1-4). Peter told the crowd to repent and be baptized. Then he said they would receive the gift of the Spirit (Acts 2:38). The Samaritans believed and were baptized (Acts 8:12-13). Later, they received the gift of the Spirit (Acts 8:17). Cornelius and his household believed as Peter was speaking. Then they immediately received the Spirit (Acts 10:44-46). There does not need to be a large gap between believing in Jesus and receiving the gift of the Spirit. But for New Testament believers, receiving Christ as Savior must come before the gift of the Spirit. The believers at Ephesus believed in Jesus and were baptized (Acts 19:1-7). Then they received the gift of the Spirit. It would have been hard for Luke to make it any plainer. The gift of the Spirit comes after believing in Jesus. And the evidence of this gift is speaking in a new language (Acts 2:4; 10:45-46; 19:6). Luke wants all believers to have the gift of the Spirit. We know we have this gift when we speak in tongues.

Q 17 ↗ *Why do Pentecostals emphasize speaking in tongues as the evidence of the baptism in the Spirit?*

Why do we emphasize this point so much? Because the gift of the Spirit is precious. Its value is beyond words. When you find something of great value, you want to share it. All who have received the gift of the Spirit want others to have the same gift. One Pentecostal pastor said it was not his responsibility to tell believers whether or not they had the gift of the Spirit.[6] We appreciate this pastor's spirit of love, humility, and unity. But is it his responsibility to help a person know whether or not he or she is born again? Or shall we just let people depend on their own feelings and opinions? Millions of us believers thought we had the gift of the Holy Spirit when we were born again. We loved God, His Word, other believers, and the lost. We had some fruit of the Spirit in our lives. We thought we had the gift of the Holy Spirit. Then we received what we thought we already had! Our experience was glorious. Our lives were filled to overflowing with the Spirit's presence. Our witness for Christ became more powerful. This new power helped us to live in victory over sin. Also, some of us began to have spiritual gifts. We all spoke in tongues! And every one of us wants other believers to receive this gift. The Bible gives one evidence that removes all doubt. When a follower of Jesus Christ speaks in a new language, we know that person is filled with the Spirit. Peter and his witnesses knew the Gentiles had received the gift of the Spirit. *"For they heard them speaking in tongues and praising God"* (Acts 10:46). We emphasize this truth so that no believer will stop short of the promise.

We often live far below what God intends. D. L. Moody used to say that God made us to soar like eagles; but we are content to scratch like sparrows. Christian, do you want to receive all that God has for you?

Lesson 26

Barnabas and Saul's Ministry at Antioch (Acts 11:19-30)

Goal: *Summarize 4 insights about the ministry in Antioch. Relate these to your context.*

Setting

Q 18 ↗ *Which city had the most people—Jerusalem, Antioch, or Corinth?*

Antioch was 300 miles (483 km) north of Jerusalem. It had a population of between 250,000[7] and 500,000.[8] This made it one of the largest cities in the ancient world. Only Rome and Alexandria were bigger.[9] The main street in Antioch was 4½ miles (7 km) long and 32 feet (10 m) wide. It had columns on both sides. Antioch was a beautiful city, but very sinful. There was a great temple to *Apollo, the Greek god of the sun. A thousand prostitutes committed sins with those who worshiped there.[10] However, this immoral city became the center of Christianity. It was Antioch, not Jerusalem, that became the key to reaching the world for Christ. Evil cities are giants of sin. But they are not too big for God. The Church should always make cities into centers of evangelism. This was Paul's strategy. Let us look at four truths related to the ministry in Antioch.

A. God has many faithful workers who are not famous.

Barnabas and Saul made the headlines in this section. But there are some other people who are just as important.

> [19]*Now those who had been scattered by the persecution in connection with Stephen traveled as far as Phoenicia, Cyprus and Antioch, telling the message only to Jews.* [20]*Some of them, however, men from Cyprus and Cyrene, went to Antioch and began to speak to Greeks also, telling them the good news about the Lord Jesus.* [21]*The Lord's hand was with them, and a great number of people believed and turned to the Lord* (Acts 11:19-21; See Figures 2.3 and 2.4).

Luke reminds us that persecution scattered believers (Acts 8:1). It was not their love for the lost that caused them to travel. Persecution scattered them. Luke also reminds us that all of the scattered believers preached as they fled. Many did as they had always done. That is, they shared the good news with Jews only (Acts 11:19). But notice the way Acts 11:20 begins. *"Some of them . . ."* Luke gives us no names here. *"Some of them"* began to speak to the Greeks. These precious believers were as much heroes as Stephen, Philip, and Peter. They were bold and Spirit filled. They obeyed God more than culture or tradition. What was the result? *"A great number of people believed and turned to the Lord"* (Acts 11:21). We honor and respect Stephen for being such a faithful witness. All believers desire to be like him. We admire Philip for winning many to the Lord in Samaria. People name their children after him! And we lift up Peter for helping the family of Cornelius. Stephen, Philip, and Peter are famous believers. Whom shall we admire for winning this great number to the Lord? *Some of them!*

Heaven will be full of faithful men and women who were never famous. We read about only one Elijah in the Bible. But there were 7,000 other faithful believers whose names we do not know (1 Kings 19:14-18). This is always true. A few believers are well known. But there are millions of faithful believers unknown to most. Revelation 11:18 assures us that God will reward the small and the great. Even those who give a cup of cold water in Christ's name will be rewarded (Matt. 10:42). *"God is not unjust; he will not forget your work and the love you have shown him as you have helped his people and continue to help them"* (Heb. 6:10).

Saul would have remained blind without an Ananias. Peter would have been wet and hungry without a Simon the tanner. Many widows would have been cold without a Dorcas. Greeks in Antioch would have been in hell without *some of them.* God will have a special place in heaven for the little people—that is, those who were faithful to Him, but whose names were seldom mentioned. People on earth may never see you as a hero. But God is keeping a record. *"Many who are first will be last, and many who are last will be first"* (Matt. 19:30).

B. There are many cultures, but only one gospel.

For 15 years the Jerusalem church had been preaching a Jewish gospel. That was all right to reach Jews in Jerusalem. Why? Because Jews were talking to Jews. Yet Jesus had told believers to go into all the world. There were only about four million Jews in the world. But there were 250 million Gentiles.[11] That is more than 60 Gentiles for each Jew. But the Jerusalem church was not reaching out to the Gentiles.

Then came persecution. Believers scattered. *Some of them* preached the good news to the Greeks in Antioch, Syria. The Greek word for a Greek person is *Hellene.* Therefore, Greek ideas are *Hellenistic. Antioch was a major center of Hellenism, that is, Greek

Figure 9.7 Carved stone head of *Apollo

Q 19 *What are the names of those who first preached to the Greeks?*

Figure 9.8 Remains of the temple to Apollo like the one in Antioch, Syria

Q 20 *How can you use Acts 11:20 to encourage yourself and others?*

Q 21 *What language do you think the Jews used to preach to the Greeks? Explain.*

ideas and culture. So the scattered Jews preached in Greek! These witnesses were probably Grecian (Hellenistic) Jews, like Stephen. They tried a new method! Amazing! The Church often likes old methods better than new ones! But these Jews preached to the Greeks. They spoke their language.[12]

Q 22 What were 4 requirements for being a member of the Jerusalem church?

To reach a person for Christ requires two things. *First,* we must speak a *language* the lost person understands. Most Greeks will not understand if a person speaks Hebrew to them. *Second,* we must speak a *message* the lost person understands. Few Greeks will understand or accept a Jewish gospel. To become a believer in Jerusalem meant being under the Law. It meant eating certain foods. It meant offering animal sacrifices in the temple. It meant circumcision for males. In Jerusalem, Judaism was the door to the church (Acts 21:17-24). The Jerusalem church was a Jewish church.

Alex and David were young believers. Full of zeal, they went out to witness. An old man welcomed them. He agreed that they could share some truth from the Bible. Alex asked, "Do you want to be washed in the blood?" The old man was shocked. "What?" he asked. "Washed in blood?" "Yes," replied Alex and David. "Do you want to be washed in the blood of the Lamb?" The old man asked, "Will you bring the blood in a bowl or a cup? How much blood will be needed?" The old man became angry. He told the young men to leave his house. They left feeling low. In time, they learned to explain the gospel message in a better way. And they were able to lead the old man to the Savior.[13]

Q 23 Does your church require all believers to dress, eat, and worship alike? Explain.

It is important to separate the gospel from every culture. The gospel is that Jesus died to take away our sins. He conquered death. And He will return to take His own and judge sinners. Jesus was a Jew. But this does not mean we need to learn Hebrew, or worship in synagogues. Gentiles do not need to become Jews to become Christians. All believers do not need to look, dress, eat, and worship alike. There is one gospel, but many cultures!

Q 24 Comment on any of the questions in the last paragraph before point C.

How does this apply today? Should a church require younger believers to dress the same as older believers? Must the youth enjoy the same music as the elders? Shall believers in the city dress like those in the country? Shall those with more education look down on believers with less education? Or shall those with less education criticize those with more? Should all believers live on the same amount of money? Must believers in Africa sing songs from America? Shall Charismatics be required to worship in the same way as Pentecostals? Do all believers need to stand up or fall down in God's presence? Must all believers study the same version of the Bible? Should all wives wear head coverings like the women at Corinth? Or do some cultures show submission in different ways? Should all believers greet each other with a holy kiss (2 Cor. 13:12)? Or is this only a custom of certain cultures? Should all believers wash each other's feet (John 13:4-17)? Or are there other ways for some cultures to show humility? Should it be a young man or an elder who starts a new church? Different cultures may have different answers to these questions. But the Jerusalem church was focused on only one culture. Persecution drove Philip to Samaria. And the Spirit led Peter to Cornelius. Even after this, there was still no rush to help the Gentiles. Even Peter continued his ministry mostly to the Jews (Gal. 2:7-9).[14] But the Lord started a new center for evangelism at Antioch. This would be a church that reached out to the whole world and not to Jews only.

C. Barnabas saw God's grace and encouraged new believers to remain true to the Lord.

²²*News of this reached the ears of the church at Jerusalem, and they sent Barnabas to Antioch.* ²³*When he arrived and saw the evidence of the grace of God, he was glad and encouraged them all to remain true to the Lord with all their hearts* (Acts 11:22-23).

Note three things in these verses.

Q 25 Would most Jerusalem believers have agreed that Christians in Antioch were saved? Explain.

First, Barnabas saw the evidence of the grace of God. The Jerusalem church sent the right man to Antioch.[15] Barnabas was a positive person. He liked to encourage people.

A negative person, like Thomas, might not have seen the evidence! He might have seen the lack of Jewish customs. These Greek believers were not wearing *phylacteries. They were not eating Jewish food. They were not offering sacrifices. And the men were not even circumcised! Many in the Jerusalem church would have doubted the salvation of Antioch believers. But Barnabas rejoiced. He *"saw the evidence of the grace of God"* (Acts 11:23).

What do you see when you look at a new convert? Some see hair that is too long. Others see a dress that is too short. Some see a person that plays loud music. Others see a person that needs to change many things. But Barnabas saw the evidence of the grace of God. Blessed is the new believer who is surrounded by people like Barnabas.

The Faith Mission was serving in Africa. Over the years, the mission had established Bible schools, churches, and other schools. Then they heard that some missionaries had come to Africa from another country. The new mission was called Hope Mission. The Faith Mission sent Frank, one of their missionaries, to meet the new visitors. Frank talked to them a few minutes. He returned with a negative report. Frank said the Hope Mission was too independent. It would be impossible to work together with its missionaries.

Second, he *"encouraged them all to remain true to the Lord"* (Acts 11:23). Barnabas, Son of Encouragement, encouraged them to remain true to the Lord. Why? Because we must remain true to the Lord to reach heaven.

Some teach once saved, always saved. And some teach that you can be a Christian without being a disciple. A disciple is a learner, a student, and a follower of Jesus. A disciple is one who learns and practices what Jesus teaches. Some falsely teach that there are many believers, but few disciples. These teach that one can believe in Jesus, but not follow His teachings.[16] This contradicts the Scriptures. In the Bible, to believe in Jesus means to follow Him.

Study the word *disciple* throughout Acts. It is the Greek word, *mathetes*. It occurs about 30 times. Disciples and believers are two words that refer to the same group of people. Disciples are not a group that is more spiritual than other believers are. There is only one group that follows Jesus. All believers are disciples. And all disciples are believers (Luke 9:23-26). *Disciple* is just another name for *Christian* (Acts 11:26).

It is true that some believe, but later turn away from Jesus. These do not *remain true to the Lord.* All who remain true believers are disciples (John 8:31-32). They turn to Jesus and continue to face Him. Those who turn away from Jesus cease to be His disciples (John 6:66-69; 1 Tim. 1:18-20; 4:1; 2 Tim. 2:18; Gal. 5:4; 2 Pet. 1:10-11; 3:17).

A person will arrive in the direction he or she walks. No one walks backwards to arrive somewhere! Jesus is in heaven. Those who turn to the Lord turn towards heaven. Those who remain true to Him continue to face toward heaven. But those who turn away from Him turn toward hell. And people will eventually arrive at the place toward which they walk.

The Bible gives many warnings about falling away from the faith. And the Bible gives no warning where there is no danger! Many Scriptures teach that heaven is only for those who remain true to the Lord (Luke 12:8-9; 2 Tim. 2:12; Rev. 3:5).

Therefore, Barnabas encouraged the new believers at Antioch. He *"encouraged them all to remain true to the Lord"* (Acts 11:23). He emphasized the Lord rather than a list of rules or customs. Only those who remain true to the Lord reach heaven.

Third, he *"encouraged them all to remain true to the Lord **with all their hearts**"* (Acts 11:23). Do not miss the words *with all their hearts.* These words give us the key to remaining true to the Lord. The Lord sees the heart of each person (Rev. 2:23). Through the Scriptures and the Spirit, He speaks to each person. Those who obey grow in grace

Q 26 *Do believers in your church expect new converts to look and act a certain way? Explain.*

Q 27 *Is it possible that Frank was wrong? Explain.*

Q 28 *Can a person remain a believer and not be a disciple? Explain.*

Q 29 *Why did Barnabas tell Antioch believers to remain true to the Lord?*

Q 30 *Why is loving the Lord with all our hearts a key to remaining true to Him?*

(2 Pet. 3:18). But those who hold back areas of their hearts have problems remaining true. A divided house cannot stand. No one can serve two masters. The key to remaining true to the Lord is to love Him with a whole heart.

Lisa had lived a hard life. Her father left the family when she was only five. She did not remember much about him. But she did remember the times he came home drunk and beat her mother. And she remembered the smell of perfume that was on his clothes. None of the family went to church. Now, at the age of 21, her life was so empty. She had two children, but had never been married. Then a neighbor witnessed to her about the love of Jesus Christ. Lisa went with her to church. At the end of the service, she went forward. She repented of her sins and invited Jesus to be her Savior. A great joy filled Lisa's heart as she was born again. She arose from the altar with a big smile on her face. An older woman named Susan was frowning at her. "My dear," said Susan, "we are glad to see you repent. Now you must get that makeup off your face. Your hair and your dress are both too short. And do not wear any jewelry again. To be a Christian, you must look like a Christian!" Lisa was no longer smiling. She felt like someone had struck her with a whip. Confused, she never attended that church again. She was afraid she would become like Susan!

Marna was divorced. She and her 12-year-old son lived in an apartment. She had a good job. Life was hard as a single parent. But she managed to make it through each day. A new couple moved into the apartment beside her. They were friendly and always smiling. She noticed that they went to church on Sundays and Wednesdays. The wife, Elizabeth, often greeted her. Sometimes they talked about the Bible. One day Elizabeth led Marna to the Lord. They cried together as Marna invited Jesus into her heart. Elizabeth encouraged Marna to remain true to the Lord with all her heart. They continued to study the Bible together. Soon, Marna was baptized and joined the church. She became friends with several women believers. It was a joy to be in God's family. After about two months, Marna knocked on Elizabeth's door. "The Lord has been speaking to me about my clothes," said Marna. "I want to dress more like you and the other women at church. Do you have a sewing machine? I would like to make my dresses a little longer on the bottom, and a little higher on the top." "Sure," replied Elizabeth. "I will be glad to help you. I'm pleased to hear that you are listening to the Lord. Remain true to Him with all your heart."

Q 31 ✎ *Why do you think the Spirit did not lead Barnabas back to Jerusalem for help?*

Luke emphasizes that Barnabas was *"a good man, full of the Holy Spirit and faith"* (Acts 11:24). He needed help. It is interesting that he did not return to get help from Jerusalem.[17] Rather, the Spirit led Barnabas to find Saul in Tarsus. He brought him to help with the ministry there. Three times in Acts 11:19-26, Luke emphasizes that great numbers of people were saved and taught. Note also that the teaching continued for a whole year, not just a few weeks. Barnabas and Saul encouraged and helped the new believers remain true to the Lord. It is important to help new converts become strong in the faith. Then they will be able to overcome sin, trials, temptations, and false teachings. Also, a good foundation helps enable them to be fruitful witnesses.

Q 32 ✎ *Who deserved to be called Christians, believers in Jerusalem or Antioch? Explain.*

The disciples were called Christians[+] first in Antioch, not Jerusalem. To be a Christian means to be a follower of Jesus. How did the believers in Antioch follow in the footsteps of Jesus? They loved people of all races and cultures. Antioch became a center for ministry to the Gentiles. Soon Barnabas and Saul would be traveling to and from there.

+ The word *Christian* occurs only three times in the New Testament (Acts 11:26; 26:28; 1 Pet. 4:16). In the beginning, a Christian was a disciple of Jesus Christ. Today, the word has lost much of its meaning. Many call themselves Christians who do not follow Christ. So to avoid confusion, we usually use the word *believer* instead of *Christian* in this book.

D. Few are prophets, but all may prophesy.

²⁷During this time some prophets came down from Jerusalem to Antioch. ²⁸One of them, named Agabus, stood up and through the Spirit predicted that a severe famine would spread over the entire Roman world. (This happened during the reign of Claudius.) (Acts 11:27-28).

A prophet is a person who speaks a revelation from God to others. Sixteen books of the Old Testament are named after prophets. Jesus was the Prophet about whom Moses prophesied (Acts 3:22-23). The New Testament emphasizes apostles more than prophets. Still, there are prophets *included in* the New Testament. Prophets are part of the Lord's gifts to the Church (Eph. 4:11). The New Testament teaches several things about prophets.

Q 33 ⟍ *Explain 2 possible purposes of a prophetic message.*

- One of a prophet's purposes is *"to prepare God's people for works of service, so that the body of Christ may be built up"* (Eph. 4:11-12).
- The message of a prophet may be to encourage, strengthen, and comfort (Acts 15:32; 1 Cor. 14:3). It may also be to warn or tell about the future (Acts 11:27-28; 13:1-2; 21:10-11). In Acts, prophets predict the future at least as often as they do other types of ministry.[18]
- We need prophets *"until we all reach unity in the faith and in the knowledge of the Son of God and become mature, attaining to the whole measure of the fullness of Christ"* (Eph. 4:13). In other words, we need prophets until we reach heaven!

It takes a calling from God to be an apostle, prophet, evangelist, pastor, or teacher. Few are called to be prophets. Still, all may prophesy. Joel gave us a special promise about the coming of the Holy Spirit.

¹⁷"'In the last days, God says, I will pour out my Spirit on all people. Your sons and daughters will prophesy, your young men will see visions, your old men will dream dreams. ¹⁸Even on my servants, both men and women, I will pour out my Spirit in those days, and they will prophesy'" (Acts 2:17-18).

God wants all believers to eagerly desire spiritual gifts, especially the gift of prophecy (1 Cor. 14:1, 31, 39). Paul taught that one who speaks in tongues in church should pray to interpret. Then, other believers will be edified. Paul emphasized that believers build themselves up by praying in tongues (1 Cor. 14:4). He prayed in tongues more than others, privately (1 Cor. 14:18-19). Paul wanted all believers to pray in tongues. Then they would be spiritually edified. Of course there are many times when believers can pray quietly in tongues while at church (1 Cor. 14:28). But Paul desired all to prophesy when believers gathered (1 Cor. 14:5). This reminds us of the words of Moses. *"I wish that all the LORD's people were prophets and that the LORD would put his Spirit on them!"* (Num. 11:29). Why should we desire to prophesy? Because prophecy builds up the entire local church (1 Cor. 14:4).

Q 34 ⟍ *Why should every believer desire to prophesy in church?*

How wonderful it would be if churches got back to God's original plan! All believers would be filled with the Spirit. They would pray in tongues at home and be built up. Then, at church, they would prophesy. That is, they would speak spiritual insights to encourage, strengthen, comfort, or warn. What a contrast this would be to the modern church. We appreciate pastors. They are one of God's gifts to the Church. But the Lord never intended for the pastor to be the only one who ministers in the church! All Spirit-filled believers may prophesy (1 Cor. 14:31)! Do not make prophecy less than it is. It is more than just preaching a sermon. Prophecy is as supernatural as speaking in tongues. Still, do not make prophecy harder than it is. Prophecy is as easy as speaking in tongues when the Spirit fills a person.

Sometimes we reach past God's gifts. Julius was a Spirit-filled believer. His friend, Amos, was a believer. But he wanted to be filled with the Spirit. The two prayed together. Amos began to beg and plead. His prayers sounded like deep groans of agony. Julius stopped him. He told Amos that he was reaching past God's gift of the

Q 35 ⟍ *Explain: Sometimes we reach past God's gifts.*

Verse	Acts
"I will pour out my Spirit on all people. Your sons and daughters will prophesy,"	2:17
"Even on my servants, both men and women, I will pour out my Spirit in those days, and they will prophesy."	2:18
22"For Moses said, 'The Lord your God will raise up for you a prophet like me from among your own people; you must listen to everything he tells you. 23Anyone who does not listen to him will be completely cut off from among his people.'"	3:22-23
"This is that Moses who told the Israelites, 'God will send you a prophet like me from your own people.'"	7:37
During this time some prophets came down from Jerusalem to Antioch.	11:27
In the church at Antioch there were prophets and teachers: Barnabas, Simeon called Niger, Lucius of Cyrene, Manaen . . . and Saul.	13:1
They traveled through the whole island until they came to Paphos. There they met a Jewish sorcerer and false prophet named Bar-Jesus,	13:6
Judas and Silas, who themselves were prophets, said much to encourage and strengthen the brothers.	15:32
When Paul placed his hands on them, the Holy Spirit came on them, and they spoke in tongues and prophesied.	19:6
He [Philip] had four unmarried daughters who prophesied.	21:9
A prophet named Agabus came down from Judea. 11Coming over to us, he took Paul's belt, tied his own hands and feet with it and said, "The Holy Spirit says, . . ."	21:10-11

Figure 9.9   Some verses in Acts about prophets and prophesying

Spirit. That is, he was trying too hard. A gift is something the giver has already decided to give. Therefore, a believer does not need to beg for it. Julius encouraged Amos to thank God for the gift, then to receive it by faith. Likewise, we do not need to convince God to give us the gift of prophecy. We need to only speak out the words of faith He brings to our minds. This is much easier for people who pray in tongues throughout the day. Why? They are already built up and sensitive to the Spirit.

On the one hand, Paul teaches us not to treat prophecies with contempt (1 Thess. 5:19-22). On the other hand, we must carefully weigh all prophecies (1 Cor. 14:29). Prophecies must never contradict Scripture. Some prophets are false (Deut. 18:22; Acts 13:6; Rev. 2:20). And some prophecies may not be correct. Notice that Agabus was a prophet they knew. He was from Jerusalem, the center of the Church (Acts 11:27). Knowing the person who prophesies helps us know his or her heart. Prophets and prophecies of the Holy Spirit are a great blessing.

How did the prophecy of Agabus help believers at Antioch? Recall that believers fled from Jerusalem. They were scattered throughout Judea and Samaria (Acts 8:1). Therefore, the famine would be very hard on these scattered believers. They had already lost their possessions. So the Greek believers at Antioch decided to help the Jewish believers in Judea.

29The disciples, each according to his ability, decided to provide help for the brothers living in Judea. 30This they did, sending their gift to the elders by Barnabas and Saul (Acts 11:29-30).

Q 36 By what standards should we examine prophecies?

The gift from Antioch served two purposes. *First,* it helped poor Jewish believers in Judea when the famine came. *Second,* it strengthened the relationship between Gentile believers in Syria and Jewish believers in Judea. And it was one prophecy that made both of these blessings possible.

Q 37 Which 2 blessings did the prophecy of Agabus make possible?

We will study more about prophesying when we reach Acts 21:9-14. Figure 9.9 summarizes verses in Acts about prophets and prophesying.

Lesson 27

Peter's Escape and Herod's Death (Acts 12:1-25)

Goal: *Explain 4 contrasts in Acts 12. Apply these to self and others.*

Setting

Luke has shown us how the gospel spread by the power of the Holy Spirit. Jesus said believers would be baptized in the Holy Spirit (Acts 1:5). The Spirit's power would enable them to be His witnesses in Jerusalem, Judea, Samaria, and the ends of the earth (Acts 1:8).

Recall that Acts 1:8 divides Acts into three parts. In the first part, Acts 1–7, the Church was planted in Jerusalem. These chapters cover about 10 years from A.D. 30-40. Then persecution scattered believers. Acts 8–12 is the second part of Acts covering about A.D. 40-47. It tells how the scattered believers witnessed as they fled. Through Philip, the gospel went to Samaria and Ethiopia. Through Peter, the gospel went to Caesarea. Through *some of them* the gospel went to Antioch, the big city in Syria. Thus we have seen the gospel spreading across miles and cultures.

Acts 12 is the final chapter in the second part of Acts. Luke uses this chapter to give us a brief update. The fire of persecution in Jerusalem had died down. Some believers had returned. But the coals of persecution were still hot.

King Herod Agrippa I became ruler over Judea in A.D. 41.[19] He is the Herod in Acts 12 (See Figure 9.11). The Church was about 11 years old when Herod began to rule over Judea. As a new ruler there, Herod wanted the favor of the Jewish leaders (Acts 12:1-3). These leaders were deeply troubled about Christianity. Thousands of Jews were following the risen Christ. Now, the gospel had spread to Samaria, Caesarea, and Antioch. Jewish leaders wanted Christianity stopped. They made it clear to Herod how he could please them. So he persecuted the Church.

Q 38 *Why did the government persecute the witnesses of Jesus?*

Ruler	Generation	Place of ruling	Time	Scripture
1. King Herod the Great (Tried to kill the baby Jesus)	1	Judea, Galilee, Iturea, Trachonitis	37–4 B.C.	Matt. 2:1-19 Luke 1:5
2. Archelaus	2	Judea & Samaria	4 B.C.–A.D. 6	Matt. 2:22
3. Herod Philip I (Uncle and first husband of Herodias)	2	None	Died about A.D. 34	Matt. 14:3 Mark 6:17
4. Herod Antipas (Uncle and second husband of Herodias; killed John the Baptist)	2	Galilee and Perea	4 B.C.–A.D. 39	Luke 3:1; 23:7-12 Matt. 14:1-12 Mark 6:14-29
5. Herod Philip II	2	Iturea and Trachonitis	4 B.C.–A.D. 34	Luke 3:1
6. Herod Agrippa I (Killed the apostle James)	3	King of Judea, Samaria, Galilee, and Perea	A.D. 37–44	Acts 12:1-24
7. Herod Agrippa II (Listened to Paul's defense)	4	King of part of Judea	A.D. 52–59	Acts 26:1-32

Figure 9.10   Herod the Great, and the rulers who descended from him[20]

Herod was one of many little kings. But God is the only big King. The greatest theme in Acts 12 is that God is sovereign. That is, He reigns and is in control. Let us look at four contrasts related to the fact that God reigns.

Q 39 *What do we mean by "God is sovereign"?*

A. The contrast between James, the martyred, and Peter, the delivered

[1]It was about this time that King Herod arrested some who belonged to the church, intending to persecute them. [2]He had James, the brother of John, put to death with the sword. [3]When he saw that this pleased the Jews, he proceeded to seize Peter also. This happened during the Feast of Unleavened Bread (Acts 12:1-3).

About this time refers to the time Antioch believers sent their gift to Judea. While they were showing love, others were showing hate. Herod arrested some (Acts 12:1). There is that word *some* again. *Some* were put in prison. We know only what happened to the famous. James was martyred. And Peter was delivered. We do not know what happened to the other believers. But God knows!

Herod had James murdered with the sword. The Roman way of killing a prisoner with the sword was to cut off his head.[21] John the Baptist was also beheaded this way (Matt. 14:1-12).

James, his brother John, and Peter were great apostles. These were the three whom Jesus kept the closest to Him. When He raised the daughter of Jairus from the dead, He

Figure 9.11   Districts of the New Testament

allowed only Peter, James, and John in the room with Him (Luke 8:40-56). And when He prayed on the mountain, He took only these three apostles with Him (Luke 9:28-36). None were dearer to Jesus than Peter, James, and John.

Q 40 ➤ *Was the apostle James a man of holiness, faith, and prayer? Explain.*

This brings us to a problem. Why did Jesus deliver Peter, but not James? James was a godly man. He was a man of prayer. Why did God not deliver him from evil? What was the purpose of the death of James? Whom did it help?

Our questions do not end with James. Why did God allow Stephen to be stoned? Or why did God raise Dorcas from the dead, but leave Stephen in the grave? Stephen was doing so much for the Kingdom. He was one of the best preachers in the Church. God could have raised him up. But He left him in the grave. Instead, He raised up Dorcas to continue sewing! This is hard for us to understand.

[33]*Oh, the depth of the riches of the wisdom and knowledge of God! How unsearchable his judgments, and his paths beyond tracing out!* [34]*"Who has known the mind of the Lord? Or who has been his counselor?"* (Rom. 11:33-34).

Q 41 ➤ *False teachers say that Stephen and James died for what reasons?*

Some, like Job's friends, have simple answers (Job 4–25). They teach that bad things happen only to bad people. They teach that faith delivers us from the trials that killed Stephen and James. These hypocrites claim to have more faith than James and Paul. But time has a way of humbling the proud. There is no easy answer to the death of James. We do not know why God allowed his death. Still, like Job, we trust God.

Possible explanation of hard times	Scriptures
1. **The Galilee principle:** The storm helps us appreciate the calm. The night helps us appreciate the day.	Luke 8:22-25 Acts 9:31
2. **The Hebrews principle:** God disciplines those He loves. *"Before I was afflicted, I went astray, but now I obey . . ."*	Heb. 12:7; Ps. 119:67 Acts 5:1-16
3. **The Paul principle:** We comfort others with the comfort we receive.	Acts 14:8-22; 27:21-26 2 Cor. 1:4
4. **The Stephen principle:** God is doing a deeper and wider work in our lives or in the Church.	Acts 8:1; Gen. 50:20
5. **The James principle:** We don't know yet! But God is sovereign.	Acts 12:2; Deut. 29:29

Figure 9.12   Five possible ways to understand hard times

Q 42 ➤ *Summarize each of the 5 principles that may explain hard times.*

Life has many hard questions. Why do children die? Why do accidents kill believers? Why do believers sometimes have financial problems? Why do the righteous suffer while the ungodly prosper? Why does divorce come to some godly people? These are hard questions.[+] Figure 9.12 gives five possible explanations. Each of these applies to different situations.[22] Take time to look up the Scriptures in Figure 9.12. These Scriptures give illustrations of each of the five principles. Every pastor should preach a message on these five principles.

Q 43 ➤ *Do you spend more time counting blessings or problems? Explain.*

The just live by faith. In hard times believers should search their souls. It is good to see which of the five principles apply. There is a time to ask "Why?" But there is also a time to stop asking why. Sometimes, as in the death of James, we must rest in God. There is a time to stop mourning for James and rejoice for Peter! And that is what we will do right now! In Acts 12 Luke writes two verses about James and sixteen about Peter. It is wise to spend most of our time thinking about the good things God does!

B. The contrast between Peter's part and God's part

Peter was an average student. He was not always at the top of the class (Matt. 16:23). He learned some lessons slowly and others quickly. It took Peter years to learn that

---

+ See *The Life & Teachings of Christ* in the *Faith & Action Series,* chapter 5, Lesson 14 (Matt. 11:1-6).

all foods are clean. Jesus told the disciples that no food makes a person unclean (Matt. 15:10-20). Years later, Peter still had not learned that lesson. He refused to eat food God told him to eat (Acts 10:9-16). But Peter did learn to trust in God. Once, Peter worried while Jesus slept (Luke 8:22-25). However, in the prison, worry did not rob Peter of sleep. A soldier was chained to each of his wrists. It was not comfortable. And Herod planned to kill him in the morning. Once Peter would have been worried. But he learned to put his trust in Jesus. The Lord had let him out of prison before (Acts 5:17-20). If God desired, He would do it again. If not, Peter could do nothing. He said his prayers and went to sleep. Even the light from the angel did not awaken him (Acts 12:7). Peter had learned the difference between his part and God's part.

Q 44 ⟩ What enabled Peter to sleep the night before his scheduled death?

It took a miracle for Peter to escape from the prison. Peter had a part. But consider the contrast between Peter's part and God's part.

Peter's part	God's part
Peter stood up.	God caused the chains to fall off.
Peter put on his sandals and clothes.	God caused the soldiers to keep sleeping.
Peter followed the angel.	God opened the prison doors.
Peter kept walking.	God opened the iron gate of the city.

Figure 9.13   Peter's part and God's part in the escape from prison

What a team God and Peter made!

A mouse climbed on the back of an elephant. He held on as the elephant walked across a bridge. The bridge trembled beneath the feet of the heavy elephant. Finally they reached the other side. The mouse said, "We sure made that bridge shake!"

Sometimes we take ourselves too seriously. We make our part too big and God's part too small. "Lord, teach us to rest in you. Help us to do the little You ask. Then help us trust You to do the rest."

C. The contrast between our weak faith and God's strong love

Mary, the mother of Mark, was wealthy. She lived in a big house and had at least one servant. Many people gathered at her house to pray for Peter (Acts 12:12). Notice that they gathered in one place. There is a time to gather together for prayer.

Q 45 ⟩ Give 3 examples showing that God honors weak faith.

Their faith was weak and imperfect. But they were using the little faith they had. They were praying for God to help Peter. God answered their prayers. Peter was free. He was knocking at the front door. Still, they did not believe!

God does not wait for perfect faith. Jesus healed a leper half-full of doubt. The diseased man did not even know if Jesus wanted to heal him. But the Lord answered his weak prayer (Luke 5:12-14). Another time, He helped a father with weak faith. Jesus encouraged the dad to believe. *"Immediately the boy's father exclaimed, 'I do believe; help me overcome my unbelief!'"* (Mark 9:24).

Use whatever faith God has given you. Do not wait to pray until you feel that your faith is strong enough. God loves His children. He loves to give good gifts to those who ask Him (Luke 11:5-13). He sometimes answers prayers that seem to contain no faith at all! The death of James shocked believers. But it did not stop them from praying. Weak faith works. God's love is so strong that He answers weak prayers.

Prayer is a powerful force. We must learn to change things through prayer. Criticism complains about the way things are. Worry frets about the way things are or may become. But prayer changes the way things are. Believers see things as they are. We do not deny that our problems exist. But we also see solutions. We must learn to think of things the way God and we want them to be. Then we can pray until God changes things.

Q 46 *How is prayer like a magnifying glass?*

Figure 9.14   A magnifying glass can focus light into a fire.

A Bible teacher named Jerry gave an example of prayer. He took a small magnifying glass (Figure 9.14). It was about as thick as the bottom of a Coke bottle. Its main purpose was to cause small letters on a page to look bigger. Some glasses people wear have lenses shaped like magnifying glasses. But the teacher knew this special glass lens could do something else. He took the students outside. The sun was shining brightly. The teacher and the students knelt on the ground in a circle. He held the glass so the light shone through it onto a piece of paper. The glass caused the sun's power to focus on one small spot. At first, nothing happened. But Jerry continued to hold the glass still. After a short time smoke began to rise from the paper. The spot was getting very hot. After a few minutes the light burned a hole in the paper! Prayer is like a magnifying glass. It allows the Light of the World to focus on one earthly problem. He works through prayer. Sometimes we quit praying too soon. We do not know how many days the believers had been praying for Peter. But as they continued, the power of God worked through their prayers.

A large snake moved on the ground. Slowly it slithered toward a nest of baby birds. The father and mother birds saw the snake. It was too big for them to fight. All they could do was make sounds through their beaks. Other birds heard. They recognized that the sounds were protests. Soon there were several different kinds of birds above the snake. All of them together could not stop the snake. All they could do was make bird sounds. The snake was getting closer to the nest. Then a farmer heard the birds protesting. He had heard those sounds before. He knew they meant the birds were in danger. So he took a long stick and went to give the snake a headache. In a short time the snake was dead. The birds returned to singing their beautiful songs.

D. The contrast between a dead king and the living Word

Herod killed the four guards instead of Peter. The king was embarrassed. He left Judea and went to Caesarea, where he had a palace.

Q 47 *Why did the citizens of Tyre and Sidon flatter Herod and seek peace with him?*

The people of Tyre and Sidon had been quarreling with Herod. But something caused them to seek peace. Remember that Paul and Barnabas had traveled to Judea with a gift. Antioch believers sent relief for the famine victims. It is likely that people in Tyre and Sidon were suffering from the famine. These two cities were located between the sea and the mountains.[23] Their food supply came from Judea. If food was scarce, they must make peace with Herod. So they found a way to meet with him.

The meeting day arrived (Acts 12:21). Herod dressed up in his royal robes. He sat on his throne and made a speech to them. *"They shouted, 'This is the voice of a god, not of a man'"* (Acts 12:22).

Do you think Herod's speech was so great? Or did they flatter him to get the food they needed? Compliments are given for various reasons! Herod thought they meant it. Their praise puffed him up.

Whoever flatters his neighbor is spreading a net for his feet (Prov. 29:5).

Q 48 *For whom shall we mourn the most, James or Herod?*

Immediately, God sent an angel to strike Herod down. Josephus, the Jewish historian, adds a few details. He says that Herod lived five more days with great pains in his stomach.[24] Herod began ruling Judea in A.D. 41. He died in A.D. 44.

Q 49 *What is a great contrast between Herod and God's Word?*

Worms ate Herod and he died (Acts 12:23). Slowly, his body began to return to the dust. In contrast, *"the word of God continued to increase and spread"* (Acts 12:24).

[24]*"All men are like grass, and all their glory is like the flowers of the field; the grass withers and the flowers fall,* [25]*but the word of the Lord stands forever."* And this is the word that was preached to you (1 Pet. 1:24-25).

Test Yourself: Circle the letter by the *best* completion to each question or statement.

1. Peter showed the greatest maturity by preaching in
a) Jerusalem.
b) Samaria.
c) Joppa.
d) Caesarea.

2. Jews did not associate with one like Simon the tanner because they thought he was
a) unclean.
b) unsaved.
c) a Samaritan.
d) a Roman.

3. A Roman centurion was over at least
a) 10 soldiers.
b) 100 soldiers.
c) 1,000 soldiers.
d) 10,000 soldiers.

4. Peter knew Cornelius had been filled with the Spirit because
a) all who believe in Jesus are filled with the Spirit.
b) Cornelius showed new joy and love.
c) he heard Cornelius speak in tongues.
d) Cornelius prayed, fasted, and saw a vision.

5. Which of the following cities was largest in Paul's time?
a) Jerusalem
b) Caesarea
c) Antioch
d) Athens

6. Being a member of the Jerusalem church required
a) only faith in Jesus Christ as Savior and Lord.
b) faith in Christ plus keeping the law of Moses.
c) faith in Christ plus tithing to the high priest.
d) faith in Christ plus selling one's possessions.

7. Those who first preached to the Greeks were
a) the twelve apostles.
b) the seven deacons.
c) Paul and Barnabas.
d) common believers.

8. Prophecy is one of God's promises for
a) the entire period of the Church.
b) the time of the apostles.
c) those believers who are prophets.
d) Pentecostals and Charismatics.

9. The death of James emphasizes the truth that God is
a) the same.
b) sovereign.
c) omnipotent.
d) faithful.

10. "We comfort others with the comfort we receive" states the
a) Galilee principle.
b) Hebrews principle.
c) Paul principle.
d) James principle.

 Essay Test Topics: Write 50-100 words on each of these goals that you studied in this chapter.

Peter's Ministry to Cornelius (Acts 9:32–11:18)

Goal: *Identify and apply 4 truths from Peter's ministry to Cornelius.*

Barnabas and Saul's Ministry at Antioch (Acts 11:19-30)

Goal: *Summarize 4 insights about the ministry in Antioch. Relate these to your context.*

Peter's Escape and Herod's Death (Acts 12:1-25)

Goal: *Explain 4 contrasts in Acts 12. Apply these to self and others.*

Figure 9.15   Samaria: Columns of Forum (Acts 8)

Figure 9.16   Caesarea: Roman ruins

Figure 9.17   Tarsus: Gate in wall of Byzantine town.
Paul was from Tarsus.

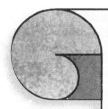

Unit 4:
The Witness of the Church
to the Ends of the Earth (Acts 13–28)

We are now entering the third and final part of Acts. Recall that Acts 1:8 reveals the structure of the whole book. The theme of Acts is the spread of the gospel from Jerusalem to Rome by the power of the Spirit (Figure 1.9).

In Chapter 10 you will travel with Paul on his first missionary journey. How did Paul grow from a new convert to a powerful apostle (Acts 13–14)? How did other apostles relate to his ministry to the Gentiles (Acts 15)? To answer these questions you will:

* *Explain and apply four keys to spiritual growth from Paul's first missionary trip.*
* *Identify and apply four more keys to spiritual growth from Paul's first missionary trip.*
* *Summarize five biblical steps to solving a problem. Relate these to your context.*

In Chapter 11 you will trace the steps of Paul on his second missionary trip (Acts 15:36–18:22). This second journey is especially important. Why? Because it includes most of the places he traveled on the first and third trips. Study this trip well. It is the key to mastering all three of Paul's misisonary trips. In this action-filled chapter you will:

* *Identify 11 provinces or districts, and 15 cities of Paul's second missionary trip.*
* *Summarize and apply what Acts 15–16 teaches about harvest, disagreements, guidance, attitudes, cultures, and citizens.*
* *State and explain five principles based on Acts 17.*
* *Explain and follow five steps for making new friends.*
* *Give four examples of Paul's friends in Acts 18.*

In Chapter 12 you will reach the mountaintop of Paul's missionary trips (Acts 18:23– 21:16). Finally, God knew Paul was ready for Ephesus. It is one of the most important cities in the New Testament. In this chapter you will:

* *Examine four principles from Paul's ministry in Ephesus. Relate these truths to your context.*
* *Explain what Paul's Ephesian ministry teaches about discussions, casting out demons, and public confession. Apply these teachings to your situation.*
* *Analyze four attitudes seen in Paul's travels from Ephesus to Jerusalem. Compare and contrast these with attitudes you have seen.*

In Chapter 13 you will travel with Paul on his journey to Rome (Acts 21:17–28:31). For years Paul had wanted to go there. It was the center of the Roman Empire. Luke has been telling us how the gospel spread from Jerusalem to Rome. The Church began so small it would fit in one upper room. Then, there were only a few local Jews. They spoke the same language and had the same culture. But as Acts closes, you will realize that the Church has spread across the Roman Empire. In only 30 years it has expanded to include many nations, languages, and cultures. In this final chapter you will:

* *Evaluate and apply three challenges of being a human bridge.*
* *Summarize what Acts 21–23 teaches about rumors, testifying, and protection.*
* *Explain and apply two ways Acts 21–28 relates to the purposes of Luke.*
* *Analyze and apply the roles of conscience and preachers in Acts 24–26.*
* *Relate Paul's faith in Acts 27 to the storms of life.*
* *Identify two truths in Acts 28. Apply these to your context.*

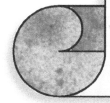

Chapter 10:

Paul's First Missionary Journey and Report at Jerusalem

(Acts 13:1–15:35)

Figure 10.1   Remains in Antioch, a city of Galatia

Introduction

It was 1934. Missionary George Roy Wood was dying. He tried to break his watch so his wife would know the time he died. But he was too weak to break the glass. Wood and two Chinese evangelists had traveled on horses. They visited a place in Hsiang Hsien Si. Many Buddhist priests lived there. Wood told the leader he had a gift for all the priests. The gift was a printed portion of Scripture. The leader of the priests said the priests were afraid. Wood was the first white man they had seen. He told Wood to wait. Meanwhile, following the custom of *Tibet, they served Wood a dish called *tsamba*. They dropped fresh butter into a wooden bowl. Then they poured hot tea over it. Wood knew the custom. He blew back the butter and drank the tea. Then they poured barley flour over what remained. To Wood, it tasted like eating sand! The priest praised Wood for knowing the language and the custom of *tsamba*. Then he left for a few minutes.

Wood was thinking about handing out the Scriptures. Focusing on this, he did not notice that the priest had not offered him a scarf. This was an important custom in Tibet. It showed that a visitor was welcome and would be safe. But the Chinese evangelists sensed danger. They urged Wood to leave immediately. So they all climbed on their horses and left. Soon, Wood became very sick. They stopped to rest, but the missionary grew worse and worse. He lay in the darkness awaiting death. But God awakened his wife to pray for him. She prayed until she felt peace. About that time, Wood vomited a green substance. At once he began to feel better. Later, some priests from Hsiang Hsien Si saw him. They said to him, "We thought you were dead." These reported the matter to another head priest. He wrote Wood a letter of apology. "They gave you enough poison to kill ten men," said the Buddhist priest. "Your God is greater than ours. Please come and tell us about Him."[1]

In Lystra, Jews who hated Paul stoned him. They thought he was dead. So they dragged him outside the city (Acts 14:19). But the power of God raised him up from the doors of death. Likewise, God still does miracles today. *"Is anything too hard for the LORD?"* (Gen. 18:14). *"Is the LORD's arm too short?"* (Num. 11:22).

Lessons:

Paul and Barnabas at Cyprus and Antioch in Pisidia (Acts 13:1-51)
Goal: *Explain and apply 4 keys to spiritual growth from Paul's first missionary trip.*

Paul and Barnabas in Iconium, Lystra, and Derbe, Then Back to Antioch (Acts 14:1-28)
Goal: *Identify and apply 4 more keys to spiritual growth from Paul's first missionary trip.*

The Important Church Meeting in Jerusalem (Acts 15:1-35)
Goal: *Summarize 5 biblical steps to solving a problem. Relate these to your context.*

                    Key Words

Galatian churches   anointing
proconsul   Judaizers   Jerusalem Council

Paul and Barnabas at Cyprus and Antioch in Pisidia (Acts 13:1-51)

Goal: *Explain and apply 4 keys to spiritual growth from Paul's first missionary trip.*

Setting

We have come to the third and final part of Acts. In part one, we saw the gospel spread in Jerusalem (Acts 1–7). In part two, we studied the spread of the gospel in Judea and Samaria (Acts 8–12). Now, in this final part, we will see the gospel spreading toward the ends of the earth (Acts 13–28).

Acts 13–21 includes three missionary journeys of Paul. Figures 10.2, 10.3, and 10.4 are maps of Paul's three trips. Take time to compare them. Notice that each new journey takes the gospel further than before.

Acts 13–14 tells about Paul's first missionary trip. He travels as far as Galatia. Galatia was a province that included the district of Pisidia. Paul establishes four Galatian churches. These include Pisidion Antioch, Iconium, Lystra, and Derbe. Many Bible teachers believe Paul's letter to the Galatians was to these four churches. His first missionary trip to them probably took 1 or 2 years. Then he wrote to them about A.D. 49.[2] This was just before he went to the church meeting in Jerusalem (Acts 15). We will study more about his letter to the Galatian churches in Lesson 30 of this chapter.

We want to look at the facts and learn the places of Paul's first missionary trip. But we want to do more than just gain knowledge. We want to study in a way that applies Scripture to our lives. A big theme in these chapters is spiritual growth. Therefore, as we study Acts 13–14, we will examine eight keys to growing in Christ. We will look at four keys in this lesson, and four in the next lesson.[3]

A. Key: Relate well to other believers.

Jesus calls us to be a part of His body. Each believer is a part of the whole. No believer should live as if other believers did not exist. He calls us all to relate to each other. An African proverb says *Kiara kimwe gitiuragaga ndaa*. That is, one thumb cannot kill a louse![4] Likewise, it is hard for a person to cut the hair on the back of his or her head. We need each other!

Sometimes churches put too much emphasis on one leader. Notice that the church at Antioch had a pastoral team.

[1]In the church at Antioch there were prophets and teachers: Barnabas, Simeon called Niger,

Q 1 *What are the 4 churches that Paul started in the province of Galatia?*

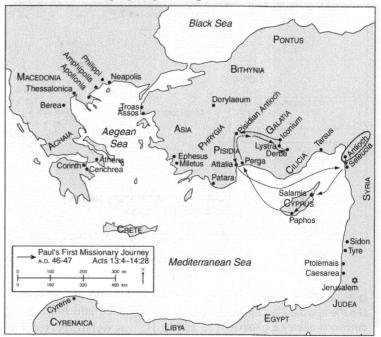

Figure 10.2 Paul's first missionary journey from Antioch in Syria

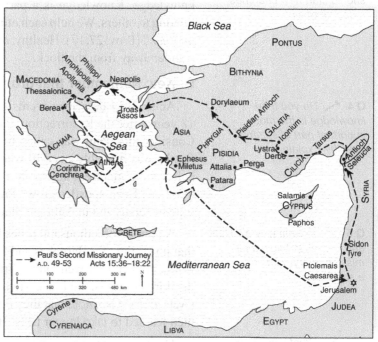

Figure 10.3 Paul's second missionary journey from Antioch in Syria

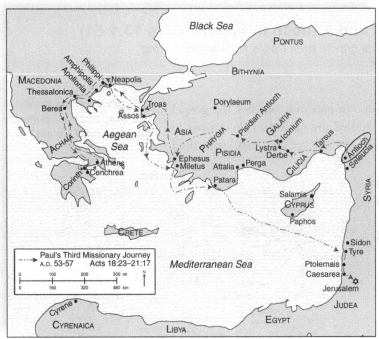

Figure 10.4   Paul's third missionary journey from Antioch in Syria

Q 2 *Did a spiritual man like the apostle Paul make decisions alone? Explain.*

Q 3 *Who do you think should start new churches today? Explain.*

Q 4 *Do you think knowledge is the most important part of spiritual growth? Explain.*

Q 5 *In what way did Paul and Barnabas begin their missionary trip with a small step?*

Q 6 *What steps can believers you know take to grow?*

Lucius of Cyrene, Manaen (who had been brought up with Herod the tetrarch) and Saul. ²While they were worshiping the Lord and fasting, the Holy Spirit said, "Set apart for me Barnabas and Saul for the work to which I have called them" (Acts 13:1-2).

Saul was a spiritual leader. But he served in relation to at least four other leaders. Five men made a decision together. The Spirit guided them to plan the first missionary trip. Two of the five were chosen.

Notice that the Holy Spirit did not pick the weakest and the youngest to go. Rather, He picked the strongest, best, most mature leaders they had. Churches today should follow the biblical pattern. We should choose the best leaders we have to start new churches. Send the leaders with the most experience to do the hardest work. Never send a boy to do a man's job! Even if he does his best, he may fail.

A company wanted to start a new business in a big city. Several of the leaders met. Together they planned their strategy. Whom should they send to start the new business? There were many to choose from. Some had just graduated from school. Others had been doing this work for many years. They decided it was best to send one of their top leaders. He had 10 years of experience. This man had already seen and helped solve many problems. His income and his family were stable. He was well respected. And he related well to others. The group agreed. The new business went well.

Some think that the main part of spiritual growth is reading books and gaining knowledge. Knowledge is a part. But the most important part of spiritual growth is relating to others. We help each other grow. *"As iron sharpens iron, so one man sharpens another"* (Prov. 27:17). Healthy, mature sheep are in flocks. Wild animals eat sheep that wander away from the flock.

B. Key: Remember that growth comes step by step.

Acts 13–14 describes events that happened about A.D. 46-48.⁵ This was about 16-18 years after the Resurrection. Paul had probably been a believer for at least 10 years. Consider this: Paul was called to be an apostle from his mother's womb (Gal. 1:15). But he was probably over 40 when he made his first missionary trip! It takes time for believers to mature. Paul spent a number of years growing in knowledge and relation to others. Even apostles grow slowly! He spent time studying the Scriptures. He spent time in Tarsus and in Antioch. Step by step he became the apostle God called him to be.

A journey of a thousand miles begins with the first step. The Holy Spirit announced that it was time for Barnabas and Saul to go. But they did not sail to a faraway place like Rome. Rather, they went only a little distance to Cyprus. Locate Cyprus on the map. It is the third largest island in the Mediterranean Sea. Recall that Barnabas was from Cyprus (Acts 4:36). Also, note that they began in a synagogue. This was familiar to them. These men learned to take longer trips. But they started with small steps.

Do you want to grow into what God has called you to be? Take small steps. Increase your giving 1 percent at a time. Agree to the responsibilities that are only a step in front of you. Attend Bible studies near you. Help children in your neighborhood. Teach a class. Work with youth. Visit the sick you know. These things are small steps that God has for you. And you will grow one step at a time. Growth is never from A to Z. It is always from A to B, B to C, C to D, and so on.

One young man felt called to be a great missionary. The pastor and elders offered him some responsibilities in the church. But they seemed small to him. He said he felt like an eagle asked to sit on a sparrow's nest. His pastor encouraged him not to despise the day of small things (Zech. 4:10). He said if the young man was faithful with a small nest, God would give him a bigger nest (Luke 16:10-12; 19:11-27). In school and in life we move up only one grade at a time.

C. Key: Expect opposition to God's will.

Satan does not clap for believers who want to grow. He opposes them. Paul and Barnabas got a good opportunity. A government ruler, Sergius Paulus, wanted to hear the Word of God (Acts 13:7). He was a *proconsul (See Figure 10.5). Luke records that many government rulers respected Christianity. One of Luke's purposes was to defend Christianity. Acts shows that Christianity related well to the government.

Q 7 ↗ *Name 5 Roman rulers in Acts who were friendly or helpful to Paul.*

Ruler's Title	Explanation	Rulers in Acts (⁺ shows rulers who helped Christians)	Acts
1. Caesar or Emperor	The top ruler of the Roman empire or kingdom	Caesar (Nero)	25:8-12
2. King	King Herod Agrippa I (Acts 12:1), was the grandson of Herod the Great (Matt. 2:1). Luke notes that Agrippa II would have freed Paul, but Paul appealed to Caesar.	⁺Herod Agrippa II	25:13-27 26:32
3. Tetrarch	Ruler of ¼ of a region (Luke 9:7-9)	Herod Antipas	13:1
4. Governor or Procurator	Appointed by Caesar to rule rebellious areas (Luke notes Pilate wanted to free Jesus, Luke 23; this attitude was helpful to believers.)	⁺ Pilate Felix Porcius Festus	3:13 23:26 24:27
5. Proconsul	Appointed by the Roman Senate to rule peaceful areas	⁺ Sergius Paulus ⁺ Gallio	13:6-12 18:12-17; 19:38
6. Officials of the Province	Men of wealth and influence who were part of a council. They were loyal to the emperor.	⁺ Friends of Paul	19:31
7. City officials	Local rulers of a city	⁺ No names given	17:6-9
8. City clerk	The most important local official—he was between a city and the Roman government.	⁺ No names given	19:35
9. Commander	Military officer in charge of at least six centurions and 600 soldiers	⁺ Claudius Lysias	21:30–23:30 24:22
10. Centurion	Military officer in charge of at least 100 soldiers	⁺ Cornelius ⁺ Julius	10:1–11:18 27:1-44

Figure 10.5   Rulers Luke mentions who are related to the Roman government

Sergius Paulus sent for Paul and Barnabas (Acts 13:6-7). Luke notes that this ruler was an intelligent man. All who are both intelligent and wise seek the Word. But Satan tried to hinder through Elymas. This man was a Jewish sorcerer. This is strange. The Jewish Scriptures teach against magic and witchcraft. Still, one often finds various religions mixed together. Such was the case with Elymas. And he stayed close to Sergius Paulus. He tried to prevent the government ruler from believing. Satan is never far from those who seek Christ.

Q 8 ✎ *Give an example from your culture of those who mix religious ideas.*

Opposition comes in many forms to those seeking to do God's will. Family members may discourage believers. Friends may become enemies. Employers may persecute those following Jesus. Sickness, laziness, temptations, and various trials oppose those

Q 9 ✎ *What types of opposition face believers you know?*

who desire to grow in Christ. Opposition is the common problem of all believers seeking to grow spiritually. Therefore, expect opposition. Do not take it personally. Opposition comes to every believer. The road to heaven is not all on flat ground. There are some hills to climb. *"Dear friends, do not be surprised at the painful trial you are suffering, as though something strange were happening to you"* (1 Pet. 4:12).

One wonders if the opposition surprised John Mark. He decided to go home to Jerusalem (Acts 13:13). He was a good young man and a cousin of Barnabas. Perhaps the missionary trip was too big a step in his spiritual growth (Acts 13:5, 13; 15:38). Later, after he grew some more, he wrote the Gospel of Mark.

D. Key: Stay filled with the Spirit.

Q 10 ↗ *Did Paul often speak harshly to those who opposed him? Explain.*

Paul was ready for opposition because he was filled with the Spirit. He had the spiritual power he needed to confront Satan (Acts 13:8-12). Paul spoke harsh words to Elymas. They remind us of the harsh words Peter spoke to Simon in Samaria (Acts 8:20-23). This is certainly not the gentle way Paul told Timothy to treat those who oppose (2 Tim. 2:24-26). This was one of those rare times when God spoke a strong judgment through a believer. In fact, Paul did more than speak. This is one of the few times in the New Testament when God's power harmed someone (Acts 9:8; 12:23; 13:11-12; 1 Cor. 11:30; Rev. 6). Why did Paul strike Elymas with blindness? There could be many possible reasons. But remember that God once struck Saul with blindness. And blindness helped Saul find the right road. So perhaps the blindness on Elymas was a severe mercy. It is better to face judgment now than after death.

Q 11 ↖ *Do Spirit-filled believers become gentler as they mature? Explain.*

The Spirit led Paul to be harsh with Elymas. But some believers are harsh because they are led by the flesh. The Spirit rarely desires a sinner to be blind! In most cases, the Spirit is gentle. As a young apostle, John wanted to call down fire from heaven on the Samaritans (Luke 9:54). As an old apostle, he was more gentle when people opposed him (3 John 9-11). Over the years, the Spirit changed John from the *Son of Thunder* to the *Apostle of Love*. Be sure the Spirit is leading you if you speak harsh words! Otherwise, be prepared to move from town to town! Usually, the wisdom from above is peaceful and full of mercy (James 3:17-18).

Staying filled with the Spirit is a theme in Acts. Luke emphasizes that Paul was filled with the Spirit (Acts 13:9). Later, he tells us that all the disciples were filled with the Spirit (Acts 13:52).

Q 12 ↗ *What are 4 physical needs that recur?*

God has made us to depend on Him daily. This is easy to see in the physical world. Yesterday's food is not enough for today. So the Lord taught us to ask Him for daily bread. Likewise, yesterday's water and rest are not enough for today. And were you healed in the past by the Lord's stripes (1 Pet. 2:24)? If so, that is wonderful. But you may need to be healed again. Many physical needs recur. They come back time after time.

Q 13 ↗ *What are 4 spiritual needs that recur?*

Spiritual needs also recur. Yesterday's prayers are not enough for today. Yesterday's devotions and Bible study are not enough for today. Both physical and spiritual needs recur. A person's sins are forgiven at the time of the new birth. Still, there may be times that we need God's forgiveness again. At conversion we received forgiveness for our past sins. But we did not receive forgiveness for future sins. However, as we confess our sins, God is faithful and just to forgive and cleanse us (1 John 1:9). Forgiveness is a recurring need.

Being filled with the Spirit is also a recurring need. Last year's filling of God's presence is not enough for today. The great men and women of God have always sought God's presence daily. They have hungered and thirsted after God on a daily basis. They have begun each day seeking to be filled with the Spirit. How shall we continue to grow spiritually? By daily seeking to be filled with the Spirit.

There is only one baptism in the Spirit. But there are many fillings. Fill up again. Each new day calls for a fresh filling of the Holy Spirit. New challenges require new power. New responsibilities call for more of God's help. The filling Paul had after conversion was glorious. But he needed a fresh filling to face Elymas. The *anointing he had as a new convert was precious. But it was not sufficient for the task that faced him in Cyprus. Paul kept growing in grace and in the Spirit of grace (2 Pet. 3:18; Heb. 10:29). Do not try to fight today's battles with yesterday's power. Keep growing and winning by staying filled with the Spirit.

The apostles learned the need for renewed faith and power each day. Read Luke 9:1-6. Notice that Jesus gave them power to drive out all demons. Later, they were surprised and defeated. Read Luke 9:37-40.

Q 14 ⟩ *What happened to the disciples' power between Luke 9:1-6 and Luke 9:40? Explain.*

Matthew tells us that their power was low because their faith was low (Matt. 17:19-20). And how do we build up our faith? We need daily prayer, fasting, and study of the Bible. Yesterday's faith and power will not win today's battles. Stay filled up!

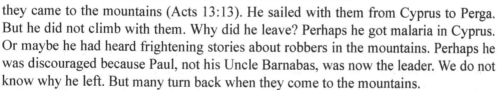

Lesson 29 **Paul and Barnabas in Iconium, Lystra, and Derbe, Then Back to Antioch (Acts 14:1-28)**
Goal: *Identify and apply 4 more keys to spiritual growth from Paul's first missionary trip.*

Setting

We are studying the first missionary trip of Paul. It is important to understand the geography of the places where he traveled. Paul and Barnabas started their journey from the city of Antioch in the province of Syria. From there they took a small step to Cyprus. This was home to Barnabas. They preached in Salamis on the east end of Cyprus. John Mark, the cousin of Barnabas, was with them there. They crossed the island from east to west. It was at Paphos, on the west end of Cyprus, that Sergius Paulus accepted Jesus.

Figure 10.6   Coastline near Paphos on the Island of Cyprus

Cyprus is the third largest island in the Mediterranean Sea. Low geographical areas, such as islands, are sources of malaria. We do not know if Paul, Barnabas, or John Mark became sick there. The three sailed north to Perga. Now the sea was behind them. But a hard journey was before them. Going north they must climb the Taurus Mountains. Lawless tribes and bandits lived in these mountains. No government could rule them.[6] There were many places to hide. And it was hard to travel in the mountains. Paul may refer to these bandits in 2 Corinthians 11:26. John Mark left them before they came to the mountains (Acts 13:13). He sailed with them from Cyprus to Perga. But he did not climb with them. Why did he leave? Perhaps he got malaria in Cyprus. Or maybe he had heard frightening stories about robbers in the mountains. Perhaps he was discouraged because Paul, not his Uncle Barnabas, was now the leader. We do not know why he left. But many turn back when they come to the mountains.

Q 15 ⟩ *What was facing John Mark when he chose to turn back?*

Besides knowing the geography, it is good to understand the political structure of places Paul went. The Roman kingdom was made up of many provinces. These were large areas of land. There was a Roman ruler over each province. Provinces were divided into smaller regions.[7] For example, the province of Galatia contained the district of Pisidia[8] (See Figure 10.2). Also, Pamphylia was part of Galatia from 25 B.C. to A.D. 43. Then the Emperor Claudius formed the province of Lycia-Pamphylia (See Figure 10.2). Sometimes the districts and provinces were named after the tribes who lived there.[9]

Q 16 ⟩ *Which is bigger, a province or a district? Explain.*

We have made a quick summary of the geography and political setting. Now let us continue studying Paul's first missionary journey. Our theme in this journey is "keys to spiritual growth." We examined four keys in the last lesson. Let us study four more.

A. Key: Do not quit. Have the courage to face suffering.

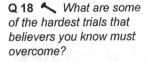 *Q 17 What are some things that could have caused Paul to quit?*

Paul was not a quitter. Perhaps that is why he marveled when some of the Galatians deserted the faith (Gal. 1:6). He did not quit when Elymas opposed him. He did not quit when John Mark left them. He kept climbing when he came to the mountains. Dark nights among robbers did not cause him to turn back. He kept going from Perga to Antioch. Many Jews turned to Jesus in Antioch of Pisidia. Paul and Barnabas urged them not to quit. They encouraged them to continue in the grace of God (Acts 13:43). Not all in Antioch believed. Some of the Jews were jealous. They criticized the apostles. Paul did not turn away from Jesus. But he turned from the Jews to the Gentiles (Acts 13:46-48). This made some Jews angrier. They stirred up leading citizens against Paul and Barnabas. These forced the two apostles to leave the city. Did Paul quit? He did not! He went on to the city of Iconium. Some Jews there rejected him. He had to flee to Lystra for his life. Did they appreciate Paul in Lystra? No! They stoned him and dragged him outside the city (Acts 14:19). Did he quit? Never! Paul was filled with great courage. He stood up. He wiped the blood off himself. Then he went back into the city that had stoned him (Acts 14:20). Paul was not a quitter. The Spirit gave him great courage to face suffering and persecution.

Q 18 What are some of the hardest trials that believers you know must overcome?

To grow spiritually, we need the attitude Paul had towards suffering. Do not quit when robbers steal your money. Do not give up when other believers desert you. Do not turn back when people do not appreciate you. Do not desert when people criticize you. *"Do not throw away your confidence"* in Jesus Christ (Heb. 10:35). Endure! Persevere! Keep climbing! Grow in grace. The person who endures to the end will be saved. Do not be offended when trials come. Do not be like the seed that withered up when hard times came (Matt. 13:6, 20-21). Have the courage to continue.

 A young preacher was doing his best to start a new church. One Sunday morning he was trying to preach to about fifteen people. Suddenly, a man stood to his feet in the middle of the message. Angry, he turned and marched out of the building. Later, the preacher discovered the reason. The angry man wanted to sing a song, but no one asked him! It does not take much to offend some people! Still, the young pastor learned to remain kind when others are rude. And he did not allow the childish Christian to discourage him.

 John the Baptist was a great man. But he became discouraged. He almost lost his faith. John suffered in prison. There were many things he did not understand. Why was Herod free? Why did Jesus allow John to remain in prison? Jesus did not give John all the answers. But He sent him a message to increase his courage. He told John to think on the good things. Then He added, *"Blessed is the man who does not fall away on account of me"* (Luke 7:23).

 A young, 16-year-old boy named Nelson walked slowly. His eyes looked at the floor as he dragged his feet along. He did not want to tell his coach the bad news. But he was quitting the football team. His finger was swollen. It hurt every time his heart beat. Likewise, his rib ached with every breath. Surely the coach would understand. Nelson looked up as he approached Coach Landon. The coach greeted him with a smile. They sat and talked for a few minutes. Nelson explained that he was quitting. But the coach would not agree. He encouraged Nelson in many ways. And he insisted that the young man continue. So that is what Nelson did. Three years later, Nelson's athletic skills opened a door for him. A university paid all of his school fees for him to play ball for them. But Coach Landon helped Nelson with more than an education. He taught him not to quit in hard times. And that attitude is the difference between going to heaven or hell. *"He who stands firm to the end will be saved"* (Matt. 24:13).

Do not be a quitter. Do not fall away or turn back for any reason. Humble yourself when you need to. Encourage yourself from time to time. But do not quit! Let us review the keys we have examined so far.

- Relate well to others.
- Remember that growth comes step by step.
- Expect opposition.
- Stay filled with the Spirit.
- Do not quit. Have the courage to face suffering.

B. Key: Watch out for trouble after a victory.

Some fall away in hard times. Others fall away in easy times. Ninety-nine out of one hundred believers may survive suffering, poverty, and persecution. But only one out of a hundred will survive great success. No time is more dangerous than the days just after success.

Q 19 ✎ *Do you know any leaders who have fallen after great success? Explain.*

In our hard times we tend to lean toward God. But in our times of ease and plenty we tend to lean away from God. Satan fell to earth after being exalted in heaven (Isa. 14). Adam lost his innocence after God gave him paradise (Gen. 3). Nebuchadnezzar lost his mind and kingdom after he made it to the top (Dan. 4). Samson lost his eyes after great victories (Judg. 16). Saul lost his throne after winning a war (1 Sam. 31). David lost his good name after he became king of all Israel (2 Sam. 11). The Israelites lost the Promised Land after they became wealthy and prospered (2 Kings 17; 25). Laodicea lost its relationship with Christ after great blessings (Rev. 3:17). *"Pride goes before destruction, a haughty spirit before a fall"* (Prov. 16:18). The greatest dangers may be just past the hill of success.

The greatest miracle we know of in Paul's early ministry is in Acts 14:8-10. At Lystra, a man crippled from birth listened as Paul preached. Paul looked directly at him (Acts 14:9). These words remind us of the way he looked directly at Elymas (Acts 13:9). Likewise, Peter looked straight at a crippled beggar (Acts 3:4). This direct look into the eyes seems to emphasize a type of spiritual communication. Paul looked directly into the eyes of the cripple. He discerned that the man had faith to be healed. Paul told him to stand up. The crippled man jumped up and began to walk. This was a great miracle! But one of Paul's greatest trials was only minutes away. The people thought their Greek gods had come down to earth. They thought Paul was the god Hermes,[+] and Barnabas was Zeus.[+] Zeus was the main god they worshiped in Lystra. His temple was there. When Paul refused their worship, they stoned him! Still, Paul continued. He learned how to handle the hard times that follow the easy times (Phil. 4:11-13). Beware of the valley past the hill of success.

Figure 10.7   At Lystra, people worshiped the Greek gods Hermes and Zeus. Above are the ruins of a temple of Zeus.

Q 20 ✎ *How were Peter and Paul able to discern that a person had faith to be healed?*

+ The Roman name for Hermes is Mercury. The Roman name for Zeus is Jupiter.

Q 21 ✎ *Explain: Success can cause your head to swell and your heart to shrink.*

Jesus spent the night praying after feeding the multitude (Matt. 14:22-23). To keep growing in Christ, watch out after victories. Success can cause your head to swell and your heart to shrink.

C. Key: Allow God to work in you while He's working through you.

Paul's first missionary journey was a wonderful success. After it, there were new churches in the province of Galatia. These included churches in the Galatian cities of Antioch, Iconium, Lystra, and Derbe. Praise the Lord for what He did *through* Paul.

It is also wonderful to see what God did *in* Paul. Good believers become better. They grow in grace. In the next lesson, we will note that Paul wrote to the Galatian churches. He probably wrote his letter to the Galatians between Acts 14 and 15. This was just after he returned from Galatia. One of the things he emphasized to them was the fruit of the Spirit. [22]*"But the fruit of the Spirit is love, joy, peace, patience, kindness, goodness, faithfulness, [23]gentleness and self-control"* (Gal. 5:22-23).

Q 22 ↗ *When does God do the most in us? Explain.*

Where does this fruit grow best? Some may think the fruit of the Spirit grows best in the easiest places. They may imagine the fruit of the Spirit growing in a shady place beside a cool stream and green grass. But Paul writes about the Spirit's fruit after a tough trip in Acts 13–14. He writes about the fruit of love after people stoned him. He emphasizes the fruit of joy with new believers (Acts 13:52). This joy was not in the shade beside a stream. It was after he climbed the Taurus Mountains and passed through robbers. He had the fruit of peace in him during the stormiest times. He wrote the Galatians about patience, kindness, and goodness after he was rejected, deserted, and persecuted. He wrote about the fruit of faithfulness because he learned it. God taught him to be faithful in the hardest times. He wrote about gentleness and self-control after people criticized and attacked him! We enjoy the easy times the most. But God does the most in us during our hardest times. That is, if we let Him! The trial of our faith is precious (1 Pet. 1:7 KJV). Some false teachers say believers should not go through trials. But notice what Paul said after he was stoned.

> [21]*They preached the good news in that city and won a large number of disciples. Then they returned to Lystra, Iconium and Antioch, [22]strengthening the disciples and encouraging them to remain true to the faith. "We must go through many hardships to enter the kingdom of God," they said* (Acts 14:21-22).

Especially note Acts 14:22. We must go through many hardships to enter God's kingdom. These hard times are more precious than gold (1 Pet. 1:7 KJV). We would prefer the gold. But the trials are more precious. For in them, God develops the Spirit's fruit in us—if we allow Him.

Q 23 ✎ *Has the Lord taught you anything through the trials of others? Explain.*

Also, others are always watching us during our hard times. Timothy lived in Lystra (Acts 16:1). This is the place they stoned Paul. But God's apostle did not become bitter. He returned to the town to preach and encourage others. Paul's attitude in Lystra preached louder than his words. And it was in Lystra that Paul met Timothy. God bound their hearts together. Timothy became Paul's son in the faith and his most valued person on earth.

> [19]*I hope in the Lord Jesus to send Timothy to you soon, that I also may be cheered when I receive news about you. [20]I have no one else like him, who takes a genuine interest in your welfare. [21]For everyone looks out for his own interests, not those of Jesus Christ. [22]But you know that Timothy has proved himself, because as a son with his father he has served with me in the work of the gospel* (Phil. 2:19-22).

We never know who is watching during our trials and temptations. As a young man, Timothy was looking out of a window in Lystra.

D. Key: Keep the focus on God, not self.

Look what the Lord has done! This was the theme of Paul and Barnabas. They could have said, "This is what we did." Or, "This happened to us." Or, "We healed a cripple." But instead, they gave God all the credit.

On arriving there, they gathered the church together and reported all that God had done through them and how he had opened the door of faith to the Gentiles (Acts 14:27).

Q 24 *What are some ways in which a believer may show pride?*

Luke's Gospel emphasizes that God is the One who deserves the credit.

51 "He has performed mighty deeds with his arm; he has scattered those who are proud in their inmost thoughts. 52He has brought down rulers from their thrones but has lifted up the humble. 53He has filled the hungry with good things but has sent the rich away empty" (Luke 1:51-53).

Herod is an example of a ruler that God brought down. Why? Because the little king did not give God the praise (Acts 12:23).

God uses those He chooses. But He wants the praise to come upward to His throne. Humans are like pencils in God's hand. He does the writing. Pencils should not brag! God once used the nation of Assyria like a rod to punish Israel. Then the king of Assyria became proud. This man wanted the praise for what God did. Therefore, Isaiah prophesied his judgment. Read Isaiah 10:12-19.

Q 25 *Does an ax raise itself above him who swings it? Explain.*

The king of Assyria fell because of pride. Later, God judged Nebuchadnezzar, king of Babylon, for the same reason. He ate grass for 7 years (Dan. 4:1-37)! God is able to humble those who walk in pride (Dan. 4:37). The Most High is sovereign over the kingdoms of men. He gives them to anyone He wishes. And He sets the lowliest of men over them (Dan. 4:17).

The tongue is a little member that boasts great things (James 3:5). No man can tame it. But the Spirit can help us control our tongues. How? By filling our hearts with God's presence. For if our hearts are right, our words will be right (Luke 6:45).

Solomon gave us wisdom about bragging. *"Let another praise you, and not your own mouth; someone else, and not your own lips"* (Prov. 27:2).

Humans should not crow like a rooster, gobble like a proud turkey, or strut like a peacock. God uses those who see themselves as foolish, weak, lowly, and despised. Why? So that no one will boast before Him (1 Cor. 1:26-29). *"Therefore, as it is written: 'Let him who boasts boast in the Lord' "* (1 Cor. 1:31).

Remember what Paul wrote to the Galatians he visited in Acts 13–14 (Gal. 6:14). May we never boast, except in the cross of our Lord Jesus Christ!

Do you want to grow in grace? Then remain humble. *"God opposes the proud, but gives grace to the humble"* (James 4:6).

Paul was a great apostle. But he thought of himself as an unprofitable, unworthy servant (See Luke 17:10).

9For I am the least of the apostles and do not even deserve to be called an apostle, because I persecuted the church of God. 10But by the grace of God I am what I am, and his grace to me was not without effect. No, I worked harder than all of them—yet not I, but the grace of God that was with me (1 Cor. 15:9-10).

Too many songs sound like the singers are looking in the mirror. In contrast, consider the worship song that follows.

There is a name I love to hear, I love to sing its worth;
It sounds like music in my ear, the sweetest name on earth.
Oh, how I love Jesus, Oh, how I love Jesus;
Oh, how I love Jesus, because He first loved me.[10]

Let us keep the focus on Jesus, not self.

Lesson 30 The Important Church Meeting in Jerusalem (Acts 15:1-35)

Goal: *Summarize 5 biblical steps to solving a problem. Relate these to your context.*

Setting

Our theme for Acts 15:1-35 is "A biblical pattern for solving problems." Acts 15 records the second big problem the Church faced. We studied the first problem in Acts 6. Some of the Grecian Jews complained that their widows were being neglected. The Church solved that problem and continued to grow.

It is always important to solve problems. The Church should never ignore them. We should not pretend that a problem does not exist. This would be like trying to sleep with a large rock under the mattress. The Church has peace and growth when she admits and solves her problems.

The problem of Acts 6 was smaller than the problem of Acts 15. In fact, the problem of Acts 15 is one of the biggest problems in Scripture. The problem came because of a weakness in the Jerusalem church. This was a great church in many ways.

- They had the apostles and deacons as leaders.
- The believers were filled with the Spirit.
- There were signs and wonders.
- Believers had great love for one another.
- They were faithful in persecution.

Yet with all these good things, the Jerusalem church still had a weakness. This should not surprise us. No church is perfect. One man searched for a perfect church. But he always found some weakness in every church he attended. A wise elder gave him some good advice. The elder said, "If you find a perfect church, don't join it. Because then it will not be perfect!" Church members are only people. Since none of us is perfect, no church is perfect.

Q 26 *Is your church obeying the Great Commission? Explain.*

The Jerusalem church was a great church. But it had one big weakness. It did not choose to obey the Great Commission. Philip only went to Samaria because of persecution. Believers from Jerusalem did not go to Antioch because of love. They fled Jerusalem because of fear. They were afraid of persecution. Later, the Jerusalem church heard of the revival in Antioch, Syria. But none of the apostles went there at once. Rather, they sent Barnabas, a lesser leader.

The Jerusalem church was a Jewish church. Many priests became believers (Acts 6:7). These probably continued to sacrifice animals in the temple. And some Pharisees became believers (Acts 15:5). These taught that all believers must obey the law of Moses! Acts 21:20 says that all of the believers in Jerusalem were zealous for the Law. To be a member of the Jerusalem church, a believer had to become a Jew first. Judaism was the door to the Jerusalem church. This was the root of the problem. In this lesson we will look at five biblical steps to solving a problem.

A. Identify the problem before you try to solve it!

Q 27 *What was the big question or problem at the Jerusalem Council?*

What is the problem? That is the first question to ask. We see the problem at the beginning of Acts 15.

> ¹*Some men came down from Judea to Antioch and were teaching the brothers: "Unless you are circumcised, according to the custom taught by Moses, you cannot be saved." ²This brought Paul and Barnabas into sharp dispute and debate with them. So Paul and Barnabas were appointed, along with some other believers, to go up to Jerusalem to see the apostles and elders about this question* (Acts 15:1-2).

It is good to state the problem as a question or a group of questions. Does a person need two Saviors? Do we need Moses and Jesus to save us? Or is following Jesus enough? Does a believer need to follow Jesus and follow some laws Moses taught (Acts 15:1, 5)? Must a person be circumcised to be saved? These were the hot questions. And believers did not agree on the answers. So they called a big meeting or *council in Jerusalem.

Before you look for the answer, be sure you can state the question in your own words. Otherwise, you will not recognize the answer when you find it!

B. Allow full and open discussion at a meeting.

Notice the words *"after much discussion"* in Acts 15:7. This shows us that they gave people time to talk.

Paul and Barnabas *"reported everything God had done through them"* (Acts 15:4). This report may have taken several hours or days. They reported about the work in Antioch, Cyprus, Perga, and Galatia. All took time to listen.

Then others began to give a different view. Leaders gave them time to talk.

Then some of the believers who belonged to the party of the Pharisees stood up and said, "The Gentiles must be circumcised and required to obey the law of Moses" (Acts 15:5).

Another name for these born-again Pharisees is *Judaizers. They emphasized Judaism, the religion of the Jews. They were believers. But they needed to grow in grace. They were still depending on the Law, rather than grace alone. In Jerusalem, most all believers were Jewish. So emphasizing Jewish customs did not offend those in Jerusalem. But outside of Jerusalem, some Judaizers were stumbling blocks to the Gentiles. A few of them went to Antioch. There, they troubled Gentile believers. Likewise, in Galatia, they led Gentile believers away from Christ to Moses (Gal. 5:1-4). In Jerusalem, Paul walked in step with Jewish believers. There, he even paid for animal sacrifices (Acts 21:17-26). To those under Law, Paul became under Law (1 Cor. 9:19-23). But he did not allow the Judaizers to force their Jewish culture on the Gentiles. In the end, Paul and the Jerusalem leaders rejected the view of the Judaizers (Acts 15:24). We do not need two Saviors. Following Moses is not necessary. Faith in Jesus Christ is enough!

Q 28 ↗ *What did Judaizers believe?*

There was once an evangelist named Freeman. He was talking on the phone to a pastor named Strictland. Both of them were members of the same group of churches. Freeman wanted to preach at Strictland's church. Pastor Strictland was a godly man. He prayed much and loved the lost. Strictland asked Freeman many questions in a holy voice. "Will you be wearing a suit that is all black? Will you wear a white shirt with long sleeves? Will you wear a narrow black tie? Will you have a mustache or a beard? Will your hair be touching your ears or your collar? Will your wife have long hair? Will she wear any makeup or jewelry?" Evangelist Freeman asked, "Why do you ask me all of these questions?" Pastor Strictland replied, "Because at our church we believe in holiness!" Evangelist Freeman agreed that he and his wife would dress according to Strictland's standards while at that church. Freeman preached a good revival. Several were saved. Strictland's church members were edified. Freeman and Strictland became good friends. Both men learned to love and respect each other. Years later, Freeman saw Strictland at a church meeting. He noticed that Strictland was wearing a brown suit. He also had on a blue shirt and a wide tie. Freeman smiled a little. Some believers have too many rules. Others have too few. Fellowship helps us find the balance.

Q 29 ↖ *How do standards of holiness differ among believers? Who is right?*

Then there was much discussion at the meeting in Jerusalem (Acts 15:7). This took time. But to solve problems, people must discuss things. There are at least three rules to remember about a discussion.

Q 30 ↗ *What are the 3 rules for a discussion?*

- **Be polite.** Never tell someone that what he or she says is stupid. Always show respect and courtesy for another person's point of view. Otherwise, you will create more problems than you solve. Love is never rude (1 Cor. 13:5).

- **Talk about issues, not people.** Never use words to attack someone who disagrees with you. For example, someone could have said Paul was too educated or did not speak well. He could have said Paul had a big nose and a bald head. That would have been attacking the person instead of the problem!

- **Do not allow tongues and interpretation or prophecy to end discussion.** Why? Because some pretend to use spiritual gifts against their enemies. No one can argue with "Thus says the Lord." Therefore, do not allow either side to take this approach. This would be an abuse of spiritual gifts. Allow free discussion. Then the group can come to its own conclusion. The group does not need one person to tell them what God thinks!

C. Listen to those with experience related to the problem.

They took time to listen to the experiences of Paul and Barnabas (Acts 15:4). These men told about the Greek believers in Antioch, Syria. And they told about their first missionary trip.

People in Africa respect the elders. They believe that the longer you live the more knowledge and experience you gain. A Swahili proverb says: *Kuishi nyingi ni kuona mengi.* It means, "to live much is to see much."[11] The Africans encourage us to listen to those with experience.

Q 31 *Do you think Paul rebuked Peter in Antioch before the Jerusalem Council? Explain.*

Next, everyone in the Jerusalem meeting took time to listen to Peter's experience. He told about what God did at the home of Cornelius. God saved this centurion and his household. Then He filled them with the Holy Spirit. They heard them speak in tongues. Only God could have done this. Peter said God treated Gentiles the same as Jews. So why try to change the Gentiles into Jews? God accepted them as Gentiles (Acts 15:7-11). Thus Peter advised that the Church should not require Gentiles to keep the Law. That would be putting a yoke on their necks that was too heavy, even for Jews (Acts 15:12). Peter emphasizes salvation by grace. Note his words. *"No! We believe it is through the grace of our Lord Jesus that we are saved, just as they are"* (Acts 15:11).

It is interesting to compare Peter's words in Acts 15:11 with Galatians. Take a few minutes to read Galatians 2:1-21. There, Paul rebukes Peter for forcing *"Gentiles to follow Jewish customs"* (Gal. 2:14). Paul emphasizes to Peter that Jews are *"justified by faith in Christ and not by observing the law"* (Gal. 2:16). Paul says that no one will be justified by keeping the Law. This is the same message we hear Peter giving in Acts 15:11. Paul probably wrote to the Galatians before the Jerusalem meeting of Acts 15.[12] And it is likely that Peter's trip to Antioch (Gal. 2:11) was also before the Jerusalem meeting of Acts 15. (Bible teachers are not sure about the order of these events. Figure 10.8 gives a possible order and approximate dates.[13])

Event	Scripture	Date (A.D.)
Jesus ascended to the Father in heaven.	Acts 1:9	30
Paul met Jesus on the road from Jerusalem to Damascus.	Acts 9:1-19	31-32
Paul studied the Scriptures for 3 years in Arabia.	Between Acts 9:21-22 Gal. 1:17-18	32-34
Paul proved to the Jews in Damascus that Jesus is the Christ.	Acts 9:22; Gal. 1:17 2 Cor. 11:32-33	34

Continued on next page

Event	Scripture	Date (A.D.)
Paul took his first trip, as a believer, to Jerusalem. He met Peter and James.	Acts 9:26-27 Gal. 1:18-19	35
Paul and Barnabas taught in Antioch, Syria for 1 year.	Acts 11:25-26 Gal. 1:20	39
Paul took his second trip to Jerusalem. He and Barnabas carried an offering from Antioch.[14] This was to help during the famine. On this visit, they met privately with Jerusalem church leaders.	Acts 11:27-30 Gal. 2:1-10	44
Paul and Barnabas went on their first missionary trip.[15]	Acts 13–14	46-47
Peter went to Antioch, Syria.	Between Acts 14:28 & 15:1; Gal. 2:11	48-49
Judaizers who claimed to be from James went to Antioch. They influenced Peter, Barnabas, and others. Paul rebuked Peter in front of them all.	Acts 15:24 Gal. 2:12-21	48-49
Judaizers led the Galatians astray from grace.	Gal. 5:1-4	48-49
Paul wrote to the Galatians.	Gal. 1–6	49
Paul went to Jerusalem a third time. He and Barnabas went for the Church council.	Acts 15	49

Figure 10.8   Possible time and order of some events in Acts and Galatians

After Peter spoke in the Jerusalem meeting, Paul and Barnabas spoke again.

The whole assembly became silent as they listened to Barnabas and Paul telling about the miraculous signs and wonders God had done among the Gentiles through them (Acts 15:12).

Experience did not decide the case. But neither did the lack of experience decide the case. Some accuse Pentecostals of basing belief on experience. We do not base belief completely on experience. But we do listen to it. Experience is a good teacher. Experience is one of the things to consider when looking for the solution to a problem. Usually, those who argue against experience do not have it! Or they have a different experience. Thus some base their beliefs on their lack of experience. But the early church placed some value on experience. They listened to those who had preached to Gentiles and not just to Jews.

Q 32 *How much value does your culture place on experience? Explain.*

D. Apply the Scriptures to the problem.

The Word is a light for our paths (Ps. 119:105). The Scriptures are our guide. They are the foundation for our faith (2 Tim. 3:16). James, the brother of Jesus, quoted a verse from Amos 9:11-12 (Acts 15:16-18). The verses from Amos focused on God's big purpose. Why did God restore David's fallen tent or kingdom through Christ? So that the Gentiles would seek the Lord.

Q 33 *How did the Lord rebuild David's fallen tent (Acts 15:16-17)? Why?*

James appears to have been the leader of the Jerusalem meeting. He concluded that Jewish believers should not make it too hard for Gentiles turning to God. And his advice agreed with the Scriptures. We must always submit to the Bible. However, different verses may lead us to more than one conclusion. We will give two examples near the close of this chapter.

E. Separate the greatest issue from the lesser parts of the problem.

Sometimes there may be several issues or parts of a problem. But there is usually one part of a problem that is more important than the other parts. This was true at the Jerusalem meeting. The biggest question was "How can Gentiles be saved?" The

Q 34 *What were the greater and lesser issues in Acts 15?*

answer was by trusting in Christ without following Moses. Thus the council or meeting in Jerusalem solved the big part of the problem. They decided how Gentiles should relate to God.

Every church should tell people the requirements for relating to God. We should emphasize the basic things the Bible teaches. We should not reject those whom Christ receives. Our standards should not be stricter than His standards. Nor should we accept people whom He does not receive. The Church's standards for membership should be the same as God's standards. Various churches have biblical reasons for their teachings. They can teach these in love. But churches should agree on the basics of salvation.[16]

There was also a lesser part of the problem. The lesser question was "How can Gentiles relate to Jewish believers?" The Jewish believers followed strict rules about eating. Moses had given them these rules. Therefore, the Jerusalem Council asked the Gentile believers to do three things related to food. *"You are to abstain from food sacrificed to idols, from blood, from the meat of strangled animals and from sexual immorality"* (Acts 15:29).

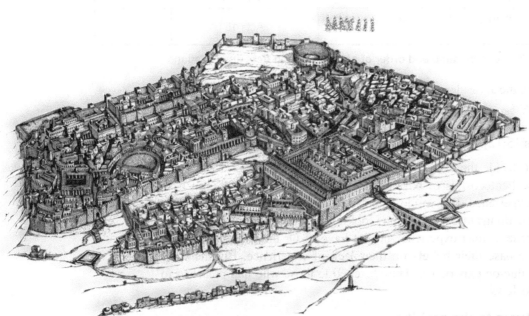

Figure 10.9 A drawing of old Jerusalem

These three food requests would help keep peace between Jews and Gentiles. It would keep the Gentiles from being a stumbling block to the Jews.

Also, notice that there is a fourth thing the Jerusalem Council required of Gentiles. That was to abstain from sexual immorality (Acts 15:29). Why are sexual sins linked with food laws? Unsaved Gentiles worshiped in pagan temples. They had feasts in these temples. There was food offered to idols and meat filled with blood. In addition, at the feasts there were hundreds of prostitutes. Pagan Gentiles ate bloody meat and had sex with prostitutes at the temple feasts. Therefore, it was natural to mention sexual purity along with food rules. We know that God requires all believers to be pure sexually. But in the Gentile world, food and sexual sins went together in the temples. Therefore, the Jerusalem Council mentioned them together.

Q 35 *Why was sexual purity linked with food laws in Acts 15?*

The Jerusalem meeting solved the greater and the lesser parts of the problem. They decided how Gentiles should relate to God and others. The second commandment is like the first (Matt. 22:37-40). How we relate to God comes first. But it is also important how we relate to others. So the Jerusalem Council asked the Gentiles to give up a little of their freedom. That way, all believers could relate to each other. How believers relate to each other is always part of the problems we must solve.

Conclusion

We have studied five biblical keys the group used to solve the problem. Afterwards, they made their decision known to all involved. They sent a letter and two of their members to Antioch (Acts 15:22-34). Solving problems helps only as we share the solutions with others.

Also, there were probably some who did not agree with the group. Often there are those who will not submit to godly leaders or the Holy Spirit. Eventually, rebels like these will wither and die spiritually.

Two case studies follow. Practice the five steps for solving a problem on each of these case studies.

Case Study 1:   *Diwali is a yearly festival time in India. It celebrates the victory of the Hindu god Siva over the evil god Narakhasura. Each family lights little clay-pot lamps. They put them around their houses. These little lights appear all over each village. Also, people put new grass on their roofs. And they buy new clothes to celebrate the feast. It is a special time of year for the people of India. But it can be a lonely time for some believers.

Q 36 ⬉ *Should a believer celebrate Diwali?*

The Prasad family lives in a small village. There are no other believers nearby. Their friends and family have rejected them. Now, their house is the only dark house in the village. All the other houses have pretty lamps glowing around them. Is there any way they can celebrate? The Christians in Europe found a way to celebrate during the pagan Festival of Winter. These European believers changed the meaning of the pagan symbols. They took the green tree the pagans used at their festival. They used candles on the tree, just like the unbelievers used. But when believers looked at the tree, they worshiped Christ. Should the Prasads put lamps around their house to worship Jesus during Diwali? Or will this be a bad testimony to others? Will the lamps be a link with their old way of Hinduism?[17]

Case Study 2:   Sabado was sick with a high fever in Papua, New Guinea. His wife and five children were worried. The medicine from the hospital did not help. So his father, a mabonong or pagan priest, decided to help him. Sabado's father began to contact the spirits. It came out that the problem was with Sabado's uncle. He had died in the war. His place in the other world was cold. He needed a new blanket. The old blanket had become thin with use. Sabado's father called a feast. They killed fifteen pigs, two cows, and a carabao (water buffalo). The fever left Sabado the day after they killed the last pig. And the fever never returned. Sabado was thankful. He killed a pig and vowed to kill another pig one year later.

But after six months, Sabado became a believer. He went to classes about following Jesus. He learned a lot about the Bible and taught others. Now, the time has come for baptism. Twenty-two of the 35 families in the village have become believers. Sabado, his wife and five children, and all of the other believers are ready to be baptized. But the time is near to kill the pig.

Sabado's father is not a believer. He feels responsible for Sabado's vow. He thinks the fever will return on both of them if Sabado does not kill the pig. Sabado is caught in the middle. He does not believe his uncle's spirit has power over him because Jesus is stronger. But he is also afraid for his father. He does not want to be a stumbling block to him. And his father is not under the protection of Jesus. Refusing to kill the pig would be like spitting in his father's face. Does God want him to do that? The Bible says he must be willing to forsake his father (Matt. 10:37; Luke 14:26). But the Bible also says he should honor his father and mother (Matt. 15:4). Sabado thinks he should delay his baptism. He thinks he should kill the pig on the day he vowed. Then he can be baptized later.[18]

Q 37 ⬉ *Should Sabado keep his vow?*

Test Yourself: Circle the letter by the ***best*** completion to each question or statement.

1. Which of the following is a Galatian church?
a) Cyprus
b) Lystra
c) Damascus
d) Ephesus

2. The most important key to growing in grace is
a) gaining new knowledge.
b) having spiritual gifts.
c) relating to others.
d) increasing in faith.

3. How does Luke mostly describe the government's attitude toward believers?
a) Helpful
b) Hostile
c) Neutral
d) Fearful

4. Believers need to be filled with the Spirit many times because
a) there is one baptism and many fillings.
b) God resists those with a haughty spirit.
c) physical needs recur many times in life.
d) yesterday's power will not meet today's needs.

5. Where did Paul begin his three missionary trips?
a) Antioch
b) Corinth
c) Jerusalem
d) Tarsus

6. No time is more dangerous than the days
a) just before a storm.
b) just after success.
c) of hard times.
d) of temptation.

7. The fruit of the Spirit grows best in times of
a) peace.
b) prosperity.
c) poverty.
d) difficulty.

8. God punished the king of Assyria because he
a) persecuted Israel.
b) was proud.
c) lacked mercy.
d) wasted wealth.

9. An important step in solving a problem is to
a) limit discussion to 2 or 3 people.
b) encourage tongues and interpretations.
c) state the problem as a question.
d) review solutions of other problems.

10. In solving a problem, it is important to
a) require the youngest to speak the least.
b) encourage the oldest to speak the most.
c) listen to those with experience.
d) silence those who oppose you.

 Essay Test Topics: Write 50-100 words on each of these goals that you studied in this chapter.

Paul and Barnabas at Cyprus and Antioch in Pisidia (Acts 13:1-51)

Goal: *Explain and apply 4 keys to spiritual growth from Paul's first missionary trip.*

Paul and Barnabas in Iconium, Lystra, and Derbe, Then Back to Antioch (Acts 14:1-28)

Goal: *Identify and apply 4 more keys to spiritual growth from Paul's first missionary trip.*

The Important Church Meeting in Jerusalem (Acts 15:1-35)

Goal: *Summarize 5 biblical steps to solving a problem. Relate these to your context.*

Figure 10.10   Damascus: Street called Straight. Saul was converted on the road to Damascus. Then the Lord told Ananias, *"Go to the house of Judas on Straight Street and ask for a man from Tarsus named Saul, for he is praying"* (Acts 9:11).

Figure 10.11   Damascus: Roman gate (Acts 9)

Figure 10.12   Damascus city wall. Paul escaped the city in a basket.

Chapter 11:
Paul's Second Missionary Journey

(Acts 15:36–18:22)

Introduction

About 8,000 people gathered for an outdoor gospel meeting in Trincomalee, Sri Lanka. They were mostly Hindus. Pastors and believers from several churches were working together, praying and fasting for the meeting. That evening began with singing. Then, Christopher stood to preach in the Tamil language. After a few minutes of preaching, a problem arose. A woman stood up and began to shout. She appeared to be about 30 years old. Her eyes were full of hate. "I curse your God and I curse your message," she screamed. Several pastors on the platform stood up. In the name of Jesus, they began to rebuke the demons in the woman. They commanded the demons to be silent and come out of her. But the woman continued to scream. Her whole body shook. Her long, black hair was blowing around in the wind. Suddenly, she stood still, breathing deeply. Then she walked straight

Figure 11.1   Paul preaching to the Thessalonians

toward the platform. There, she demanded a blood sacrifice. This was a common demand of witch doctors in that area. But Christopher answered, "Jesus shed His blood once for all. His blood delivers us from the kingdom of Satan." The pastors continued to pray. Victory came through the power of Jesus' name. In time, the woman fell as if she were dead. The crowd was shocked. Several women believers came to help the woman. As they prayed, she became calm before the crowd. Then she went quietly to one side for prayer and counseling. "Glory to God," said Christopher. He explained to the crowd what had happened. The power of Jesus had broken Satan's power in the woman's life. As a result, most of the crowd wanted to accept Jesus as Savior. They had seen that His power was greater than Satan's power.[1]

Likewise, people in Philippi saw Paul cast a demon out of a slave girl. Demons submit to believers in the name of Jesus (Luke 10:17).

Lessons:

Paul and Silas Extend the Gospel to Philippi (Acts 15:36–16:40)
Goal A: *Identify 11 provinces or districts and 15 cities of Paul's second missionary trip.*
Goal B: *Summarize and apply what Acts 15–16 teaches about harvest, disagreements, guidance, attitudes, cultures, and citizens.*

Paul and Silas in Thessalonica, Berea, and Athens (Acts 17:1-34)
Goal: *State and explain 5 principles based on Acts 17.*

Paul and Silas Extend the Gospel to Corinth (Acts 18:1-22)
Goal A: *Explain and follow 5 steps for making new friends.*
Goal B: *Give 4 examples of Paul's friends in Acts 18.*

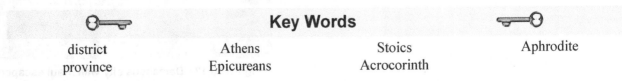

Key Words

| district | Athens | Stoics | Aphrodite |
| province | Epicureans | Acrocorinth | |

174

Paul and Silas Extend the Gospel to Philippi (Acts 15:36–16:40)

Goal A: *Identify 11 provinces or districts and 15 cities of Paul's second missionary trip.*

Goal B: *Summarize and apply what Acts 15–16 teaches about harvest, disagreements, guidance, attitudes, cultures, and citizens.*

Setting

We are in the third and final part of Acts. In the first part of Acts, believers witnessed in Jerusalem (Acts 1–7). In the second part, persecution drove them to witness in Judea and Samaria (Acts 8–12). This third part of Acts tells how the good news spread into their entire world (Acts 13–28).

We have seen that it took time for the Church to expand. Jesus ascended to heaven about A.D. 30. But Paul's first missionary trip was not until about A.D. 46. Building the foundation for a great work always takes time. We should not despise the day of small beginnings (Zech. 4:9-10).

Q 1 *What are 4 reasons why the geography of Paul's second trip is important?*

Now we have come to Paul's second journey. The biblical geography of this second trip is very important for four reasons.

- The second trip includes most of the first and third trips. So learn the geography of this trip. Then you will know most of the places Paul went on all three trips.
- Studying biblical geography will help you understand the Bible. Many people stumble over biblical geography. They trip over the names of places. This hinders them in understanding the Bible. So we will help you learn a few districts and cities. Then we can focus on the message of the Bible.
- Knowing biblical geography will help your memory. We will teach you to remember people and events by relating them to a map. You will learn to recall what happened at places like Antioch, Troas, and Ephesus. See Figure 13.15.
- Knowing biblical geography will help when you study Paul's letters. He wrote to believers in Rome, Corinth, Galatia, Ephesus, Philippi, and Thessalonica. These towns are important because believers lived there!

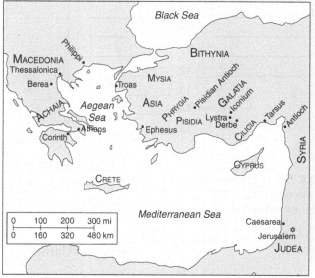

Figure 11.2   Seven provinces, four districts, and fifteen cities of Paul's second missionary trip

Let us identify 7 provinces, 4 districts, and 15 cities Paul visited. On the map, notice that cities, like Ephesus, begin with capital letters. But we use all capital letters for names of provinces or districts. Also, notice that on the map the capital letters of provinces, like GALATIA, are larger than the capital letters of districts, like Pisidia (See Figure 11.2). Why are the capital letters of provinces larger? Because provinces were larger than districts. For example, the province of ASIA contained three districts (Acts 16:12).[2]

Q 2 *Why are some names in all capital letters?*

We have had a quick look at the places Paul traveled. Now, let us look at six principles related to Paul's second missionary trip.

A. It is important to conserve the harvest.

Some time later Paul said to Barnabas, "Let us go back and visit the brothers in all the towns where we preached the word of the Lord and see how they are doing" (Acts 15:36).

Paul did not want to plow new ground until he checked on the old. He did not want to build more until he examined the foundation. He did not want to extend the gospel further until he strengthened the base of believers. So they walked about 400 miles (644 km) from Antioch in Syria to Antioch in Pisidia. This was hard walking over a lot of mountains. But the Spirit led them in this type of follow-up ministry.

Q 3 *Did Paul spend all of his time preaching in new places? Explain.*

Q 4 ✏ *Fill in the blanks below that go with Figure 11.3. A–G are for provinces, H–K for districts, and 1–15 for cities.*

Farmers know it is important to care for the grain they reap. It takes several months of hard work to get a harvest. This work includes moving rocks and burning stumps. It includes plowing, sowing, hoeing, and reaping. We can write about the cost of harvest with a pen. But it takes blisters and sweat to get a real harvest. After all the work, a farmer is careful to conserve the reward. He puts the harvest in a barn. He keeps it in a place that will be safe from wild animals, rats, birds, and thieves. A farmer does a lot of work to get a harvest. So he makes sure his labor is not in vain.

A. _____   1. _____
B. _____   2. _____
C. _____   3. _____
D. _____   4. _____
E. _____   5. _____
F. _____   6. _____
G. _____   7. _____
                     8. _____
H. _____   9. _____
I. _____   10. _____
J. _____   11. _____
K. _____   12. _____
                     13. _____
                     14. _____
                     15. _____

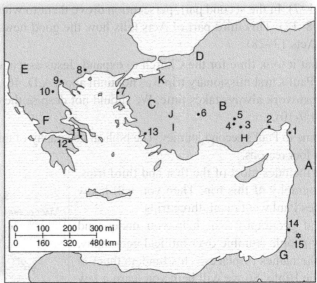

Figure 11.3   Practice map of Paul's second trip

The Church needs to learn from the farmers. It is one thing to get people in the front door of the church. We emphasize this. But sometimes people walk in a church's front door and leave out the back door. That is, they leave without believers noticing them.

It is good to focus on the lost. Jesus came to seek and save them. The Savior paid a great price for the harvest. Heaven rejoices when one sinner comes to Christ. But it is easy to focus on the lost and forget the found! New believers are like babies. They must be fed to grow. They must be cared for, or they will die. So let us remember to teach those we reach. The Great Commission includes more than preaching. We obey the command of Christ only as we make disciples out of those we reach (Matt. 28:19-20).

Q 5 ✏ *Has your church learned a lesson from farmers? Explain.*

Q 6 ✏ *How are some believers like Nimrod?*

Three men went hunting for wild pigs. The two brothers took guns. But Nimrod took only a small knife for a weapon. The brothers laughed. They asked, "How will you kill a wild pig with only a small knife?" "You will see," replied Nimrod. So they traveled to the woods. There was a very small, old house they stayed in. Many wild pigs lived nearby. The next morning Nimrod arose early. It was still dark outside. He dressed quietly. The brothers were still sleeping. Nimrod opened a window above his bed. Then he sneaked out of the house. He left the front door open a little. All he carried was a flashlight and his knife. Smiling, he began to search for the home of some wild pigs. In time he saw a hole in the ground. The tracks of pigs were all around the hole. He knew this was the entrance to their house. Quietly, he shined the light into the hole. A big pig was there, sleeping well. Its long teeth looked dangerous. Nimrod tightened the strings on his shoes. He did not want them to come loose. Then he poked the pig with his knife. The big pig awoke with a squeal. In a rage, it charged out of the hole. The angry pig quickly went after Nimrod who was running back toward the house. It was a good race. Nimrod reached the open door a few feet ahead of the angry pig. He ran into the house and jumped out the open window above his bed. The brothers woke up to see the mad pig run into the house. Then they heard Nimrod say, "Pig hunting is easy. I got this one. Now, I'm going after another!"

B. Sometimes two people who disagree are both right.

Q 7 ✏ *Is it necessary for believers to agree on everything? Explain.*

Believers must agree upon many things. We must agree that Jesus died for our sins and rose from the grave. We must agree that Jesus is God. We must agree that the Bible is the Word of God. Those who disagree with the Bible are wrong. But two believers may disagree with each other and both be right.

> ³⁷*Barnabas wanted to take John, also called Mark, with them, ³⁸but Paul did not think it wise to take him, because he had deserted them in Pamphylia and had not continued with them in the work. ³⁹They had such a sharp disagreement that they parted company. Barnabas took Mark and sailed for Cyprus, ⁴⁰but Paul chose Silas and left, commended by the brothers to the grace of the Lord. ⁴¹He went through Syria and Cilicia, strengthening the churches* (Acts 15:37-41).

Paul was an apostle. Everyone knows he was a godly man. But Barnabas was also a spiritual man. He was generous (Acts 4:36-37). He was committed. It appears that he, like Paul, chose not to marry (1 Cor. 9:5-6). Barnabas is listed among the prophets and teachers (Acts 13:1).

Barnabas was a chosen man. The Jerusalem church chose him to go to the new believers in Antioch (Acts 11:22). The Antioch believers chose him to help carry the offering to Judea (Acts 11:30). The Holy Spirit chose him to be a missionary (Acts 13:2).

Barnabas liked to help others grow. His name means *Son of Encouragement*. And encouragement always brings out the best in others.[3] Barnabas was among the first to welcome Saul as a brother (Acts 9:27). And it was Barnabas who searched for Saul in Tarsus and brought him to help teach at Antioch (Acts 11:25). Barnabas helped bring out the best in Saul. And he wanted to help bring out the best in his nephew, John Mark.

Q 8 *Why does encouragement bring out the best in people?*

Was Barnabas right to give Mark a second chance? Yes, he was right! John Mark grew stronger as a man of God. He and Barnabas strengthened the churches in Cyprus. And the trip with Barnabas strengthened Mark. Mark deserted Paul about A.D. 46 on the first journey. Twenty years later, Paul's attitude toward Mark had changed. Paul asked Timothy to bring Mark who was useful for ministry (2 Tim. 4:11). Also, Mark traveled with Peter to help minister (1 Pet. 5:13).[4] Mark grew up and wrote the Gospel of Mark. The encouragement of Barnabas brought out the best in him. Blessed is the young person who has a Barnabas to encourage him.

Was Paul right in his opinion about Mark? Yes, he was probably right also. Recall Paul's opinion. *"Paul did not think it wise to take him"* (Acts 15:38).

Q 9 *Why was it not wise for Mark to travel with Paul on the second trip?*

Paul was not an easy man to travel with. He was an apostle with skin like leather. He knew only one direction—that was forward! He never turned back. There was no reverse gear in Paul. Many think Paul was sick when Mark left. We do not know when Paul became sick on the first missionary trip. But we do know he was sick when he preached to the Galatians (Gal. 4:13-14).

Paul had a job to do. He chose to do it or die. He would not quit or turn back. Some stoned him. Did he quit? No! He wiped off the blood and went back into town (Acts 14:19-20). Some beat him and put him in jail. Did this cause him to turn back? No! He sang praises at midnight (Acts 16:25). Persecution did not cause Paul to turn back. He was different from most of us. The normal human does not choose hard times. But recall the words Paul wrote about A.D. 55-56. *"For Christ's sake, I delight in weaknesses, in insults, in hardships, in persecutions, in difficulties. For when I am weak, then I am strong"* (2 Cor. 12:10).

The standard Paul set was probably too high for Mark, especially as a young man. It was too high for most of us! Review the list of Paul's persecutions (2 Cor. 11:23-29). The only good reason Paul saw for turning back was death! Trophimus tried to travel with Paul. Paul left him sick at Miletus (2 Tim. 4:20). Was it wise for a young man like Mark to travel with Paul? Probably not. Mark might have been beaten at Philippi. This would have given him a good reason to turn back. We admire Paul as an apostle. But who among us would make a good companion to travel beside him? It would not be wise for 99.9 percent of the church to travel with Paul! He needed a mature, unmarried man like Barnabas or Silas. Paul needed one who would forsake all family and friends. It was not wise for young Mark to travel with Paul.

Q 10 ✎ *Give an example of believers who disagree, and both are right.*

The point is this: Believers who disagree may both be right. Yet they are right from different points of view. Believers who see the value of choruses are right. But those who see the value of hymns are also right. Those who want resident Bible schools are right. But those who want extension Bible schools are also right. Those who say a certain version of the Bible is best may be right. But those who say other versions of the Bible help make some verses more clear are also right. Barnabas and Paul were both right about Mark.

Prayer: "Lord, help us to listen for truth from those who disagree with us. It may be that they are right about something we have not seen. We are a body, and we need each other. Teach us to value the opinions of others. Each person sees only a part of the truth. We are wiser together."

C. God guides in at least five different ways.

Every believer struggles with how to know the will of God. A believer may ask many questions about guidance. Whom should I marry? What courses should I study in school? What type of work should I do in life? These are a few of the common questions.

Q 11 ✎ *Do you think we already know about 95 percent of God's will for us? Explain.*

God leads His children step by step. Usually, we cannot see very far ahead. James warns us not to boast about what we will do next year. Rather, he says we should always say, *"If it is the Lord's will"* (James 4:15). Likewise, Paul did not claim to be certain about God's will for the future (Rom. 1:10; 15:32). God intends for us to depend on Him. He guides us as we walk with Him step by step.

Walking with God is the most important part of guidance. Why? Because who we are is more important than what we do. About 95 percent of God's will for each believer is already known. God's will is for us to be like Jesus (Rom. 8:29). His will is for us to love one another. His will is for us to obey His commandments. His will is for us to be His witnesses. Therefore, we should spend 95 percent of our time working at what we know God wants. Then we will *be* the believers God wants us to be. And it is easy for Him to guide those who walk close to Him. Guidance is 95 percent *being* and only 5 percent *doing*. Some have trouble knowing the will of God. Why? Because they are not growing in grace. They are focusing too much on *doing* and not enough on *being*.

We have emphasized that guidance comes to believers who focus on being like Jesus. Acts reveals that God guides these believers in at least five ways (Figure 11.4).

Method of Guidance	Example	Acts
1. The Word of God	The words of Jesus guided believers to wait in Jerusalem. The Scriptures guided believers to replace Judas. The Scriptures guided the lost to understand Pentecost and to accept Christ. The Scriptures guided the lost away from scoffing. The Scriptures guided the Church to accept the Gentiles.	1:4 1:20-21 2:16-28 3:22-26 13:40-41 15:15-21
2. Supernatural revelation (Angels, visions, dreams, and spiritual gifts)	An angel guided Philip to the Ethiopian. Jesus appeared to Saul and directed him to Damascus. Jesus appeared to Saul in a vision, preparing him to meet Ananias. The Lord appeared to Ananias and guided him to Saul. God used a vision to guide Peter to Cornelius. God used a vision to guide Paul to Macedonia.	8:26 9:1-9 9:11-12 9:10-19 10:9-16 16:9-10
3. Circumstances	Circumstances guided the Church to choose seven deacons. Circumstances guided believers to flee from Jerusalem. God used circumstances to guide Paul from Jerusalem to Caesarea.	6:1-6 8:1-3 23:23-35
4. An inner witness (Some gifts of the Spirit, such as an inner word of knowledge or wisdom, overlap with #2 above.)	The Holy Spirit guided Peter in the message he preached. The Holy Spirit guided Peter to deal with Ananias and Sapphira. The Holy Spirit guided Stephen in the words he spoke. The Holy Spirit guided Paul to return to where he and Barnabas had already preached. The Holy Spirit guided Paul to expect hard times in every city.	2:14-41 5:1-10 6:15–7:60 15:36 20:22-23

Continued on next page

Method of Guidance	Example	Acts
5. An outer witness	God guided Matthias through the church's decision. God guided seven men through the church's decision. Prophets confirmed Paul's call to be a missionary. God guided Timothy through Paul's decision.	1:23-26 6:5-6 13:1-3 16:1-3

Figure 11.4 Five ways God guided people in Acts

The Spirit may use any one of these ways to guide us. Or He may use some of them together. God guides us as we live close to Him. He speaks to us as we spend time in His Word and in His presence. Learn to trust what the Father puts in your heart in His presence.

Morris Williams was a missionary to Africa for many years. He served in Malawi and South Africa for 26 years. Then, for 15 more years, he was the leader of a group of 300 missionaries in Africa.[5] A pastor once asked Morris how God guided him to become a missionary. Morris replied, "When I was a young man, I wanted to do something for God. I didn't get any clear sense of a call. But I decided that the Lord was looking for volunteers. So I volunteered to help." In time this decision led him to Africa. Likewise, Isaiah was a volunteer prophet. In God's presence he saw a need. Then he volunteered to help (Isa. 6:8). An inner witness led both Morris and Isaiah. They responded to desires that God put in their hearts. When we walk close to God, the desires in our hearts come from Him.

John Karanja felt a great burden. He prayed often for God to call missionaries from his country of Kenya. As he continued to pray he sensed a change coming in his ministry. Then, the church leaders asked him to be the first missionary from Kenya to Malawi. He was surprised to be part of the answer to his own prayers.[6]

D. We need good attitudes to be fruitful workers for God.

Notice three things about Paul's attitude.

First, **he had a servant's attitude toward other believers.**   Paul wanted Timothy to travel with him. One reason why they traveled was to announce that Jewish customs were not necessary for Gentiles (Acts 16:4). And Timothy was half Greek. Still, Paul had Timothy circumcised. Why? To relate well to Jewish believers. Paul gave up some of his rights so he would not offend others (Matt. 17:27). He had the humble attitude of a servant.

Second, **he had a humble attitude toward God.** Paul did not demand clear directions from God. Rather, he started walking, then he expected God to guide him. Paul started walking west from Antioch in Pisidia (See Figure 11.2). He wanted to preach in Ephesus, the capital of Asia. But the Holy Spirit said *"No"* (Acts 16:6). This did not discourage Paul. He did not know where God wanted him to preach next. But he knew the Lord did not want him to walk west. The timing was not right. So Paul turned north and kept walking. He had already walked over 400 miles (644 km)! After a while, he turned east toward the district of Bithynia. We do not know how long he walked east. But in time, the Spirit said *"No"!* Paul did not complain or get upset. The Black Sea was north of him. To go that direction meant walking on water. So he turned back west again and kept walking. Still, God had not told Paul where to go. He told him only where he should *not* go! Finally, Paul came to Troas. This was near the site of the old Greek city of Troy.[7] It was at the northeast edge of the Aegean Sea. Paul had walked as far as he could go. There was no more land. Then God gave him a vision. A man in Macedonia begged Paul to come over and help (Acts 16:9). So Paul sailed that direction. God does not need to guide us if we are walking in the right direction. But He tells us if we take a wrong turn. Paul was humble toward God. He did not become upset when God said *"No"*. Paul knew that a closed door can be as much of a blessing as an open door. A *no* from God is as helpful as a *yes* from Him.

One year a teacher named Quentin spent all of his Christmas holidays working on a teaching method. Each hour he prayed for God to guide him. Finally, after about 50 hours of work, he finished. A few months later, the Holy Spirit showed him a better

Q 12 *Which of the 5 methods in Figure 11.4 has God used to guide you? Explain.*

Q 13 *Which 2 of the methods in Figure 11.4 did God use to guide John Karanja?*

Q 14 *Why did Paul have Timothy circumcised?*

Q 15 *How did Paul serve Gentiles by refusing to have Titus circumcised (Gal. 2:3)?*

Q 16 *Have you ever, like Paul, walked and prayed on a road, and then heard God say, "No"? If so, how did you feel toward God?*

Q 17 ➤ Is it hardest to have a good attitude toward believers, God, or sinners? Explain.

way. Quentin threw all of the former work in the trash. He wondered why the Lord had not guided him earlier. Sometimes we do not listen well. Other times, seeing His will is like climbing a hill. We cannot see some things until we reach a certain height.

Thomas Edison invented the lightbulb. But he tried hundreds of times before succeeding. The steps of a righteous person are guided by the Lord (Ps. 37:23). But sometimes we must walk a kilometer to find a solution that was only a meter away.

Third, **he had a loving attitude toward sinners.** At Philippi, Paul did not complain. The first convert was a woman, not the man he saw in a vision. Paul was thankful that the Lord opened her heart (Acts 16:14). He loved both men and women who were lost. Later in Philippi, the town leaders had Paul beaten severely (Acts 16:22). But his heart did not fill up with hatred or bitterness. At midnight he was praying and singing to God (Acts 16:25)! What an attitude! He did not say, "God, I do not deserve to be treated like this!" He was not angry with God or men. He sang praises when he was stepped on!

No wonder Paul was such a fruitful worker. He had good attitudes toward believers, toward God, and toward sinners.

E. The Church of Jesus Christ includes people of all levels and cultures.

A Roman road, the Egnatian Way, connected Rome and Philippi. This road enabled travel from the Aegean Sea to the Adriatic Sea.[8] Philippi was about 8 miles (13 km) from the port city of Neapolis[9] (See Figure 10.2). The Egnatian Way ended in Neapolis. Philippi was a great city. It was a Roman colony. Many Roman veterans raised families there. But Philippi prospered because of the Egnatian Way. This road brought much business to Philippi. The city was named after Philip II, the father of Alexander the Great. Cities along the Egnatian road were about 30 miles (48 km) apart. This was a day's journey on foot.[10]

In the Spirit John saw a multitude that no one could number. They were the redeemed from every nation, tribe, people, and language (Rev. 7:9). Likewise, the church at Philippi included people who differed greatly. Luke contrasts three people the gospel touched there.

First, **the gospel touched Lydia, a rich Gentile woman.**[11] (Acts 16:13-15). She sold purple cloth from Thyatira. This was a city about 75 miles (120 km) northeast of Ephesus, and 20 miles (32 km) southeast of Pergamum. The purple cloth was expensive.[12] She may have had several people working for her. We know she was rich because she had a big house. Lydia invited Paul, Silas, Timothy, and Luke to stay in her house. That is too many visitors for a small house! Lydia was a successful businesswoman.

Second, **the gospel touched a slave girl.** In the Greek the biblical text says she had a spirit associated with the python snake. This large snake was the symbol of Apollo, the sun god of the Greeks.[13] People worshiped Apollo in various temples they built for him. They believed that the spirit of the snake spoke through the girl.[14] The owners of the slave girl claimed that her voice was the voice of Apollo.[15] The demon in her spoke against her will. The Scripture does not tell us how well she predicted the future. But the Bible forbids God's people to seek the counsel of Satan's prophets (Deut. 18:9-12; Lev. 19:31; 20:36). Her testimony did not bring glory to God. It was not the kind of witness Paul wanted. So he commanded the spirit to come out of her. Notice that he

Figure 11.5   Paul and Silas prayed and sang in prison at Philippi.

Figure 11.6   The Gangites River where Paul met Lydia

Figure 11.7   Corinth— Temple of Apollo, the Greek sun god

spoke directly to the spirit in the name of Jesus. Immediately the slave girl was set free! There is power in the name of Jesus. And His power touches rich business people and poor slaves.

Today, the python is a symbol of spiritual power in Ouidah, Benin. There is a temple for the python in this city of West Africa. Priests wrap live python snakes around themselves. They claim spiritual power to tell people things about themselves. A missionary from Burkina Faso went to Ouidah to start a church. A priest appeared at the time of prayer. Only his head was visible. The rest of his body was covered with python snakes! He claimed to be the devil, and he commanded believers to leave the town. But they stayed in the name of Jesus. Today, there is a strong church in Ouidah, Benin.[16] The One who is in us is greater than the one in the world (1 John 4:4).

Third, the gospel changed the life of a Roman jailer. He was a respected Roman citizen. He was not as rich as Lydia. But he was not as poor as the slave girl. He was the man in the middle. This jailer asked a question that every person should ask: *"What must I do to be saved?"* (Acts 16:30). Paul answered that believing in Christ is all that is necessary to save one person or a household. We are saved by faith, not works. But the faith that saves works! A person with saving faith follows in the footsteps of Jesus. The rich young ruler once asked a question similar to the Philippian jailer's question: *"Good teacher, what must I do to inherit eternal life?"* (Luke 18:18). The thing that he lacked was to follow Jesus (Luke 18:22). Jesus has different demands for each person. But all who are saved have one thing in common: They believe in Jesus. And to believe in Him means to follow and obey Him. The jailer at Philippi believed in Jesus. Immediately, he began to obey Jesus by being baptized. In Luke 15, there are three examples of heaven's joy over a sinner's salvation. And in Acts 16 Luke shows us three sinners the gospel touched. Luke assures us that Lydia and the jailer were saved. And we hope the slave girl entrusted her life to Christ.

Philippi is a model church. Jesus died for the rich, the poor, and those in the middle! These three people were far apart. Yet in Christ they could all be close together.

Jesus does not ask us whom He can save. But He commands us to love all who come to Him. In Christ, people are equal from the top to the bottom of the social ladder.

F. Believers should use their rights as citizens.

"There is a time for everything" (Eccl. 3:1). There is a time to give up our rights. And there is a time to use them. Early in Acts 16 we saw Paul giving up some of his rights. He had Timothy circumcised in Lystra. He did this to relate better to Jewish believers in that area. Paul knew that circumcision had nothing to do with salvation. He did not mention it to the Philippian jailer. Why? Because there were few Jews to relate to in Philippi. Luke mentions no synagogue there. And there was a synagogue in any city that had ten Jewish men.[17] So Paul emphasized salvation by faith alone.

Paul used his rights as a Roman citizen in Philippi. It was a Roman city. There, they beat Paul without a trial. Since he was a Roman citizen, the beating was illegal (Acts 16:37). The crowd was loud (Acts 16:22). Paul probably had no chance to tell them he was a Roman citizen before they beat him. But when things became calm, he stood on his rights. The city officials and the people broke a Roman law by beating Paul without a trial. Paul could have taken them to court. He did not use his rights that much. But he did require the city officials to apologize (Acts 16:38-39). The officials in Philippi would always remember that Paul could have taken them to court. And they would remember that he forgave them. Thus he used his rights as a citizen to help the church.

Q 18 *How did Philippi get its name?*

Q 19 *Contrast 3 people the gospel touched at Philippi.*

Q 20 *Does your church reach out to people of all levels and cultures? Explain.*

Q 21 *How did Paul use his government rights in Philippi?*

Figure 11.8 The Roman Forum and related ruins at Philippi

Q 22 ➤ *What are some ways for believers to use their rights as citizens?*

Q 23 ✎ *Do you think the believers were right or wrong? Explain.*

There are times when Christians should use their rights as citizens. If possible, believers should vote in political elections. In this way they help elect leaders who honor God. Likewise, they should serve on court juries when asked. Also, there is a time for believers to emphasize the law. This is one of their rights as a citizen.

A storeowner was breaking the law. He was selling alcohol to children. And he was also selling magazines that contained illegal sexual pictures. Several believers noticed this. They decided to use their rights as citizens. First, they asked him to please stop breaking the law. He was having an evil influence on the youth. He refused to change. Next, the believers warned him that they were going to act. He only laughed at them. Finally, a large group of believers went to the city officials. They told the officials about the problem. Within a few days the storeowner stopped breaking the law. There is a time for believers to use their rights as citizens.

Lesson 32 — Paul and Silas in Thessalonica, Berea, and Athens (Acts 17:1-34)
Goal: *State and explain 5 principles based on Acts 17.*

Setting

In Acts 16 Luke showed us three different people the gospel touched. In Acts 17 he shows us three cities the gospel touched. Each of these cities responded in a different way.[18] Let us note several key principles as we study these three cities of Thessalonica, Berea, and Athens.

A. Most spiritual growth must be planned.

Q 24 ✎ *Do you agree with Paul's strategy of focusing on the larger cities? Explain.*

This is true for a church or just one believer. We see this principle in relation to Thessalonica (Acts 17:1-9). Paul planned for church growth. He had a strategy. He focused on starting churches in the big cities. His eye was on Thessalonica. It was the chief city of Macedonia. And it had a population of 200,000.[19] Notice that Paul passed through the two cities of Amphipolis and Apollonia. They needed the gospel. But Paul did not try to meet every need by himself. The person who tries to do everything will not do well at anything. So Paul focused on the big cities. He planted churches in key cities like Thessalonica. Then believers there could reach out to others. Paul made a plan and followed it. And the plan worked. The Bible contains two letters Paul wrote to the church at Thessalonica. A church was started there because Paul followed a plan.

Q 25 ✎ *What are some ways in which believers must plan to grow spiritually?*

Each believer needs a plan for spiritual growth. We need targets to aim at. We need goals to focus on. Some think they will grow by just attending church or standing beside good people. But growing in grace requires a plan. How much will you study the Bible each day? When will you study? When will you pray each day? How long will you pray? When will you witness to your neighbors? How will you approach them? How much will you give to the church this year? None of these things just happens. They all usually require a plan. If we do not plan our schedules for spiritual growth, we will not grow much. Paul is a good example for us. He succeeded because of goals and plans. Very little happens in the kingdom of God unless believers plan.

B. We should harvest the ripest grain first.

Q 26 ➤ *Why did Paul go to the synagogues first? Explain.*

We should witness first to those who are the most ready for the gospel. Paul practiced this principle. In each new town, he went first to the synagogue. This was partly to honor the Jews. But it was also to find those reaching out to God. There was no synagogue in Philippi. So he looked for a place where people were praying. He found them by a river. But in Thessalonica, Berea, and Athens, Paul went straight to the synagogue (Acts 17:1, 10, 17). There he was sure to find some Jews searching for God. Also, away from Jerusalem, there was a place in the synagogue for Gentiles. They were allowed in the courtyards or outer courts. These Gentiles, like Cornelius, are often called God-fearers

(Acts 10:2; 17:4).[20] They liked Judaism because it emphasized one God, high ethical standards, and a coming Messiah.[21]

If you have food to give away, look for a hungry person. If you have water, look for a thirsty person. If you have a coat to give, look for a person who is cold. If you have a spiritual message, do not offer it first to those without eyes to see or ears to hear. Be alert for those who perceive they have a spiritual need. If adults are not ready for the gospel, perhaps you can still reach the children. Plant your seed on plowed ground.

Paul went straight to the synagogue in Thessalonica. People there already believed in one God and in His Word. So he used the Scriptures people were already studying. He reasoned with them (Acts 17:2). He explained and proved that Jesus was the Christ (Acts 17:3). He persuaded some. God always allows people to choose. But it is His will for us to try to influence people's choices. *"Some of the Jews were persuaded and joined Paul and Silas, as did a large number of God-fearing Greeks and not a few prominent women"* (Acts 17:4).

Q 27 *Is it right to try to persuade people? Explain.*

Many people in the synagogue were close to God. Thus Paul did not need to lead them very far to find the Father. Others in Thessalonica were jealous. They opposed Paul and the gospel (Acts 17:5-9). These enemies of Christ caused Paul to flee by night (Acts 17:10). He traveled to Berea.

C. Expect to find some like the Bereans (Acts 17:10-15).

This third principle is very encouraging. It reminds us that God will lead us to those we can help. Some are like Paul's enemies at Thessalonica. They oppose the gospel. Others are like the Bereans. They are eager to find the truth.

[11]*Now the Bereans were of more noble character than the Thessalonians, for they received the message with great eagerness and examined the Scriptures every day to see if what Paul said was true.* [12]*Many of the Jews believed, as did also a number of prominent Greek women and many Greek men* (Acts 17:11-12).

Q 28 *What was noble about the Berean Jews?*

Some seed falls on the hardened path. Some falls on rocky soil. Other seed falls among thorns. But there is always some seed that falls upon good ground (Luke 8:4-15). Hallelujah! What a joy and a delight! What an encouragement to witness!

Sometimes believers get discouraged in witnessing. We may feel like Peter—he fished all night but caught nothing. The Bereans encourage us. Keep fishing. Continue telling others about Jesus. Keep sowing the seed. In due season we will reap if we do not give up (Gal. 6:9). Think of what it means to rescue one person from hell. Imagine how you will feel in heaven standing beside the one you helped on earth. Keep praying, witnessing, and teaching. Some success is certain. Remember the Bereans.

Q 29 *Have you known the joy of helping someone like those at Berea? Explain.*

D. Adapt the gospel message to the listeners (Acts 17:16-34).

Paul traveled from the joy of Berea to the distress of Athens. Athens may have had a population of less than 10,000.[22] It was famous for its stone carvings, buildings, books, and speakers. Famous Greek philosophers like Socrates, Plato, Aristotle, Epicurus, and Zeno called Athens home. This city had its greatest glory in the fifth and fourth centuries B.C. But even in Paul's day, it was known for its culture.[23] Athens, Tarsus, and Alexandria had the top universities of the world.[24] Those who visit Athens today admire its sculptures and buildings. But in Paul's day the stone carvings were idols. And the buildings were temples for demons (1 Cor. 10:20). *"While Paul was waiting for them in Athens, he was greatly distressed to see that the city was full of idols"* (Acts 17:16).

Q 30 *Describe the reputation of Athens.*

In Athens Paul went as usual to the synagogues. But he also preached in the marketplace (*agora*). It was there that he met the idol worshipers and the philosophers. These people were highly educated. And they were proud of their education. Luke gives us the names of two groups that argued with Paul (Acts 17:18). The *Epicureans followed the teachings of Epicurus. They believed God was in everything. Also, they

Figure 11.9   Entrance to Acropolis in Athens with Temple of Athena Nike (on right)

Figure 11.10   Close-up of the Porch of the Maidens on the Acropolis at Athens

Q 31 ➤ How did the Epicureans and Stoics differ?

Q 32 ➤ In Paul's day, to what did "Areopagus" refer?

Q 33 ➤ How did Paul's method in the synagogue differ from his method in the marketplace?

Q 34 ➤ What bridge or door did Paul find? Explain.

Figure 11.11   Athens—Areopagus (Mars' Hill) where Paul preached about the Unknown God

thought pleasure was the main goal in life.[25] They said *"Let us eat and drink, for tomorrow we die"* (1 Cor. 15:32). The *Stoics had a contrasting view. They followed the teachings of Zeno. He used to speak in Athens on a *stoa* or covered porch (*portico*) that was decorated with paintings and had large stone columns. The Stoics taught that man should not pay attention to pleasure or pain.[26] These two groups, the Epicureans and the Stoics, brought Paul to a meeting of the *Areopagus. The Greek word *Areopagus* means "the hill (*pagus*) of Ares." Ares was the Greek god of thunder and war. In Paul's day, the word *Areopagus* referred to a council or group of leaders.[+] They examined religious teachings.[27]

Paul had only one message. But he used different methods. The method he used in the synagogue was not the method he used in the marketplace. In the synagogue, people knew the Scriptures. So he explained, reasoned, and persuaded from the Scriptures they knew (Acts 17:17). He showed that Jesus fulfilled the Jewish prophecies. But the people in the marketplace did not accept the Jewish Scriptures. Therefore, Paul did not quote from them. To persuade people, we must refer to things they understand and accept. It is not enough to have the right message. We must also have the right method to present the message.

Paul was a careful observer. He studied people and their beliefs. Wise witnesses search for a door into a person's life. They look for a bridge. They pray about an opportunity to relate the gospel well. All learning must be related to what people already know. The new must be tied to the old. Paul found the door he sought.

"For as I walked around and looked carefully at your objects of worship, I even found an altar with this inscription: TO AN UNKNOWN GOD. Now what you worship as something unknown I am going to proclaim to you" (Acts 17:23).

He told them about the unknown god whom they worshiped. The people of Athens did not want to offend any god. So they put up an altar to the unknown god. Thus they hoped to avoid offending a god they didn't know.[28]

Paul preached the gospel message in the market. But he did not quote Scripture. Instead, he quoted poets they knew (Acts 17:28). He used the poets to illustrate the truth. Jesus often used things people knew to illustrate the truth. He talked about bread, birds, fish, foxes, sowing, money, renters, banquets, sons, kings, weddings, and so on. The stories Jesus used were seldom quotations from the Bible. Rather, His method was to talk about things people knew well. Illustrations, like those Jesus used, help people understand and accept a message.

Paul praised the people of Athens for being religious (Acts 17:22). It is always good to give people a sincere compliment. His words were kind and gracious. Still, he spoke clearly against their temples and idols (Acts 17:24-31). He did not quote verses from the Bible. But his thoughts came from the Bible. He described God as our Creator and Jesus as our Judge.[29]

The results were wonderful. Some measure success with numbers. But heaven rejoices when one person accepts Christ. Paul's wise method won a few to the Master.

+ The Areopagus was located near the Acropolis, which was a citadel or strong tower.

A few men became followers of Paul and believed. Among them was Dionysius, a member of the Areopagus, also a woman named Damaris, and a number of others (Acts 17:34).

Wise witnesses use different methods for different people. Puppets work well for children. Drama reaches many that sermons will not reach. Singing may open hearts that are closed to preaching. Films touch people of all ages. Crusades reach people who will never come to Christ in a church. Home meetings bring the Savior to neighbors that are not open to church meetings. We become all things to all people that we might win some (1 Cor. 9:22). If you are preaching in the city, do not dress like you are in a small village. And if you are preaching in a small village, do not dress like you are meeting with the President. The messenger and the message should fit the context or local situation.

Q 35 ↖ *What are some methods your church uses to reach various people?*

Q 36 ↖ *Which word do you think Ivan should use to describe God? Explain.*

Figure 11.12 Athens—Temple of *Athena Parthenos or the Parthenon, dedicated in 438 B.C.

Ivan threw up his hands in frustration. He was trying to translate the Bible into Telugu, a language in South India. He was looking for a word that meant *God*. He wanted a word to show that God is the Creator and above all. But he also wanted a word to show that God is personal and likes to talk to us. The Telugu language does not have a word for *creator*. Hinduism has influenced the languages in India. Hindus believe that *Brahman* is a force without feelings. They think Brahman is the highest power, but it does not love or talk. Brahman is a power, not a person. It is a force like the wind. Hindus also believe all life is one. That is, plants, animals, humans, and gods all have the same kind of life. In the Telugu language the word *deva* means "god." They believe the gods come to earth as humans *(avatars)* to help people. But they believe that the gods sin. Hindus believe that the gods who sin are reborn as humans, animals, or even ants. Ivan thought about using the English word *God,* without translating it. But then, it would be a foreign word the people would not understand. He was confused. Should he use the word *Brahman, deva,* or *God?* He did not know which word would be best for his message.[30]

Note: The Parthenon was home to a 40-foot (12 m) high gold and ivory statue of the goddess Athena.

This temple was built on the *Acropolis*. The Greek word *Acro* means "high place." *Polis* means "city" or "state."

Cities had high places where their idols and shrines were kept. What seem to be magnificent ruins today were evil places of idolatry in Paul's time.

E. The challenge of higher learning is keeping it low enough to help people on earth.

"(All the Athenians and the foreigners who lived there spent their time doing nothing but talking about and listening to the latest ideas)" (Acts 17:21).

Ideas are interesting. And the more a person studies, the more that student enjoys listening to ideas. Some like a cup of coffee. But one cup of coffee often causes a person to want another cup. Some people drink many cups of coffee in one day. Doctors tell us that too much coffee is harmful. Likewise, too much studying can do more harm than good.

The people at Athens studied too much. Luke says, they *"spent their time doing nothing but talking about and listening to the latest ideas"* (Acts 17:21). There is a balance between learning and doing other things. Those who study too much are like a balloon that rises further and further away from earth. They spend their time thinking about ideas that have little or nothing to do with life. They forget the daily problems of common people. Studying can be helpful. We are glad you are studying this book! But a wise old teacher gave good advice to his students. He said, "Never get more education than you can recover from!"

Q 37 ↗ *What problem did the people at Athens have?*

Paul was persecuted almost everywhere he went except Athens. Why? Because the people at Athens did not have strong beliefs. They listened to everyone's ideas. They tolerated what everyone said. But they did not take a stand for what was right or wrong. Studying too much may cause some people to lose their beliefs.

Q 38 ↗ *Why did the citizens of Athens not persecute Paul?*

The people at Athens responded to Paul in a mental manner. They did not have strong emotional feelings about religious teachings. Rather, they just thought about what each person said. Therefore, nothing Paul said could make them angry. So how did they respond

Q 39 ↗ *How did the citizens of Athens respond to Paul's message?*

Figure 11.13   Statue of a philosopher like the ones in Athens

Q 40 ✎ *Why do you think the people stopped tithing?*

mentally to Paul? They responded in two ways. *First,* they scoffed at him. They looked down at him like he was ignorant. They called him a *babbler.* This word in the Greek is "seed-picker" (Acts 17:18).[31] They said Paul was like a bird that flew around picking up seeds here and there. They compared him to a beggar who went around picking up scraps. They likened him to an ignorant man who picked up ideas from place to place. They said Paul was not smart enough to understand much. He could grasp only a little here and there. This is the way some with much education ridicule others. They look down on them with contempt. Those who have studied too much ridicule great apostles. They pretend to know more than the greatest of God's servants. *Second,* they closed the discussion. *"When they heard about the resurrection of the dead, some of them sneered, but others said, 'We want to hear you again on this subject' "* (Acts 17:32).

A young man graduated from Bible school. Other students had made lower grades. But he had been at the top in all of his studies. However, studying pushed other things out of his schedule. He did not take time to pray much. And he seldom had time to witness. In his 4 years as a student, he preached only four times. He paid a big price to make the best grades. Now, it was time to pastor. His church leaders sent him to a small church in a village. He expected them to send him to a big church in the city. Still, he agreed to be the shepherd of the small flock. But the people did not like his preaching. He talked often about the meaning of Greek and Hebrew words. His sentences were long and difficult to understand. He seldom talked about the problems they were facing. And he often talked about things they did not care about. Instead of explaining a Bible verse, he told them three things it might mean. His messages raised more questions than they answered. They created more doubt than faith. The people were not sure what he believed. And his illustrations were as few as eager donkeys. They were as rare as cornfields in the city. He was working very hard to prepare his sermons. But he did not discern why the believers did not like them. Another question troubled him. Why had people stopped paying their tithes?

Lesson 33   Paul and Silas Extend the Gospel to Corinth (Acts 18:1-22)

Goal A: *Explain and follow 5 steps for making new friends.*
Goal B: *Give 4 examples of Paul's friends in Acts 18.*

Setting

Athens was an educational and cultural mountain of the ancient world. In contrast, Corinth was a deep moral valley. It was a city of the world and the flesh. To act like a Corinthian meant to commit sexual sins.[32] Behind the city was the Acrocorinth, or hill of Corinth. It stood like a tower, about 1,500 feet (457 m) above the city.[33] On it was a temple to Aphrodite (Greek name) or Venus (Roman name). Venus was the goddess of love[34] and sex.[35] In this temple about 1,000 female slaves committed sexual sins with those who came to worship. At night, they walked the streets as prostitutes.[36] Paul reminds the Corinthians of their life before they met Jesus. Read 1 Corinthians 6:9-11.

Q 41 ➚ *What were the Corinthians like before Jesus changed them?*

Jesus made some big changes in people at Corinth.

Corinth was famous for sin and also for business. Locate Corinth on the map (See Figure 11.15). This huge city was located 50 miles (80 km) west of Athens. Paul walked on a short neck of land from Athens to Corinth. Sailors dragged smaller ships 4 miles over this neck or *isthmus. It connected the Aegean and Adriatic Seas. These 4 miles over land saved them days of sailing 200 miles (322 km) around the southern part of Achaia.[37] Ships from the east and the west came to Corinth. Sailors worked on the water and played in the temple.[38]

Q 42 ➚ *Did Athens and Corinth have the same number of people? Explain.*

Corinth was a big city. Athens may have had a population of less than 10,000. But Corinth was much larger. Estimates range from 100,000 to several hundred thousand people.[39] Scholars of the NIV Study Bible think Corinth may have had 250,000 free people and as many as 400,000 slaves.[40] Most scholars agree that the most populated city of Paul's day was Rome, followed by Alexandria, and then Antioch. But cities like Ephesus, Philippi, and Corinth were also large. Now, there are over 400 cities larger than a million.[41] Over half the world lives in big cities. But there have not always been so many large cities. In 1850, there were only four cities in the world with populations over one million.[42] Corinth was a big city in its day! And big cities were Paul's favorite targets for the gospel.

Figure 11.14   Corinth: Acrocorinth with Temple of Apollo in foreground

In Corinth, friendship stands out as a theme of Paul's ministry. Let us look at four examples of Paul's friends.

A. Paul makes two new friends (Acts 18:1-4).

Christian friendship is a great treasure. Jesus called His followers *friends* (John 15:14-15). Since that time, believers have understood better the value of friendship.

Paul made many friends. His list of friends included Barnabas, Mark, Silas, Timothy, Luke, Aquila, Priscilla, Titus, Tychicus, Trophimus, Sopater, Aristarchus, Secondus, Gaius, Epaphras, Epaphroditus, Artemas, Apollos, Zenas, Onesiphorus, Eubulus, Pudens, Linus, Claudia, Philemon, and Onesimus.[43] Most of these are not listed among his 30 friends in Romans 16.

Q 43 ⟋ *Who are 2 new friends Paul made in Corinth (Acts 18:1-3)?*

Sometimes it takes a little work to make a friend. It is natural for some to make friends. Others must learn the skill of making friends. But all can make new friends if they pray and practice five steps.

The *first* step in making a new friend is meeting a new person.It is easy to walk past people without meeting them. Seeing is not meeting. Sometimes neighbors see each other, but they do not meet each other! In fact, people may see each other at church but never meet each other! Simple but amazing! To make a new friend you must meet a new person. So practice taking the first step toward friendship. Meet those you see. Paul saw a man. Then he met him (Acts 18:2). He found out that the man's name was Aquila. This was the first step toward friendship. And Paul took it with a purpose.

Figure 11.15   Corinth was located in a great place for business.

The *second* step toward friendship is talking. We meet many people in life. But friendship is a few steps beyond meeting a person. Paul met Aquila. At that point, Paul and Aquila were not friends. So Paul took the second step toward making a new friend. He spent some time talking to the person he met. Talking, Paul learned that Aquila and his wife Priscilla were from Italy. Aquila was a Jew. And the Roman Caesar Claudius had ordered all the Jews to leave Rome (Acts 18:2). This probably refers to Jewish Christians. History tells us that Claudius expelled Jews because of trouble related to Christ. It appears that the unbelieving Jews stirred up trouble for Jewish believers. As a result, the Roman Emperor Claudius made Jewish believers move from Rome.[44] Thus, Aquila and Priscilla had to leave their home and friends. A new friend would mean a lot to them.

Paul continued to talk and listen. He was taking the *third* step toward making a new friend. That step is finding something in common. Paul learned that Aquila and Priscilla made tents. Since Paul also made tents, this gave them something in common. Friends must share some common interests.

Q 44 ⟋ *What are the first 3 steps toward making a new friend?*

Next, Paul took the *fourth* step. He *"went to see them"* (Acts 18:2). Paul met Aquila. He talked and listened. He found something they had in common. Then he went to visit him. Friendship begins as a small seed. But it can grow until it becomes like a tall tree. First, Paul planted a seed. Then he watered it. Next they began to hoe a little. The roots of friendship were growing. Paul worked side by side with Aquila. They sewed tents together. Paul was not ashamed to work. Many ministers must do work besides preaching. Paul often sewed tents to earn money. He and Aquila made tents during the week. They spent time together.

Q 45 ⟋ *Summarize steps 4 and 5 for making new friends.*

Finally, Paul took the *fifth* step toward a deeper friendship. He studied the Scriptures and worshiped with his new friends. It is almost certain that they attended the synagogue with Paul (Acts 18:4).[45] During the week they sewed tents together. And on the Sabbath they worshiped together. In time, they became very close. In fact, they became such close friends that they went with Paul when he traveled to Ephesus (Acts 18:18-19). Thus Aquila and Priscilla became two of Paul's many friends. We do not know if Aquila and Priscilla were believers before they met Paul. But he certainly helped them know God better. In the next chapter of this book we will see how this husband and wife team helped Apollos.

Q 46 *Give an example of how you made a friend.*

Friendships do not just happen. If you want a new friend, you must take steps toward that person. He who wants friends must act friendly (Prov. 18:24 KJV). Are you a social person? Do you try to make new friends in the church? Or do you just wait for others to take steps toward you? Do you greet new people? Do you take time to find out about their background, family, and interests? Have you learned the skill of making new friends?

Friendship is a great tool of evangelism. Do you take steps of friendship toward the lost around you? Influence increases with relationship. It is easier to lead a friend to Christ than it is to lead a stranger.

Q 47 *Do you practice the skills of making and keeping friends? Explain.*

Adam was a believer. He liked to make new friends and then lead them to Jesus. Near his home he met a man named Val. Val was the manager of a group of apartments. It was easy to see that Val was not a believer. He had many sinful habits. So Adam began to take the steps of becoming a friend to Val. First, they talked. Adam learned a lot about the work Val did. He learned that many of the renters complained. Also, Adam learned that Val often fixed things like broken windows and doors. Adam knew a little about fixing things. Therefore, they had a little in common. Adam took the third step toward friendship. He visited Val often. He

Q 48 *How did Paul's old friends help him in Corinth?*

went by to see Val two or three times a week. Val smoked a lot of cigarettes. And he was often drunk. But Adam did not mention these things. Rather, he spent a lot of time listening. He knew that Val's greatest need was not to change his habits. After a year they became good friends. Then Adam introduced Val to another friend named Jesus. The roots of their friendship went deeper as they began to study the Scriptures and worship together.

Figure 11.16   Corinth: Temple of Apollo

B. Paul's old friends help him in the ministry (Acts 18:5-8).

Silas and Timothy were two of Paul's friends. They joined him in Corinth about A.D. 50. They had stayed in Berea for a time (Acts 17:14). Then they visited Thessalonica (1 Thess. 3:2). They brought a good report about the faith of the Thessalonians (1 Thess. 3:6). The Thessalonian believers had stood firm against their enemies. Thus Paul's friends brought a very encouraging message. And they brought a financial gift from some of Paul's other friends (See Phil. 4:14 and 2 Cor. 11:8-9). This gift enabled Paul to stop making tents for a while. Then he began to preach every day (Acts 18:5).[46] Also, he wrote 1 Thessalonians shortly after Silas and Timothy came to Corinth. We know this from 1 Thessalonians 3:6-10.[47] Paul had many friends who shared with him in the work of God.

Figure 11.17   Interior view of the Temple of Apollo at Corinth

Unbelieving Jews in Corinth opposed Paul. They became abusive. This probably means they blasphemed against Paul and his gospel.[48] This caused Paul to turn to the Gentiles. He left the synagogue and shook off his cloak. He did not want a speck of dust from the synagogue to remain on his clothes. Jesus had told his disciples to do this when rejected (Luke

9:5). Paul and Barnabas shook the dust off their feet at Antioch in Pisidia (Acts 13:51). This sign was a protest against the unbelievers. To the outward sign, Paul added a spoken testimony. He declared he was innocent of their blood. He said the guilt of their blood was upon their own heads, not his (Acts 18:6). These terrible words remind us of Ezekiel 33:1-6. Read these verses.

Paul moved next door to the house of Titius Justus. His full name was probably Gaius Titius Justus (Acts 18:7; Rom. 16:23; 1 Cor. 1:14).[49] Thus Paul shifted his ministry from the Jews to the Gentiles. Crispus believed. Paul baptized him and his household (1 Cor. 1:14). Also, many others, probably Gentiles, believed (Acts 18:8). Note the emphasis here and throughout Acts on households and house churches. The churches in Acts met often in homes (See Figure 11.19).

Figure 11.18 Corinthian columns

For sure, Paul enjoyed the fellowship and support of his friends. Make new friends and keep the old. One is silver and the other is gold!

Acts	Scripture
2:46	*They broke bread in their homes and ate together with glad and sincere hearts.*
9:11	*"Go to the house of Judas on Straight Street and ask for a man from Tarsus named Saul."*
10:6	*"He is staying with Simon the tanner, whose house is by the sea."*
10:25	*As Peter entered the house, Cornelius met him and fell at his feet. . .*
12:12	*He went to the house of Mary, . . . where many people . . . were praying.*
16:15	*When she and the members of her household were baptized, she invited us to her home.*
17:7	*"Jason has welcomed them into his house."*
18:7	*Paul left the synagogue and went next door to the house of Titius Justus.*
18:26	*When Priscilla and Aquila heard him, they invited him to their home.*
28:7	*Publius, the chief official of the island, . . .welcomed us to his home . . .*
28:30	*Paul stayed there in his own rented house and welcomed all who came to see him.*

Figure 11.19 Believers in Acts met often in homes for prayer, Bible study, and fellowship.

C. Paul's best friend comforts him (Acts 18:9-11).

No doubt the unbelieving Jews were angry enough to murder Paul. Imagine him as a stranger in this huge city of Corinth. Hundreds of powerful Jews wanted to see him dead. It must have been a frightening time for Paul. He was preaching daily next door to a den of roaring lions!

In this fearful moment a message came from Paul's best friend.

Q 49 How did Paul's best friend help him at Corinth?

⁹One night the Lord spoke to Paul in a vision: "Do not be afraid; keep on speaking, do not be silent. ¹⁰For I am with you, and no one is going to attack and harm you, because I have many people in this city" (Acts 18:9-10).

Jesus knows the future and all who are His. What a friend we have in Jesus!

Jesus has promised to be with us always (Matt. 28:20; Heb. 13:5-6). He is the friend who sticks closer than a brother (Prov. 18:24). So Paul stayed in Corinth for about 2 years![50] Consider the courage Jesus gave Paul to preach beside the angry lions for 2 years!

"Hallelujah, what a Savior; Hallelujah, what a friend;
Saving, keeping, helping, loving; He is with us to the end!"[51]

Polycarp was pastor of the church at Smyrna. He had been a disciple of the apostle John. When Polycarp was 86 years old, the Roman government tried to get him to deny Jesus. He replied, "Eighty and six years have I served him. And he never did me any harm. How then can I blaspheme my King and my Savior?"[52] So they prepared to burn him alive. He replied that if they would give him an hour to pray, they would not even need to tie him.

D. Paul finds a new friend in the government (Acts 18:12-17).

[12]*While Gallio was proconsul of Achaia, the Jews made a united attack on Paul and brought him into court.* [13]*"This man," they charged, "is persuading the people to worship God in ways contrary to the law."* [14]*Just as Paul was about to speak, Gallio said to the Jews, "If you Jews were making a complaint about some misdemeanor or serious crime, it would be reasonable for me to listen to you.* [15]*But since it involves questions about words and names and your own law—settle the matter yourselves. I will not be a judge of such things."* [16]*So he had them ejected from the court* (Acts 18:12-16).

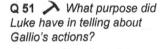

Q 50 *How was Gallio linked to Nero?*

Achaia was a big and important province. So Gallio was an important Roman ruler. He was the younger brother of Seneca. Seneca was a famous philosopher. Also, he was the tutor of Nero who became the Emperor of Rome![53] Nero was the Roman Caesar at the time of Paul's trial in Rome, about A.D. 63.

Gallio threw Paul's case out of the Roman court system. This was a huge decision in favor of Christianity. The Roman government allowed Jews to worship God rather than Caesar. Gallio's decision meant that Christianity was protected under the umbrella of Judaism. Gallio ruled that Christianity was not breaking Roman law. He said that Christianity and Judaism needed to settle their own disagreements. This prevented the unbelieving Jews from using Roman law against believers. Wow! Gallio's decision helped believers in Achaia and probably many other places.

Q 51 *What purpose did Luke have in telling about Gallio's actions?*

Recall Luke's purposes for writing Acts. One of these was to defend Christianity and show it was friendly to the government. Thus, Luke had a big reason to include this court case under Gallio. Gallio's decision may have helped Paul in his trial at Rome. Gallio ruled that Paul was not guilty of breaking Roman law. This may have influenced Nero, the Roman ruler at Paul's trial in Rome. Many Bible teachers believe that Nero set Paul free after his first trial in Rome about A.D. 63.[54] Gallio was a friend of Paul, of believers, and of justice.

Conclusion

We are near the end of Paul's second missionary trip. From Corinth, he travels 6 miles (10 km) southeast to the port city of Cenchrea (See Figure 10.2). There, he had his hair cut (Acts 18:18). Shaving his head meant he had completed a vow.[55] We know almost nothing about this vow. It was probably a form of a Nazirite vow. This involved not drinking wine or cutting one's hair for a period of time[56] (See Num. 6:1-21 and Acts 21:24).

Figure 11.20
Music Theater of Herod Atticus in Athens

Paul sailed from Cenchrea to Ephesus. This time the Spirit did not forbid him. A door that God closes today may be open tomorrow. Timing is important in God's work.

The Jews at Ephesus did not oppose Paul like the Jews of Corinth. Perhaps this was partly because his head was shaved.[57] The shaved hair showed that he was loyal to Judaism.

Paul did not stay long in Ephesus. Some Greek versions of the Bible explain why Paul was in a hurry. He wanted to go to a feast in Jerusalem. This was probably the Passover Feast. He met with the church in Jerusalem. No doubt he told about obeying the Church council of Acts 15. He strengthened relationships for a time. Then he sailed back to Antioch, Syria. This completed the second missionary trip (See Figure 10.3).

Test Yourself: Circle the letter by the *best* completion to each question or statement.

1. Corinth is in the province of
a) Galatia.
b) Asia.
c) Macedonia.
d) Achaia.

2. Of Paul and Barnabas, who was right about John Mark?
a) Paul
b) Barnabas
c) Both
d) Neither

3. What guided believers to flee from Jerusalem after Stephen's death?
a) The Word of God
b) Supernatural revelation
c) Circumstances
d) An outer witness

4. Paul used his rights as a Roman citizen in
a) Lystra.
b) Philippi.
c) Athens.
d) Thessalonica.

5. People were described as "noble" in
a) Berea.
b) Thessalonica.
c) Athens.
d) Corinth.

6. Paul quoted from the Scriptures the least in
a) Jerusalem.
b) Iconium.
c) Thessalonica.
d) Athens.

7. The social level of Lydia was
a) very low.
b) low.
c) average.
d) high.

8. Which city of Paul's second journey had the greatest reputation for sin?
a) Corinth
b) Athens
c) Thessalonica
d) Rome

9. The first step in making a new friend is
a) meeting.
b) eating.
c) talking.
d) praying.

10. In Corinth, Paul found a new friend in
a) Pontus.
b) Claudius.
c) Gallio.
d) Timothy.

 Essay Test Topics: Write 50-100 words on each of these goals that you studied in this chapter.

Paul and Silas Extend the Gospel to Philippi (Acts 15:36–16:40)

Goal: *Identify 11 provinces or districts and 15 cities of Paul's second missionary trip.*

Goal: *Summarize and apply what Acts 15–16 teaches about harvest, disagreements, guidance, attitudes, cultures, and citizens.*

Paul and Silas in Thessalonica, Berea, and Athens (Acts 17:1-34)

Goal: *Contrast 3 reactions to the gospel in Acts 17. Relate these to those you know.*

Paul and Silas Extend the Gospel to Corinth (Acts 18:1-22)

Goal: *Explain and follow 5 steps for making new friends.*

Goal: *Give 4 examples of Paul's friends in Acts 18.*

Chapter 12:
Paul's Third Missionary Journey

(Acts 18:23–21:16)

Introduction

Evangelist Ben Tipton tried to lift his voice above the noisy crowd. He was preaching the gospel in Pendembu, Sierra Leone, in 1970. This small city in West Africa was mostly Muslim. Ben and his friend, Faya, had rented a building for the gospel meeting. It was a courtroom just opposite the mosque. Now, the Muslim prayers in the mosque were over. People were coming out of the mosque. From the street, they shouted words of ridicule into the courtroom. It was very hard to hear.

Figure 12.1 At Ephesus, new believers burned their scrolls about magic and sorcery.

Ben was standing on a table at the front of the courtroom. For three days, he and Faya had been praying and fasting. They took turns. One prayed six hours, then the other prayed the same amount of time. In this way, there was prayer day and night for the gospel meeting. It was the third day. Still, there were only about ten people in the courtroom. But there were many shouting in the street. Suddenly, Ben felt the presence of the Holy Spirit in a special way. The Spirit led Ben's attention to an old man by the door. The old man had fallen and was trying to get up. Ben called out to the crowd, "Help the old man stand up. He has fallen and no one is helping him." At once, some stepped forward to help the old man. "Now," said Ben, "bring the old man to the front of the room." Ben held his Bible high. "You are going to see that this book has the power of God." People laughed. But they helped the old man to the front of the room. He was bent over and gasping for breath. Ben prayed for him in the name of Jesus. Immediately, the old man straightened up. His breathing became normal. He turned to Ben and smiled. "Thank you," said the old man. "All of my pain suddenly left me." He started to walk away, but turned again and said, "Thank you very much." The people were silent now. And Ben preached. Before the week was over, three blind people had received their sight. A paralyzed woman was also healed. The old Muslim man gave property to start a church. Many turned to Christ.[1] The power of God underlined the truth of the gospel. The apostle Paul had similar miracles in Ephesus, about 1,900 years earlier.

Lessons:

Paul Travels to Ephesus—Part 1 (Acts 18:23–19:20)
Goal: *Examine 4 principles from Paul's ministry in Ephesus. Relate these truths to your context.*

Paul Travels to Ephesus—Part 2 (Acts 18:23–19:20)
Goal: *Explain what Paul's Ephesian ministry teaches about discussions, casting out demons, and public confession. Apply these teachings to your situation.*

Paul's Travels from Ephesus to Jerusalem (Acts 19:21–21:16)
Goal: *Analyze 4 attitudes seen in Paul's travels from Ephesus to Jerusalem. Compare and contrast these with attitudes you have seen.*

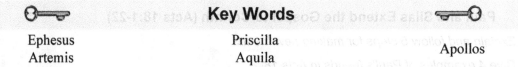

Key Words

Ephesus
Artemis

Priscilla
Aquila

Apollos

Lesson 34 — Paul Travels to Ephesus—Part 1 (Acts 18:23–19:20)

Goal: *Examine 4 principles from Paul's ministry in Ephesus. Relate these truths to your context.*

Setting

Recall that Acts 1:8 is a good outline for Acts. Jesus commanded His followers to wait in Jerusalem for the promise of the Father (Acts 1:4). He said the Holy Spirit would give them power to witness for Him. Those filled with the Spirit became His witnesses. They witnessed in Jerusalem, Judea, Samaria, and to the ends of the earth (Acts 1:8).

In Units 1 and 2 we studied the witness of the Church in Jerusalem (Acts 1–7). In Unit 3 we saw believers in Judea and Samaria (Acts 8–12). Now, in Unit 4, we are exploring the witness of the Church to the ends of the earth (Acts 13–28). This final unit includes the three missionary trips of Paul. Figure 12.2 summarizes some details of Paul's three trips.

Missionary Trip	Acts	Date (A.D.)	Beginning Place	First Stop	Farthest Place from Antioch, Syria
1	13:1–14:28	46-48	Antioch, Syria	Cyprus	Antioch, Pisidia
2	15:36–18:22	49-52	Antioch, Syria	Tarsus	Berea
3	18:23–21:16	53-57	Antioch, Syria	Tarsus	Berea

Figure 12.2   Chart of Paul's three missionary journeys

Paul began the first missionary trip with Barnabas and John Mark. He began the second trip with Silas. But he started the third trip alone. It was a trip of over 1,500 miles or 2,400 kilometers.[2] However, the first parts of the journey were to places Paul had already been. And old friends joined him when he reached the new territory of Ephesus.

Q1 *With which friends did Paul begin each of his 3 trips?*

The third missionary trip focuses mostly on Ephesus. Pergamum was the capital of the province of Asia. But Ephesus was the most important city in Asia.[3] It was located on the eastern shore of the Aegean Sea. Some say 250,000[4] to a third of a million[5] lived in Ephesus. Others think Ephesus had a population of a half million[6] to 600,000.[7] Let us look at four principles that flow out of Paul's ministry in Ephesus.

A. Sometimes God allows us to know why He once closed a door.

Earlier, on the second trip, the Spirit forbade Paul to enter Ephesus (Acts 16:6). But now, the Spirit led Paul to minister in Ephesus for 3 years (Acts 19:8-9; 20:31). This was the longest he stayed in one place on his three trips. Why did the Holy Spirit delay Paul's ministry in Ephesus? Why did God once close the door there? There are at least two possible reasons.[8]

Q2 *On which city does Paul's third trip focus?*

First, **Ephesus is located in the center of the churches Paul planted.** East of Ephesus are the Galatian churches of Pisidian Antioch, Iconium, Lystra, and Derbe. Northwest of Ephesus are the churches of Philippi, Thessalonica, and Berea. And straight west of Ephesus, across the Aegean Sea, are Athens and Corinth. Thus Ephesus was like the hub of a wheel. It was the center of God's strategy for a big area. *To Ephesus,* the churches could send messengers to Paul with questions or offerings. And *from Ephesus* Paul could send messengers to the churches he planted. Therefore, Ephesus became a new center for God's mission to the Gentiles. It was second only to Antioch, Syria, as a base for Gentile missions.[9]

Figure 12.3   Ruins of Temple of Artemis (Diana)

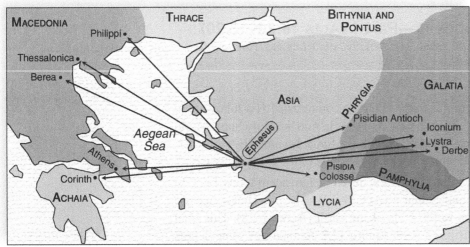

Figure 12.4   Ephesus was a strategic center for missions.

Second, **Ephesus was a powerful center of Satan's kingdom.** It was a stronghold of the devil. In Ephesus, thousands worshiped the goddess Artemis (Diana). They built her a great temple there (Figure 12.3). It was four times bigger than the Parthenon at Athens.[10] The temple was one of the seven wonders of the ancient world. Local craftsmen made statues of the goddess. These statues had many breasts. The Ephesians believed that men communicated with Artemis through the prostitutes in the temple.[11] Paul's preaching lessened the sale of idols. Thus the business people became angry. Opposition to the gospel was never greater than at Ephesus. Paul learned many things on his first two trips. No doubt this prepared him for the spiritual warfare in Ephesus. Remember that even apostles grow in grace.

Q 3 ⟋ *State 2 possible reasons why the Spirit delayed Paul's ministry in Ephesus.*

Q 4 ⟍ *Have you learned to trust God when He closes doors to you? Explain.*

Looking back, Paul probably realized why God once closed the door to Ephesus. *"There is a time for everything"* (Eccl. 3:1). Has God closed a door to you? Be patient. *"What he opens no one can shut, and what he shuts no one can open"* (Rev. 3:7). Be content to walk through the doors He opens. And be thankful for the doors He closes. God knows best. He does all things well. Many believe Ephesus was the crown of Paul's ministry in the cities. But there was a right time for putting on the crown.

B. The private ministry of laypeople is as important as the public ministry of apostles.

Q 5 ⟍ *In your culture, is it usually best to correct people in private? Explain.*

We read about Priscilla and Aquila six times in the New Testament (Acts 18:2, 18-19, 26; Rom. 16:3; 1 Cor. 16:19; 2 Tim. 4:19). Four of these times Priscilla's name comes first. This is probably because she was the main teacher of the two. This man and wife were laypeople. Planting churches was not their ministry. Paul left them at Ephesus. They did not plant a church there. And they probably did not speak in the synagogue. They were a quiet couple who sewed tents for a living. But they had a very important private ministry. It was Priscilla and Aquila who helped Apollos mature (Acts 18:26). They heard him in public. But they helped him in private. This was wise. It is wiser to correct a preacher privately than to rebuke one in public.

Q 6 ⟋ *What were 5 strengths of Apollos?*

Apollos had a destiny. He would become a great champion of the Christian faith. But without Priscilla and Aquila, he was a weak witness. Consider the condition of Apollos when Priscilla and Aquila first heard him.

- *"He was a learned man"* (Acts 18:24). He came from Alexandria, the capital of Egypt at that time. This city was second only to Rome in size. It was located on the northern coast of Egypt. Alexandria, Athens, and Tarsus were famous for their universities. Thus, Apollos had a good education.

- He had a thorough knowledge of the Old Testament Scriptures.

- *"He had been instructed in the way of the Lord"* (Acts 18:25). That is, someone taught him about Jesus.[12] Who taught him? How much did he know? We are not sure. Many think he believed in the death and resurrection of Jesus.[13]

- *"He spoke with great fervor"* (Acts 18:25). This is unusual for a person with higher learning. Sometimes education cools down the emotions. Students may gain degrees but lose heat! But this did not happen to Apollos. The fire in his soul burned throughout university study.

- He *"taught about Jesus accurately"* (Acts 18:25). There was no false doctrine in his teaching.

- *"He knew only the baptism of John"* (Acts 18:25). This reveals the great weakness of Apollos. It appears that he was born again. But he knew only about the cold water baptism of John. He needed the fiery baptism of Jesus. Apollos was educated at the university. He was trained in the Scriptures. He was instructed in the way of the Lord. He spoke with great fervor. He taught about Jesus accurately. But he lacked the power of the Holy Spirit. He was a great man in many ways. But without Pentecostal power, "Peter the fisherman was worth a thousand of him."[14] No amount of human training or talent compares with Pentecostal power. Apollos knew only the baptism of John. But he needed the baptism in the Holy Spirit.

Q 7 ↗ *What was the great weakness of Apollos? Explain.*

Priscilla and Aquila saw what Apollos could become. So they invited him to their home. They did not embarrass him in public. But in private, they *"explained to him the way of God"* in a better way (Acts 18:26). Thus these tent sewers enabled Apollos to become a champion. Later, he went on to Corinth. Filled with the Spirit, Apollos became a great blessing. Luke says, *"He was a great help to those who by grace had believed"* (Acts 18:27). Paul *"planted the seed, Apollos watered it, but God made it grow"* (1 Cor. 3:6). But do not forget the tent sewers, Priscilla and Aquila. These laypeople helped change Apollos from a weak witness into a champion.

Q 8 ↗ *How did Priscilla and Aquila help Apollos?*

The private ministry of laypeople is as important as the public ministry of apostles. In fact, you do not have one without the other. For every Apollos in public, there must be many private lay teams like Priscilla and Aquila. Behind every apostle like Paul, there must be hundreds of laypeople like Ananias to pray for him. For every hero in battle, there are thousands of common soldiers who help. Wars are not won by heroes alone.

Q 9 ↖ *Explain the proverb, "Wars are not won by heroes alone."*

A young man stood tall before a great crowd. Their applause sounded like thunder as he received an award. At first, he was tempted to feel proud. A voice whispered that he deserved all the credit and glory. Then he began to look at the faces in the crowd. He owed something to each of them. Without a farmer, he would never have eaten. Without a tailor, he would have been naked. Without his teachers, he would have been ignorant. Without a policeman, he would have been robbed. Without a doctor, he would have died. Without a carpenter, he would have been homeless. Without a friend, he would have been lonely. Without a father, he would not have been conceived. Without a mother, he would not have been born. And without a crowd, there would have been no one to clap for him! So he held the award high, for all to share the credit. Those who receive awards never deserve all the credit.

C. The baptism in the Holy Spirit is for all, after salvation.

Read Acts 19:1-5. Paul arrived in Ephesus after Apollos left. He met twelve men. They remind us of Apollos. Note that Luke carefully placed the account of Apollos beside the twelve disciples at Ephesus.[15] Like Apollos, they knew only of John's baptism. Apollos probably taught these twelve before he met Priscilla and Aquila. People are like their spiritual leader.

Q 10 ↗ *What prevented the 12 men from being baptized in the Spirit before Paul came?*

These twelve men were disciples. Everywhere else in Acts, Luke refers to those who follow Jesus as disciples.[16] Therefore, it is likely that these men were believers.[17] Paul did not question the fact that they were believers. In fact, he refers to the time they believed (Acts 19:2). But he sensed that something was missing in their lives. They lacked the same power that Apollos once lacked.

Q 11 ↗ *What shows that the 12 men may have been saved before Paul arrived?*

So Paul asked them if they had received the Holy Spirit after they believed. Their response is surprising. They said they had not heard of the Holy Spirit (Acts 19:2). This

Q 12 ➤ At what point are we sure the 12 men were saved?

caused Paul to question their baptism. Why? Because disciples were baptized in the name of the Father, the Son, and the Holy Spirit. Thus Paul asked what type of baptism they had received. Like Apollos, they knew only of John's baptism. This seems strange to us today. We have the Bible, many preachers and teachers, and a lot of helpful books. But remember that there was not even one church in Ephesus then. These twelve men were disciples. They had received bits and pieces of the gospel. Someone had witnessed to them. And they had believed. But no one had led them into Christian baptism. So Paul explained to them the relationship between John the Baptist and Jesus. Then they were baptized into the name of the Lord Jesus. At this point, we are certain that they were born again. They had believed and been baptized in water. Their names were written in the book of life. Still, they needed to be baptized in the Spirit. So Paul prayed for them.

> [6]*When Paul placed his hands on them, the Holy Spirit came on them, and they spoke in tongues and prophesied.* [7]*There were about twelve men in all* (Acts 19:6-7).

Q 13 ➤ What shows that the baptism in the Spirit is for all believers?

All twelve men were baptized in the Holy Spirit. This gift is for all believers. John baptized in water. But Jesus baptizes in the Holy Spirit (Acts 11:16). The baptism in the Holy Spirit is for all who repent, believe in Christ, and are baptized in water (Acts 2:38). The gift Father promised is for all believers. Do not stop short of it. Be like the twelve disciples at Ephesus. After you are baptized in water, be baptized in the Spirit.

D. The evidence of the baptism in the Spirit is speaking in tongues.

Q 14 ➤ Summarize 5 cases in Acts that support tongues as the evidence of the baptism in the Spirit.

Acts 19 is the *fifth* time in Acts we see believers baptized in the Holy Spirit. (Review Figure 3.4.) The *first* time was in Jerusalem (Acts 2:4). There, they all spoke in tongues. The *second* was in Samaria (Acts 8:14-19). The Samaritans believed in Christ and were baptized in water. Then the apostles prayed for them to be baptized in the Spirit. Something outstanding happened. Simon saw something that convinced him they had received. A reasonable explanation is that they spoke in tongues. *Third*, Paul was filled with the Spirit in Damascus (Acts 9:17). There are several reasons why we believe Paul spoke in tongues when he was baptized in the Spirit. He was not inferior to any of the apostles. He spoke in tongues more than all the believers at Corinth (1 Cor. 14:18). And he would not have prayed for believers at Ephesus to receive a gift he had not already received. Paul went to Ephesus 25 years after he walked blindly into Damascus. But he still wanted believers to receive the Spirit in the same way he received Him. *Fourth*, Cornelius and his household were baptized in the Spirit. Peter knew because he heard them speak in tongues (Acts 10:45-46). The *fifth* time was in Ephesus. Paul baptized twelve believers who believed in Jesus. Then he prayed for them to be baptized in the Spirit. They all spoke in tongues as the Spirit filled them (Acts 19:6).

We have looked at the five passages in Acts where believers were first filled with the Spirit. In three of these passages, the Scriptures plainly state that believers spoke in tongues when the Spirit filled them. That is, in 60 percent of the cases in Acts, the Bible states that believers spoke in tongues. In the other two cases, speaking in tongues is the best explanation. The Scriptures are our guide.

Q 15 ➤ Is tongues the purpose of the message of Pentecost? Explain.

The purpose of Pentecost is not tongues. It is power. And the message of Pentecost is not tongues. It is Jesus. How then is speaking in tongues related to Pentecost and the baptism in the Spirit? Tongues is the first, outward evidence of the baptism in the Spirit. Tongues show that the Holy Spirit has prepared a believer to witness for Jesus. Speaking in tongues was a common experience of the apostles and early believers.

Q 16 ➤ Why does Luke not mention tongues every time believers were filled with the Spirit?

Some wonder why Luke did not mention tongues more in Acts. They ask, "If tongues is important, why does Luke not mention it on every occasion?" Recall that Luke chose few things to emphasize. He leaves out many things that we know are important. For example, Luke usually omits water baptism. Conversions occur at least 30 times in

Acts. In these, a person, a family, or a large group was converted. Luke records these 30 cases of conversion. But he mentions water baptism in only 9 of the 30 cases (See Figure 12.5). Does this mean water baptism is not important? Does it mean that only 30 percent of the converts in Acts were baptized in water? No! We all agree that water baptism is important. Still, Luke mentions it only 30 percent of the time. Likewise, we believe speaking in tongues is important. And Luke mentions tongues 60 percent of the time when people were baptized in the Spirit.[18]

Acts	Conversion (Person, Family, or Group)	Water Baptism Mentioned?
2:41	3,000 were saved.	Yes
4:4	Many believed. The number of men grew to 5,000.	No
5:14	More and more men and women believed.	No
6:7	The number of disciples increased rapidly, including a large number of priests.	No
8:12	Men and women in Samaria believed Philip.	Yes
8:35-38	An Ethiopian heard the gospel and was baptized in water.	Yes
9:18	Saul met Jesus on the road to Damascus.	Yes
9:31	The church throughout Judea, Galilee, and Samaria grew in numbers.	No
9:35	All those in Lydda and Sharon saw Aeneas and turned to the Lord.	No
9:42	Many heard about Dorcas and believed in the Lord.	No
10:48	Cornelius, his family, and friends accepted Jesus.	Yes
11:21	A great number believed and turned to the Lord.	No
11:24	A great number of people were brought to the Lord.	No
12:24	Herod died, but the Word of God continued to increase and spread.	No
13:12	Sergius Paulus, the proconsul, was amazed and believed.	No
13:43	Many of the Jews and devout converts to Judaism followed Paul and Barnabas in Pisidian Antioch.	No
13:48	The Gentiles honored the Word of the Lord and believed.	No
14:1	At Iconium a great number of Jews and Gentiles believed.	No
14:21	In Derbe, they won a large number of disciples	No
16:1-2	Paul won Timothy and others at Lystra.	No
16:5	The churches grew daily in numbers.	No
16:14-15	Lydia and her household believed.	Yes
16:33-34	A jailer and his household believed at Philippi.	Yes
17:4	In Thessalonica some of the Jews and Greeks believed.	No
17:12	In Berea many of the Jews and Greeks believed.	No
17:34	In Athens some of the Jews and Greeks believed.	No
18:8	In Corinth, Crispus, his household, and many Corinthians believed.	Yes
19:5	In Ephesus, Paul met twelve disciples who had believed.	Yes
19:19-26	In Ephesus and most of Asia, large numbers believed.	No
28:24	In Rome, some were convinced by what Paul said.	No

**Figure 12.5   Acts describes 30 times that people were converted.
But it mentions water baptism on only 9 of these occasions.**

Today, God saves us in the same way He saved the first believers. We are baptized in water the same way they were. And God still fills us with the Spirit in the same way He filled them. When we are baptized in water, we get wet. That is part of the experience. When we get baptized in the Spirit, we get tongues. That is part of the experience.

Q 17 ✎ *Have the experiences of being born again, baptized in water, and baptized in the Spirit changed? Explain.*

Lesson 35 Paul Travels to Ephesus—Part 2 (Acts 18:23–19:20)

Goal: *Explain what Paul's Ephesian ministry teaches about discussions, casting out demons, and public confession. Apply these teachings to your situation.*

Setting

Q 18 *What are 5 great cities mentioned in Acts?*

We are studying Paul's ministry in Ephesus. He stayed there for 3 years (Acts 19:8-9; 20:31). Paul used Ephesus as a center for evangelism and church growth. From there he communicated with churches he started. Recall that it was a big city with perhaps 500,000 to 600,000 people.

Ephesus was famous for business. In the book of Revelation, Ephesus is the first of the seven churches. Why? Probably because it was the greatest city in the province of Asia (now Turkey). It was located 3 miles from the Aegean Sea. The Cayster River connected the city to the sea.[19] The biggest ships in the world could come to Ephesus. Also, a Roman road connected Ephesus with the eastern parts of the Roman kingdom. Ephesus was a great city, like Rome, Corinth, Alexandria, and Antioch, Syria.

In the last section we studied four principles. These flowed out of Paul's ministry in Ephesus. In this section we will examine three more Christian principles.

Figure 12.6   The Celsus Library at Ephesus had many scrolls.

A. Paul used discussions as a teaching method.

But some of them became obstinate; they refused to believe and publicly maligned the Way. So Paul left them. He took the disciples with him and had discussions daily in the lecture hall of Tyrannus (Acts 19:9).

Acts 19:9 is one of the most wonderful verses in the Bible. Paul moved into the lecture hall. It was a place famous for lectures. It was a building where one person stood up and did all the talking. It was a place where students listened, took notes, or slept. The lecture hall of Tyrannus was the perfect place for one more lecture. But Paul was a spiritual teacher. He knew that teaching is more than telling, and learning more than listening. So Paul did not fill up the hours using the lecture method. Rather, he led discussions.

**Figure 12.7
Close-up of a library pillar at Ephesus**

Q 19 *Is telling teaching? Explain.*

You cannot know what people are learning if they are only listening. Students may say "Amen." They may nod their heads to show they agree. But the best teachers never lecture for long. They guide students in discussions. People learn as they ask questions and discuss.

Listening to a lecture is like smelling food. But discussing is like eating.

People do not grow stronger by smelling food. And they do not learn through listening alone. Smelling may lead people toward food. But the benefit comes only as people eat. A very short lecture may introduce new ideas. Then, through discussions, people apply new truths to their lives. Lectures give people ideas. But discussions change lives and beliefs. In the western world, many think lectures are the key to success. They think that telling is teaching. They believe information changes people. But Paul knew this is not true. His longest lecture in Scripture is less than 2 minutes. Through discussions, he brought people face to face with the truth.

**Figure 12.8
Ephesus had a marble road that led to the sea**

A professor taught a class on principles of teaching. He warned his students not to lecture much. He said that people quickly forget what they hear. He reminded them that his lecture from Monday was forgotten by Friday. The students listened and agreed. They knew his words were true. But after 3 days they forgot what he said. When they became teachers, they lectured as he had done.

A lecture may tell people about a new pair of shoes. But a discussion hands the shoes to the listeners. It enables people to put on the shoes and walk around in them. Discussion asks people how the shoes feel. And it enables people to take the shoes home with them. What people discuss, they may choose to possess.

Today, many churches and classrooms are full of lectures. Words bounce off the walls. Many sermons are like lectures. People endure them. Many Sunday school classes are only lectures. People come to church. They sit, listen, and then go home. The next week they do the same thing. If lectures were the key to success, the Church would be very successful. How successful has the Church been? We have had some success. But half of the world is still waiting to hear the gospel! Let us add more discussion to our methods. Paul did not use the lecture method much. He used discussions as a teaching method. Was Paul successful? Did the discussion method work for him?

> [9]*He took the disciples with him and had discussions daily in the lecture hall of Tyrannus.* [10]*This went on for two years, so that all the Jews and Greeks who lived in the province of Asia heard the word of the Lord* (Acts 19:9-10).

The entire province of Asia heard the Word in only 2 years! That was success! Paul talked a little to people. Then they talked a little to him and to each other. Then Paul talked a little more. Little by little he guided people to truth. Daily discussions were the key to spreading the gospel. Why? Because one discussion led to another. Discussions in the classroom led to discussions outside the classroom. All of Asia did not come to the classroom. But those from the classroom went throughout all of Asia. And what they discussed in the classroom, they continued to discuss throughout Asia. Lectures touch the head. But discussions touch the heart. And people talk about what touches their feelings and hearts.

At Corinth women could not ask questions during the church service. Do you think men asked questions during the services?

So what are some keys to having more discussion in the classroom? At least four things are important. *First*, we must avoid teaching too much content in one course. Western books tend to have too many facts and details. More discussion means less content. Why? Because discussion takes time. Sometimes we need less of the *what* (content) and more of the *so what* (discussion and application)! Some, like the disciples at Ephesus, needed more content. They had not heard of the Holy Spirit. But for many, the greatest need is not more content. Many of us need to apply what we already know. May the Lord help us find the balance between lectures and discussion.

Second, we must begin to emphasize thinking more than memorizing.[20] We need less value on recall and more value on people. People do not grow by memorizing. They grow by thinking and talking. Students can memorize without understanding. As we emphasize discussions, we place a higher value on teaching people to apply new knowledge. *Third*, we must build the class around discussion. Discussion should not be left until the last 10 minutes of class. It should be planned throughout the class. How? By planning questions and life examples for students to discuss. In this

Q 20 ✎ *Why do we have so many lectures and few discussions in classrooms?*

Q 21 ✎ *Are there too many lectures in your church or school? Explain.*

Q 22 ↗ *What resulted from Paul's use of the discussion method?*

Q 23 ✎ *Why does the discussion method change lives?*

Q 24 ✎ *Should we encourage more discussion during our church services? Explain.*

Figure 12.9   The great outdoor theater at Ephesus had 24,000 seats.

Q 25 ✎ *Does your school ask students to memorize too much and talk too little? Explain.*

Q 26 ⟍ *When should discussion take place in a class? Explain.*

Q 27 ⟍ *State 2 reasons why the Faith & Action Series should promote discussion.*

Q 28 ⟍ *Give 5 examples showing that power flows through relationships, not mere words.*

book, there are many questions and case studies to encourage discussion. *Fourth*, have books that students can read and understand outside of class. Then class time can be used for discussion. Some books are too hard for students to understand alone. Then discussion time is lost. Why? Because the teacher must spend most of the class time explaining the book! The *Faith & Action Series* is especially designed for discussions. We hope you use it for that purpose. A growing number of teachers are discerning the value of discussion.

B. The power in the name of Jesus flows through believers.

[13]Some Jews who went around driving out evil spirits tried to invoke the name of the Lord Jesus over those who were demon-possessed. They would say, "In the name of Jesus, whom Paul preaches, I command you to come out." [14]Seven sons of Sceva, a Jewish chief priest, were doing this. [15]One day the evil spirit answered them, "Jesus I know, and I know about Paul, but who are you?" [16]Then the man who had the evil spirit jumped on them and overpowered them all. He gave them such a beating that they ran out of the house naked and bleeding (Acts 19:13-16).

Power does not flow through words. It flows through relationships. A Roman centurion who came to Jesus knew this (Luke 7:1-10). He had authority because he was under authority. The centurion was under the authority of the Roman government. He submitted to it. So as he did his job, the authority of Rome flowed through his words. He told soldiers under him to go or come and they obeyed. There was nothing magic about the words in his commands. Soldiers obeyed him because of his relationship with Rome.

The Roman centurion knew Jesus had authority from God. The Lord had power over demons because of His relationship to the Father. Authority always flows through relationships, not mere words.

The seven sons of Sceva wanted authority without relationship. They tried to pray in the name of Jesus. But they were not under the authority of Jesus. Therefore, they had no power. For sure, Jesus is the name above all names (Phil. 2:9). But God's power does not flow through the name of Jesus alone. It flows only through those rightly related to the Father. Electricity is powerful. But it flows only through wires that are plugged into the source. Power flowed through handkerchiefs sent by Paul (Acts 19:11-12). But no power flowed through the name of Jesus spoken by unbelievers. The seven sons of the Jewish priest learned a painful lesson. Power flows through relationships.

Do you pray in the name of Jesus? Do you expect God's power to flow through you? Be sure you are connected to the source. Do not allow sin or the cares of the world to block your relationship with God. God answers our prayers as we walk in obedience. As we abide in the vine, He gives us all we ask in His name (John 14:12-14; 15:7).

C. Believers should make a public break with past sins.

Read Acts 19:17-20. There was a great revival in Ephesus. Receiving Jesus made a difference in the way people lived. Notice Acts 19:19. In those days scrolls were more popular than books. People had many scrolls about *sorcery. Some new believers still had their old, evil scrolls. But the beating of the sons of Sceva brought insight. It helped the new believers discern the conflict between Jesus and evil forces. So they decided to honor Jesus fully and reject evil. This decision led them to burn their sorcery scrolls. The value of the scrolls was 50,000 drachmas. A drachma was a silver coin worth about one day's wage. So imagine the value of the scrolls they burned. The wages of 50,000 days went up in smoke. That is the total wages of 50 people working for about 3 years! That is a lot of money to burn.

They could have sold these scrolls for a lot of money. How much is a day's wage in the place where you live? Multiply the local daily wage by 50,000. This was enough

Q 29 ✎ *What is the total value of 50,000 days' wages where you live?*

money to make people millionaires! So why did they burn the scrolls instead of selling them?

There are two reasons why they burned the scrolls. *First*, if something is evil, it should be burned—not sold to others. Believers should not sell any product that is evil. It is wrong for a believer to make profit from things that cause others to stumble or be lost. *Second*, sin is strong in the dark. It grows in secret. But the power of sin is broken as we confess and forsake it publicly. When you receive Christ as your Savior, get rid of the sinful things that relate to your past. Burn the bridges between you and your past sins. Destroy the links between you and evil. These evil things may include books, magazines, drugs, videos, cassettes, pictures, CDs, charms, idols, and so forth. Burn them in your earliest days of following Jesus. Then you will be free from them. They will never again be a stumbling block to you or others. If you have things that oppose Jesus, honor Him by turning them to ashes.

Q 30 *Do you agree with the 2 reasons why Ephesian believers burned their scrolls?*

A drunkard named Festus wanted to be free from the bondage of alcohol. It had stolen his respect. Often his children had needed the money he spent on beer and wine. Sometimes they slept with empty stomachs. Their shoes had holes in the soles. Their clothes looked like rags. When he was drunk, he beat his wife. When he was sober, he looked for more alcohol. It had been his cruel master for many years. Two deacons urged Festus to receive the Savior. He agreed. They prayed together. In a moment, the Savior broke the chains of alcohol. Immediately, they urged Festus to destroy the alcohol in his home. He agreed. He was completely free. And he never went back to his old master. From that day forward, he could not stand the smell of beer.

A person will be free only from the things he or she is willing to destroy. Only Jesus can break the chains of sin that bind us. But we should not leave the old chains lying around the house. Satan may seek an opportunity to put them on us again. Flee from the appearance of evil. *"Hate what is evil; cling to what is good"* (Rom. 12:9). Kill a poisonous snake when you get the chance. Then it will not bite you or anyone else. Each year 20,000 people die from snakebites in India.[21] If people killed the snakes, the snakes would not kill the people. Dead snakes do not bite! Do not keep evil close enough to reach out and take in a moment of weakness. A wise person will not stand on the edge of a deep pit.

Q 31 *What types of things in your culture should new believers destroy?*

Lesson 36 — Paul's Travels From Ephesus to Jerusalem (Acts 19:21–21:16)
Goal: *Analyze 4 attitudes seen in Paul's travels from Ephesus to Jerusalem. Compare and contrast these with attitudes you have seen.*

Setting

Paul completed 3 years of ministry in Ephesus. He had sought to go there earlier, on his second missionary trip. But then, it was not God's timing. When the time became right, Paul had a great ministry to the Ephesians. The beating of the seven sons of Sceva in Ephesus opened the eyes of new believers. They realized the powerful conflict between God and evil. This led them to make a clean and public break with their evil past. The sky turned black with smoke from their magic books.

Luke shows us that this big fire brought a great peace to Paul. The Ephesians had made a public break with the past. They had burned the bridges between them and sin. Now the church in Ephesus would do well. God's apostle could move on.

Q 32 *Why did the big fire in Ephesus fill Paul with peace?*

A big goal of Paul was to reach Rome. Recall Luke's purposes. One of these was to show how the gospel spread from Jerusalem to Rome by the power of the Spirit. Acts 19:21 to the end of Acts tells how Paul traveled to Rome. This is a big theme in Acts. We will give it special attention in the next chapter of this book.

Q 33 To what does "after all this" refer (Acts 19:21)?

²¹After all this had happened, Paul decided to go to Jerusalem, passing through Macedonia and Achaia. "After I have been there," he said, "I must visit Rome also." ²²He sent two of his helpers, Timothy and Erastus, to Macedonia, while he stayed in the province of Asia a little longer (Acts 19:21-22).

Review the map in Figure 10.4. Paul decided to move on to Jerusalem. On the way he visited churches he planted in the districts of Macedonia and Achaia. God's apostle was careful to care for his spiritual children.

Q 34 Did the government defend Paul or Demetrius? Explain.

A riot occurred in Ephesus as Paul was about to travel north to Troas (Acts 19:23-41). The local government defended Paul. It said he was innocent. The city clerk said Paul had *"neither robbed temples nor blasphemed our goddess"* (Acts 19:37). Also notice that some of the *"officials of the province"* were *"friends of Paul"* (Acts 19:31). Do not miss the significance of these statements. One of Luke's purposes is to defend Christianity. Throughout Acts, Paul always finds favor in the eyes of the government. Christianity is the source of solutions, not problems. The problems come from jealous Jews and greedy businessmen, like Demetrius. In the chapters of Acts that follow, Luke shows that the government leaders say Paul is innocent.

The city clerk said Paul was right and the crowd was wrong. The clerk warned them not to riot. And he told them to follow the proper legal paths. Then he dismissed them all. Acts 20:1-6 tells of Paul's travels and the men who joined him.

We have surveyed the setting. Now let us examine four attitudes seen in Paul's travels from Ephesus to Jerusalem. Read Acts 19:21–21:16.

A. The attitude of Demetrius: Oppose the truth to keep your customers.

Figure 12.10   Statue of the goddess Artemis (Diana)

Demetrius saw truth as an enemy. He made and sold little silver gods. These idols were called images of Artemis, or Diana. Images of Artemis varied. In Ephesus, the idol of Artemis was linked to childbirth. She had many breasts that looked like ostrich eggs.²² Demetrius was the head of a group of craftsmen. They made these idols with their hands. Paul preached the truth. He said that *"man-made gods are no gods at all"* (Acts 19:26). Did Demetrius believe man could create God? Paul spoke the truth! Still, many worship *"idols that cannot see or hear or walk"* (Rev. 9:20). Ephesus had a big library (Figure 12.6). But the educated people at Ephesus shouted for 2 hours about a god that was blind, deaf, lame, and lifeless!

Q 35 Why did the gospel cause Demetrius to lose money?

Demetrius opposed truth. His first concern was his income. Sinners become angry in a hurry when the gospel affects their pocketbooks! Those who earn their living from evil often oppose the gospel.

Q 36 How has the gospel affected the economy or society in your area?

Magic books were burning. Idol sales were falling. Demetrius was upset. Once again the preaching of the gospel had affected the economy. This was also true in Samaria and in Philippi (Acts 8:9-25; 16:16-40). Sinful businesses always suffer when people accept Jesus. Sometimes revivals close bars and houses of harlots. Those selling false religion, *pornography, drugs, or abortions lose customers to the Savior. So those who value money more than people oppose truth. Demetrius represents those who see people as customers, not neighbors.

B. The attitude of false shepherds: Distort the truth to seduce followers.

Demetrius opposed the gospel because it hurt his business. In contrast, false shepherds turn the gospel into a business. They use the truth as a business tool. It is not an accident that these false shepherds distort truth. They twist truth for a purpose.

Q 37 Why does Acts 20:30 say false shepherds twist the truth?

²⁹I know that after I leave, savage wolves will come in among you and will not spare the flock. ³⁰Even from your own number men will arise and distort the truth in order to draw away disciples after them (Acts 20:29-30).

False shepherds twist truth to draw disciples. They want to draw believers away from Jesus. Why? Because these false teachers want the attention and the money of believers. The attitude of false teachers is, "Listen to me, clap for me, pay me!" They do not love or care about the sheep. False shepherds care only about themselves. They believe the sheep should lay down their lives for the shepherd. False shepherds see life as a mirror, not a window.[23]

The sons of Eli were false shepherds (1 Sam. 2:12-25). They stole the Lord's offerings for themselves. They committed sexual sins with the Lord's women servants. They used their positions to serve themselves rather than others.

The false apostles at Corinth served themselves. They used and abused believers (2 Cor. 11:20). These proud and greedy leaders sacrificed the sheep for their own lusts. Paul wrote about people like these in 2 Timothy 2:1-9. In Acts 20:29 he called these false shepherds *"savage wolves."* Jesus referred to them as wolves in sheep's clothing (Matt. 7:15). They attract believers by twisting Scripture into new teachings. They seduce sheep away from the flock, and then destroy them.

Q 38 ✎ *How do false shepherds you know twist the truth?*

A man from Uganda claimed to be a prophet. He visited Malawi and preached in a church. After the service, he invited people to private prayers for healing or prophecy. When they came, he said, "You cannot come empty-handed to see the prophet of God." He reminded them that Naaman carried a gift when he sought the prophet (2 Kings 5). So people began to bring gifts to the man from Uganda. This false prophet used the Word of God for his own profit.[24]

Luke records Paul's parting words about these false teachers. *"So be on your guard! Remember that for three years I never stopped warning each of you night and day with tears"* (Acts 20:31).

Q 39 ↗ *Was Paul an emotional preacher? Explain.*

C. The attitude of Paul: Preach the truth to help people.

Demetrius opposed the truth to keep customers. False shepherds distort the truth to seduce followers. But Paul preached the truth to help people.

"You know that I have not hesitated to preach anything that would be helpful to you but have taught you publicly and from house to house" (Acts 20:20).

Paul lived to help others. Note the characteristics of his ministry in Acts 20:17-35.

Q 40 ✎ *Which characteristics of Paul are the most rare today?*

- He was humble and compassionate.
  [17]*From Miletus, Paul sent to Ephesus for the elders of the church.* [18]*When they arrived, he said to them: "You know how I lived the whole time I was with you, from the first day I came into the province of Asia.* [19]*I served the Lord with great humility and with tears"* (Acts 20:17-19).

- He persevered through hard times.
  "I was severely tested by the plots of the Jews" (Acts 20:19).

- He did not hide the truth from anyone. He showed neither fear nor favoritism.
  "I have declared to both Jews and Greeks that they must turn to God in repentance and have faith in our Lord Jesus" (Acts 20:21).
  [26]*"I declare to you today that I am innocent of the blood of all men.* [27]*For I have not hesitated to proclaim to you the whole will of God"* (Acts 20:26-27).

- He valued his life for only one reason. He lived for only one purpose.
  [24]*"However, I consider my life worth nothing to me, if only I may finish the race and complete the task the Lord Jesus has given me—the task of testifying to the gospel of God's grace"* (Acts 20:24).
  "I am ready not only to be bound, but also to die in Jerusalem for the name of the Lord Jesus" (Acts 21:13).

- He loved people, not things (See Romans 9:1-3).
  "I have not coveted anyone's silver or gold or clothing" (Acts 20:33).

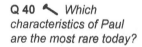

Figure 12.11a - d Ephesus: Monuments along Marble Way showing gladiators (trained fighters)

Q 41 *Is it right for preachers to work like other believers? Explain.*

Figure 12.11b

Q 42 *What does Acts 20:28 teach about the deity of Christ? Explain.*

Q 43 *Why did God want the Ephesians to know they would never see Paul again?*

Q 44 *Was the prophecy at Tyre to enlighten Paul or the disciples? Explain.*

Figure 12.11c

- He worked hard to supply his own needs and help others.

He taught publicly in the lecture hall of Tyrannus. Some Greek texts say this teaching was from 11:00 a.m. to 4:00 p.m. This was the hot part of the day when the lecture hall was available.[25] Others used it during the cooler, morning hours. In the cool hours he made tents to sell. In the hot hours of the day he taught in the hall of Tyrannus. And at night he taught from house to house (Acts 20:20). Paul was a busy servant of Jesus Christ. He worked hard to help others. It is not a disgrace for preachers to have blisters and calluses. It is a glory!

[34] *"You yourselves know that these hands of mine have supplied my own needs and the needs of my companions.* [35]*In everything I did, I showed you that by this kind of hard work we must help the weak, remembering the words the Lord Jesus himself said: 'It is more blessed to give than to receive' "* (Acts 20:34-35).

- He was a model for Christian leaders. He told the Ephesian elders to do two things.
  "Keep watch over yourselves and all the flock of which the Holy Spirit has made you overseers. Be shepherds of the church of God, which he bought with his own blood" (Acts 20:28).

Church leaders must watch out for themselves and others. They are shepherds of God's Church. This brings us to our final thought of this chapter.

D. The attitude of God: Reveal the truth so people can walk in it.

The Church belongs to God. *"He bought* [her] *with his own blood"* (Acts 20:28). The blood of Jesus was the blood of God. This is true because Jesus was God in the flesh.

Jesus was also the Word of God. That is, He was the message of God's truth to us. In Him, we see truth as a person. He showed us what God is like. He revealed God's truth to us. A part of this truth is that God loves us. He loves us so much that He bought us with His own blood. God reveals truth so people can walk in it.

Acts 20–21 gives us four examples of God revealing truth about the future. Let us look at the purpose of these four prophecies.

- The Holy Spirit revealed to Paul that the Ephesians would never see his face again. The Spirit had already told Paul to expect prison and hard times in every city (Acts 20:23). So persecution was not a surprise to Paul. God revealed the truth to Paul to prepare him. As he walked in this truth, persecution did not shock him. Paul was ready to face his enemies because God warned him. Likewise, Paul revealed part of the future to the Ephesian elders. Paul was very dear to them. God did not want their faith to be shaken. And the Father wanted them to be able to say good-bye to their apostle. So He revealed the future to Paul. This prophecy prepared them. Likewise, Jesus prepared His disciples for His death and departure. God knows the beginning and the end. He reveals the truth to us so we can walk in the light.

- Disciples at Tyre prophesied about Paul's trials in Jerusalem (Acts 21:4). These prophecies were mostly for the disciples. Paul knew he would never be coming back. He was on a one-way trip to Rome and beyond. But the Holy Spirit was preparing the disciples to say farewell to Paul (Acts 21:5-6). Later, they were not shocked when they heard he was in prison. But notice that their prophecies got mixed up with their feelings. The Spirit was warning of Paul's trials. But the disciples interpreted the Spirit's message wrongly. The Spirit said danger was ahead. Then the disciples jumped to the conclusion that Paul should not go.

- In Caesarea, the four daughters of Philip prophesied (Acts 21:9). Philip had settled down there. And he had passed his Pentecostal faith on to his daughters. It is a great inheritance for children to receive the fullness of the Holy Spirit. Philip's daughters prophesied when Paul arrived. It is likely that these prophecies were about Paul's future trouble in Jerusalem. The Holy Spirit was revealing truth to prepare believers.

- Finally, we see a prophet named Agabus prophesying about Paul's future trouble. Prophets like Agabus are rare in the New Testament. But as we have seen, all may be filled with the Spirit and prophesy (Acts 19:6; 21:4, 9; 1 Cor. 14:1, 5, 24, 31, 39). God wants prophecy to be a common blessing among believers. But consider the purpose of the prophecy of Agabus.

Q 45 ⟩ *Does God usually guide believers through prophecy? Explain.*

¹⁰After we had been there a number of days, a prophet named Agabus came down from Judea. ¹¹Coming over to us, he took Paul's belt, tied his own hands and feet with it and said, "The Holy Spirit says, 'In this way the Jews of Jerusalem will bind the owner of this belt and will hand him over to the Gentiles'" (Acts 21:10-11).

The purpose of prophecy is rarely to direct a believer. Agabus did not tell Paul not to go to Jerusalem. He warned only about trouble. Paul already knew that trouble was ahead in Jerusalem. The prophecies along the way did not direct him. They only confirmed what the Spirit had already told him. But the main purpose of the prophecies was not for Paul. The prophecies informed younger believers of what God's mature apostle already knew. Then their faith was not shaken by his trials. Thus the prophecy was related to future comfort (Compare with Philippians 1:12-14).

Figure 12.11d

A young man preached a sermon in a church. Afterward, a young woman came forward to meet him. She prophesied that God wanted him to marry her! The young man smiled. "That may be true," he said. "But if it is, the Holy Spirit will tell me in private!" Prophecy may confirm what God has already told someone. But its purpose is rarely to direct.

God told a young prophet to go on a mission (1 Kings 13:1-32). The young man went and was successful. The Spirit of God told him not to eat or drink until he returned home. However, on the way home an old prophet met him. He falsely prophesied that God wanted the young man to come to his house and eat. God had already given the young man a message. He should have walked in the light God personally gave him. Instead, he depended on another to guide him. He went and ate with the older prophet. As a result, a lion killed him. Each believer should be filled with the Spirit. Then God can speak directly to him or her. Prophecy should confirm rather than direct. Those who seek guidance through the prophecies of others often meet the lion in the road!

Figure 12.12
Tyre—stone columns on former main street

Figure 12.13
Caesarea—port and harbor

Test Yourself: Circle the letter by the ***best*** completion to each question or statement.

1. Paul's third trip focuses on the city of
a) Jerusalem.
b) Ephesus.
c) Corinth.
d) Rome.

2. Apollos owed his successful ministry to
a) Paul.
b) John the Baptist.
c) Priscilla and Aquila.
d) Ananias.

3. The greatest weakness of Apollos was that he
a) was not filled with the Spirit.
b) had too much education.
c) did not teach correctly about Jesus.
d) did not know the Scriptures.

4. When believers in Acts are baptized in the Spirit, Luke mentions tongues
a) 10 percent of the time.
b) 30 percent of the time.
c) 60 percent of the time.
d) 100 percent of the time.

5. All the province of Asia heard the Word because Paul used which method?
a) Lectures
b) Preaching
c) Healing
d) Discussion

6. In Acts 19 we saw that the key to spiritual power is
a) fasting.
b) relationships.
c) the name of Jesus.
d) knowledge.

7. In Ephesus a great peace came over Paul after
a) the Holy Spirit spoke to him.
b) believers burned their scrolls.
c) Agabus prophesied to him.
d) the sons of Sceva fled.

8. Listening to a good lecture is like
a) cooking food.
b) eating food.
c) buying food.
d) smelling food.

9. Ephesus was famous for the temple of
a) Artemis.
b) Apollo.
c) Zeus.
d) Venus.

10. A common purpose of prophecy is to
a) guide believers in personal decisions.
b) replace the need to walk by faith.
c) provide believers with comfort.
d) clarify the meaning of Scripture.

 Essay Test Topics: Write 50-100 words on each of these goals that you studied in this chapter.

Paul Travels to Ephesus—Part 1 (Acts 18:23–19:20)

Goal: *Examine 4 principles from Paul's ministry in Ephesus. Relate these truths to your context.*

Paul Travels to Ephesus—Part 2 (Acts 18:23–19:20)

Goal: *Explain what Paul's Ephesian ministry teaches about discussions, casting out demons, and public confession. Apply these teachings to your situation.*

Paul's Travels from Ephesus to Jerusalem (Acts 19:21–21:16)

Goal: *Analyze 4 attitudes seen in Paul's travels from Ephesus to Jerusalem. Compare and contrast these with attitudes you have seen.*

Figure 12.14   Arched pillar and other ruins from Ephesus

Figure 12.15   Massive stone ruins at Ephesus

Figure 12.16
A view through two pillars at Ephesus

Chapter 13:
Paul's Journey to Rome
(Acts 21:17–28:31)

Introduction

There is a story about a pastor with a confused church elder. Many will believe this story. Others may think of it as a parable. The elder claimed to be a believer, yet he continued to practice witchcraft. In time, the elder became very sick. He visited the doctor, but his condition became worse. One day his pastor confronted him. "I don't think your ways are right with God," said the pastor. "Would you like to tell me about your personal life and relationship with the Lord?" The elder was shocked. "How did you know about my secret life?" asked the elder. "I know nothing," replied the pastor. "But I don't feel good when I pray for you. And your illness does not change." The elder began to tremble. He confessed his evil practice.

Figure 13.1   Soldiers rescued Paul in Jerusalem.

Q 1 ✎ *What message does this story have for your culture? Explain.*

The pastor asked, "What do you do?" The elder explained, "If I want to kill a person, I start rain. Then I cause lightning to strike that person." The pastor asked him to cause rain and lightning. The elder brought out the things he used. They were only an old nail and a bottle of water. He struck the bottle and rain came. He caused lightning to strike a banana tree. It immediately dried up. The pastor prayed and bound that evil power in the name of Jesus. He asked the elder to try it again. But the elder's attempt failed. The evil power was gone. The elder started crying. He repented and accepted Jesus as his Savior. At once he was delivered. His sickness ended.[1]

Throughout Acts we have seen that the power of the Holy Spirit is greater than any other power. We do not see many miracles in Acts 21–28. But God's power is always the same. Sometimes God reveals His power through signs and wonders. Other times He allows believers to face hard trials. Still, His Spirit is powerful and present at all times. The Spirit was present with Paul at his court trials and in the storm. The Spirit was present at Malta when Paul shook off a poisonous snake and healed many (Acts 28:1-9). And the Spirit was just as powerful and present the 2 years Paul was a prisoner in Rome. God is Almighty. He never changes. And He never leaves or forsakes His children (Matt. 28:20; 2 Tim. 4:16-17; Heb. 13:5).

Lessons:

Paul's Imprisonment in Jerusalem (Acts 21:17–23:35)

Goal A: *Evaluate and apply 3 challenges of being a human bridge.*
Goal B: *Summarize what Acts 21–23 teaches about rumors, testifying, and protection.*

Paul's Imprisonment in Caesarea (Acts 24–26)

Goal A: *Explain and apply 2 ways Acts 21–28 relates to the purposes of Luke.*
Goal B: *Analyze and apply the roles of conscience and preachers in Acts 24–26.*

Paul's Imprisonment in Rome (Acts 27–28)

Goal A: *Relate Paul's faith in Acts 27 to the storms of life.*
Goal B: *Identify 2 truths in Acts 28. Apply these to your context.*

 Key Words

Jerusalem	Rome	Sadducees
Caesarea	Pharisees	Malta

Paul's Imprisonment in Jerusalem (Acts 21:17–23:35)

Goal A: *Evaluate and apply 3 challenges of being a human bridge.*
Goal B: *Summarize what Acts 21–23 teaches about rumors, testifying, and protection.*

Setting

Many tried to persuade Paul not to go to Jerusalem. Disciples at Troas and Caesarea did not want him to go there. Why? Because they did not want him to suffer. It is hard for us to accept suffering as a part of God's will. We do not want to suffer. And we do not want others to suffer. Peter rebuked Jesus when the Lord spoke of suffering and death (Matt. 16:21-22). But the Lord said Peter was thinking from man's point of view, not God's (Matt. 16:23).

Suffering is often a part of God's will for believers. God does many things through our sufferings.[+] Let us consider some of the many blessings that suffering brings. *First,* suffering helps us grow in grace. Through suffering God corrects, purifies, and perfects us (1 Cor. 11:30-32; Heb. 12:3-11; James 1:2-4; 1 Pet. 1:6-7, 4:1-2). *Second,* suffering helps us relate to others who suffer. We comfort others with the comfort we receive in our sufferings (2 Cor. 1:4). *Third,* suffering brings us into contact with those who need Jesus. Through his suffering, Paul shared the gospel with the small and the great. Would the jailer at Philippi have found Christ if Paul had not been in prison? Likewise, Paul's trials enabled Felix, Festus, Herod, and Caesar to hear the gospel.

Q 2 *What are 3 purposes of suffering?*

As the Spirit said, Paul was bound in Jerusalem. Let us study four lessons related to his arrest there.

A. God calls some to become human bridges.

This is a hard saying. Not everyone can accept it. It reminds us of a passage in Scripture. Jesus said unfaithfulness in marriage was the only just cause for divorce.

> [10]*The disciples said to him, "If this is the situation between a husband and wife, it is better not to marry."* [11]*Jesus replied, "Not everyone can accept this word, but only those to whom it has been given"* (Matt. 19:10-11).

God has enabled only a few to live alone. And he has enabled only a few to become human bridges. These human bridges become all things to all people. Paul was among those few. Recall his testimony in 1 Corinthians 9:19-23.

Paul's words amaze most of us. Few free people are willing to serve as slaves. Few strong people are willing to become weak. God gave Paul special grace to relate to others. Let's consider three challenges a human bridge faces.

First, **people walk on bridges. They treat them roughly.** Critics will be hard on a human bridge. Some Jewish believers criticized Paul. They called him a traitor. They claimed he betrayed their traditions. They had heard that he taught Jews *"to turn away from Moses"* (Acts 21:21). This was not true. False teachers had slandered Paul. He did not require Gentiles to live like Jews. But neither did he teach Jews to live like Gentiles.[2] He always showed respect for Jewish customs. Paul even had Timothy circumcised to relate to the Jews (Acts 16:3). His rule was that a believer should remain in the social context of finding Christ (1 Cor. 7:17). A converted Jew should remain a Jew.[3] A converted slave should remain a slave. A converted Gentile should remain a Gentile. When possible, Paul honored society, customs, and traditions. James and the elders at Jerusalem knew this. Still, many believers talked harshly about Paul.

Q 3 *Explain the proverb, "People walk on bridges."*

Today, some continue to criticize Paul for what Luke records in Acts 21:17-26. They say Paul should not have submitted to the Jerusalem church leaders. They say he was wrong to take a vow and pay for animal sacrifices. These critics say Paul's efforts failed.

Q 4 *Why do believers criticize human bridges?*

+ See the *Revelation & Daniel* text of the *Faith & Action Series,* chapter 3, Lesson 7A.

Figure 13.2   The Fortress of Antonia, connected to the north end of the temple in Jerusalem (Acts 21:34) (The Model City)

Q 5 ➚ *What are 2 reasons why Paul wrote Galatians, Ephesians, and Romans?*

Q 6 ➚ *What were 4 characteristics of Jewish believers?*

Q 7 ➚ *Explain: "Children who eat ugali become adults who eat ugali."*

Q 8 ➘ *What types of things do groups you know emphasize?*

Q 9 ➘ *Does your church relate well to other churches and denominations? Explain.*

Q 10 ➚ *How is receiving truth like eating bread?*

But what was Paul's goal? He was trying to be a bridge between Jewish and Gentile believers. In this he succeeded. The Jewish believers in Jerusalem did not reject Paul. It was the unbelieving Jews who hated him. Those who criticize Paul do not fully understand his calling and his mission. Small people often criticize great leaders like Paul. People trample bridges.

***Second*, a bridge must relate to the land on both ends. And a human bridge must relate to two different groups.** There were serious tensions between Jewish and Gentile believers. Consider the letters Paul wrote to the Galatians, Ephesians, and Romans. These letters say a lot about salvation by faith rather than by keeping the Law. These Epistles explain how Jews and Gentiles depend on Jesus as Savior. Why did Paul write these letters? Because of Jews who wanted Gentile believers to come under the law of Moses. Also, Paul wrote to bring all believers closer together. He was trying to unite people on opposite ends of the bridge.

Read Acts 21:17-26 carefully. The Jerusalem church was a Jewish church. Look at what James and the elders at Jerusalem told Paul. Re-read Acts 21:20-22.

Acts 20:20 says that all Jewish believers were zealous for the Law. This included Ananias. He kept the law of Moses. All Jews in Damascus, even those who did not believe in Jesus, respected Ananias (Acts 22:12). These early believers had received Jesus as Messiah. But they continued sacrificing animals and circumcising their sons. They continued keeping the Sabbath and attending the feasts.

People behave in certain ways because of who they are. The Jewish believers were not just acting like Jews. They were Jews! Therefore, we should not criticize them for living like Jews. Likewise, old people like old ways and old songs. They like the ways and songs they learned when they were young. This should not surprise us. And young people like some new songs. But when they are old, they will like many of the songs from their youth! Those who eat *ugali as children eat ugali as adults. Any fool can criticize. But a wise person seeks to understand why people behave as they do.

Often, believers with differing backgrounds and views do not relate well to each other. People tend to form groups. Then each group emphasizes what it believes.

Group members may not see themselves clearly. Those who are bound often call themselves free (John 8:33). The blind believers at Laodicea claimed to see well (Rev. 3:17-18). Likewise, Paul referred to weak believers who did not eat meat (Rom. 14:19–15:1). But did these believers call themselves weak? They probably called themselves spiritual! Those who tell their own stories describe heroes.

Here is a big question. How do believers with differences relate to each other? How do those with much education relate to those with little? How do the rich relate to the poor? How do the strong relate to the weak? How do those with new ideas relate to those with old ideas? How do the young relate to the old? How do believers in one nation or tribe relate to another?

***Third*, people walk across a bridge one step at a time. Likewise, people cross cultural bridges slowly.** It took decades for the Jewish believers to understand that Jesus made animal sacrifices unnecessary. It took them more than 30 years to realize that the circumcision God wants is spiritual. Circumcision is of the heart, not the flesh (Rom. 2:29). Paul understood people. He knew that people change slowly, little by little.

Receiving truth is like eating bread. A person can eat only one bite at a time. If you offer a person a piece of warm bread with butter, the person will probably take it. Then he or she will eat it, bite by bite. But if you try to force an entire loaf down someone's throat, the person will resist. And if you succeed, the person will probably die! Likewise, people accept truth when it is offered warmly in small bites.

Paul did many little things to bring Jews and Gentiles together. He always preached in the synagogues first. He took part in Jewish religious ceremonies (Acts 18:18; 21:17-26). When there was a famine in Judea, he took an offering from the Gentile believers in Antioch (Acts 11:29). Later, he took an offering from Gentile believers in Macedonia and Achaia to help poor believers in Jerusalem (2 Cor. 8:1–9:15).[+] He attended a meeting to discuss relationships between Jewish and Gentile believers (Acts 15:1-31). He had Timothy circumcised (Acts 16:1-3). He hurried his journey to attend an important Jewish feast (Acts 20:16). Finally, late in his ministry, he wrote letters like Romans (A.D. 57), Ephesians, and Colossians (about A.D. 62). These three letters explained that Jews and Gentiles come to God by one path. That path is by faith in Jesus Christ. Paul spent a lifetime taking steps to unite Jewish and Gentile believers.

> [4]*There is one body and one Spirit—just as you were called to one hope when you were called—*[5]*one Lord, one faith, one baptism;* [6]*one God and Father of all, who is over all and through all and in all* (Eph. 4:4-6).

Paul knew that patience, understanding, effort, and God's timing are keys to unity.

Not many try to be a human bridge between groups. Do you know any who relate well to believers and sinners? Do you know any who try to be a bridge between the old and the young? Do you know any who try to understand those in the city and those in the country? Do you know any who try to connect the educated and the uneducated? Do you know any who relate well to people from various tribes or nations? We need more human bridges. Few are called to become all things to all people. But those who are not called should pray for those trying to bring unity among believers.

B. We should not believe or repeat all we hear.

More people are hurt by gossip than by bullets.[4] Bullets kill a person's body. But gossip kills a person's reputation.

In Acts 21 there are three examples of lies, false *assumptions, gossip, or rumors.
- *"They have been informed that you teach all the Jews who live among the Gentiles to turn away from Moses, telling them not to circumcise their children or live according to our customs"* (Acts 21:21). This was not true. But many believed it.
- [28]*"Men of Israel, help us! This is the man who teaches all men everywhere against our people and our law and this place. And besides, he has brought Greeks into the temple area and defiled this holy place."* [29]*(They had previously seen Trophimus the Ephesian in the city with Paul and assumed that Paul had brought him into the temple area.)* (Acts 21:28-29). The crowd believed these lies.
- *"Aren't you the Egyptian who started a revolt and led four thousand terrorists out into the desert some time ago?"* (Acts 21:38). The commander did not have the facts. He assumed Paul was an Egyptian terrorist!

Lies, false assumptions, gossip, and rumors all belong to the same family. They are all tools of the devil. We believers are too quick to believe things we hear. And we are too quick to repeat things we do not know are true. May the Lord help us to walk and talk in the light.

Consider the four sayings that follow:

If all knew what each said about the other, there would be less than five friends in the world!

Plant a little gossip and you will reap a harvest of regret.

Q 11 ➤ *What are 6 things Paul did to help be a bridge between Jews and Gentiles?*

Q 12 ✎ *Do you feel called to be a human bridge in some way? Explain.*

Q 13 ➤ *What are 3 lies or false assumptions in Acts 21?*

Q 14 ✎ *Do you and believers you know believe and repeat lies? Explain.*

+ Dr. Carl Gibbs notes that one of the reasons why God allowed the famine was so that Gentile believers could send an offering to Jewish believers. This brought Jews and Gentiles closer together.

No person can help the size of his ears, nose, or tongue. But anyone can keep all three out of other people's business.

Confess your sins, not your neighbor's sin![5]

A gossip told many lies about a preacher. Later, the gossip asked the preacher to forgive him. The preacher noticed that there were no tears in the gossip's eyes. So the preacher said, "I will forgive you. But first, I want you to understand the greatness of your sin." The preacher and the gossip caught a rooster and killed it. Together they pulled out all of the feathers and put them in a bowl. Then the preacher's wife cooked the chicken, and they all ate it together. "Now," said the preacher, "take this bowl of feathers home with you. Set it on the ground in front of your house. In the morning, bring it back with the feathers." The gossip did as he was told. The next morning, he arose to return the feathers to the preacher. But most of the feathers were gone. The night wind had scattered them in many directions. It had carried most of them out of sight. Only a few feathers remained around the yard. The gossip returned and explained what had happened. "I know," said the preacher. "And so it is with your words. I will forgive you. But the lies you have told about me are scattered far and wide." As the gossip understood, true repentance filled his heart. And he remembered the lesson every time he ate chicken!

The Old Testament records hundreds of laws God wants us to know. Of all of these, He chose ten that were the most important to Him. The Almighty wrote these ten on stone. One of God's top ten commandments is *"You shall not give false testimony against your neighbor"* (Exod. 20:16). We should never repeat anything that might not be true. Rather, we should always put others in the best light possible. This fulfills the Golden Rule.

[36]*"But I tell you that men will have to give account on the Day of Judgment for every careless word they have spoken.* [37]*For by your words you will be acquitted, and by your words you will be condemned"* (Matt. 12:36-37).

Set a guard over my mouth, O LORD; keep watch over the door of my lips (Ps. 141:3).

C. There is a time to defend what we believe.

"There is a time for everything . . . a time to be silent, and a time to speak" (Eccl. 3:1, 7).

The book of Acts emphasizes that believers are witnesses for Jesus. The power of the Holy Spirit enables us to tell others about the Savior. Sometimes we witness through good deeds, good character, and good attitudes. But there are times to speak. God can give us courage to speak at the most difficult times. The crowd was rioting. They had been beating Paul, trying to kill him. The soldiers rescued God's apostle. So Paul said, *"Brothers and fathers, listen now to my defense"* (Acts 22:1). Then he defended himself by giving his testimony of being saved.

Q 15 Why are reports of changed lives our best defense of the gospel?

Our best defense of the gospel is the testimony of lives that Jesus has changed.[6] In court, witnesses are valuable. A lawyer with two or three witnesses will probably win the case. Likewise, we silence the enemies of Christ with testimonies of what Jesus has done. Peter's accusers could not say anything because the man whom Jesus healed was there (Acts 4:14). Who can speak against the miracle of a changed life? No one can argue with a believer's testimony of what Jesus has done. Paul knew this. So to defend the gospel, he told what Jesus had done for him.

Q 16 Do you agree with the statement, "For every teacher in the classroom we need a dozen witnesses on the street"? Explain.

The Church needs scholars and teachers to defend the faith. These study more than most believers. They teach others to correct the errors of false teachers. Along with these teachers, we need an army of believers to tell what Jesus has done for them. For every teacher in the classroom, we need a dozen witnesses on the street. These tell about what Jesus has done. Trained teachers are vital. But do not underestimate the value of your personal testimony. Do not overlook the power in telling what Jesus has done for you. The greatest apostle used his personal testimony to defend the faith. Three times Luke records the story of what Jesus did for Paul (Acts 9:1-22; 22:1-21; 26:1-29).

God asked Moses, *"What is that in your hand?"* (Exod. 4:2). It was something very common to Moses. But God wanted to use that staff in a special way. Believer, what is that in your hand? It is the story of what Jesus has done for you. Use this testimony you know so well. God will do a miracle with it.

Some sinners criticized a believer. They said he thought he was better than they were. He replied, "No, I am not saying that I am better than you. I'm just saying that I am better than I was before." Then, like Paul, he told them his story. All were silenced. And some were touched.

D. Forty killers are not enough to kill one person God protects.

God is sovereign. He allows some to suffer and die. Unbelieving Jews stoned Stephen in Jerusalem (Acts 7:57-60). King Herod had James killed with a sword (Acts 12:2). Each year, unbelievers murder about 160,000 believers.[7] These martyrs are counted as sheep to be slaughtered (Rom. 8:36). Still, time will prove that they are more than conquerors (Rom. 8:37).

Q 17 *Does God choose to protect all believers from evil? Explain.*

"How long, Sovereign Lord, holy and true, until you judge the inhabitants of the earth and avenge our blood?" (Rev. 6:10). How long? Until God says the number is complete (Rev. 6:11).

On rare occasions God breaks forth into history. Acts 12 records that God protected Peter from death. No prison was strong enough to keep him. And Herod did not have enough soldiers to kill him. God opens doors that no one can shut. And He protects people that no one can harm.

God protected Paul from death. Forty men with knives could not kill him. Imagine it—forty killers possessed by hate. Each one took a vow not to eat or drink until Paul was dead in the dirt. Days went by. But they could not kill him. They either lied or they died. Twice, Jesus passed through the midst of those who wanted to kill Him (Luke 4:28-30; John 7:30). Likewise, those whom God protects will pass safely through every trial. They will escape as surely as the baby Jesus escaped King Herod (Matt. 2).

Q 18 *Can Satan kill a person God chooses to protect? Explain.*

God's greatest enemies cannot harm those He protects. Fire fell on those who came against Elijah (2 Kings 1). Blindness fell on the entire army of Aram that tried to capture Elisha (2 Kings 6:8-23). No one will harm the two witnesses in the Tribulation while God protects them (Rev. 11). And God will place the woman out of the serpent's reach (Rev. 12:14).

Our Father has all the power in the universe. He is worthy of our trust. The attitude of the three Hebrew children is good for all of us. Read Daniel 3:16-18.

Q 19 *Comment on the statement: "Some believers God protects, but all who die He resurrects."*

Remember this. Some believers God protects. But all who die He resurrects.

Lesson 38 Paul's Imprisonment in Caesarea (Acts 24–26)
Goal A: *Explain and apply 2 ways Acts 21–28 relates to the purposes of Luke.*
Goal B: *Analyze and apply the roles of conscience and preachers in Acts 24–26.*

Setting

We are studying the five trials and prison terms of Paul (Acts 21–28). Paul was on trial before the crowd, the Sanhedrin, Governor Felix, Governor Festus, and King Agrippa. Luke's biggest purpose in Acts is to show how the gospel spread from Jerusalem to Rome by the power of the Holy Spirit. But Luke has several lesser purposes. Review these in chapter 1, Lesson 2.

Paul was a loyal son of Israel. Many Jews found no fault with Paul. Unbelieving Jews from the province of Asia wanted to kill him. They used lies to stir up the people and start a riot. Soldiers rescued Paul. The next day he spoke to the Sanhedrin. They were divided.

The Pharisees found *"nothing wrong"* with Paul. They thought that perhaps an angel had appeared to him (Acts 23:9). But the Sadducees hated Paul. These religious leaders did not believe in the resurrection, spirits, or miracles (Acts 23:8). They disagreed with Paul on these supernatural issues. Likewise, they rejected his belief in Jesus.

Q 20 ↗ *How was Acts able to help Paul?*

Paul was also a loyal citizen of Rome.[8] This is a minor theme in Acts. Earlier we noted that Luke records a good relationship between Christianity and Roman centurions (See Figure 9.6). More important, Acts usually shows that government leaders found Paul innocent. Paul was probably in a prison in Rome as Luke completed Acts.[9] The apostle was waiting to be judged by Caesar. The book of Acts would have made a good defense for Paul. Luke records that Pilate found no basis for a charge against Jesus (Luke 23:4). Likewise, Acts records that government leaders charged Paul with no crimes. Figure 13.3 summarizes what governing bodies and leaders said about Paul.

Acts	Government leaders	Words or Actions in Regard to Paul
16:19-40	Magistrates in Philippi	They appeased Paul and politely escorted him from the prison. This was after their mistake of beating him, an innocent Roman citizen.
17:16-34	The Areopagus in Athens	They found no fault with Paul. One of their members became his follower.
18:14-16	Gallio, proconsul of Achaia	The Jews' complaint was not about a crime. It was about a religious question from their own law. So he refused to judge it and threw them out of court.
19:31	Officials of the province in Ephesus	These friends of Paul tried to keep him away from the rioters.
19:35-41	The city clerk in Ephesus	He said Paul had neither robbed temples nor blasphemed the goddess Diana. The clerk directed Demetrius from the street to the court and dismissed the rioters.
23:6-10 24:5-6	The Sanhedrin in Jerusalem	The Pharisees said they found nothing wrong with Paul. The Sadducees said he stirred up riots and made religious errors.
23:27-30	Claudius Lysias, the commander in Jerusalem	He said there was no charge against Paul worthy of prison or death. The Jewish accusation was a question about their law.
24:22-27	Governor Felix in Caesarea	He refused to decide the case. He hoped for a bribe and left Paul bound 2 years as a favor to the Jews.
25:18-21	Governor Festus in Caesarea	He said Paul was not charged with any crimes against the government. The only accusations against him were about Jewish religion.
26:32	King Agrippa of Galilee and Perea	*"Agrippa said to Festus, 'This man could have been set free if he had not appealed to Caesar.'"* (Agrippa said Paul was innocent. But if a citizen appealed to Rome, he had to be tried in Rome.)
28:7	Publius, chief official of Malta	He showed hospitality and allowed the people to honor Paul in many ways.

Figure 13.3   Governing bodies and leaders did not accuse Paul of any crimes.

Q 21 ↗ *Identify 5 government leaders who said Paul did no crime.*

We have looked briefly at how Acts 21–28 relates to Luke's purposes. Luke does at least three things in these chapters. *First,* he shows that the gospel is spreading toward Rome. *Second,* he shows that Paul committed no crimes against the government. Acts may have been one of the reasons why Paul was freed from a Roman prison. *Third,* Acts 21–28 contains several big truths that help believers. Let us look at two of these truths found in Acts 24–26.

A. God uses the conscience to help guide people.

The first principle is about conscience. This topic is in the setting of Paul on trial before governor Festus.

[15]*"I have the same hope in God as these men, that there will be a resurrection of both the righteous and the wicked.* [16]*So I strive always to keep my conscience clear before God and man"* (Acts 24:15-16).

Some cultures teach that a conscience is like a triangle in a circle. The conscience turns a little when a person does something wrong. The person feels this *turning* and has the chance to repent. Some people ignore the conscience when it turns. This causes the points of the conscience to wear off. Then the person does not feel the conscience when it turns.

The Bible says several things about the conscience.

- Each person has a conscience. Conscience is a gift from God. It is a lesser judge within. It is aware of all the actions, thoughts, and decisions that a person makes. A good conscience testifies that a person has done right. A guilty conscience occurs if a person sins against God or others. Paul said that conscience either accuses or excuses a person (Rom. 2:15).

- It is possible for an unbeliever to live with a clear conscience. *"Paul looked straight at the Sanhedrin and said, 'My brothers, I have fulfilled my duty to God in all good conscience to this day'"* (Acts 23:1). This verse probably includes Paul's life before he was a believer. Remember that he obeyed the Law before receiving Christ. By the Law, Paul was without fault (Phil. 3:6). Some unbelievers may live with a clear conscience.

- A conscience can make mistakes. It acts on the basis of knowledge. Knowledge is information or understanding gotten through experience. But knowledge may be incomplete. Paul's conscience did not accuse him when he rebuked the high priest (Acts 23:1-5). Why? Because Paul did not know he was talking to the high priest. Likewise, Paul once believed that persecuting believers was doing God's will (Acts 26:9; 1 Tim. 1:13). The conscience does not condemn a person for things it does not know are wrong.

Knowledge may be true or false. People know what they have learned. But there are true teachings and false teachings. Some cultures approve things that God forbids. These sins may include lying, having many wives, having sex outside of marriage, stealing, killing unborn babies, drunkenness, gossip, and so on. It is sad when a culture opposes God and truth. Then people live by standards that are false. The light that is in them is darkness (Matt. 6:23).

Conscience judges only on the basis of what it knows. Paul writes of those who have a weak conscience. He says these have a weak conscience because they lack true knowledge (1 Cor. 8:7). The consciences of many people are not accurate. Why? Because they have not been taught what God says is right and wrong. Many do what is right in their own eyes (Judg. 17:6). But they are wrong in God's eyes.

Some believers live with false knowledge. They are true to what they believe. But what they believe is not true. They grow up under false teachings in the church. These false teachings include things like false security, purgatory, salvation by works, and living unholy lives.

Martha's mother taught her that demons cause malaria. Martha grew up with this false knowledge. She married and had several children. Her first son died from malaria. She did not feel guilty that her children slept without mosquito nets. And she did not feel guilty for neglecting to give her children tablets that prevent malaria. She thought a demon was guilty of killing her son. She was guilty, but her conscience did not know it. Her conscience was blind to the truth. It did not have eyes to see. Why? Her conscience would judge in darkness until her mind saw the light. Be careful what you accept as truth. It may affect your children, their children, and their children's children.

The Jews at Berea were more noble than the Jews at Thessalonica. They searched the Scriptures to see what was true (Acts 17:11).

- A conscience can be renewed and enlightened. The Scriptures make a person's conscience more reliable. Paul argues that a person may not recognize some sins without Scripture (Rom. 7:7). God's Word is a light to our paths (Ps. 119:105). The Scriptures and the Holy Spirit enlighten the conscience.

- A conscience can be seared and ruined (1 Tim. 4:2).

- Believers who ignore their consciences will wreck their faith (1 Tim. 1:19). A guilty conscience destroys faith (1 John 3:21).

Figure 13.4   Some liken the conscience to a triangle that turns inside a circle.

Q 22 ⚒ *What does each person's conscience do?*

Q 23 ⚒ *Do some sinners have clear consciences? Explain.*

Q 24 ⚒ *On what does a conscience base its judgments?*

Q 25 ✎ *Does your culture approve things the Bible says are wrong? Explain.*

Q 26 ⚒ *How can the church help people have accurate consciences?*

Q 27 ⚒ *Can people be guilty if their consciences do not accuse them? Explain.*

Q 28 ⚒ *What happens to believers who practice ignoring their consciences?*

Q 29 ⟍ *What are
2 blessings of a clear
conscience?*

- A clear conscience strengthens faith and love (1 John 3:21-22; 1 Tim. 1:5).
- Believers should always try to obey the guidance of conscience. We should please our consciences in small things. Then we will be faithful in big decisions (Luke 16:10). We are blessed if our consciences do not condemn us for our choices (Rom. 14:22).

George Jones practiced listening to his conscience as a child. Later, as a young man he began working as a clerk in a small store. He had a reputation for being honest. His good character and skills led to a friendship. Jones and another man started a newspaper called the *New York Times*. The newspaper was a great success. It waged a war against things that were not right or fair. An opponent offered Jones a bribe of a half million dollars. The opponent wanted Jones to move to another place. Jones replied that his conscience would not allow it. Years of listening to his conscience made Jones a mature, godly man.[10]

B. God sends preachers with a message to enlighten the conscience.

Q 30 ⟍ *What political
problem was Felix facing?*

Paul stood on trial before Felix. Felix himself was about to be in court with the Jews. He would be examined for the way he handled some riots. Therefore, Felix did not want to anger the Jews he would see in a Roman court.[11] So Felix left Paul in prison for 2 years. Thus he avoided angering Paul's Jewish accusers.

Things did not go well for Felix. Festus replaced him as governor. Festus found no reason to condemn Paul. But the new governor wanted to gain favor with the Jews. So he asked Paul if he was willing to be tried in Jerusalem (Acts 25:9). Paul knew the Jerusalem Jews had vowed to kill him. So his only choice was to appeal to be tried in Rome by Caesar. This was the right of every Roman citizen.

Rulers had the custom of visiting new rulers. So King Agrippa visited the new governor, Festus. Festus consulted with Agrippa about Paul's case. Agrippa said he would like to hear Paul.

King Agrippa was also known as Herod Agrippa II. He was the son of the King Herod whom the worms ate (Acts 12:23). Agrippa was living with his widowed sister, Bernice.[12] Many thought they were committing incest. The Emperor Claudius gave Agrippa the responsibilities of caring for the temple and appointing the high priest.[13] Read Paul's defense to King Agrippa (Acts 26:1-29). It is the longest and most detailed of Paul's five defenses. In Agrippa's presence, the prophecy that Paul would testify before kings is fulfilled (Acts 9:15). Note that Paul describes three phases of his life. *First,* he speaks of being a Pharisee (Acts 26:4-8). *Second,* Paul tells of his life as a persecutor (Acts 26:9-11). *Finally,* Paul testifies of his conversion and call to be an apostle (Acts 26:12-18).[14] Let us turn now to examine Paul's role as a preaching apostle.

Q 31 ⟍ *How is preaching
related to the conscience?*

God speaks to everyone through the conscience. But He sends preachers to strengthen the work the conscience begins. Preachers bring truth that is a brighter light than conscience.

[17]*"I will rescue you from your own people and from the Gentiles. I am sending you to them* [18]*to open their eyes and turn them from darkness to light, and from the power of Satan to God, so that they may receive forgiveness of sins and a place among those who are sanctified by faith in me"* (Acts 26:17-18).

Q 32 ⟍ *Contrast the
conscience and the gospel.*

The gospel is more helpful than the conscience. The conscience may tell a person what is right or wrong. But the gospel brings the power to change a person's life. The gospel enables people to choose between darkness and light. It gives them the choice to move from Satan's kingdom to God's kingdom. The conscience condemns. But the gospel offers forgiveness and a new beginning. Those who choose to follow Jesus Christ become holy in God's sight. The conscience can tell us when we sin. But the gospel *"is the power of God for the salvation of everyone who believes: first for the Jew, then for the Gentile"* (Rom. 1:16).

Paul was not ashamed of the gospel. God sent him to turn people from darkness to light. And he obeyed the heavenly vision.

"First to those in Damascus, then to those in Jerusalem and in all Judea, and to the Gentiles also, I preached that they should repent and turn to God and prove their repentance by their deeds" (Acts 26:20).

Q 33 ⟋ *Which 3 things do preachers call people to do?*

Acts 26:20 mentions three things preachers call people to do. These three things are bound together. Let us look at each of them.

***First*, preachers call people to repent.**   This is part of a preacher's job. God uses the preacher to call attention to things that are wrong. A preacher must not neglect to declare what God says is wrong. Humans did not create the Bible. It is the Word of God. So preachers should not apologize for what is in it. It is not the preacher's responsibility to change people. Preachers identify what God says is sin and call people to repent.

Q 34 ⟋ *How can a preacher be innocent of the blood of all people?*

Paul did not hide the truth from the people of Athens. He did not tell them they could believe in Jesus and continue to worship idols (Acts 17:24-30). Likewise, he told the people at Lystra to turn from the worthless things they worshiped (Acts 14:15). They wanted to honor him until he told them the full truth. Then they stoned Paul. He told them the truth because it was his duty. Later, in Ephesus, he told people that man-made gods were no gods at all (Acts 19:26). Paul was not popular, but he told them the truth! He was innocent of all men's blood. Why? Because he proclaimed the whole will of God (Acts 20:26-27). It is not enough for a preacher to tell people to repent. Every preacher must answer the question, Repent of what? The Holy Spirit helps in this area. But preachers must be specific. Throughout Acts, God's preachers talked about specific sins. And throughout the New Testament, preachers mentioned the sins they knew about.

To *repent*, people must change their thinking. Sinners are facing sin. The preacher calls them to turn their backs toward things that are wrong.

***Second*, preachers call people to turn to God.**   Those whom God sends do more than condemn sin. They offer help. Preachers announce that there is forgiveness and freedom through Jesus Christ. They do not ask people to obey conscience in their own strength. They emphasize that God sent a Savior for us sinners. Those living in sin have their backs toward God. Preachers call people to turn from sin toward Jesus.

Q 35 ⟋ *Is it possible to face God and sin at the same time? Explain.*

"Everyone who calls on the name of the Lord will be saved" (Acts 2:21).

"Salvation is found in no one else, for there is no other name under heaven given to men by which we must be saved" (Acts 4:12).

Philip went down to a city in Samaria and proclaimed the Christ there (Acts 8:5).

Q 36 ⟋ *Do preachers declare the problem and the solution? Explain.*

42 *"He commanded us to preach to the people and to testify that he is the one whom God appointed as judge of the living and the dead. *43*All the prophets testify about him that everyone who believes in him receives forgiveness of sins through his name"* (Acts 10:42-43).

38 *"Therefore, my brothers, I want you to know that through Jesus the forgiveness of sins is proclaimed to you. *39*Through him everyone who believes is justified from everything you could not be justified from by the law of Moses"* (Acts 13:38-39).

They replied, "Believe in the Lord Jesus, and you will be saved—you and your household" (Acts 16:31).

***Third*, preachers call people to prove their repentance by their deeds.**   In the New Testament, good deeds are always the evidence of true repentance and faith.

John the Baptist linked repentance and right living.

8 *"Produce fruit in keeping with repentance. . . *9*The ax is already at the root of the trees, and every tree that does not produce good fruit will be cut down and thrown into the fire"* (Luke 3:8-9).

Paul did not preach, as some do, that a believer's part is only trusting in Christ as Savior. Paul insisted that the only ones who will be saved are those who prove their repentance by their actions (Acts 26:20).15 Paul linked righteousness and self-control.

Q 37 ⟋ *According to Paul, what proves true repentance?*

As Paul discoursed on righteousness, self-control and the judgment to come, Felix was afraid and said, "That's enough for now! You may leave. When I find it convenient, I will send for you" (Acts 24:25).

Felix needed to hear that there is a relationship between righteousness and self-control. He was living with his third wife, Drusilla. She was the sister of King Agrippa II and Bernice. Luke will introduce these two in the next chapter. Felix had used a magician to seduce the young, beautiful Drusilla from her husband. Their lack of morals helps us understand why Paul spoke to them about righteousness and self-control.[16] Those who follow their fleshly desires cannot be righteous. Read Titus 2:11-14.

 Q 38 *Is it possible for God's children to live like Satan's children? Explain.*

Paul taught the Romans that God's only children are those led by the Spirit, not the flesh (Rom. 8:9-14). He warned the Corinthians that those who practice evil deeds would not inherit the Kingdom. Read 1 Corinthians 6:9-11.

Q 39 *How are righteousness and self-control related?*

Faith without works is not saving faith. Faith without works is useless (James 2:14-26). Righteous living is present wherever an attitude of repentance exists. Repentance, faith, and actions exist together. They are like fire, light, and heat in the fireplace. Two cannot exist without the third.

Lesson 39 Paul's Imprisonment in Rome (Acts 27–28)

Goal A: *Relate Paul's faith in Acts 27 to the storms of life.*
Goal B: *Identify 2 truths in Acts 28. Apply these to your context.*

Figure 13.5   The Pantheon (on left) was a famous pagan temple in Rome.

Setting

Rome was the largest city of Paul's day. It was the capital and symbol of the Roman Empire. Rome was famous for its sin. Seneca said Rome was a *sewer of sin. The apostle John referred to Rome as a prostitute and the mother of all harlots (Rev. 17:1-18). Rome was also famous for its buildings. The Colosseum was completed by A.D. 80. And Rome was the home of the Pantheon (See Figure 13.5). To a Roman, Rome was the center of the world. Its roads and government went out into the entire world.[17]

For at least 3 years, Paul had wanted to reach Rome.[18] He arrived there about A.D. 60. But earlier, he wrote to the Roman believers about A.D. 57.[19] Many think he wrote from Corinth on his third missionary trip. Figure 13.6 lists verses in Romans that refer to Paul's desire to visit Rome.

Romans	Scripture
1:10	*I pray that now at last by God's will the way may be opened for me to come to you.*
1:11-12	[11]*I long to see you so that I may impart to you some spiritual gift to make you strong—*[12]*that is, that you and I may be mutually encouraged by each other's faith.*
1:13	*I planned many times to come to you (but have been prevented from doing so until now) in order that I might have a harvest among you, just as I have had among the other Gentiles.*
1:15	*That is why I am so eager to preach the gospel also to you who are at Rome.*
15:20, 22	[20]*It has always been my ambition to preach the gospel where Christ was not known, . . .* [22]*This is why I have often been hindered from coming to you.*
15:23-24	[23]*But now that there is no more place for me to work in these regions, and since I have been longing for many years to see you,* [24]*I plan to do so when I go to Spain. I hope to visit you while passing through and to have you assist me on my journey there, after I have enjoyed your company for a while.*
15:25-26, 28-29	[25]*Now, however, I am on my way to Jerusalem in the service of the saints there.* [26]*For Macedonia and Achaia were pleased to make a contribution for the poor among the saints in Jerusalem. . .* [28]*I will go to Spain and visit you on the way.* [29]*I know that when I come to you, I will come in the full measure of the blessing of Christ.*
15:31-32	[31]*Pray that I may be rescued from the unbelievers in Judea and that my service in Jerusalem may be acceptable to the saints there,* [32]*so that by God's will I may come to you with joy and together with you be refreshed.*

Figure 13.6   Verses in Romans tell of Paul's desire to visit Rome.

The final third of Acts describes Paul's journey from Jerusalem to Rome.[20] Paul liked to see strong churches in big cities. No doubt he wanted to help make Rome a great center for spreading the gospel.

We do not know when the Roman church began. Luke records that visitors from Rome were in Jerusalem on the Day of Pentecost (Acts 2:10). Perhaps they were converted and returned to Rome with the gospel. Almost 30 years after Pentecost, Roman believers traveled on the Appian Way to meet Paul (Acts 28:15).

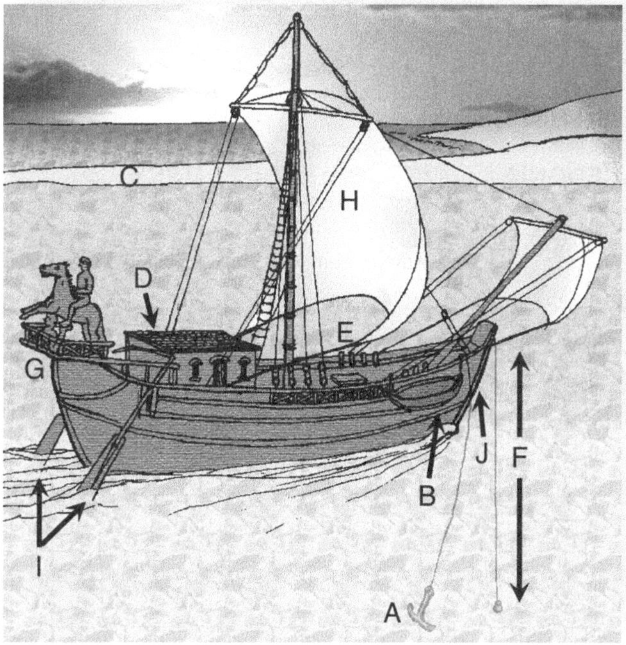

We have looked at the background and setting of Acts 27–28. Now, let us focus on three truths that stand out in these chapters.

A. Faith enables us to survive the storms of life (Acts 27:13-44).

It took three ships to get Paul from Caesarea to Rome. First, he sailed from Caesarea to Myra. This took place on a ship from Adramyttium, a city just south of Troas. Notice that Julius had become a friend to Paul. This centurion allowed Paul to visit friends in Sidon. Acts does not tell us of a church there. But Paul made friends everywhere he went. The second ship was from Alexandria, Egypt. It was carrying grain from Egypt to Rome. The winds were strong. Therefore, they sailed to the lee of Cyprus and Crete. The *lee* refers to the side protected from the wind.

It was after the Fast (Acts 27:9). This means that it was after the Jewish Day of Atonement in late September or October. This was a dangerous time. Paul warned that they should not sail. How did he know more than the pilot and the owner of the ship? Some think his knowledge came from experience. They note

Figure 13.7 A ship like the ones Paul sailed on

Q 40 How many passages in Romans show that Paul wrote to believers there before he went there?

Q 41 Who started the church in Rome? Explain.

Q 42 Identify parts A–J (Fig. 13.7 and Fig. 13.8) on the picture of the ship.

Letter	Term	Explanation	Acts 27:
A	anchor	Heavy metal weights to help prevent the boat from moving	13, 17, 29, 30, 40
B	lifeboat	A small boat carried on the side of a big ship	16, 30
C	sandbar	A long finger-shaped portion of earth or sand that stuck out into a sea	17
D	cargo	Grain or valuable things carried on a ship	18
E	tackle	Planks of wood, ropes, and cloth sails	19
F	soundings	Measurements of the distance to the bottom of the sea, using a long rope with a weight on one end	28
G	stern	The rear or back part of a ship	29
H	sail	Cloth used to catch the wind and cause motion	40
I	rudders	Pieces of wood or oars used to guide a ship	40
J	bow	The front part of a ship	41

Figure 13.8 Terms related to a ship like the one Paul sailed on to Rome

Q 43 Does God still give believers supernatural insights like He gave Paul (Figure 13.9)? Explain.

Acts	Insight or Prophecy
27:10	*"Men, I can see that our voyage is going to be disastrous and bring great loss to ship and cargo, and to our own lives also."*
27:22	*"Not one of you will be lost; only the ship will be destroyed."*
27:24	*"Do not be afraid, Paul. You must stand trial before Caesar. And God has graciously given you all the lives of those who sail with you."*
27:26	*"We must run aground on some island."*
27:31	*"Unless these men stay with the ship, you cannot be saved."*

Figure 13.9 Insights or prophecies that God gave to Paul in Acts 27

Figure 13.10   Paul's journey from Jerusalem to Rome

that Paul had been on eleven voyages at sea before his trip to Rome.[21] Also, he had been in three shipwrecks already (2 Cor. 11:25).[22] In contrast, the pilot and sailors had probably sailed much more than Paul had. In addition to experience, Paul was filled with the Spirit. Some think Paul's knowledge of the storm was from the Holy Spirit.[23] Figure 13.9 lists several insights that God gave Paul.

The centurion listened to the majority instead of the man of God (Acts 27:11-12). A gentle wind lured them out to sea. This gentle wind deceived them. A terrible wind was hiding behind the gentle breeze. This angry wind had the force of a hurricane (Acts 27:14). It drove them wildly out to sea. Their voyage started with the temptation of a gentle wind. But suddenly, the fist of danger seized them.

Q 44 ✎ *Do deadly sins today sometimes hide behind gentle temptations? Explain.*

Luke describes the scene with much detail. The wind was so strong that men had to hold on. The ropes stretched as the wind tore through the sails. The waves beat against the boat and splashed into it. The storm was violent. Those on board feared the storm would tear the ship into pieces. So they tied strong ropes around the boat to help hold it together (Acts 27:17). Meanwhile, the warnings of God's apostle echoed in their ears. All wished they had discerned the dragon behind the gentle wind.

Q 45 ✎ *In your own words, describe the storm.*

The fierce storm continued. It was dark. They did not see the sun, moon, or stars for 14 days. And in those times, sailors used the stars for guidance. Therefore, in the darkness, they were lost. They did not know where they were going.

Q 46 ➤ *How do people's values change in the storms of life?*

Their values changed during the storm. Early in the storm, they threw some of the cargo into the sea (Acts 27:18). Why? Perhaps the boat was too heavy. Maybe it would not sink if they threw some of the cargo away. But even this did not help. Later, they threw all of the grain into the sea (Acts 27:38). This was like throwing away money. But in a deadly storm, people do not care about money. They care only about staying alive. Hard times bring us back to the basics.

Q 47 ➤ *Summarize 5 different attitudes in the storm.*

After many days of darkness and fasting, they did a terrible thing. They threw their hope over the side of the ship (Acts 27:20). Note the various attitudes of people in the storm.[24]

- The pilot and the owner lost all hope.
- The centurion did not know what orders to give.
- The soldiers thought only of killing. They knew they would be responsible if their prisoners escaped.
- The sailors cared only about saving their own lives.
- Only Paul, the Christian, had a message of hope. Because of his faith, the 276 people on the ship all lived. Nineveh was spared because of Jonah. Likewise, the 276 were spared because Paul prayed and believed.[25]

Faith in God is the only thing that helps during great trouble. Storms cause people's hearts to fail with fear and discouragement. But those with faith in God can stand fast in the darkest trials. Our faith is built on the promises of God. Like Paul, we can say, *"So keep up your courage, men, for I have faith in God that it will happen just as he told me"* (Acts 27:25).

Many have been through various kinds of storms. These storms may be social, political, financial, national, moral, physical, or spiritual. Crises are everywhere in our world. Not long ago, several Japanese leaders committed suicide. They could not stand up against the financial storm in their country. When the sky is dark and little light shines, faith in God is the only answer.

A believer sat crying in a dark room. His father and mother had recently died of cancer. He himself had been sick for several weeks. He had lost about 35 pounds (16 kg) during his illness. His body was thin and weak. Doctors had not been able to help him. For weeks he had not slept at night. Had

Figure 13.11   The lives of all were saved as Paul said.

God forgotten him? Why were there no answers to his prayers for help? He knew of no reason to repent. He loved God, His Word, His work, and His people. He felt like a man whom God had abandoned. Perhaps Job felt this way. The man was in a storm like the one of Acts 27. He had not seen any light for many days. His values were changing. He had begun to throw away some of the things he cared about. He had not felt the presence of God for many weeks. Darkness surrounded him. He was in an ocean of sorrow. And he was going under. But the Holy Spirit helped him turn to the promises of God. Scripture is a rock we can stand on in the storm. He began to quote Bible verses. He did this each day and through the sleepless nights. He stopped worrying about the storm. He quit thinking about how sick he was. He focused only on the Word of God. After several days, a peace came over him. The strong wind stopped blowing. In time, the sun appeared. Today, he is helping create the *Faith & Action Series*. God is faithful in the storms of life. Do not throw away your hope in God during the storm (Heb. 10:35). It is the one thing that will save you.

Q 48 ✎ *Describe a storm that faith in God helped you survive.*

B. Some people's theology is confused (Acts 28:1-10).

Read Acts 28:1-6. The people on the island had a confused theology. When a snake bit Paul, they believed he was a murderer. These people believed that bad things happen only to bad people. But Paul's hand did not swell from the snakebite. And he did not die. So the people concluded that Paul was a god. They thought that miracles happen only to the gods!

Q 49 ⚐ *What were 2 false beliefs of the people of Malta?*

The people on the island were wrong twice. Bad things do happen to bad people. But bad things also happen to good people. Good people like Paul were beaten, robbed, and shipwrecked. Good people like Timothy, Trophimus, and Epaphroditus were sick at times. Likewise, good things happen to both bad and good people. God causes His sun to rise on the evil and the good. He sends the rain on the righteous and the unrighteous (Matt. 5:45). Trials and blessings visit the good and the bad.

Q 50 ✎ *Do people you know think bad things happen only to bad people? Explain.*

God used Paul to teach the people on the island. Paul healed many, including the father of Publius. They learned that healings and miracles are for common people, not gods. God does not give us healings and miracles because we deserve them. He blesses us because He loves us. We do not need to be gods to receive God's blessings.

Figure 13.12 The twin gods Castor and Pollux. They were called guardians of sailors. Many believed they were sons of *Zeus (Acts 28:11).

Q 51 ➚ *What happens to those who refuse to listen to and obey God?*

Q 52 ✎ *Practice recalling one thing from each chapter in Acts.*

C. People lose what they refuse to use (Acts 28:11-31).

Paul traveled on three ships toward Rome. The third ship had idols representing Castor and Pollux. These were twin Greek gods. Many believed these gods shone as two bright stars in the sky.[26] Those who had been in the storm knew the truth. The stars are not gods. When the stars refuse to shine, the true God is still ready to help.

After leaving the ship at Puteoli, Paul walked on the Appian Way to reach Rome. The brothers from Rome came down to the forum of Appius to meet Paul and talk with him. In the city, Paul called the leaders of the Jews together (Acts 28:17). He lived in a house that he rented (Acts 28:16, 30). A Roman soldier guarded him at all times. Some think the soldier was chained to him (Acts 28:16; Eph. 6:20; Phil. 1:13-14, 16; Col. 4:3, 18; Philem. 10, 13). The Jewish leaders and many other Jews came to Paul's house. From morning until evening he explained and declared the kingdom of God to them. He tried to convince them about Jesus from Moses and the Prophets (Acts 28:23). As usual, the response was mixed. Some were convinced. Others refused to believe. The rejection of the gospel by the Jews brought a strong word from Paul. Read Acts 28:25-27.

Note the reason why the Jews did not understand. Their hearts had become calloused (Acts 28:27). This happened as they rebelled against God. And note the reason they could not see the truth. They had closed their eyes (Acts 28:27). No one becomes more deaf than those who refuse to listen. And no one becomes more blind than those who refuse to see.[27]

Here then is a solemn warning to us. We lose what we refuse to use (Matt. 13:11-15; Mark 4:12; Luke 8:10; John 12:39-40; Rom. 11:8). If we refuse to listen to God's voice, we will lose our ability to hear it. If we refuse to obey the truth, we will lose our ability to see it. This explains why many in cults today were once in churches.

Acts ends with a great contrast. Many Jews rejected the gospel. But many Gentiles listened and received it (Acts 28:28-30). Some reject the blessings of God. These lose all that God wants them to have. But many others accept the good news of Jesus Christ (Matt. 22:1-10). Thus Acts ends in Rome the way it began in Jerusalem, with the preaching of the kingdom.[28]

Conclusion

Take a few minutes to review Acts. Look at the chart that follows, and recall some of the things we studied. Learn to recall something from each chapter in Acts. Practice by writing numbers from 1-28. Then try to describe something from each chapter. Refer to the chart as needed.

Acts	Person or Event	Place	Date[+] (A.D.)
1	Jesus ascended to heaven.	Jerusalem	30
2	The 120 were filled with the Spirit.	Jerusalem	30
2	Peter preached his first sermon.	Jerusalem	30
3	Peter healed the crippled beggar.	Jerusalem	30-31
4	Peter and John were called before the Sanhedrin.	Jerusalem	30-31
5	Ananias and Sapphira died suddenly.	Jerusalem	30-31
6	The believers chose seven deacons.	Jerusalem	31-32
7	Stephen preached his final message.	Jerusalem	31-32

Continued on next page

[+] We do not know the exact dates.

Acts	Person or Event	Place	Date (A.D.)
8	Philip had a great revival.	Samaria	31-32
8	An Ethiopian turned to Christ.	Road to Gaza	31-32
9	Saul was converted and baptized in water.	Damascus	31-32
9	Peter healed Aeneas.	Lydda	
9	Peter healed Dorcas.	Joppa	
10	Cornelius turned to Christ.	Caesarea	39-40
11	Barnabas and Saul taught for a year.	Antioch, Syria	39-40
12	Believers prayed for Peter at Mary's house.	Jerusalem	
12	Worms ate King Herod.	Caesarea	44
13	Paul and Barnabas began their first trip.	Antioch, Syria	46-47
13	Paul blinded Elymas.	Cyprus	46-47
13	John Mark left Paul and Barnabas.	Perga	46-47
13–14	Paul and Barnabas planted churches on their first missionary trip.	Galatia	46-47
15	The first big Church council took place.	Jerusalem	49
15	Paul and Silas began the second trip.	Antioch, Syria	49-52
16	Timothy joined Paul and Silas.	Lystra	49-52
16	Paul received the Macedonian vision.	Troas	
16	Lydia and a jailer turned to Christ.	Philippi	
16	A slave girl was set free from a demon.	Philippi	
17	Jason was persecuted for welcoming Paul into his home.	Thessalonica	
17	Noble Jews searched the Scriptures.	Berea	
17	Paul preached to the Areopagus.	Athens	
18	Gallio threw Paul's accusers out of court.	Corinth	53
18	Paul and Silas began the third trip.	Antioch, Syria	53
18	Aquila and Priscilla taught Apollos.	Ephesus	53
19	12 men were baptized; 7 others fled.	Ephesus	56
19	The city clerk quieted a riot.	Ephesus	57
20	Eutychus was raised from the dead.	Troas	57
20	Paul said farewell to the Ephesian elders.	Miletus	57
21	Paul was beaten, arrested, and protected.	Jerusalem	57
22	Paul gave his testimony to an angry crowd.	Jerusalem	57
23	40 Jews took a vow to murder Paul.	Jerusalem	57
24–26	Paul stood trial before Felix, Festus, and King Agrippa.	Caesarea	58-60
27–28	Paul and others sailed on toward Rome. His faith in God enabled them to survive a storm and a shipwreck. Finally, he arrived in Rome and stayed there 2 years.	Rome	60-62

Figure 13.15   Matching people and events with places in Acts 1–28

Figure 13.13 Drawing of Christian symbols in Roman Catacombs

Figure 13.14   Good Shepherd drawing in Roman Catacombs

Test Yourself: Circle the letter by the *best* completion to each question or statement.

1. An example of a human bridge is
a) Caiaphas the high priest.
b) Stephen the deacon.
c) Alexander the Great.
d) Paul the apostle.

2. Acts teaches that believers in Jerusalem
a) were zealous for the law of Moses.
b) taught salvation by faith alone.
c) realized that animal sacrifices were past.
d) were eager to evangelize the world.

3. Claudius Lysias thought Paul was
a) a great apostle.
b) an Egyptian terrorist.
c) a Jewish rabbi.
d) a humble servant.

4. Our best defense of the gospel is the testimony of
a) Bible scholars.
b) ancient history.
c) signs and wonders.
d) changed lives.

5. According to Acts, how often does God protect believers from persecution?
a) Always
b) Usually
c) Rarely
d) Never

6. One of Luke's purposes in Acts 21–28 is to show that
a) government leaders charged Paul with no crimes.
b) persecution spread the gospel from Jerusalem to Antioch.
c) there were many signs and wonders in Paul's ministry.
d) God protects the believers He respects.

7. Those who have a clear conscience
a) are free from guilt.
b) do not know the Bible.
c) are justified by God.
d) may be living in sin.

8. In the presence of King Agrippa, Paul linked repentance with
a) forgiveness.
b) good deeds.
c) eternal life.
d) the blood.

9. Many on the island of Malta believed that
a) bad things happen only to bad people.
b) bad things happen to good and bad people.
c) good things happen to bad people.
d) good things happen to good and bad people.

10. Paul told some Jews in Rome that they did not see well because they
a) had few opportunities.
b) had poor physicians.
c) had closed their eyes.
d) were born blind.

 Essay Test Topics: Write 50-100 words on each of these goals that you studied in this chapter.

Paul's Imprisonment in Jerusalem (Acts 21:17–23:35)

Goal: *Evaluate and apply 3 challenges of being a human bridge.*

Goal: *Summarize what Acts 21–23 teaches about rumors, testifying, and protection.*

Paul's Imprisonment in Caesarea (Acts 24–26)

Goal: *Explain and apply 2 ways Acts 21–28 relates to the purposes of Luke.*

Goal: *Analyze and apply the roles of conscience and preachers in Acts 24–26.*

Paul's Imprisonment in Rome (Acts 27–28)

Goal: *Relate Paul's faith in Acts 27 to the storms of life.*

Goal: *Identify 2 truths in Acts 28. Apply these to your context.*

Figure 13.16   The Egnatian Way went from Rome through Philippi.

Figure 13.17   The Colosseum (theater) in Rome where people came to see wild beasts kill believers

Figure 13.18   Inside the Colosseum

Definitions

The right-hand column lists the chapter in the textbook in which the word is used.

breaking of bread—sharing bread together at a meal; sometimes believers ate a meal together. They celebrated the Lord's Supper by breaking bread at this meal (1 Cor. 11:17-34). — 4

Caesar—the highest earthly ruler of the Roman kingdom. Nero was the Caesar to whom Paul appealed (Acts 25:11). He ruled Rome A.D. 54-68. — 1, 13

Caesarea—a city on the coast of Judea, named in honor of Augustus Caesar. Herod rebuilt Caesarea with a good harbor. The city was a military base and the home of Cornelius. It was about 30 miles (48 km) north of Joppa, and 50 miles (80 km) northwest of Jerusalem. — 9, 13

capacity—amount that a person or thing can contain — 5

caste—the level of society that a person is born into, as in India — 8

centurion—a Roman military commander over at least 100 soldiers — 9

Charismatics—a term that became popular in the 1960s. Then it referred to believers in various denominations who were filled with the Spirit. Many Charismatics have remained in their denominations. But some have left their denominations and started or joined Charismatic churches. Charismatics emphasize the *charismata* (Greek for "gifts of the Spirit"). However, unlike Pentecostals, they do not always emphasize the Pentecostal experience or the initial, outward sign of tongues. — 3

checkers—a game played by two people. Players sit and face each other with a board between them. Each player begins with 12 checkers, which are objects shaped like the caps on Coke bottles. Checkers sit on a board divided into 32 black squares and 32 white squares. Each square is about two inches on a side. Players take turns trying to jump, and thus remove the other player's checkers. — 4

cholera—a serious, sometimes deadly disease that can be passed from one person to another. Its symptoms include fever and disorders in the intestines. A vaccine will prevent it. — 4

Cilicia—the province whose capital was Tarsus — 7

communism—a system of government in which the state owns everything — 6

Cyrene—a province in North Africa. The capital city of this province is also called Cyrene. The city is about 500 miles (805 km) west of Alexandria. (See Figure 7.2.) — 7

Damascus—a city in Syria. It is located about 150 miles (242 km) north of Jerusalem. It is about halfway between Jerusalem and Tarsus. Damascus was famous for business. — 8

diary—a blank book into which people write daily summaries of thoughts or events — 5

district—an area or part of a province. Examples of provinces are Pisidia, Phrygia, and Mysia. — 11

Diwali—a yearly festival time in India. It celebrates the victory of the Hindu god Siva over the evil god Narakhasura. During this time people light small clay lamps around their homes. — 10

Ephesus—the leading city of Asia. Paul ministered there for 3 years. Ephesus was a great center for evangelism. From there, all Asia heard the Word. — 12

Epicureans—people who followed the teachings of Epicurus. They believed God was in everything. Also, they thought pleasure was the main goal in life. — 11

epistles—letters — 1

eunuch—the person in Acts 8 from the nation of Ethiopia in East Africa. A eunuch was one who could not have sexual relations with a woman. Some are born eunuchs. Others are made eunuchs when men cut away part of their sexual organs (Matt. 19:12). — 8

evangelism—telling the good new of Jesus Christ to an unbeliever — 8

Galatian churches—churches, such as Pisidian Antioch, Iconium, Lystra, and Derbe in the province of Galatia. Paul established these on his first trip and visited them on his second and third trips. He wrote the letter of Galatians to them between his first and second missionary trips. — 10

geographically—refers to various places on the earth — 1

gift of the Holy Spirit—the baptism in the Holy Spirit; the full measure of the Spirit we receive after the new birth — 4

Great Commission Christians—believers who obey the command of Matthew 28:19-20. They try to do their   6
   part in reaching the lost for Christ.

Grecian Jews—Jews from outside Palestine who spoke Greek. They did not know Hebrew well.   7

Hebraic Jews—Jews who were mostly from Palestine. These spoke Hebrew in their homes.   7

Hellenistic—the Greek word for a Greek person is *Hellene*. Therefore, Greek ideas and culture are Hellenistic.   7, 9
   Antioch was a major center of Hellenism, that is, Greek ideas and culture.

Hindu—a person whose religion is Hinduism. Hinduism is a religious umbrella over 3 million gods. Hindus   8
   pick the gods they want to worship. Also, Hindus believe that when a person suffers, it is always because
   of his or her past actions.

Holy Spirit—the third member of the Trinity or Godhead. He comes to live in each believer at the time of the   1
   new birth. He fills a believer at the time of the baptism in the Holy Spirit.

hyperbole—a method in which a writer or speaker exaggerates or overstates a truth to emphasize a point   4

Imperial—associated with or belonging to Caesar, the emperor   9

isthmus—a short neck of land like the one between Athens and Corinth that connected the Aegean and   11
   Adriatic Seas

Jerusalem—the capital city of the Jews in New Testament times. The final part of the word, *salem*, means   1, 13
   "peace." David was the first of Israel to conquer the city, sometimes referred to as *Zion* (2 Sam. 5:6-8). It
   became his capital. Later, Solomon built the temple there.[2]

Jerusalem Council—the big church meeting of Acts 15. Leaders gathered to discuss whether or not Gentiles   10
   must obey the law of Moses.

Judaizers—born-again Jewish believers who were Pharisees. They accepted Jesus, but still taught that all   10
   believers must obey the law of Moses. Thus they emphasized circumcision for Gentiles.

Judea—the southern part or region of ancient Palestine. It is just north of the region of Idumea (See Figure 1.10).   1

last days—the period that began with the first coming of Christ and ends with his Second Coming   4

laypeople—common believers who serve in the church. These are often part-time volunteers who may not   1
   have as much training as formal leaders, such as pastors. Still, laypeople have helpful skills and gain
   training as they minister.

legion—a group of 6,000 Roman soldiers. A legion contained 10 regiments, each of which had 600 soldiers in it.   9

Malta—an island known as Melita by the Greeks and Romans. It was located 58 miles (93 km) south of Sicily.   13

Matthias—the disciple chosen to replace Judas as an apostle   2

Parousia—a Greek word referring to the coming of Christ at the end of this age   2

patriarch—one of the fathers of the Hebrew race, such as Abraham, Isaac, Jacob, or his sons   7

Pentecost—means "fifty." It was a Jewish feast celebrating the summer harvest. It took place 50 days after   2
   the Passover Feast. Pentecost has also come to refer to being baptized in the Spirit. This is because the
   disciples were first filled with the Spirit on the Day of Pentecost.

Pentecostals—believers who emphasize and practice being filled with the Spirit, like the 120 on the Day of   3
   Pentecost, with the outward sign of speaking in tongues. Pentecostals believe that the baptism in the Spirit
   is a spiritual experience that comes after the new birth and empowers a believer for service. Pentecostals
   emphasize evangelism and missions.

Pharisees—means "the separate people." They were members of a Jewish group. These strictly followed the law   13
   of Moses and Jewish religious customs. Many did not like Jesus because He did not follow all of their rules.

phylacteries—small boxes the Jews wore on the forehead or left arm (Deut. 6:8; 11:18). These boxes   9
   contained Scripture verses.

pornography—sinful writing or pictures of a sexual nature. *Porno* is a form of the Greek word for prostitute   12
   or harlot.

portico—the Greek word for a porch   11

Priscilla—wife of Aquila. This husband and wife team sewed tents. They were laypeople who helped Paul and others, like Apollos. Priscilla seems to be the leading teacher of the team.   12

proconsul—a ruler appointed by the Roman Senate. Proconsuls ruled over peaceful areas. Examples of proconsuls in Acts are Sergius Paulus and Gallio.   10

prophesy—to speak spiritual insights to encourage, strengthen, comfort, or warn. Few are prophets, but all believers may prophesy.   9

Protestant—a member of a group of believers that began in the Reformation period. Protestant was the name given to followers of Christ who protested against the unbiblical doctrines and practices of the Roman Catholic Church. Today, the three major groups of Christianity are Protestants, Roman Catholics, and Eastern Orthodox.   6

province—a region that is part of a kingdom or empire, and subject to that kingdom's government. Provinces of Rome included Achaia, Macedonia, Asia, Galatia, and others.   1, 11

regiment—a group of 600 Roman soldiers. It contained 6 centurions. Each of these was over at least 100 soldiers.   9

Rome—the capital of the Roman empire or kingdom. Rome was built upon seven hills.   13

Sadducees—a wealthy, important, Jewish religious group. They believed that the only true Scriptures were the Pentateuch. They did not believe in angels or the resurrection. They lost their power after the destruction of Jerusalem in A.D. 70.   5, 13

Samaria—the biblical part or region of Palestine just north of Judea in New Testament times. There was also a city called Samaria within the region of Samaria.   1, 8

Samaritans—those who lived in the region of Samaria. They were the descendants of Jews who had married non-Jews.   8

Sanhedrin—a council or group of Jewish leaders who judged religious matters. It was the highest Jewish court in the days of Jesus and the early church. The men of the council sat in a half-circle to judge.[3]   5

Sapphira—the wife of Ananias. Together, they agreed to lie about the sale of their property.   6

sewer—a place filled with human excrement   13

Simon the sorcerer—the man of Acts 8 who was saved under Philip's ministry. Simon either claimed to be God, or His representative.[4] For years he had deceived the people through witchcraft or sorcery.   8

socialism—a system of government based on the theory that all people are equal owners of everything and live by the same financial standards   6

sorcery—witchcraft; using evil spirits to gain knowledge or advantage. The Bible says God forbids any form of sorcery. He invites His people to seek Him, not those outside of His kingdom.   12

sovereign—Almighty; the highest power or authority who rules   5, 9

Stephen—a Hellenistic, or Greek-speaking, Jew of Acts 6–7. He was chosen to be one of the first deacons. Some call him *the Father of the Book of Hebrews.*   7

stoa—the Greek word for a large porch surrounding the marketplace. It was decorated with paintings and had stone columns.   11

Stoics—those who followed the teachings of Zeno. He used to speak in Athens on a porch (*stoa) with large stone columns. Stoics taught that man should not pay attention to pleasure or pain.   11

synagogue—building where Jews met. In biblical times, the purposes of synagogues were worship, education, and government.   7

Theophilus—a common Greek name meaning "one who loves God"   2

Tibet—a region of southwestern China. It is located high in the mountains. At times it has governed itself as an independent state. At other times it has been associated with China at various levels, such as a province.   10

tongues—a supernatural, verbal sign that the Holy Spirit has filled a believer. Tongues refers to a language the Spirit inspires that the believer has never learned. It may be a language known or unknown on earth.[5]   3

ugali—a common food in East Africa. It is white cornmeal, cooked until it is very difficult to stir.   13

Zeus—the highest god in ancient Greek beliefs. The Romans called this top ruler Jupiter.   13

Scripture List

Bibliography

Austin, Colonel Charles F. *Management's Self-Inflicted Wounds*. London: Holt, Rinehart and Winston, 1966.

Barker, Kenneth, gen. ed. *The NIV Study Bible*. Grand Rapids, Michigan: Zondervan Publishing House, 1985.

Barrett, C. K. *The First Epistle to the Corinthians*. New York: Harper and Row, 1968.

Barrett, David. *International Bulletin of Missionary Research*. (January 1997): 25.

_____. *International Bulletin of Missionary Research*. (January 2000): 25.

_____. *International Bulletin of Missionary Research*. (Fall 2000): 25.

Brisco, Thomas. *Holman Bible Atlas*. Nashville, Tennessee: Broadman & Holman Publishers, 1998.

Bruce, F. F. *The Book of the Acts*. Grand Rapids, Michigan: Wm. B. Eerdmans Publishing Co., 1974.

Burtner, Robert W., and Robert E. Chiles. *John Wesley's Theology: A Collection From His Works*. Nashville, Tennessee: Abingdon Press, 1982.

Carter, Tom. *Spurgeon At His Best*. Grand Rapids, Michigan: Baker Book House, 1988.

_____. *2200 Quotations from the Writings of Charles H. Spurgeon*. Grand Rapids, Michigan: Baker Book House, 1988.

Chadwick, Samuel. *The Way to Pentecost*. London: Hodder and Stroughton, 1972.

Chapman, J. Wilbur. "What a Savior," *Hymns of Glorious Praise*. Springfield, Missouri: Gospel Publishing House, 1969, p. 23.

Cole, Glen D. Sermon notes on Acts 17.

_____. "Waiting for the Promise," *Cassette Series on Acts*, Sermon Number One. Sacramento, California: Capital Christian Center.

Douglas, J. D., ed. *The New Bible Dictionary*. Grand Rapids, Michigan: Wm. B. Eerdmans Publishing Co., 1978.

Duffield, Guy, and Nathaniel M. Van Cleave. *Foundations of Pentecostal Theology*. Los Angeles, California: L.I.F.E. Bible College, 1983.

Earle, Ralph. *The Acts of the Apostles*. Kansas City, Missouri: Beacon Hill Press, 1965.

Elmer, Duane, and Lois McKinney. *With an Eye on the Future*. Monrovia, California: MARC, 1996.

Fee, Gordon D. *New International Commentary on the New Testament: The First Epistle to the Corinthians*. Grand Rapids, Michigan: Wm. B. Eerdmans Publishing Co., 1987.

Gibbs, Carl, gen. ed. *Barnabas Series: Acts*. Springfield, Missouri: Global University, 2001.

Glasser, Arthur J. *Worldwide Perspectives–A Text for Use with Perspectives on the World Christian Movement*. Pasadena, California: William Carey Library, 1996.

Green, Michael. *I Believe in the Holy Spirit*. Grand Rapids, Michigan: Wm. B. Eerdmans Publishing Co., 1975.

Guthrie, Donald. *The Apostles*. Grand Rapids, Michigan: Zondervan Publishing House, 1975.

Haenchen, Ernst. *The Acts of the Apostles, a Commentary*. Philadelphia, Pennsylvania: The Westminster Press, 1971.

Hanegraaff, Hank. *Christianity in Crisis*. (cassette tape) San Juan Capistrano, California: Christian Research Institute, 1993.

Harris, Ralph W. *Acts Today, Signs and Wonders of the Holy Spirit*. Springfield, Missouri: Gospel Publishing House, 1995.

_____, ed. *The Complete Biblical Library: The New Testament Study Bible Acts*, Vol. 6. Springfield, Missouri: The Complete Biblical Library, 1991.

Harrison, E. F. *Acts: The Expanding Church*. Chicago, Illinois: Moody Press, 1975.

Harrison, Everett F., ed. *Baker's Dictionary of Theology*. Grand Rapids, Michigan: Baker Book House, 1975.

Hayford, Jack. *The Beauty of Spiritual Language*. Nashville, Tennessee: Thomas Nelson Publishers, 1996.

Hewett, James S., ed. *Illustrations Unlimited*. Wheaton, Illinois: Tyndale House Publishers, 1968.

Hiebert, Paul G. *Case Studies in Missions*. Grand Rapids, Michigan: Baker Book House, 1987.

Hodges, Melvin. *The Indigenous Church*. Springfield, Missouri: Gospel Publishing House, 1976.

Holdcroft, L. Thomas. *The Holy Spirit*. Springfield, Missouri: Gospel Publishing House, 1971.

Horton, Stanley M. *The Book of Acts*. Springfield, Missouri: Gospel Publishing House, 1994.

_____, and William Menzies. *Bible Doctrines*. Springfield, Missouri: Gospel Publishing House, 1993.

Hughes, Philip. *New International Commentary on the New Testament: The Second Epistle to the Corinthians*. Grand Rapids, Michigan: Wm. B. Eerdmans Publishing Co., 1977.

Jones, Doyle G. *Be Filled With the Spirit*. Waxahachie, Texas: Doyle G. Jones, 1997.

Landau, Sidney I. *Funk and Wagnall's Standard Desk Dictionary*. New York: Funk and Wagnall, 1974.

Larson, Bob. *Larson's New Book of Cults*. Wheaton, Illinois: Tyndale House Publishers, Inc., 1989.

Lindsell, Harold. *My Daily Quiet Time*. Grand Rapids, Michigan: Zondervan Publishing House, 1970.

MacPhearson, Ian. *The Art of Illustrating Sermons*. Grand Rapids, Michigan: Baker Book House, 1976.

Marshall, I. Howard. *Acts*. Grand Rapids, Michigan: Wm. B. Eerdmans Publishing Co., 1996.

Mayfield, Joseph H., and Ralph Earle. *Beacon Bible Commentary: Acts,* Vol. 7. Kansas City, Missouri: Beacon Hill Press, 1965.

McGee, Gary B. *Initial Evidence*. Peabody, Massachusetts: Hendrickson Publishers, 1991.

_____. cited in *Transcendence/Immanence and the Emerging Pentecostal Academy* by Del Tarr, 1995, p. 7.

McKenzie, E. C. *Mac's Giant Book of Quips and Quotes*. Grand Rapids, Michigan: Baker Book House, 1980.

Menzies, William W., and Robert Menzies. *Spirit and Power*. Grand Rapids, Michigan: Zondervan Publishing House, 2000.

Mounce, Robert H. *New International Commentary on the New Testament*: *The Book of Revelation*. Grand Rapids, Michigan: Wm. B. Eerdmans Publishing Co., 1977.

Pfeiffer, Charles F. and Howard F. Vos, eds. *The Wycliffe Historical Geography of Bible Lands*. Chicago: Moody Press, 1967.

Pfeiffer, Charles, Howard Vos, and John Rea, eds. *Wycliffe Bible Encyclopedia,* Vol. 1. Chicago, Illinois: Moody Press, 1975.

Rumph, Jane. *Stories from the Front Lines*. Grand Rapids, Michigan: Chosen Books, A Division of Baker Book House, 1996.

Sammis, John H. "Trust and Obey," *Sing His Praise*. Springfield, Missouri: Gospel Publishing House, 1991, p. 195.

Stamps, Don, gen. ed. *The Full Life Study Bible*. Grand Rapids, Michigan: Zondervan Publishing House, 1992.

Stiles, J. E. *The Gift of the Holy Spirit*. Old Tappan, New Jersey: Fleming H. Revell Co., 1971.

Stott, John R. W. *The Message of Acts: The Spirit, the Church and the World*. Downers Grove, Illinois: Inter-Varsity Press, 1994.

Stronstad, Roger. *Spirit, Scripture & Theology*. Baguio City, Philippines: Asia Pacific Theological Seminary Press, 1995.

_____. *The Charismatic Theology of St. Luke*. Peabody, Massachusetts: Hendrickson Publishers, 1984.

Tan, Paul Lee. *Encyclopedia of 7700 Illustrations*. Rockville, Maryland: Assurance Publishers, 1979.

Tenney, Merrill C. *New Testament Survey*. Grand Rapids, Michigan: Wm. B. Eerdmans Publishing Co., 1961.

Turnbull, Ralph G. *Proclaiming the New Testament*. Grand Rapids, Michigan: Baker Book House, 1972.

_____. *The Acts of the Apostles*. Grand Rapids, Michigan: Baker Book House, 1972.

Wagner, C. Peter. *Blazing the Way, A New Look at Acts–Sharing God's Power Throughout the World*, Acts 15–28. Ventura, California: Regal Books, 1995.

_____. *Lighting the World–A New Look At Acts*, Acts 9–15. Ventura, California: Regal Books, 1995.

_____. *Spiritual Power and Church Growth*. Altamonte Springs, Florida: Strang Communications Co., 1986.

Walker, Thomas. *The Acts of the Apostles*. Chicago, Illinois: Moody Press, 1965.

Waller, Lynn. *International Children's Bible Dictionary*. Dallas, Texas: Word, 1987.

Walvoord, John F., and Roy B. Zuck. *The Bible Knowledge Commentary*. Wheaton, Illinois: Victor Books, 1997.

Whitfield, Frederick. "Oh, How I Love Jesus," *Sing His Praise*. Springfield, Missouri: Gospel Publishing House, 1991, p. 73.

Wiersbe, Warren. *Bible Exposition Commentary: Matthew–Galatians,* Vol. 1. Wheaton, Illinois: Victor Books, 1994.

Williams, Morris. *Toughness & Trivia*. A compilation of writings and poems by Morris Williams published by the family, 1991, back cover.

Wimber, John and Kevin Springer. *Power Evangelism*. San Francisco, California: Harper and Row, 1986.

Wood, George O. *Acts–A Study Guide*. Irving, Texas: ICI University Press, 1996.

_____. *Study in Acts*, Introduction (cassette tape) Costa Mesa, California: Newport-Mesa Christian Center, 1987.

_____. *Study in Acts*, Acts 3:1-10 (cassette tape) Costa Mesa, California: Newport-Mesa Christian Center, 1987.

_____. *Study in Acts*, Acts 3:11-26 (cassette tape) Costa Mesa, California: Newport-Mesa Christian Center, 1987.

_____. *Study in Acts*, Acts 4 (cassette tape) Costa Mesa, California: Newport-Mesa Christian Center, 1987.

_____. *Study in Acts*, Acts 6 (cassette tape) Costa Mesa, California: Newport-Mesa Christian Center, 1987.

_____. *Study in Acts*, Acts 8 (cassette tape) Costa Mesa, California: Newport-Mesa Christian Center, 1987.

_____. *Study in Acts*, Acts 9 (cassette tape) Costa Mesa, California: Newport-Mesa Christian Center, 1987.

_____. *Study in Acts*, Acts 9:32–11:18 (cassette tape) Costa Mesa, California: Newport-Mesa Christian Center, 1988.

_____. *Study in Acts*, Acts 12 (cassette tape) Costa Mesa, California: Newport-Mesa Christian Center, 1988.

_____. *Study in Acts*, Acts 13–14 (cassette tape) Costa Mesa, California: Newport-Mesa Christian Center, 1988.

_____. *Study in Acts*, Acts 15 (cassette tape) Costa Mesa, California: Newport-Mesa Christian Center, 1988.

_____. *Study in Acts*, Acts 18 (cassette tape) Costa Mesa, California: Newport-Mesa Christian Center, 1988.

_____. *Study in Acts*, Acts 19 (cassette tape) Costa Mesa, California: Newport-Mesa Christian Center, 1988.

York, John. *Missions in the Age of the Spirit*. Springfield, Missouri: Logion Press, 2000.

Endnotes

Chapter 1

1 Carl Gibbs, *Barnabas Series: Acts* (Springfield, Missouri: Global University, 2001), p. 33.

2 Stanley M. Horton, *The Book of Acts* (Springfield, Missouri: Gospel Publishing House, 1994), p. 9.

3 George O. Wood, *Study in Acts*, Introduction, cassette tape (Costa Mesa, California: Newport-Mesa Christian Center, 1987).

4 Horton, p. 11.

5 Roger Stronstad, *Spirit, Scripture & Theology* (Baguio City, Philippines: Asia Pacific Theological Seminary Press, 1995), p. 47.

6 John F. Walvoord and Roy B. Zuck, *The Bible Knowledge Commentary* (Wheaton, Illinois: Victor Books, 1997), p. 389.

7 George O. Wood, *Acts—A Study Guide* (Irving, Texas: ICI University Press, 1996), p. 7.

8 Horton, p. 10.

9 Horton, p. 184.

10 William W. Menzies and Robert Menzies, *Spirit and Power* (Grand Rapids, Michigan: Zondervan Publishing House, 2000), p. 41.

11 Bill Lasley, Missionary and editor at Global University, Interview on the relationship between history and doctrine, July, 2000.

12 Stronstad, p. 42.

13 Kenneth Barker, gen. ed., *The NIV Study Bible* (Grand Rapids, Michigan: Zondervan Publishing House, 1985), p. 1642.

14 Glen D. Cole, "Waiting for the Promise," Cassette Series on Acts, Sermon Number One (Sacramento, California: Capital Christian Center).

15 John Lindell, Pastor at James River Assembly in Springfield, Missouri, Sermon on Romans 12, September 2000.

16 Walvoord and Zuck, p. 349.

17 Walvoord and Zuck, p. 355.

Chapter 2

1 F. F. Bruce, *The Book of the Acts* (Grand Rapids, Michigan: Wm. B. Eerdmans Publishing Co., 1974), pp. 31-32.

2 *The NIV Study Bible*, p. 1522.

3 Based on a conversation with Paul York, Assemblies of God missionary in Ethiopia, January 6, 2000.

4 J. D. Douglas, ed., *The New Bible Dictionary* (Grand Rapids, Michigan: Wm. B. Eerdmans Publishing Co., 1978), p. 964.

5 Harold Lindsell, *My Daily Quiet Time* (Grand Rapids, Michigan: Zondervan Publishing House, 1970), pp. 13-14.

6 Horton, p. 16.

7 Stronstad, pp. 189-192.

8 Gary B. McGee, *Initial Evidence* (Peabody, Massachusetts: Hendrickson Publishers, 1991), p. 164.

9 Elizabeth Karanja, Interview about Kikuyu proverbs from Kenya, October 26, 2000.

10 Ralph G. Turnbull, *Proclaiming the New Testament* (Grand Rapids, Michigan: Baker Book House, 1972), p. 8.

11 Based on *The NIV Study Bible*, pp. 1643, 1668.

12 Melvin Hodges, *The Indigenous Church* (Springfield, Missouri: Gospel Publishing House, 1976), p. 153.

13 John R. W. Stott, *The Message of Acts: The Spirit, the Church and the World* (Downers Grove, Illinois: InterVarsity Press, 1994), p. 51.

14 Stott, p. 51.

15 Stott, p. 51.

16 Paul Lee Tan, *Encyclopedia of 7700 Illustrations* (Rockville, Maryland: Assurance Publishers, 1979), p. 1630.

17 John H. Sammis, "Trust and Obey," *Sing His Praise* (Springfield, Missouri: Gospel Publishing House, 1991), p. 195.

18 Horton, pp. 25-26.

19 Horton, p. 24.

20 Lindsell, p. 156.

21 Lindsell, p. 116.

22 Horton, p. 26.

23 Stott, pp. 55-56.

24 Bruce, p. 49.

25 Horton, p. 27.

26 E. F. Harrison, *Acts: The Expanding Church* (Chicago, Illinois: Moody Press, 1975), p. 48.

27 Horton, p. 28.

Chapter 3

1 Doyle G. Jones, *Be Filled with the Spirit* (Waxahachie, Texas: Doyle G. Jones, 1997), p. 12.

2 Horton, p. 29.

3 John York, *Missions in the Age of the Spirit* (Springfield, Missouri: Logion Press, 2000), pp. 80-81.

4 Roger Stronstad, *The Charismatic Theology of St. Luke* (Peabody, Massachusetts: Hendrickson Publishers, 1984), pp. 20-26.

5 Stronstad, *The Charismatic Theology of St. Luke*, p. 62.

6 Horton, pp. 30-31.

7   Ralph W. Harris, ed., *The Complete Biblical Library: The New Testament Study Bible Acts*, vol. 6 (Springfield, Missouri: The Complete Biblical Library, 1991), p. 39.

8   David Barrett, *International Bulletin of Missionary Research* (Fall 2000): p. 25.

9   Ernst Haenchen, *The Acts of the Apostles, a Commentary* (Philadelphia, Pennsylvania: The Westminster Press, 1971), p. 304.

10 Horton, p. 106.

11 Horton, p. 119.

12 L. Thomas Holdcroft, *The Holy Spirit* (Springfield, Missouri: Gospel Publishing House, 1971), p. 112.

13 Robert W. Burtner and Robert E. Chiles, *John Wesley's Theology: A Collection From His Works* (Nashville, Tennessee: Abingdon Press, 1982), pp. 17-18.

14 Barrett, p. 25.

15 J. E. Stiles, *The Gift of the Holy Spirit* (Old Tappan, New Jersey: Fleming H. Revell Co., 1971), p. 36.

16 Guy Duffield and Nathaniel M. Van Cleave, *Foundations of Pentecostal Theology* (Los Angeles, California: L.I.F.E. Bible College, 1983), p. 320.

17 McGee, p. 122.

18 Ralph W. Harris, *Acts Today, Signs and Wonders of the Holy Spirit* (Springfield, Missouri: Gospel Publishing House, 1995), pp. 111-112.

19 McGee, p. 49.

20 McGee, p. 124.

21 Burtner and Chiles, pp. 17-18.

22 Elizabeth Karanja, Interview of November 21, 2000.

23 Stronstad, *Spirit, Scripture & Theology*, p. 123.

24 Stronstad, *Spirit, Scripture & Theology*, p. 67.

25 Barrett, p. 25.

26 Gordon D. Fee, *New International Commentary on the New Testament: The First Epistle to the Corinthians* (Grand Rapids, Michigan: Wm. B. Eerdmans Publishing Co., 1987), p. 625.

27 Jones, p. 12.

Chapter 4

1   Jack Hayford, *The Beauty of Spiritual Language* (Nashville, Tennessee: Thomas Nelson Publishers, 1996), pp. 75-82.

2   Horton, p. 34.

3   Donald Guthrie, *The Apostles* (Grand Rapids, Michigan: Zondervan Publishing House, 1975), p. 27.

4   Harris, pp. 43-45.

5   Don Stamps, gen. ed., *Full Life Study Bible* (Grand Rapids, Michigan: Zondervan Publishing House, 1992), p. 1647, Acts 2:17.

6   Horton, p. 42.

7   Everett F. Harrison, *Baker's Dictionary of Theology* (Grand Rapids, Michigan: Baker Book House, 1975), p. 298.

8   Horton, p. 46.

9   Horton, p. 46.

10 Barrett, p. 25.

11 Stanley M. Horton and William Menzies, *Bible Doctrines* (Springfield, Missouri: Gospel Publishing House, 1993), pp. 157-158.

12 Horton, *Acts*, p. 48.

13 Horton, *Acts*, p. 49.

14 Tom Carter, *2200 Quotations from the Writings of Charles H. Spurgeon* (Grand Rapids, Michigan: Baker Book House, 1988), p. 142.

15 Carter, p. 143.

16 Carter, pp. 145-146.

17 Carter, p. 144.

18 Horton, *Acts*, p. 49.

19 Carter, p. 179.

20 Jim Hall, Evangelism and Discipleship Coordinator for Intercultural Ministries of the Assemblies of God, Springfield, Missouri, Interview, May 12, 2001.

Chapter 5

1   Carter, pp. 209-210.

2   George O. Wood, *Study in Acts*, Acts 3, cassette tape (Costa Mesa, California: Newport-Mesa Christian Center, 1987).

3   Stott, p. 90.

4   *The NIV Study Bible*, p. 1688, Acts 21:24.

5   Philip Hughes, *New International Commentary on the New Testament: The Second Epistle to the Corinthians* (Grand Rapids, Michigan: Wm. B. Eerdmans Publishing Co., 1977), pp. 201-204.

6   Horton, *Acts*, p. 53.

7   *The NIV Study Bible*, p. 1651, Acts 3:2. This was probably the gate that Nicanor, a Greek Hebrew, gave to the temple. Some call it the Nicanor Gate.

8   Bruce, p. 83.

9   Douglas, pp. 79, 1245-1247, and plate XIV.

10 Stott, p. 90.

11 Merrill C. Tenney, *New Testament Survey* (Grand Rapids, Michigan: Wm. B. Eerdmans Publishing Co., 1961), p. 91. Dr. C. Schick's model of Herod's Temple, based on his research.

12 George O. Wood, *Study in Acts*, Acts 3, cassette tape (Costa Mesa, California: Newport-Mesa Christian Center, 1987).

13 Tom Wilson, Pastor of Oak Cliff Assembly of God in Dallas, Texas, Sermon on Acts, March 26, 2000.

14 Thomas Walker, *The Acts of the Apostles* (Chicago, Illinois: Moody Press, 1965), p. 67.

15 George O. Wood, *Study in Acts*, Acts 3, cassette tape (Costa Mesa, California: Newport-Mesa Christian Center, 1987).

16 Horton, *Acts*, p. 64.

17 Bruce, p. 102.

18 *The NIV Study Bible*, p. 1650, Acts 4:5.

19 Horton, *Acts*, p. 68.

20 Horton, *Acts*, p. 67.

21 George O. Wood, *Study in Acts*, Acts 4, cassette tape (Costa Mesa, California: Newport-Mesa Christian Center, 1987).

22 Bruce, p. 100.

23 George O. Wood, *Study in Acts*, Part 9, cassette tape (Costa Mesa, California: Newport-Mesa Christian Center, 1987).

24 Horton, *Acts*, p. 68.

Chapter 6

1 Harris, pp. 159-160.

2 Wood, *Study in Acts*, Part 9, cassette tape

3 Elizabeth Karanja, Interview of October, 2000, Kikuyu proverb.

4 Elizabeth Karanja, Interview of October, 2000.

5 Ian MacPhearson, *The Art of Illustrating Sermons* (Grand Rapids, Michigan: Baker Book House, 1976), p. 40.

6 *The NIV Study Bible*, p. 1651, Acts 4:36.

7 Ralph Earle, *The Acts of the Apostles* (Kansas City, Missouri: Beacon Hill Press, 1965), p. 307.

8 Horton, *Acts*, p. 70.

9 Horton, *Acts*, p. 72.

10 Joseph H. Mayfield and Ralph Earle, *Beacon Bible Commentary: Acts,* vol. 7 (Kansas City, Missouri: Beacon Hill Press, 1965), p. 309.

11 Horton, *Acts*, p. 72.

12 Warren Wiersbe, *Bible Exposition Commentary: Matthew–Galatians*, vol. 1 (Wheaton, Illinois: Victor Books, 1994), p. 420.

13 Wiersbe, p. 422.

14 Horton, *Acts*, p. 75.

15 Bruce, pp. 117-118.

16 Bruce, pp. 117-118.

17 I. Howard Marshall, *Acts* (Grand Rapids, Michigan: Wm. B. Eerdmans Publishing Co., 1996), p. 115.

18 C. Peter Wagner, *Spiritual Power and Church Growth* (Altamonte Springs, Florida: Strang Communications Co., 1986), pp. 83-93.

19 John Wimber and Kevin Springer, *Power Evangelism* (San Francisco, California: Harper and Row, 1986), pp. 107-115.

20 Gary McGee, cited in *Transcendence/Immanence and the Emerging Pentecostal Academy*, a paper by Del Tarr, 1995, p. 7.

21 Wimber and Springer, p. 110.

22 Wimber and Springer, p. 107.

23 Horton, *Acts*, p. 76.

24 Michael Green, *I Believe in the Holy Spirit* (Grand Rapids, Michigan: Wm. B. Eerdmans Publishing Co., 1975), p. 12.

25 Wimber and Springer, pp. 157-174.

26 Wimber and Springer, pp. 175-185.

27 Jane Rumph, *Stories from the Front Lines* (Grand Rapids, Michigan: Chosen Books, A Division of Baker Book House, 1996).

28 Harris, *Acts Today,* pp. Forward-160.

29 David Barrett, *International Bulletin of Missionary Research* (January 2000): p. 25.

30 Barrett, (January 2000): p. 25.

31 Barrett, (January 2000): p. 25.

32 Barrett, (January 2000): p. 25.

Chapter 7

1 Rumph, pp. 16-18.

2 Horton, *Acts*, pp. 83-84.

3 *The NIV Study Bible*, p. 1653, Acts 6:1.

4 Horton, *Acts*, pp. 83-84.

5 Bruce, p. 128.

6 Stott, p. 120.

7 Stott, p. 120.

8 Horton, *Acts*, p. 84.

9 Bruce, p. 128.

10 George O. Wood, *Study in Acts*, Acts 6, cassette tape (Costa Mesa, California: Newport-Mesa Christian Center, 1987).

11 Hank Hanegraaff, *Christianity in Crisis*, cassette tape (San Juan Capistrano, California: Christian Research Institute, 1993).

12 E. C. McKenzie, *Mac's Giant Boook of Quips & Quotes* (Grand Rapids, Michigan: Baker Book House, 1980). p. 64.

13 Horton, *Acts*, p. 84.

14 Douglas, pp. 1227-1229.

15 Walvoord and Zuck, p. 368.

16 Horton, *Acts*, p. 88.

17 George O. Wood, *Study in Acts*, Acts 7, cassette tape (Costa Mesa, California: Newport-Mesa Christian Center, 1987).

18 Walvoord and Zuck, p. 370.

19 Wood, *Acts* (ICI), p. 127.

20 Colonel Charles F. Austin, *Management's Self-Inflicted Wounds* (London: Holt, Rinehart and Winston, 1966), pp. 88-90.

21 Elizabeth Karanja, Interview of October, 2000.

22 Walvoord and Zuck, p. 369.

23 Walvoord and Zuck, p. 369.

24 *The NIV Study Bible*, p. 1657, Acts 7:49.

25 Wood, *Acts* (ICI), p. 124.

26 James S. Hewett, ed., *Illustrations Unlimited* (Wheaton, Illinois: Tyndale House Publishers, 1968), p. 202.

27 Horton, *Acts*, p. 98.

Chapter 8

1 Rumph, pp. 49-53.
2 George O. Wood, *Study in Acts*, Acts 8, cassette tape (Costa Mesa, California: Newport-Mesa Christian Center, 1987).
3 Stott, p. 148.
4 *The NIV Study Bible*, p. 57, Genesis 34:2.
5 *The NIV Study Bible*, p. 1600, John 4:9.
6 Horton, *Acts*, p. 102.
7 Dr. Robert E. Cooley, notes on Acts 8.
8 Douglas, pp. 463-464.
9 Marshall, p. 152.
10 Paul G. Hiebert, *Case Studies in Missions* (Grand Rapids, Michigan: Baker Book House, 1987), pp. 173-176.
11 Stott, p. 150.
12 Marshall, p. 157.
13 Wood, *Study in Acts*, Acts 8, cassette tape.
14 Haenchen, p. 304.
15 Horton, *Acts*, p. 108.
16 Wood, *Study in Acts*, Acts 8, cassette tape.
17 Robert Holmes, Assemblies of God missionary, Sermon in Irving, Texas, 1998.
18 Ralph G. Turnbull, *The Acts of the Apostles* (Grand Rapids, Michigan: Baker Book House, 1972), p. 53.
19 Tom Carter, *Spurgeon At His Best* (Grand Rapids, Michigan: Baker Book House, 1988), p. 70.
20 Tan, p. 1319, #5871.
21 Barrett, (January 2000): p. 25.
22 Wimber and Springer, p. 118.
23 *The NIV Study Bible*, p. 1661.
24 George O. Wood, *Study in Acts*, Acts 9, cassette tape (Costa Mesa, California: Newport-Mesa Christian Center, 1987).
25 Walvoord and Zuck, p. 376.
26 Wood, *Study in Acts*, Acts 9, cassette tape.
27 Wood, *Study in Acts*, Acts 9, cassette tape.
28 Walvoord and Zuck, p. 378.

Chapter 9

1 Rumph, pp. 85-92.
2 *The NIV Study Bible*, p. 1660, Acts 8:40.
3 George O. Wood, *Study in Acts*, Acts 9:32–11:18, cassette tape (Costa Mesa, California: Newport-Mesa Christian Center, 1988).
4 Hiebert, pp. 173-176.
5 *The NIV Study Bible*, p. 1662, Acts 10:1.
6 Hayford, p. 98.
7 Thomas Brisco, *Holman Bible Atlas* (Nashville, Tennessee: Broadman & Holman Publishers, 1998), p. 244.
8 Stott, p. 203.
9 Bruce, p. 238.
10 Wood, *Acts* (ICI), p. 194.
11 Wood, *Acts* (ICI), p. 201.
12 Wood, *Acts* (ICI), p. 195.

13 Elizabeth Karanja, Interview of November 16, 2000.
14 Horton, *Acts*, p. 139.
15 George O. Wood, *Study in Acts*, Acts 9:32-11:18, cassette tape.
16 Wiersbe, pp. 231-232.
17 Horton, *Acts*, pp. 141-142.
18 *The NIV Study Bible*, p. 1667, Acts 11:28.
19 Horton, *Acts*, p. 145.
20 *The NIV Study Bible*, p. 1443.
21 Horton, *Acts*, p. 146.
22 George O. Wood, *Study in Acts*, Acts 12, cassette tape.
23 Horton, *Acts*, p. 152.
24 Horton, *Acts*, p. 153.

Chapter 10

1 Harris, pp. 88-90.
2 *Full Life Study Bible*, pp. 1806-1807.
3 George O. Wood, *Study in Acts*, Acts 13–14, cassette tape (Costa Mesa, California: Newport-Mesa Christian Center, 1988).
4 Kikuyu proverb from Elizabeth Karanja.
5 *The NIV Study Bible*, p. 1672.
6 Douglas, p. 1000.
7 Bruce, pp. 266-267.
8 Douglas, p. 1000.
9 Douglas, pp. 446-447.
10 Frederick Whitfield, "Oh, How I Love Jesus," *Sing His Praise* (Springfield, Missouri: Gospel Publishing House, 1991), p. 73.
11 Elizabeth Karanja, Interview of November 16, 2000.
12 *Full Life Study Bible*, pp. 1806-1807.
13 Wood, *Acts* (ICI), pp. 257-260.
14 Wood, *Acts* (ICI), p. 204.
15 Wood, *Acts* (ICI), p. 220.
16 George O. Wood, *Study in Acts*, Acts 15, cassette tape (Costa Mesa, California: Newport-Mesa Christian Center, 1988).
17 Hiebert, pp. 84-85.
18 Hiebert, pp. 86-89.

Chapter 11

1 Rumph, pp. 199-203.
2 *The NIV Study Bible*, p. 1676, Acts 16:12.
3 John Palmer, Pastor of First Assembly of God in Des Moines, Iowa, Sermon on Acts, Naivasha, Kenya, December, 1987.
4 Horton, *Acts*, pp. 187-188.
5 Morris Williams, Toughness & Trivia, A compilation of writings and poems by Morris Williams published by the family, 1991, back cover.
6 Elizabeth Karanja, Interview of November 16, 2000.
7 Douglas, pp. 1300.
8 Bruce, pp. 329-330.

9 Douglas, p. 985.

10 *The NIV Study Bible*, p. 1679, Acts 17:1.

11 Horton, *Acts*, p. 194.

12 Stott, p. 262.

13 Horton, *Acts*, p. 194.

14 *The NIV Study Bible*, p. 1678, Acts 16:16.

15 Horton, *Acts*, p. 194.

16 Dr. Willard Teague, Dean of the School of Bible and Theology, Global University, Interview of June 19, 2000.

17 Horton, *Acts*, p. 93.

18 Glen D. Cole, Former pastor of Capital Christian Center in Sacramento, California, Sermon notes on Acts 17.

19 *The NIV Study Bible*, p. 1679, Acts 17:1.

20 C. Peter Wagner, *Lighting the World—A New Look At Acts*, Acts 9–15 (Ventura, California: Regal Books, 1995), pp. 69-71.

21 Arthur J. Glasser, *Worldwide Perspectives—A Text for Use with Perspectives on the World Christian Movement* (Pasadena, California: William Carey Library, 1996), pp. 320-321.

22 Stott, p. 293.

23 Bruce, p. 348.

24 Douglas, p. 107.

25 Bruce, p. 351.

26 Sidney I. Landau, *Funk and Wagnall's Standard Desk Dictionary* (New York: Funk and Wagnall, 1974), p. 663.

27 *The NIV Study Bible*, p. 1680, Acts 17:19.

28 *The NIV Study Bible*, p. 1680, Acts 17:23.

29 Turnbull, p. 101.

30 Hiebert, pp. 155-157.

31 Bruce, p. 351.

32 Bruce, p. 367.

33 Charles F. Pfeiffer and Howard F. Vos, eds., *The Wycliffe Historical Geography of Bible Lands* (Chicago, Illinois: Moody Press, 1967), p. 481.

34 Stott, p. 296.

35 Wood, *Acts* (ICI), p. 289.

36 Stott, pp. 295-296.

37 Wood, *Acts* (ICI), p. 289.

38 George O. Wood, *Study in Acts*, Acts 18, cassette tape (Costa Mesa, California: Newport-Mesa Christian Center, 1988).

39 Charles Pfeiffer, Howard Vos, and John Rea, eds., *Wycliffe Bible Encyclopedia*, vol. 1 (Chicago, Illinois: Moody Press, 1975), p. 380.

40 *NIV Study Bible*, p. 1732.

41 Barrett, (Fall 2000): p. 25.

42 Stott, p. 292.

43 Turnbull, p. 104.

44 Stott, p. 296.

45 Horton, *Acts*, p. 212.

46 Stott, p. 297.

47 Horton, *Acts*, p. 213.

48 Horton, *Acts*, p. 213.

49 Bruce, p. 371.

50 Stott, p. 300.

51 J. Wilbur Chapman, "What A Savior," *Hymns of Glorious Praise* (Springfield: Gospel Publishing House, 1969), p. 23.

52 Tan, p. 787.

53 Stott, p. 299.

54 *Full Life Study Bible*, p. 1704, Acts 28:30.

55 Horton, *Acts*, p. 216.

56 Stott, p. 300.

57 Stott, p. 301.

Chapter 12

1 Ben Tipton, Assemblies of God missionary-evangelist, Interview of October 3, 2000.

2 Horton, *Acts*, p. 217.

3 Douglas, p. 380.

4 Robert H. Mounce, *New International Commentary on the New Testament: The Book of Revelation* (Grand Rapids, Michigan: Wm. B. Eerdmans Publishing Co., 1977), p. 85.

5 Douglas, p. 380.

6 Stott, p. 293.

7 Wood, *Acts* (ICI), p. 304.

8 Wood, *Acts* (ICI), pp. 306-307.

9 Bruce, p. 387.

10 Douglas, p. 381.

11 Wood, *Study in Acts*, Acts 18, cassette tape.

12 Bruce, p. 382.

13 Stott, p. 302.

14 Samuel Chadwick, *The Way to Pentecost* (London: Hodder and Stroughton, 1972), p. 17.

15 Menzies and Menzies, p. 74.

16 Horton, *Acts*, p. 221.

17 Bruce, pp. 384-385.

18 George O. Wood, *Study in Acts*, Acts 19, cassette tape (Costa Mesa, California: Newport-Mesa Christian Center, 1988).

19 *The NIV Study Bible*, p. 1789.

20 Duane Elmer and Lois McKinney, *With an Eye on the Future* (Monrovia, California: MARC, 1996), p. 21.

21 Bob Larson, *Larson's New Book of Cults*, (Wheaton, Illinois: Tyndale House Publishers, Inc., 1989), p. 9.

22 *The NIV Study Bible*, p. 1684, Acts 19:24.

23 Lazarus Chakwera, Graduation message at East Africa School of Theology, Nairobi, Kenya, 1994.

24 Elizabeth Karanja, Interview of November 16, 2000.

25 *The NIV Study Bible*, p. 1683, Acts 19:9.

Chapter 13

1 Elizabeth Karanja, Interview of October, 2000.

2 Horton, *Acts*, p. 249.

3 C. K. Barrett, *The First Epistle to the Corinthians* (New York: Harper and Row, 1968), p. 168.

[4]   McKenzie, p. 214.

[5]   McKenzie, pp. 213-215.

[6]   Turnbull, p. 128.

[7]   David Barrett, *International Bulletin of Missionary Research* (January 1997): p. 25.

[8]   Stott, p. 359.

[9]   Carl Gibbs, Dean of the School of Graduate Studies, Global University, Interview of August 30, 2000.

[10] Tan, p. 616.

[11] *The NIV Study Bible*, p. 1693, Acts 24:27.

[12] Horton, *Acts*, p. 272.

[13] Stott, p. 368.

[14] Stott, pp. 370-374.

[15] *Full Life Study Bible*, p. 1700.

[16] Stott, p. 363.

[17] Stott, p. 383.

[18] Wood, *Acts* (ICI), p. 388.

[19] *Full Life Study Bible*, p. 1705.

[20] Stott, p. 385.

[21] Haenchen, pp. 702-703.

[22] Horton, *Acts*, p. 283.

[23] C. Peter Wagner, *Blazing the Way, A New Look at Acts—Sharing God's Power Throughout the World*, Acts 15–28 (Ventura, California: Regal Books, 1995), p. 237.

[24] Turnbull, pp. 150-151.

[25] Wagner, p. 241.

[26] *Funk and Wagnall's Standard Desk Dictionary*, p. 97.

[27] Bruce, p. 533.

[28] Wagner, p. 249.

Definitions

[1]   Douglas, p. 24.

[2]   Douglas, pp. 614-615.

[3]   Lynn Waller, *International Children's Bible Dictionary* (Dallas, Texas: Word, 1987), p. 25.

[4]   *The NIV Study Bible*, p. 1658, Acts 8:10.

[5]   *Full Life Study Bible*, p. 1646, Acts 2:4.

God's Plan of Salvation

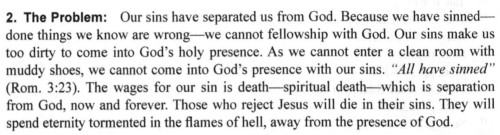

1. Introduction: God is holy, good, and pure—completely righteous. *"God is light; in him there is no darkness at all"* (1 John 1:5).

2. The Problem: Our sins have separated us from God. Because we have sinned—done things we know are wrong—we cannot fellowship with God. Our sins make us too dirty to come into God's holy presence. As we cannot enter a clean room with muddy shoes, we cannot come into God's presence with our sins. *"All have sinned"* (Rom. 3:23). The wages for our sin is death—spiritual death—which is separation from God, now and forever. Those who reject Jesus will die in their sins. They will spend eternity tormented in the flames of hell, away from the presence of God.

3. God's Solution: God loves us so much that he sent Jesus to rescue us. Jesus said, *"I am the way and the truth and the life. No one comes to the Father except through me"* (John 14:6). His name is Jesus, which means Savior, because He saves us from our sins (Matt. 1:21). Jesus saves us from both the penalty and the power of sin–now and forever. Jesus, the Son of God, became a man and lived a perfect, sinless life (John 1:14; Heb. 4:15). He died on the cross as our substitute—He took the penalty for our sins (Rom. 6:23; 2 Cor. 5:21; 1 Pet. 2:24-25. Those who submit their lives to Jesus—God declares to be forgiven, clean and righteous (Rom. 5:1-2).

4. God's Invitation: Jesus says, *"Here I am! I stand at the door (of your heart) and knock. If anyone hears my voice and opens the door, I will come in"* (Rev. 3:20). God's favorite word is "Come". He wants to come to all people, and He wants them to come to him. *"The Spirit and the bride say, "Come!" And let him who hears say, "Come!" Whoever is thirsty, let him come; and whoever wishes, let him take the free gift of the water of life"* (Rev. 22:17). Accept God's invitation. Come to Jesus. Repent of your sins, that is, turn away from what you know is wrong. Put your trust in Jesus as your Savior and Lord. Believe that He died to save you from your sins. Ask Him to forgive your past sins and free you from being a slave to sin. *"If we confess our sins, He is faithful and just and will forgive us our sins, and cleanse us from all unrighteousness"* (1 John 1:9). Welcome Jesus into your life and He will enter. To all who receive Him, He gives the right to become God's children (1 John 1:12).

5. Your Commitment: Welcome to the family of God! God's plan of salvation has a beginning, a middle, and a completion–when we reach heaven. By walking through steps 1–4 above, you have begun to follow God's plan of salvation. Your name is now written in God's book of life (Phil. 4:3; Rev. 3:5; 20:12). The middle part of God's plan is following Jesus as we live on earth. As a child of God, seek to obey the teachings of Jesus in the Bible (Matt. 28:19-20). As you follow Him, He will lead and strengthen you in your relationship with God. As a baby grows into an adult, you will grow from a new child of God into to a mature family member. Be baptized in water (Matt. 28:19; Acts 8:36-38; Rom. 6:4; Mark 16:16). Become part of a local church that preaches and teaches the Bible (Acts 2:41; 9:31). Seek to be filled with the Holy Spirit (Acts 1:8; 2:4; 4:31; 8:17; 10:44-46; 19:1-7; Eph. 5:18-20). Learn to walk in the Spirit, so you can overcome sinful desires that come through the flesh (Rom. 8:5; Gal. 5:16). Grow in grace, and in the knowledge of our Lord and Savior Jesus Christ, and in maturity (2 Pet. 3:18; 2 Pet. 1:5-18). Fellowship with other believers who will encourage you. Share your testimony with others, and lead them to Jesus (John 1:40-42; 4:39). The completion of salvation occurs when Jesus Christ returns. At that time, He will give you a new body, and complete His glorious plan of salvation in your life (Rom. 8:18-25; 1 Cor. 15:20-58; 1 Thess. 4:13-17). We do not know the exact time Jesus will return. For now, enjoy the presence of God, and His Spirit in you, as you grow in grace. You have been saved from your past sins. You are being saved daily, as you abide and grow in Christ. And your salvation has a glorious completion ahead.